"... the true ... be, a party ma... or wrong, is not our slogan. All Fabians have their price, which is always the adoption of Fabian measures, no matter by what party." —George Bernard Shaw

Planners and Permeators

In this fascinating volume, a noted scholar and author analyzes the aims and accomplishments of the Fabians—the unique band of intellectuals who played a vital role in the planning and legislation of British social reforms.

Tracing the growth and development of this society, Anne Fremantle shows how the Fabians developed from a drawing room study group to a behind-the-scenes power that drafted a social reform program which served as a blueprint for the Labor Government's welfare state. She discusses the careers and personalities of the Fabian leaders, their research work, their lectures, their writings, and assesses the extent and areas of their influence—past, present and future.

Penetrating and provocative, this dynamic book presents an exciting, informal history of an influential movement that enlisted some of the most brilliant minds of the twentieth century.

*12, 28, 64, 75, 82 CONSTANCE GARNETT = FABIAN
37 - LADY SOCIALISTS
38 - WEBB AS DISCIPLE of Mill
new Statesman = FABIAN
99-100, 143 LIBERAL BETRAYAL 1892 (Ch. Gen.)

Other MENTOR Books You Will Enjoy

The Age of Belief: The Medieval Philosophers
Selected and edited by Anne Fremantle
Basic writings of the most important philosophers from the 5th to the 15th century. (#MD126—50¢)

The Papal Encyclicals in Their Historical Context
edited by Anne Fremantle
For the first time in one volume, the teachings of the Catholic Church as expressed by the Popes in their official letters on doctrine, family relationships, and moral questions that have vexed mankind in the past and present. (#MT256—75¢)

The Theory of the Leisure Class *by Thorstein Veblen.*
Introduction by C. Wright Mills
A challenging and ironic analysis of social and economic conduct. (#MD93—50¢)

Ideas of the Great Economists *by George Soule*
Examines the views, times and lives of over 50 great economists from ancient days to the present.
(#MD143—50¢)

Anne Fremantle

THIS LITTLE
BAND OF
PROPHETS

The British Fabians

NAL MENTOR BOOKS

A MENTOR BOOK PUBLISHED BY
THE NEW AMERICAN LIBRARY

(The page following constitutes an extension of this copyright page.)

For permission to print excerpts from copyrighted publications the author wishes to thank the following authors, publishers, and authorized representatives:

GEORGE ALLEN & UNWIN, LTD.:
From *A History of British Socialism* by Max Beer, published by George Allen & Unwin, Ltd. (London) and Harcourt, Brace & Co., Inc. (New York); from *The History of the Fabian Society* by Edward R. Pease, published by George Allen & Unwin, Ltd. (London).

GEORGE ALLEN & UNWIN, LTD. and THE FABIAN SOCIETY OF LONDON:
From *Fabian Essays*, edited by G. B. Shaw, published by George Allen & Unwin, Ltd. (London) and The Macmillan Co. (New York).

APPLETON-CENTURY-CROFTS, INC. and ARCHIBALD HENDERSON:
From *George Bernard Shaw: Man of the Century* by Archibald Henderson, published by Appleton-Century-Crofts, Inc. (New York).

THE CLARENDON PRESS:
From *England 1870-1919* by Sir Robert Ensor, published by The Clarendon Press (Oxford).

MISS D. E. COLLINS and SHEED & WARD:
From the *Autobiography* by G. K. Chesterton, published by Messrs. Hutchinson (London) and Sheed & Ward (New York). With permission of Miss D. E. Collins.

MISS D. E. COLLINS, SHEED & WARD, and MAISIE WARD:
From *Gilbert Keith Chesterton* by Maisie Ward, published by Sheed & Ward (London and New York). Copyright, 1943, Sheed & Ward, Inc.

ST. JOHN ERVINE and WILLIAM MORROW & CO., INC.:
From *Bernard Shaw, His Life, Work and Friends* by St. John Ervine, published by Constable & Co., Ltd. (London) and William Morrow & Co., Inc. (New York).

EXECUTORS OF LORD HALDANE and HODDER & STOUGHTON, LTD.:
From *Richard Burdon Haldane: An Autobiography.* Published by Hodder & Stoughton, Ltd. (London) and Doubleday & Company, Inc. (New York). By permission of the Executors and Hodder & Stoughton.

HARCOURT, BRACE & CO., INC.:
From *My Years of Exile: Reminiscences of a Socialist* by Eduard Bernstein, published by Leonard Parsons (London) and Harcourt, Brace & Co., Inc. (New York).

DAVID HIGHAM ASSOCIATES, LTD.:
From *Growing Up Into Revolution* by Margaret I. Cole, published by Longmans, Green & Co., Ltd. (London and New York).

Library of Congress Catalog Card No. 60-7644

MENTOR BOOKS are published by
The New American Library of World Literature, Inc.
501 Madison Avenue, New York 22, New York

PRINTED IN THE UNITED STATES OF AMERICA

for VIRGILIA *and* VICTOR: *their book*

The third current of fin de siècle *Socialism, and the most important, was the Fabian doctrine, specially connected with Mr. and Mrs. Sidney Webb. The Fabian Society was founded in 1883. Its name recalls a Roman general whose motto was 'slow but sure.' Eschewing revolution, and intent on the actualities of England at the end of the nineteenth century, Fabians exonerated socialists from the heavy obligation of reading Karl Marx. Without dogmatising as to the ultimate future of industrial organisation, they preached practical possibilities, here and now—municipal socialism and state control of conditions of labour. Equally far from Marx and Morris, they left the New Jerusalem alone, and sought to impregnate the existing forces of society with collectivist ideals. The Fabians became experts in bringing electoral, journalistic and personal pressure to bear on local bodies, and on the Liberal or Conservative Government of the hour. By the end of the century it is in Fabianism that we find the nearest approach to a body of doctrine directly affecting the laws and administration of the time, like the doctrines of Bentham and Mill in the past. The Fabians were intelligence officers without an army—there was no Fabian party in parliament—but they influenced the strategy and even the direction of the great host's moving under other banners.*

—G. M. Trevelyan
British History in the Nineteenth Century

CONTENTS

CHAPTER ONE

Milling around the corridors of the Mother of Parliaments at Westminster in 1945 after the King's Speech had ended, were 394 newly elected Socialist members of the House of Commons and their wives. "It's just like a Fabian Summer School," cooed one wife to another, "all the same faces." For the first time in British history, Labor had come into power with a majority—and what a majority! Labor had beaten the archenemy, Winston Churchill, in the hour of his greatest triumph; it had gone to the country with an unequivocally Socialist program, and received the wholehearted endorsement of the British people. Among the dense crowd of Socialists were the Fabian Prime Minister, Clement (now Earl) Attlee, and 229 other Fabians, of whom 41 were in the government.

Who the Fabians were, how, why, and when they came together; what was the extent of their influence and where it was most felt, how much they actually accomplished, how powerful they once were and still are; their growth from a handful of drawing-room would-be do-gooders in London in the 1880's, to a society numbering thousands in the 1940's, this book attempts to discover. It also discusses the famous Fabian tactics of "permeation" and the various Fabian "deviationists" and their failure.

"The Fabian Society consists of Socialists." So read the famous first line of the Fabian Basis of 1886, and so, as revised in 1919 and again in 1949, it still reads today. The Fabian Society is the oldest Socialist society, and the most successful, in the world; it has never had a split, and its tenets and methods are today the same as when it was founded in 1884. Yet the word "Socialist" did not occur in the Fabian Society's minutes until its sixth meeting, nor did it appear in the Society's literature until the publication of its third tract, and then half-facetiously! George Bernard Shaw, who wrote this tract, declared that

> The Fabian Society having in view the advance of Socialism and the threatened subversion of the powers hitherto exercised by private proprietors of the national land and capital, ventures plainly to warn all such proprietors that the establishment of Socialism means nothing less than the compulsion of all members of the upper class, without regard to sex or condition, to work for their living.

What did Shaw, and what did, and do, the Fabians mean by Socialism? Dicey, the great nineteenth-century English historian, first equated collectivism with Socialism, and the Christian Socialists had declared, in mid-nineteenth century, that "Socialist legislation is religion functioning through the State." But it was an early Fabian, Belfort Bax, who introduced a deft definition when he said, "Socialism is the system of society the material basis of which is social production for social use."

Graham Wallas, one of the Founding Fabians, described Socialism as "a movement towards economic equality to be achieved by democracy." Finally, Sidney Webb, the most important thinker among the Fabians and the third most influential of British Socialists (Robert Owen and John Stuart Mill being his two predecessors), most authoritatively defined Socialism as first the Fabians and thereafter British Labor saw it: "Socialism," he wrote, "is the conscious and deliberate substitution, in industrial as well as political matters, of the collective self-government of the community as a whole, organized on a democratic basis, for the individual control over other men's lives, which the unrestrained private ownership of land and industrial capital inevitably involves." The ethics of Socialism, the *Encyclopaedia Britannica* declares, are identical with those of Christianity; other authorities have felt, and continue to feel, the relationship to be somewhat less intimate than identity.

The Fabians thought pretty much as many other people around them thought. But they instantly and constantly put their thoughts tidily down on paper and published them as tracts, thus making a series of blueprints of them. Then they trained themselves, and others, to convert those blueprints into action at every level—local, municipal, and national. *Scripta manent,* what is written, remains; and during Labor's first post-World War II government —that is, during the first Labor Government with a working majority—the Labor Party in six years enacted almost the whole of a program that had been completely outlined fifty years before by the Fabian Society. Their ideas were not even then original—they were not, even in 1900, very novel, but the fact that they were spelled out by the Fabians, and half a century later enacted as they had been drafted by Fabians, indicates continuity and a permanence rare in the fluctuating world of political and social ideas.

Lord Attlee, a lifelong Fabian, has put into simple words what these changes mean in actual solid fact. "I've seen the sweating of women go, I've seen child labor go, I've seen abject poverty go. And there's a real change in the climate of opinion as well," he told a United States newspaper reporter lately. "Today your ordinary Conservative is, by the standards of fifty years ago, a terrible revolutionary." The London *Times* could not possibly maintain in a lead article—as it did in 1890—that to suggest that a man has the right to work or eat is "a wild proposition." Lord Attlee comments on some other significant changes that have taken place in his lifetime, and for which the Fabians must take at least some of the credit. "When I was young," he notes, "there was a definitely working-class type of dress. A working-class home had a sink, but no bath, the family lived in the kitchen. Now the typical working-class home is typically lower-middle-class."

Although seventy-five years after the foundation of the Fabian Society in the rooms of Mr. E. L. Pease at 17 Osnaburgh Street, in London, on Friday, January 4, 1884, the Society may not have completely succeeded in compelling every single British peer to earn his bread by the sweat of his brow, it certainly has succeeded in its more general aim, that of "reconstructing society, as based on the competitive system, in such a manner as to secure the general welfare and happiness." When the Fabian Society was founded, there were only 30,000 Socialist votes in the whole world. Since British Labor's defeat in 1951, owing to the local Labor parties' falling down on their job of educating and training their members, the Fabian Society has come very much to the fore again, and its erstwhile weaknesses—lack of emphasis on a positive colonial policy and ignorance of foreign policy—have been converted into a new strength.

Today the Fabian Colonial Bureau is responsible for the briefing, and indeed for much of the training, of the local leadership in such new members of the British Commonwealth as Ghana, and for the planning from the blueprint stage on up of such experiments as the Central African Federation. The extent to which Fabian foreign policy has matured can be judged by comparing the total absence of any essay on foreign affairs in the original volume of Fabian essays, with the whole well-informed book on the subject, recently published in Britain, edited by Kenneth Younger and T. McKitterick.

The complete reorientation and reorganization of England since World War II cannot be ascribed to any one cause. Two world wars and the Russian Revolution, together with the staggering increase in world population and the scientific discoveries which have underscored the abiding possibility of dictatorship, reducing space, time, and the areas in which the exercise of free will is possible, are obviously causes no less than they are effects. But the Fabians not only caught the tide that had set in against nineteenth-century laissez-faire liberalism, but were themselves the most powerful, because the most widely diffused, expression of that tide in Britain. Indeed, they not only were, but are, the wave of the Welfare State and of the Socialist ideal. And they are also the most contemporary expression of the resilience of the British body politic. The fact that today it matters less than ever before in British history what party is in power, since the Welfare State has now been accepted by both the Conservative and Labor parties as the successor of the Watchdog State and as the only possible preventative against, and alternative to, the Police State, is a vindication of Fabian ideas and methods. It has been said that the distance between Jeremy Bentham's nineteenth-century fear of the state and Sidney Webb's twentieth-century faith in it is the economic and intellectual—and perhaps even spiritual —measure of the distance between yesterday's Victorians and today's Elizabethans.

Indeed, by 1947 Socialism, as Shaw put it, had become as respectable as the Old School ties worn by Lord Attlee and many of his colleagues. H. M. Hyndman, in 1881, was thrown out of the New University Club for being a Socialist, although his father was an Old Etonian, and although Hyndman himself dressed in an everlasting silk-faced frock coat and wore a respectable long-flowing dark-brown beard. (Frank Harris called him the "incorruptible work-horse of Socialism, a plodder with the figure of a grocer.") Herbert Spencer, Beatrice Potter's "revered and respected mentor," revoked his will naming her his literary executrix when he learned of her engagement to a Socialist, Sidney Webb. Recently a *Conservative* Government appointed Lord Listowel, a lifelong Socialist, to the important post of governor of the newly created state of Ghana.

Few today will deny that the Welfare State, of which today's England is a working model, is a Fabian blueprint fairly successfully executed. But this success of their ideas was not achieved by Fabians only. They have been, and are still, the planners and permeaters, rather than the pioneers, in such areas as social legislation, municipal housing, nationalization. "The Welfare State is an association with a Socialist philosophy but in the Liberal tradition," as Roy Harrod has said.

G. M. Trevelyan[1] * called the Fabians "intelligence officers without an army who influenced the strategy and even the direction of the great hosts moving under other banners." For the Fabians never became a political party, never ran a single candidate for Parliament as a Fabian; their speakers never urged anyone to become a Fabian or to join the Fabian Society—not even in 1892, when 3,400 lectures were given by 113 Fabians in a twelvemonth. The Fabian Society has never had more than 4,000 members; at the time of its greatest influence, which then extended into both the Liberal and Conservative parties, it had under 1,500. Nor is the Fabian Society a school of Socialist doctrine; rather it was, and is, a group of men and women who spread practical views on current needs and immediate social problems, and indicate the way these problems may be met by legislative or administrative reforms. Over its seventy-five years of existence, the Fabian Society has in fact produced a collective body of Socialist doctrine tested at every step by constant concrete experience.

The Fabians did for British Socialism at the end of the nineteenth century almost exactly what their predecessors, the Utilitarians, did for British Liberalism at the beginning of the same century; and they were adept at using the basic Utilitarian instrument for carrying out the reforms they advocated: the British Civil Service, an instrument originally forged by Jeremy Bentham and the Utilitarians. The Fabians, many of them, were career civil servants—Sidney Webb and Sydney Olivier were clerks in the Colonial Office; Frank Podmore, who gave the Society its name of "Fabian," was in the Post Office, and many others were in other branches. This gave the Fabians an acquaintance with the actual functions of government, which was of great practical advantage to them in keeping their schemes concrete and in helping their realization; the machinery of government in all its details was

[1] p. 403.

* Footnotes such as this are used when a specific year, page, or additional name is needed to complete a reference. The rest of the reference may be found in the bibliography, pp. 308-14. Page references are for the first edition listed.

familiar to them; they could and did execute their own blueprints. This combining of planning and executive functions in the same individuals was a disadvantage, however, in that it tended to confound in Fabian minds the state and the government; a confusion always dangerous and recently often fatal. The Fabians, during their seventy-five years, have given Socialism its bureaucracy, a necessary servant; but in so doing they also have made Socialist society into a bureaucracy, an inestimable liability.

Indeed, the Fabian success is not universally endorsed even by members of hierarchically Fabian families. A niece of Mrs. Sidney Webb's[2] strikes a somewhat acid note writing in reference to the Fabian triumph.

> Such a loathsome world the Fabians have saddled us with. Aunt Bo's ideas were terrifying in their boredom. A sort of lower-middle-class inferno (in the sense that there was *no* possibility of escape from it) was her idea of a brave new world. We have almost reached it in this country [England]. Everyone has a boring degree of comfort, a horrid little house with a TV set, a garage and a sitting room furnished exactly like everyone else's with what is naively known as contemporary furniture. As soon as you become a nuisance to the younger generation, you are put to die into a soul-less institution, run at appalling expense by the country.

In his preface to the 1931 edition of what he calls the "apparently indestructible" *Fabian Essays,* first published in 1889, which have sold over two million copies, Shaw, the first of the seven essayists and the meticulously painstaking editor of the volume, notes that "the distinctive mark of the Fabian Society among the rival bodies of Socialists with which it came into conflict in its early days was its resolute constitutionalism." It still is. And the "seemingly immortal" volume, published in a jubilee edition in 1948 with still another preface by its original editor, then well over ninety, was, he noted, "still doing its old work, the rescuing of Socialism . . . from the barricades . . . from confusion with the traditional heterodoxies of anti-clericalism, individualism, anti-State republicanism, and middle-class Bohemian anarchism." Also from Utopianism, Meliorism, and Marxism.

For, from 1900, when the Taff Vale dispute brought the British trade-union leaders to reject Marx, the Fabian out-

---

[2] My sister Konradin, wife of Sir Arthur Hobhouse, a former Liberal Member of Parliament, and chairman of the County Councils Association, in a letter to me dated January 21, 1957.

look has dominated the Socialist outlook in Britain. Even
earlier than 1900, the Fabian Society, from its drawing-
room days on, has been professedly anti-Marxist. Sidney
Webb and Graham Wallas followed Shaw in demonstrating
how J. S. Mill and Stanley Jevons broke the spell of Marxism
so that it was not the Marxist theory of value but the Jevonian theory of marginal utility which has proved to be the
foundation stone of British labor economics. The fact that
the Fabians in the 1920's never faced the loss of foreign
markets led to the discrediting of their economic theory, and
their theory of value was dropped from economic textbooks
from World War I on, although in a closed economy it could
have continued to be a plausible assumption.

The tools forged by the Fabians to do the job they had set
themselves, that of socializing Britain, did just that job.
These tools were three in number: the Labor Party, the
London School of Economics, and the weekly magazine,
the *New Statesman*. The Labor Party, founded jointly by the
Fabians and the trade unions, always had two wings, the
"gas-and-water" Fabian wing, and the doctrinaire Socialism
of the Trades Union Council (TUC); these two wings have
kept apart and distinct. The London School of Economics,
founded by the Webbs in 1895, has never been Socialist-
directed, although it has always had Socialists on its staff,
and has "raised" and trained many, if not all, of the Socialist
leaders. But from the School's first arch-conservative director, W. A. Hewins, through others such as the Liberal Sir
William Beveridge and the Tory Sir A. M. Carr-Saunders,
to the present time, "LSE" has proved to be something of a
cuckoo in the Webb nest. It has nourished not only many
non-Socialists but even many anti-Socialists too. The *New
Statesman*, founded as a weekly by the Webbs in 1912, on
the other hand, has gone from Fabian strength to strength
and may be said today to represent the Fabian outlook
most fully.

Although as long ago as in good old W. E. Gladstone's
days, Sir William Harcourt could announce that "we are all
Socialists now," it has taken a long while to eradicate the
natural deep-down snobbishness of even devoutly theoretical
Socialists. H. M. Hyndman, for example, who spent his life
and fortune in the Socialist cause, still could describe the
misery and embarrassment he felt when Henry George, the
American, stopped a barrow at the corner of Great Port-
land Street and stood beside it eating whelks. Shaw, a confirmed Socialist for more than seventy years, yet did not
admit to anyone, until nearly the end of his life, that he had

been to a school open also to the sons of tradespeople. Today British Labor has proved its Socialism to be, as G.B.S.
said, a constitutional movement in which the most respectable
citizens and their families can enlist without forfeiting the
least scrap of their social or spiritual standing. And this is
without any doubt the work of the Fabian Society. For, as
the basic motif of Robert Owen's ideas was idealism, and
of Karl Marx revolution, that of Fabianism was, and is,
social regeneration.

How incredulous the original members of the Fabian Society would have been could they have foreseen what their Society, founded with such bombastic aspirations toward a Fellowship of the New Life, was actually to accomplish. These
founding Fabians were a cranky lot, full of the dietetic and
sartorial fads of their age, "cycling along country lanes, the
ladies in bloomers, their consorts sandalled . . . innocuous
enough, if not a little absurd," as Malcolm Muggeridge, married to a Webb niece, describes them. Nevertheless, among
these nut-cutlet-eating cultists were at least half a dozen of
the most brilliant minds of the twentieth century: George
Bernard Shaw, Sidney Webb, Graham Wallas, and Sydney
Olivier, the "Four" as the other Fabians called them; also,
later, Bertrand Russell, H. G. Wells, John Galsworthy, Mrs.
Sidney Webb, R. H. Tawney, G. D. H. Cole, and Harold
Laski. All these brought to the Society, from conscience or
conviction, or from both, their brains, their time and their
energy.

The history of the Fabian Society can be divided into five
periods. The first, from 1884 to 1907, might be described as
the second spring of Socialism in England—an evolutionary
spring, compared with the earlier revolutionary and Chartist
spring of the 1830's. This period was the heyday of Fabian
permeation and initiative. During the second period, from
1907 to 1917, the wind seemed to be taken out of the
Fabian sails by the Liberals, whose great social enact-
ments were drawn, almost literally, from Fabian Tracts.
Meanwhile, the real struggle for the working class—and
within it—was at that time between the Liberals and the
young Labor Party, with the Fabians somewhat schizophren-
ically running with the hare and hunting with the hounds.
The third period, between 1917 and 1931, was a time when,
in Europe, revolution and counterrevolution were increasingly substituted for progress, when the Labor Party learned
the hard way that foreign affairs, and, above all, foreign
markets, are also matters of vital importance to the British
workingman. And here the Fabians continued to be individu-

ally of great importance, although their economic theory—
and everybody else's—went down like tenpins before the triumphant genius of John Maynard Keynes. The Labor Party
split of 1931 did not affect the Fabians, for the Society held
no truck with the so-called National Government, but it realized sadly that its work was all to do again, and that the Labor Party had to be retrained from the nursery up. The
fourth period, of anxious and attentive reappraisal, lasted
from 1931 until the Labor victory of 1945; the fifth period, a
new era of expansion and influence, carried on from that victory until the present day.

When the Fabians came to power in 1945 it was to discover that, alas, it is not possible to make people good by
making them happy, well, and comfortable. Today's Fabians,
rethinking back to ethics, are trying, on a colonial and international scale, to help other countries, whether capitalist or
Communist, realize some of the things the Fabians were to
some extent able to make the English governing classes realize in the eighties and nineties; that beggars are bad business,
and that the half-fed and the half-free are not only a blight
on the conscience of individual or nation, but also a threat
to the pocketbooks and even to the lives of the highly indus-
trialized nations. The countries with underdeveloped economies and the countries with underdeveloped consciences are
both faced by today's Fabians in the same mildly missionary
spirit with which the famous early Fabians proselytized all
who would listen, from the policemen set to watch him in
Hyde Park whom Shaw succeeded in interesting, to Mr. R. B.
Haldane, later Lord Chancellor, "butchered to make a Fabian holiday" on March 16, 1888, in a very public debate.

Many questions arise from a study of the Fabians, and not
all of them have single or simple answers. To take a few examples: Why did so many of the leading Fabians become
Marxists in the 1930's, when the Fabian Society was, one
might almost say, founded to bypass Marx and elevate Jevons
and Ricardo? Why had Fabianism, which interested so many
brilliant minds, so little influence outside England, either in
the U.S.A. or in Europe, or in the Near or Far East? Why
have the two wings of British Socialism, the "gas-and-water"
Fabian wing and the doctrinaire TUC wing, always kept so
distinct? Is it basically, as G.B.S. suggested, an intellectual or
educational and social distinction, or is it not rather ideologi-
cal? Why have the Fabians, so long on economic theory, been
so short on political theory? Why were the Fabians, professionally Socialist and internationalist, Imperialists during the
Boer War? Why were so few of them pacifist during World

Wars I and II? And why, in spite of socialized medicine and social legislation from cradle to grave, has the governess-state they achieved caused such a delinquent and dissatisfied reaction in today's spiv or beat generation of young people who have really nothing whatever to grumble at? Finally, why, in spite of several notorious individual secessions, and some other defections, have the Fabians never splintered? What secret homogeneity accounts for their survival, and for such an organic, structurally complete survival? In searching for answers to such questions as these, it is necessary to look back to the beginnings of the Fabian Society.

WELFARE STATE OR
POLICE STATE

CHAPTER TWO

W ITH THE SUPPRES-
sion of the Paris Commune in 1871, the era of what George
Bernard Shaw called "the romantic revolutionary Liberalism
and Radicalism of 1848" may be said to have come to an
end. Shaw said that the Liberals and the Radicals had a common object in democracy, and a common concept of method
in revolution, and that both were catastrophic. Most Radicals
of the 1890's, as G.B.S. twitted, thought that cutting off the
king's head and leaving the rest to nature would produce, if
not the millennium, at least a clean slate. The Utopias of the
1820-28 phase of Socialism, as dreamed of by Robert Owen
and Fourier and Saint-Simon, were still the carrots held out to
the donkeys who died on the barricades in Europe in 1848,
although each new prophet had a different method and suggested a different instrument for reaching these Utopias.
Proudhon offered the minimum wage; Georges Sorel the general strike; Marx, according to Shaw, declared that force is
the midwife of progress without reminding us that force is
equally the midwife of chaos; Bentham proposed universal
male suffrage and annual parliaments. John Stuart Mill, in
spite of his outrageous optimism ("happily there is nothing in
the laws of value which remains for the present or any future
writer to clear up"), considered that the social problem of the
future was that of uniting the greatest individual liberty of
action with a common ownership in the raw materials of the
globe and an equal participation of all in the benefits of combined labor, equally distributed.

In England the economic slump of 1879 shook the calm
and complacency of the mid-Victorians, and ended a time
when, as J. A. Hobson put it, peace, prosperity, and progress
appeared to be the permanent possession of most civilized nations.

Eighteen eighty-one saw the publication in England of two
vitally important books: Henry George's *Progress and Pov-*

erty and H. M. Hyndman's *England for All*. Henry George's book had been published in his native United States two years earlier and had already sold over 100,000 copies there before he arrived in England to lecture on his theory of the single tax.

Shaw was profoundly influenced by hearing George's argument that nowhere in the civilized world had labor received its just due: "Over-production could not possibly exist as long as there were men suffering from hunger, wearing bad clothes and living in ramshackle houses." The fundamental cause of the whole evil was to be sought in the fact "that people were shut off from the land which, combined with human labor, formed the source of all wealth . . . in a newly opened country it was best to regard the land as belonging to all, and to permit everyone to take possession of and cultivate as much as he required . . . in old countries, however, the taxation of rent was the best remedy." [1]

Shaw has said that five-sixths of those who like himself were swept into the great Socialist revival of 1888 had been converted by Henry George. Shaw himself heard George speak in the Farringdon Street Memorial Hall on the land question for the Land Reform Union, an organization founded by Sydney Olivier, who was then one of the two resident clerks in the Colonial Office, and H. H. Champion, a former army officer.

"To George," E. R. Pease[2] has noted, "belongs the extraordinary merit of recognizing the right way to social salvation. The earlier Socialists had proposed segregated communities; the Co-operators had tried voluntary associations; the Positivists advocated moral suasion; the Chartists favored force, physical or political; the Marxists talked revolution . . . George wrote in a land where people ruled themselves, not only in fact but also in name."

Henry George did not impress only the Socialists. Wilfred Ward has described how when he brought him to Cardinal Manning, the Cardinal told George that he loved Christ and Christ brought him to the people He loved; George in turn told the Cardinal he loved the people and the people had brought him to Christ Who loved them. (Later in 1888 when there was a possibility that George's book would be put on the Catholic Index, Cardinal Gibbons appealed to Manning, and Manning was able to give assurances that this would not happen.)

In the same year that Henry George's book appeared in

[1] Beer, II, p. 243.
[2] p. 20.

England, H. M. Hyndman, a rich, eccentric patrician and indefatigable diner-out, published his *England for All*, which, he admits himself, was the result of his conversations with Karl Marx and of his conversion to Marxism. He had discovered Karl Marx through reading *Das Kapital* in the French translation. Karl Marx was then living at 41 Maitland Park Road on Haverstock Hill in London, and arriving daily at the British Museum Reading Room when it opened, leaving only when it closed, and writing far into the night. Hyndman sought out Marx, and he and Hyndman would pace up and down Marx's studio, smoking cigars provided by Hyndman.

To the end of his life, Hyndman, perhaps in unconscious imitation of his idol, would walk up and down, rising on his toes at each point he made in the conversation. His second wife begged him, "My darling, I do wish you would stand still, you go up and down and down and up and up and down until it makes me dizzy. I've poured six cups of tea and we are only three." Eleanor (Tussy), Marx's youngest daughter, then a blooming twenty-four-year-old, with black hair and black eyes and an exceptionally musical voice, took care of her father. Marx told Hyndman that "England is the one country in the world in which a peaceful revolution is possible," cautiously adding: "history does not tell us so." Hyndman absorbed Marx's ideas and in his book published them without acknowledgment. Marx was deeply hurt. On December 15, he wrote in a letter to Friedrich Engels,

> In the beginning of June there was published a little book called *England for All*. It pretends to be written as an exposé of the propositions of the Democratic Federation, a recently formed association of different English and Scotch Radical Socialists . . . the chapters on Labor and Capital are . . . literally extracted from, or circumlocutions of, *Das Kapital*, but the author does not quote the book or its author . . . he wrote letters of excuse for instance that "the English don't like to be taught by foreigners" and that "my name was so much detested." With all that, his little book, in so far as it pilfers *Das Kapital*, makes good proposals, although the man is a weak vessel.

Actually, Hyndman had, albeit rather cursorily, acknowledged his debt to Marx in the preface, by noting that "for the ideas and much of the matter contained in Chapters 2 and 3 I am indebted to the work of a great thinker and original writer" whose works he hoped would soon become accessible in English. Max Beer[3] says that Hyndman was quite unaware of the inordinate desire of Marx for public recognition of his work: ". . . no amount of privation, distress, and suffering would deter him . . . his whole being came finally to be bound up with the fate of his book."

Yet in spite of the resulting personal rift between Hyndman and Marx, Beer adds that it was really due to Hyndman that Marx found a footing on British soil. Hyndman even endeavored to create an organization based wholly on the Marxian doctrines. This organization, the Democratic Federation, later the Social-Democratic Federation, was formed by Hyndman on June 8, 1881, with a program calling for universal suffrage, triennial Parliaments, equal electoral divisions, payments of members, corruption and bribery of the electors to be made a criminal offense, abolition of the House of Lords as a legislative body, home rule for Ireland, self-governments for the colonies, nationalization of the land. Only the last point could be considered a Socialist proposal —the other points were all old-hat radical. Among the members of the new Federation were J. L. Joynes, an Eton master, who had accompanied Henry George on his speaking tour, and had been arrested and briefly imprisoned with George as a suspected Fenian; William Morris, the poet and artist; Ernest Belfort Bax; Eleanor Marx, and her odious lover, Dr. Edward Aveling; Henry H. Champion; and Walter Crane, the artist and illustrator.

So out of the picture, however, was Socialism in England at this time that the Russian Prince Peter Kropotkin, who had fled to London after escaping from a French prison, found the 1881 atmosphere one in which a man who held advanced opinions could not breathe. For John Burns, Keir Hardie, and the later-famous Labor leaders were still at the beginning of their careers, and John Bright had entirely gone over to the Right, even speaking in public in 1883 to expose the fallacies underlying Henry George's theory of land nationalization. "The working classes," Max Beer noted, "had definitely abandoned all socialist agitation and class warfare, and not even the genius of Marx could bring them back to Chartism." [4] For Chartism, that from the thirties until the seventies had been the core of British radical expression (William Lovett's *People's Charter* had been published in 1838), had finally petered out, after a desperate contest of fully thirty years' duration. It had not been a struggle of the plebs for equal rights, but a class war aiming at the over-

[3] II, pp. 229-30.
[4] II, p. 191.

throw of capitalist society and putting production, distribution, and exchange on a co-operative basis. The working class was apparently defeated. In 1881, H. M. Hyndman and his wife, with a few workers grouped around them, were practically the only "out and out" representatives of Socialism. Prince Kropotkin describes how that year, in the fall, a small Socialist Congress was held

and we used to say jokingly—but it was very true—that Mrs. Hyndman had received all the Congress in her house. We had ridiculously small audiences, seldom consisting of much more than a dozen men. Occasionally some gray-bearded Chartist would rise and tell us that all we were saying had been said forty years before and was greeted then by crowds of workers but that now all was dead and there was no way of reviving it.

After speaking before the Durham miners in broken English, Prince Kropotkin[5] confessed,

My wife and I were so lonely in London, and our efforts to awaken a socialist movement in England seemed so hopeless, that in 1882 we decided to move again to France. We were sure that in France I would soon be arrested, but we often said to each other, "Better a French prison than this grave."

In the summer of 1882 the *Spectator*, then, as now, a sedately middle-of-the-road magazine, declared that Britain as a whole had never been more tranquil and happy. No class was at war with society or the government; there was no dissatisfaction anywhere; the treasury was fairly full and the accumulations of capital, vast. But in September of the same year, it noted warningly that the Trades Union Congress had just passed a resolution asking the government to institute an inquiry with a view to relaxing the stringency of Poor Law administration. This, the *Spectator* considered, was beginning to tamper with natural conditions, and it warned that there was no logical halting place between the theory that it is the duty of the state to make the poor comfortable, and Socialism.

The poor were not of course comfortable at all. Men, women, and children worked from 5:30 A.M. to 7:00 or 8:00 P.M., as their normal working day, and children often had a working week of sixty hours, earning thereby an average of one shilling and sixpence per week. Keir Hardie earned four shillings and sixpence a week at the age of twelve, on which

[5] 1899, p. 169.

he supported his whole family during his father's last illness; Will Thorne, at six, considered himself fortunate to earn two shillings and sixpence a week, working twelve hours a day. Yet, while the trade depression grew worse, and unemployment rose, Mr. Gladstone, who as Prime Minister incarnated laissez-faire Liberalism, was still apparently entrenched in the public favor. But perhaps even he felt the *status quo* could not last; when Hyndman asked him, "Would you not say, sir, that the world will consider you the last of our great commercial statesmen?" the Prime Minister hesitated, and then said, "Yes."

For the recurrent economic crises with their concomitant misery, and the memory of Chartism, proved to many in the late seventies the bankruptcy of Liberalism. As Yves Simon[6] has said, "At the heart of Liberalism lies an almost religious belief in a kind of Demiurge imminent in the stream of contingent events, or, better, identical with the very stream of contingencies. . . . Owing to this benevolent Spirit of Nature contingency and chance are supposed to result indefectibly in happy achievements." The fact that nature, like water and clocks, runs down instead of up, had, after some forty years of triumphant liberalism, resulted in more misery, not less, more poverty, more depression. And, above all, for many more people.

Housing, as Sir Robert Ensor[7] points out, instead of catching population up, was still actually falling behind it. The very blackest scandals were being lessened; the number of one-room tenements containing nine persons and upward had fallen, but the situation was so bad that in 1884 the Royal Commission on Housing was appointed. On this the Prince of Wales, Cardinal Manning, Lord Salisbury, and others, sat under Sir Charles Dilke's chairmanship. The Prince of Wales himself visited dwellings in St. Pancras and Holborn, on which his comment was that their state was disgraceful.

The reaction to this sorry state of affairs was varied. Some men who had been lifelong Liberals, became, as did John Stuart Mill, Socialists at the end of their lives, because, as Shaw[8] put it, "Socialism implies the introduction of design, contrivance and co-ordination, by a nation consciously seeking its own collective welfare, into the present industrial scramble for private gain." John Morley, the last of "the great, the true liberals," though Shaw accused him of eight-

[6] p. 52.
[7] p. 301.
[8] 1948, p. xxx.

housing conditions as impulse to leave liberalism for socialism —very few c eenth-century Rip-van-Winkleism, was yet radical enough to declare on July 30, 1884, in the St. James Hall, "Be sure that no power on earth can separate the question of mending the House of Commons from the question of mending, or ending, the House of Lords." But the great crowds of between fifty and a hundred thousand unemployed that massed in London's Trafalgar Square for the July 21st meeting, 1884, were given scant courtesy by Lord Salisbury. "Does the Government imagine," he asked, "that 30,000 Radicals going to amuse themselves in London on a given day express the public opinion of the country? They are merely attempting legislation by picnic." It was no wonder that the essence of Fabianism was the rejection of laissez faire, which apportioned the products of labor almost in inverse proportion to the labor involved, the largest part going to those who never worked at all, the next largest to those whose work was almost nominal, and so in descending scale, the remuneration descending as the work grew harder and more disagreeable, until the most fatiguing bodily labor could not with certitude count on being able to earn even the necessities of life.[9] In fact, in 1881, only one quarter of the national income went to the working classes, who accounted for some 85 per cent of the population, while one-eighth of the total area of England was owned by 600 noblemen; one-third by 7,400 individuals.

As Keith Hutchison[10] put it, "The paradoxical mission of nineteenth-century liberalism was to create both the free-market economy and the democracy that was to destroy it." And the misery that resulted from the economic position of free-trade England competing with tariff-protected nations, moved some of the governing classes to pity—and these founded such settlements as Toynbee Hall, or worked with the Charity Organization Society—and others to propitiatory fear. As A. J. Balfour pointedly remarked, social legislation was not merely to be distinguished from Socialist legislation; it was its most effective antidote. Still others, like Lady Dorothy Nevill, felt neither pity nor fear: to H. M. Hyndman[11] she said,

> The turn of the people will come some day, I see that quite as clearly as you do. But not yet, not yet. You will educate some of the working class . . . and when you have educated them, we shall buy them, or, if we don't, the Liberals will. Besides we shall never offer any obstinate or bit-

[9] *See* Slesser, 1941.
[10] p. xiii.
[11] 1911, p. 353.

cf. JUNKERS

in Germany

ter resistance . . . when your agitation becomes really serious we shall give way a little . . . our object is to avoid any direct conflict in order to gain time.

When Karl Marx died in London on March 14, 1883, E. R. Pease noted that nobody in England was aware how great would be his influence, and added that he did not think that any of the original Fabians had read the book or had assimilated its ideas at the time the Fabian Society was founded. Very many of the first Fabians were instead influenced by Robert Owen, and some by the Christian Socialists whose leader, the Rev. Stewart D. Headlam, a devotee of Henry George, advocated the Single Tax. Charles Kingsley and F. D. Maurice had preached Socialist ideas derived from the early Fathers, from St. Thomas Aquinas, from the Abbé Lammenais, and from the Rev. Rosmini-Serbati. By a curious irony of fate at that time Protestants such as Kingsley and Maurice were discovering Rosmini and St. Thomas, while Catholics were ignoring them. It was the actual initiator, or founder *malgré lui* of the Fabian Society, Thomas Davidson, a Presbyterian born of crofter (small farmer) parents near Aberdeen, Scotland, who set himself the task of editing and translating the works of Rosmini, and of writing his life, at a time when the great social reformer was under a cloud in Vatican circles. Davidson became a schoolmaster and later a peripatetic philosopher, and was then dubbed currently the "Wandering Scholar." During a visit to Rome, where he had half an hour's conversation in Latin with Pope Leo XIII, he suggested to the Pontiff a new, complete edition of the works of St. Thomas Aquinas, at the very time that the Papacy was bringing a new emphasis to bear on social theory and labor legislation. Davidson came to London in 1883 from the United States, where he had already founded, on Rosminian principles, his Fellowship of the New Life. He collected a few interested young people; his first meetings were held in a large, bare room in Chelsea. His three earliest recruits were Havelock Ellis, William Clarke, and Henry Hyde Champion. Davidson, according to Havelock Ellis, was convinced of the absolute necessity of founding practical life on philosophical conceptions, of living a simple, strenuous life, so far as possible communistically, and on a basis of natural religion. This was Rosminianism, carried a step further—quite a step. For Rosmini, a loyal and devout Catholic priest and the founder of a religious order, had noted that:

In modern times the people have risen against the absolutism of their rulers, but they fought merely a special form of absolutism instead of absolutism itself. They substituted . . . popular despotism for monarchical . . . the question is, how can despotism in all its forms be destroyed? Only by recognising the fact that above civil society and the people and human nature there is eternal justice which comes, not from legislators or from the people or from the will of man, it does not "come" at all: it *is*. That is the source of human rights, and of all authority.

To subsequent meetings of Thomas Davidson's held throughout 1883 came Frank Podmore, E. R. Pease, Hubert Bland, Miss Owen, a granddaughter of Robert Owen, and Mrs. and Miss Hinton, the widow and daughter of the Rev. James Hinton, a celebrated preacher and advocate of polygamy, who said of himself, "Christ was the Saviour of men . . . I am the Saviour of women, and I don't envy Him one bit." All of these subsequently became prominent Fabians.

To these, Thomas Davidson proposed the foundation of a society modeled on the one he had already established in the U.S.A., to be called the Vita Nuova, or the Fellowship of the New Life, whose object was to be: "the cultivation of a perfect character in each and all." A number of other people interested in religious thought, in ethical problems, and in social reform formed with the above-named the nucleus of the Fellowship, and after Davidson's departure, the aspirants continued to meet in E. R. Pease's room at 17 Osnaburgh Street, Regent's Park. The English organizer or secretary of the embryonic society was Percival Chubb, then working for the Local Government Board and subsequently head of an Ethical church in New York. At the first duly constituted meeting of the Fellowship, on October 24, 1883, the minutes, written by Mr. Chubb, note that from the general discussion emerged the possibility "for a number of persons in sympathy with the main idea to unite for the purpose of common living, as far as possible on a communistic basis, realising among themselves the higher life." The members were to "pursue their present calling in the world, but would aim to make the community as far as practicable self-contained and self-supporting." But from the first some members were obviously animated by a passion primarily for social, rather than individual, betterment. The young leaders of the more socially minded of Davidson's adherents were Frank Podmore and E. R. Pease, then working on the Stock Exchange. Messrs. Podmore and Pease were also interested in psychical research, and it was while vainly waiting for a ghost to appear in an empty, supposedly haunted house at Notting Hill that they discussed Henry George's teachings in *Progress and Poverty,* and found they had a common interest in social as well as in psychical progress.

At the meeting of the Fellowship of the New Life held in E. R. Pease's rooms on November 28, thirty-one people were present, including Frederick Keddell, the first secretary of the Fabian Society. H. H. Champion introduced as the third resolution that "the competitive system ensures the happiness and comfort of the few at the expense of the suffering of the many, and . . . Society must be reconstituted in such a manner as to secure the general welfare and happiness." This was carried unanimously, but at a subsequent meeting on December 15, when another resolution was introduced stating that the principle of the Fellowship would be "the subordination of material things to spiritual," nine members demurred. Frank Podmore wrote to Percival Chubb the next day, to the effect that "some of us, after talking the matter over, cannot submit to the resolution moved by Dr. Burns Gibson. At the same time, we wish to have a society on more general lines . . . we are anxious not to have any discussion of any kind." At the next meeting, therefore, held at 17 Osnaburgh Street on Friday, January 4, 1884, Mr. Frank Podmore moved an amendment to the series of resolutions read at the previous meeting, and proposed as Resolution 1 the formation of a second society to be called the Fabian Society. This was carried by 9 votes to 2, and a second resolution promised that for the present the Fabian Society should not pledge its members to anything further than the basis of agreement unanimously carried on November 20, 1883.

Frank Podmore explained that the name Fabian was an allusion to the victorious policy of Fabius Cunctator (Fabius the Delayer). Frank Podmore, who is traditionally supposed to have written the two mottoes on the title page of Fabian Tract No. 1, refers to Fabius and his tactics in the second motto, which runs, "For the right moment you must wait, as Fabius did, most patiently, when warring against Hannibal, though many censured his delays; but when the time comes you must strike hard, as Fabius did, or your waiting will be in vain and fruitless." (H. G. Wells pointed out insultingly, but inaccurately, that Fabius never did strike hard. In fact, Fabius Cunctator inflicted a severe loss on Hannibal by the recapture of Tarentum when he was consul for the fifth time in B.C. 209.)

"On the motion of Mr. Pease, Mr. Bland, Mr. Keddell and Mr. Podmore were provisionally appointed as an Executive Committee, to serve for three months . . . a collection was made to provide funds for past expenses: the sum collected amounting to thirteen shillings and sixpence. Thus the Fabian

Society was founded," noted E. R. Pease,[12] its secretary for a quarter of a century and a Fabian until his death at ninety-seven in 1955.

The Fabians started at once to hold meetings, fortnightly, for discussion, for the reading of papers, and the hearing of reports. Members were delegated to attend meetings on social subjects, debates at Workingmen's Clubs, etc., in order that they might report the proceedings to the Society, and put forward, as occasion served, the views of the Society. The fortnightly meetings have continued practically ever since.

Thomas Davidson was not pleased. He regarded the Fabian Society as an offshoot of the one he had founded, but disapproved of it because it seemed.to tend toward an external rather than an inward ideal. Yet there was never any bitterness between the two societies, and several Fabians continued also to be members of the Fellowship of the New Life until its demise.

The Fellowship of the New Life lasted for fifteen years, publishing a quarterly, *Seed Time*. It was supported by such men as J. Ramsay MacDonald, later Labor Prime Minister, Edward Carpenter, and the Havelock Ellises. It ran a printing press, a kindergarten, and later, an Ethical church in Croydon. Co-operative residence was attempted, but, as Pease[13] blandly noted, it was singularly unsuccessful, since "close association, especially of persons with the strong and independent opinions of the average socialist, promotes discord, and against this the high ideals of the New Fellowship proved no protection." The Fellowship was dissolved in 1896.

Meanwhile, the Fabians flourished.

[12] p. 35.
[13] p. 36.

CHAPTER THREE

ALL REALITY, RABINdranath Tagore has said, is relationship, and from the first beginnings of the Fabian Society its members' relations to each other and to other societies were tremendously vital. At the Fabian Society's second meeting, reports were presented of a lecture by Henry George, and a Conference of the Democratic Federation. Shaw's conversion *by* Henry George—though not *to* him—was but one of the current attitudes. Karl Marx had sneered at Henry George's book as "the capitalist's last ditch" and Arnold Toynbee made his last public speech against George. John Bright, too, had taken upon himself publicly to expose the fallacies underlying George's theories of land nationalization. But Charles Darwin had ordered a copy of the book, and in 1881 John Morley, reading it, confessed himself electrified, and Joseph Chamberlain recommended it to Lady Dorothy Nevill,[1] saying it was being eagerly read by the working classes. George, meanwhile, expressed his own opinion of British sages: after meeting Herbert Spencer he declared him to be most horribly conceited and noted that he refused to believe that really great men were.

John Bright was far farther from the Fabians than Henry George—nothing is so Tory as an erstwhile radical. Bright has been variously castigated for making an idol of principle, and for dodging in and out of office, whether from love of influence or from dislike of measures. In political circles then it was being whispered that moral splendor is a national asset; but it has to be paid for, and few countries could bear the expense of many Brights. As seen by the Fabians, Bright combined the delight of being powerful with the enjoyment of being sinless. Henry George, on the other hand, kept the qualified admiration of many Fabians, and above all of Shaw, for the rest of his long life: "I am glad to say," wrote Shaw,

[1] pp. 20, 26.

"that I have never denied or belittled our debt to Henry George. If we [Fabians] outgrew *Progress and Poverty* in many respects, so did George himself too, but nobody ever has got away, or ever will get away, from the truths that were the centre of his propaganda—his errors anybody can get away from." [2] Hyndman, who had been endlessly good to George, even having him, his wife and children to stay for months, thought that George taught by error, which for Karl Marx was an impossibility. Fulminating against George, Marx declared that the leaving of error unrefuted was to encourage intellectual immorality, since for ten men who went further, a hundred might very easily stop with George, and the danger of this was too great to run. George's fluent inconsequence was indeed most alien to Marx's tidy German mind.

At an early Fabian meeting, Hubert Bland read a paper on the Democratic Federation, and moved "That while not entirely agreeing with the statements and phrases used in the pamphlets of the Democratic Federation, and in the speeches of Mr. Hyndman, this Society considers that the Democratic Federation is doing good and useful work and is worthy of sympathy and support"—a resolution which was carried unanimously. Hyndman was not quite so kind—nor so patronizing—about the Fabians. "Those who were not ready to accept Marx's theories or to mix familiarly with the working class went off and formed the bureaucratic Fabian Society, which has since so assiduously promulgated the doctrines of middle-class permeation and high-toned intrigue," [3] he wrote. But the members of both groups were, at this stage, fairly intimate; indeed, the handful of Socialists in London saw a great deal of each other, and their differences had not as yet crystallized. M. Gustav Le Bon has pointed out that Socialist doctrines, even as late as 1907, were of such mobility that to discuss them was a waste of time, adding that this mobility was common to, and preceded, the birth of any new belief, since dogmas did not harden until they had triumphed—until the moment of victory they remained fluid and vague. This imprecision, he insisted, was a necessary condition of their success, since it allowed them to adapt themselves to the most varied necessities, and thus to give satisfaction to the differing discontents. Socialism, as Dicey and Le Bon agree, is, philosophically speaking, a collective reaction against individualization. For its enemies, it is a re-

2 Letter from G.B.S. to Hamlin Garland, January 29, 1905. Quoted in Henderson, p. 215.
3 Hyndman, 1911, p. 310.

turn to the tribe; for its adherents, an earnest of a society where each individual truly will love his neighbor as himself. For the Socialists in England in the 1880's, whether they were Marxists, as was Hyndman, or Millites, as were the Fabians, Socialism was first of all a collective reaction against the results of nearly a century of laissez-faire liberalism as a national way of life. Today, in mid-twentieth century, the pendulum has shifted, and the individual is once more raising his bloody and bowed head after half a century of collectivization. Today's Liberals hate Socialism far more than they do Conservatism, and the Conservatives do likewise—a complete reversal of the situation fifty years ago, when the little bands of infant Socialists were petted by both the great parties and pitted by them each against the other, like bantam Davids egged on by sparring Goliaths.

Mrs. Hubert Bland has described the genesis of Fabian Tract No. 1, the four-page leaflet, "Why Are the Many Poor?" which has remained in print ever since. "Friday evening," Mrs. Bland wrote, "to Mr. Pease's for tea and after a Fabian meeting. Over at 10, but some of us stayed till 11:00, talking. The talks after the Fabian meeting are very jolly. I do think the Fabians are quite the nicest set of people I ever knew . . . we are now going to issue a *pamphlet* by Mr. Keddell, the secretary, and a Mr. Phillips (working man). Personally, I don't think much of it, but you can't expect a workingman's style to be *much* and his facts are right." [4] Mr. Pease[5] notes that "at that time, H. L. Phillips, a housepainter, was the only 'genuine working man' in our ranks. He had been introduced to me by a Positivist friend, and was in his way a remarkable man, ready at any time to talk of his experiences of liberating slaves by the 'Underground Railway' in the United States. He worked with us cordially for several years, and then gradually dropped out."

Shaw[6] explains how he became a Fabian.

I had read Marx and become a strong Socialist, but I was in doubt about throwing in my lot with the Democratic Federation, not because of snobbishness, but because I wanted to work with men of my own mental training. The Fabian Society's tract "Why Are the Many Poor?" fell into my hands. The moment I saw the words, "Fabian Society" on it I realized that here was a good title which suggested an educated body, so I found out the Society's

[4] Quoted in Moore, p. 37.

[5] p. 39.

[6] "Who I Am and What I Think," May, 1901.

address from the tract and turned up at Pease's rooms for the next meeting.

This was on May 16th, and a pencil note in Shaw's well-known handwriting, subsequently added to the minutes, reads: "This meeting was made memorable by the first appearance of Bernard Shaw." Shaw himself wrote Tract 2, read on September 19th. This was, as Pease put it, "of course, unqualified 'Shaw' and already the era of 'highest moral possibilities' seems remote." Pease[7] demurred to its last proposition: "that we had rather face a Civil War than such another century of suffering as the present one has been." But Shaw assured him that it was all right since in fact no such alternative would ever be offered. Thirty years later Shaw wrote *Misalliance* around the sixth of his Tract 2 proposals. "That the State should compete with private individuals—especially with parents—in providing happy homes for children, so that every child may have a refuge from the tyranny or neglect of its natural custodians." The seventh, "That men no longer need special political privileges to protect them against Women, and that the sexes should henceforth enjoy equal political rights," is indicative of the way the Fabians were thereafter to spice their serious intent with humor. For the most outstanding characteristic of the Fabians was their humor, that is to say, their capacity to take themselves lightly, to laugh at themselves. As wit is the capacity to laugh at others, so humor is the capacity to laugh at oneself. Shaw had both capacities in abundance, and for the Fabian Society's first twenty years he was its foremost writer and speaker, its most articulate interpreter, and its presiding genius.[8] And Shaw[9] wrote of the infant Fabian Society:

. . . it was at this period that we contracted the invaluable habit of freely laughing at ourselves which has always distinguished us, and which has saved us from becoming hampered by the pushing enthusiasts who mistake their own emotions for public movements. From the first, such people fled after one glance at us, declaring we were not serious. Our preference for practical suggestions and criti-

[7] p. 43.

[8] As Sidney Webb told Archibald Henderson, Shaw's official biographer, "Shaw has been the leading member of the Fabian Society virtually from its foundation; and . . . the Society has always expressed his political ideas and work." *See* Henderson, p. 222.

[9] 1892.

cisms, and our impatience of all general expressions of
sympathy with working-class aspirations, not to mention our
way of chaffing our opponents in preference to denouncing
them as enemies of the human race, repelled from us some
warm-hearted and eloquent Socialists, to whom it seemed
callous and cynical to be even commonly self-possessed in
the presence of the suffering upon which Socialists make
war. But there was far too much equality and personal
intimacy among the Fabians to allow of any member pre-
suming to get up and preach at the rest in the fashion
which the working-classes still tolerate submissively from
their leaders. We knew that a certain sort of oratory was
useful for "stoking up" public meetings, but we needed no
stoking up, and, when any orator tried the process on us,
soon made him understand he was wasting his time and
ours. I, for one, should be very sorry to lower the intellectual standard of the Fabian Society by making the atmosphere of its public discussions the least bit more congenial
to stale declamation than they are at present.

Many were drawn to the Fabians by just this gaiety and
youthfulness: these young men and women, all in their early
twenties, who were so determined to remold the world nearer
to their heart's desire, were just as determined not to be
pompous about it, or to pose as Paladins. They must have
seemed April-fresh at the fag end of a long reign and a
longer century. Yet Hesketh Pearson,[10] one of Shaw's biogra-
phers, would not admit that Shaw joked about Fabians, and
said, on the other hand, that he was deadly serious about
them and told him that without them he would have been as
futile as Matthew Arnold. "Socialism was our religion, and
we were as earnest about it as the Communion of Saints."
But saints are never sad, nor were the Fabians.

Eighteen eighty-three marked not only the year the German Government, under Bismarck, began a system of workmen's insurance; it was in that year, too, that Karl Marx
died. The years 1884 to 1887 were years of study and preparation for the members of the Fabian Society. They read
Marx, Lassalle, Proudhon, and Owen, as well as the English
economists, Adam Smith, Ricardo, and Mill, and gradually
shook themselves free from the old Socialist traditions.

Before he became a Fabian, Shaw had read Marx, and
he persuaded Sidney Webb, whom he had first met in 1879
upon joining the Zetetical (truth-seeking) Society, also to become a Fabian. (Sidney Webb was the other resident clerk at
the Colonial Office.) He and Sydney Olivier were great

[10] p. 22.

friends, and the two young men came into the Fabian Society
together, on May 1, 1885. William Clarke, Graham Wallas,
and Annie Besant had all joined by April 1885, when the
Society counted about thirty members. From the first, the
Fabians made it clear that they were not, and never would
be, a Socialist party, but were—and are—"a group of men
and women who are endeavoring to spread practical views
on the immediate and pressing social problems and to indicate the way for their embodiment in legislative or administrative measures." [11]

The Fabians have been accused of being almost too
brainy, of wearing their intellects indecently exposed, but the
over-all impression of them as seen by their contemporaries
is rather one of effervescent and eccentric gaiety than of egg-
head earnestness. And they vastly enjoyed each other's company. All their very varied activities, their comments on
themselves and on each other show that these gifted, often
very good-looking, very young people delighted in their ag-
nosticism, vegetarianism, and Jaegerism, in their talkfests in
gaslit Bloomsbury or Hampstead rooms, their wintry public
debates in unheated halls, their theatricals, and their sandaled
picnics. Eduard Bernstein, the leader of the German "Revi-
sionists," perhaps the only important European Socialist to be
seriously influenced by the Fabians, claims that the Fabians
wished to be "the Jesuits of Socialism." Certainly they trained
as thoroughly as do Jesuits, spending years in relentless study
and research before attempting to begin public political action. Certainly, too, being accepted as a Fabian was a commitment to a very definite way of life. It was not the least
like becoming a member of a political party, and thereafter
just voting or perhaps doing a little electioneering. You could
not *join* the Fabians: you became one, after being duly proposed and seconded, by election and grace. And thereafter
you worked at it.

Shaw has described in *The Fabian Society: What It Has
Done and How It Has Done It*[12] how

A man's Socialistic acquisitiveness must be keen enough to
make him actually prefer spending two or three nights a
week in speaking and debating, or in picking up social information even in the most dingy and scrappy way, to going to the theatre, or dancing or drinking or even sweet-
hearting, if he is to become a really competent propagandist. . . . it is at such lecturing and debating work, and on

[11] Beer, II, p. 277.
[12] 1892.

squalid little committees and ridiculous little delegations to conferences of the three tailors of Tooley Street, with perhaps a deputation to the Mayor thrown in once in a blue moon, that the ordinary Fabian workman or clerk must qualify for his future seat on the Town Council, the School Board, or perhaps in the Cabinet.

(These words were written over thirty years before any Fabian had got into the Cabinet!) As St. John Ervine[13] has noted,

> A person seeking to become a Fabian had first to provide two guarantors that he was known to be in general agreement with the Society's objects. He had also to attend several meetings before he became a candidate; and he had to promise that he would do serious work for the Society of the sort that it was accustomed to do. He was then placed on probation for a year, at the end of which time, if he satisfied the Executive of his ability and devotion, he was admitted to full membership.

Sidney Dark, a lifelong Christian and Fabian, thus accounted for his life: "I joined the Fabians to be thrilled by G.B.S. long before he wrote famous plays. I went on Sunday evenings to hear William Morris at Hammersmith. I went on the stump for the Society at weekends." Sidney Dark was one of the very High Church Fabians, and for many years was editor of the *Church Times*.

One of the things the early and very ambitious Fabians did was to walk all the way to Hampstead—about seven miles there and back—once a fortnight for meetings of the Hampstead Historic Club. This club was a systematic history class where each student took his turn at being professor. G.B.S., Sidney Webb, and Sydney Olivier were the "regulars," of course, earnestly walking their seven miles. G.B.S. at this time wore a shaggy felt hat, a Jaeger wool-jersey suit buttoned down the front, and cocked-up mustachios. Sydney Olivier was upset because Shaw's suit after a downpour of rain shrank almost visibly and when dry developed a rattle like the sound of loose wires. He told G.B.S. he must not wear this tinkling suit if he wished Olivier to walk with him. To quote himself, Shaw at that time was "uppish." His face was dead white with patches of orange whiskers about his cheek and chin (H. H. Champion said the effect was that of an unskilfully poached egg), and even poor Edith Bland, who fell dreadfully in love with Shaw, described him as *"very*

13 p. 126.

plain." Wilfred Scawen Blunt,[14] too, describes G.B.S.'s appearance unflatteringly:

> Shaw was in the papal robes in which Neville [Lytton] is painting him . . . a grotesque figure . . . he is an ugly fellow, too, his face a pasty white, with a red nose and a rusty red beard, and little slatey blue eyes. Shaw's appearance, however, matters little when he begins to talk, if he can ever be said to begin, for he talks always, in his fine Irish brogue.

Mrs. Bland comments further: "He has a fund of dry Irish humor that is simply irresistible. He is the grossest flatterer of men, women and children impartially I ever met, and is horribly untrustworthy as he repeats everything he hears and does not always stick to the truth." Shaw worked endlessly at his Socialism: "For about twelve years . . . I sermonized on Socialism at least three times a fortnight average. I preached whenever and wherever I was asked. It was first come first served with me: whether it was for a street corner, a public-house parlor, a market place, the economic section of the British Association, the City Temple, a cellar or a drawing room. My audiences varied from tens to thousands." Shaw never once in his life took payment for any political speech, although, at that time, he was horribly poor, nor did he ever refuse or break an engagement to speak on Socialism in order to pass a gallant evening.

Yet G.B.S. loved flirting, and, in the case of Mrs. Bland (whose husband was everlastingly, congenitally, gratuitously, and inconsiderately unfaithful), Shaw perhaps thought that a *public* flirtation might soothe the lady's wounded ego. But even from her, lovely as she was, the most attractive and vivacious woman among the Fabians, with her dark, beautiful eyes, and fine broad forehead half-covered with a fringe of curly brown hair, cut short of course (short hair was a *must* among Socialist ladies), he would stand no nonsense. He was "heartlessly amusing," yet refused to sit beside her at Fabian meetings unless she promised not to ask for a glass of water or stage a faint. But he was a frequent visitor at the Blands, as were all the Fabians (the Bland home was the Fabian social headquarters), and on gala occasions Edith would trail around in a long peacock-blue satin gown, with strings of beads and Indian bangles from wrist to elbow. "Madame," as she was called, smoked incessantly, and looked "like a raffish Rossetti with her long full throat and dark luxuriant hair."

[14] II, p. 141.

The assorted children—Paul, Iris, Fabian, and Rosamund, some hers, some by members of her husband's harem—were all lively and good-looking.

To Ethel Voynich, daughter of George Boole who wrote *The Laws of Thought*, G.B.S. was endlessly kind, turning her novel *The Gadfly* into a play and having it performed with one of his to protect the copyright. He also advised her on her choice of agent, "I would go to Curtis Brown," he wrote. She, however, found G.B.S. unpleasant to touch and like many other women friends of hers, did not like to shake hands with him. But then she and G.B.S. had disagreed about her interpretation on the pianoforte of the G Sharp Major in the second volume of Bach's forty-eight; so perhaps her view of him was not wholly unbiased.

Sydney Olivier says that on their fortnightly walks to the Hampstead Historic Club, G.B.S. "regarded it as his duty to talk wittily, if only for practice." But Sydney Olivier and Webb were "university graduates, I from Oxford," notes Olivier,[15] and, with true British snobbishness, they judged "Shaw's education and his appreciation of academically and socially established humanities to be sadly defective." G.B.S. was well aware of his then own attitude of priggish superiority to these social superiors, for he poked fun at this trait in himself as Cokane in *Widowers' Houses*.

G.B.S. was already at this time a fanatical vegetarian. He was a cannibal, he declared, only until his early twenties. Thereafter he never deviated from his principles, which included the rejection of all alcohol, tea, coffee, or tobacco. When the doctor told him he would die if he didn't have liver injections, he declared, in refusing, that he would go to his grave followed by a grateful procession of the animals he hadn't eaten. Asked to dine by R. B. Haldane, and told to "come in morning dress," he bought himself a suit for twenty dollars (having at that time only evening dress and tweeds), to find the other three men—his host, Asquith, and Balfour —in tails, and the women blazing in diamonds. He took Margot Asquith in, and got nothing to eat but "a scrap of bread and a glass of water," since his principles prevented him eating anything else. At his own house he always provided conventional fare, and his famous post-card invitations included the words, "my wife will provide a corpse."

G.B.S.'s greatest friend, Sidney Webb, could not have

[15] As stated by Lord Olivier in a letter to Archibald Henderson. *See* Henderson, p. 212.

offered a greater contrast. Shaw has described Sidney at their first meeting.

A few weeks after I joined the Zetetical Society I was much struck by a speaker. He was about 21, rather below middle height, with small hands and feet, and a profile that suggested an improvement on Napoleon the Third. He had a fine forehead, a long head, eyes that were built on top of two highly developed organs of speech (according to phrenologists) and remarkably thick, strong, dark hair. He knew all about the subject of debate; knew more than the lecturer; knew more than anybody present; had read everything that had ever been written; and remembered all the facts that bore on the subject. . . . This was the ablest man in England: Sidney Webb. Quite the wisest thing I ever did was to force my friendship on him and to keep it; for from that time I was not merely a futile Shaw but a committee of Webb and Shaw.

But neither Sidney Webb nor his wife Beatrice ever tasted lemonade or practiced any sort of diet. Diets to them were only fads, said Shaw.[16]

Webb, later Baron Passfield . . . now buried in Westminster Abbey at my urgent demand, proved one of the most extraordinary and capable of world-bettering administrators and historians. I somehow divined this whilst we were still both nobodies. As a disciple of John Stuart Mill he had grasped the economic certainty that private property in the sources of production plus freedom of contract must produce a plutocracy face to face with a proletariat, and substitute class war for genuine democracy . . . Webb, as a modern upper division civil servant, knew that there is a quite feasible corrective alternative in nationalization of the sources of production, and direct management of vital industries by the State, of the existence and success of which he had at his fingers' ends an overwhelming list of examples. On that basis he was a convinced Socialist. The difference between Shaw with Webb's brains, knowledge and official experience and Shaw by himself was enormous. But as I was and am an incorrigible histrionic mountebank, and Webb was the simplest of geniuses, I was often in the center of the stage whilst he was invisible in the prompter's box.

G. D. H. Cole, who was to lead the revolt against the Fabian "old guard"—Shaw and the Webbs—years later, writes of Sidney: "Fabianism was essentially his creation—

[16] 1949, p. 108.

his and no one else's. There might have been a Fabian Society
without him, but it would not have lived nor had an 'ism'
called after it. . . . His social philosophy came out of J. S.
Mill." Webb, in propounding his doctrine of the "inevitability of gradualism," made of Fabianism a peculiarly British
institution. Hyndman, for all his money, devotion, enthusiasm, and intelligence, could not turn Marxism into a language understood by the British people. As Shaw[17] pointed
out, "Marx's *Kapital* is not a treatise on Socialism; it is a
Jeremiad against the bourgeoisie," and it was the bourgeoisie who painted the flag red, while on the real Left were the
aristocratic anarchists such as Kropotkin and Bakunin, for
example. By the same token, Fabianism never had much
appeal in Europe: as a Swabian delegate put it at the International Congress of 1886—the first to which the Fabian
Society sent delegates—"Comrades, we must not allow ourselves to be carried away by patience."

H. G. Wells's description of Sidney Webb in *The New
Machiavelli* pulls no punches:

> . . . he was a short sturdy figure with a rounded protrud-
> ing abdomen and a curious broad, flattened, clean-shaven
> face that seemed nearly all forehead. He peered up with
> reddish-swollen-looking eyes over gilt-edged glasses that
> were divided horizontally into portions of different refrac-
> tive power . . . he was always just the same, a little con-
> fidential and *sotto voce,* artlessly rude and egoistic in an
> undignified way.

Yet Sidney never seemed justly sensitive to epithets like these.
Once, when Desmond MacCarthy was staying with the
Webbs and a new Wells novel had just come out, Beatrice
said, "I'm in this one, too. I'm the woman whose voice is a
strangulated contralto, but you're not in it, Sidney." He replied with a pleasant smile, "Oh, yes, I am. I'm the man who
is described as one of those supplementary males often found
among lower crustacea," exhibiting not a trace of hurt. No
one, indeed, ever saw him vexed in his long life.

H. H. Asquith, of a very different political complexion,
called Sidney Webb a saint, and certainly he was never cross
or crabbed, but always selfless and serene, "a rotund little
man, with a goatee beard, who peered . . . through thick
eyeglasses and spoke with a strong lisping Cockney accent,"
as L. S. Amery described him. Mrs. Cecil Chesterton, dining
with the Webbs, asked her host what had become of the con-
servatory she had seen on her previous visit. "Wiste of spice,"

[17] "Who I Am and What I Think," May, 1901.

replied Sidney. Amery[18] adds, "I remember walking with him once on Box Hill on a Sunday. Seeing loving couples roll each other downhill I caught the eye of the friend who was with us, and in a twinkling we had our globular little Napoleon . . . revolving helplessly down the steep grass slope." Yet Sidney remained unvexed.

W. T. Stead, then editor of the *Pall Mall Gazette,* described Sidney Webb as

> a very remarkable man, much more remarkable than anybody thinks, excepting himself. Since Mr. Chamberlain arose in Birmingham there has been no man so like him as Mr. Sidney Webb . . . to all the energy and perseverance and municipal spirit of Mr. Chamberlain, Mr. Sidney Webb adds a great literary gift and a philosophic conception of social progress to which Mr. Chamberlain can lay no claim. He is a Socialist, but he is no Utopian dreamer; he is a man crammed with facts.

Beatrice Webb,[19] Sidney's devoted wife, described him as

> an unprepossessing speaker with a husky voice, made less articulate by a rapid delivery; at times, in his haste, he omits a syllable or clips his words . . . when addressing a popular audience he is apt to be prosy and monotonous . . . as a committee man Sidney Webb excels. He is always on the spot. He thinks twice as fast as his colleagues. He is the ideal draftsman, able to express the desired conclusion in a dozen different phrases so as to disarm suspicion or prejudice . . . admirable as a social engineer, he has not the make-up of a popular magnetism; he has no liking for personal prominence; he is, in fact, not a public personage at all, he is a private citizen with public aims and expert knowledge . . . he has always been a "behind-the-scenes" man.

John Morley said, "I never can see what people see in him," to a friend—who promptly repeated it to Sidney! The caricature of him that his wife liked best was one—about 1900 —of Balfour and Asquith bobbing up and down at the end of wires handled by the "wily Fabian." "His influence," his wife concluded, "has been limited but steady." As G. D. H. Cole said, "The worst is that he is *permanent*—when you think you have disposed of him he confronts you in another part of the field."

[18] p. 229.

[19] 1948, pp. 5, 6.

The contrast between G.B.S. and Webb could not have been greater, nor could their affection. Bertrand Russell[20] once remarked to Shaw that Webb seemed somewhat deficient in kindly feeling. "No," Shaw replied, "you are quite mistaken. Webb and I were once in a tram car in Holland eating biscuits out of a bag. A handcuffed criminal was brought into the tram by policemen. All the other passengers shrank away in horror, but Webb went up to the prisoner and offered him biscuits." Also in Holland, Shaw made Webb look at pictures, though at Oberammergau Shaw could not get Webb out of their hotel. "I have very little knowledge of what has happened to me internally," Webb wrote in a rare moment of confession. "I am, I suppose, what is nowadays called an extrovert. Things impinge on me, and I re-act to their impact, occasionally with ideas and suggestions that prove interesting." [21] His future wife, after Sidney had dined for the first time at her house (February 14, 1890), noted, "a remarkable little man, with a huge head and a tiny body, a breadth of forehead quite sufficient to account for the encyclopedic character of his knowledge . . . there is a directness of speech, an open-mindedness, an imaginative warm-heartedness, which will carry him far."

There was also in Sidney an almost terrifying disregard for the means used to achieve the single goal he had set himself. "The first time I worked with Sidney," Leonard Woolf wrote, "I was puzzled and troubled by this extraordinary mixture of scrupulousness with regard to ends, and an almost ingenuous unscrupulousness with regard to means." After describing the Webbs' work, Woolf goes on,

> Their ruthless concentration upon a limited field of human life and a curious habit of open-minded dogmatism gave to their thought a dangerous narrowness . . . their politics had a reciprocal effect upon their political thought. They were entirely honest researchers and social scientists. . . . Yet to a great extent they regarded the object of their research work and books . . . to be to provide them with material for permeating and persuading practical men to do what the Webbs thought ought to be done or for blowing them up if they refused to be permeated or persuaded.[22]

Because he had an authentic preference for getting things done to being seen as doing them, and because he was utterly disinterested and genuine in his faith that collective control

[20] p. 108.
[21] *St. Martin's Review*, 1928.
[22] Margaret I. Cole (ed.), 1949, p. 267.

and collective administration would diminish, if not abolish, poverty, a grateful country has enshrined Sidney Webb, with his wife, among its greatest dead.

Shaw[23] described the "Fabian Politbureau" as "an incomparable critical threshing machine" for his ideas.

> When I seemed most original and fantastic, I was often simply an amanuensis and a mouthpiece with a rather exceptional literary and dramatic knack . . . my colleagues knocked much nonsense, ignorance, and vulgar provinciality out of me; for we were on quite ruthless critical terms with one another . . . for some years the leaders in the Politbureau or Thinking Cabinet of the Fabian policy were Webb, Olivier, Wallas, Shaw, and the Tory Democrat Hubert Bland.

G.B.S. came of "downstart" Irish gentry stock; Webb came from a working-class family, from which he early escaped through scholarships. In later life he never identified himself with working-class people, as did other Labor politicians, such as George Lansbury, J. H. Thomas, or J. R. Clynes. Rumor had it (and St. John Ervine, in his life of Shaw, endorses this rumor) that Sidney Webb was Jewish; certainly, both his appearance and his astonishing skill at languages were un-English, to say the least. Sidney Webb had come to Fabian Socialism via the "saint of Liberalism" John Stuart Mill, son of the Benthamite philosopher, James Mill. John Stuart Mill had worked himself free from a rigid utilitarianism only to become, temporarily, one of the first English disciples of the French positivist Auguste Comte. Comte's mystical adoration of humanity had led a whole generation of thinkers to substitute sociology for religion and humanitarianism for charity. Comte amalgamated the two great commandments of Christianity—to love God and to love one's neighbor—by eliminating God, and elevating the second commandment to first place. Mill, however, soon found that Comte's ideas of the relation of the individual to society were becoming increasingly totalitarian, since humanity, not the individual human being, was the God-substitute actually worshiped. For Mill, the foundations of society were the psychological laws of association and motivation which cannot be regulated by self-evident truths, categorical imperatives, or any other "oughts." For Mill, all knowledge, every given or supposed fact, must be tested by experience, which for him was the sole criterion of truth. Mill was radically empirical, and his great essay *On Liberty* is one of the classics of human

23 1949, p. 111.

J. S. M. languages also

reason. "His whole philosophy, whatever its faults, is perhaps the greatest nineteenth century symbol of spiritual liberality." [24] But though Mill insisted that the only valid criterion is experience, he knew that not all valid propositions are reports of immediate experience; the lessons of history are not an adequate basis for the conduct of political affairs; real continuities in nature do not always lie upon the surface of experience. Like Bentham, Mill declared that actions are to be judged by their consequences, and that morality is the deliberate choice by the individual of what leads to the greatest good, individual and collective. For Mill the greatest good is the harmonious satisfaction of all the desires of the individual, who is a social being, dependent for his happiness on the satisfaction of his social impulses and other-regarding sentiments. A life of personal pleasure is as self-frustrating for Mill as any other pattern of conduct which does not satisfy the total demands of the human personality.

Sidney Webb's devotion to Mill matched Wallas's to Bentham. Webb's colleague and great friend, Sydney Olivier, was equally intelligent and studious. He and Webb had both passed their civil-service examinations brilliantly, being placed in the upper division, and Olivier headed the competition list. Both these young men became Cabinet Ministers and peers, though, at this time, when both were in their early twenties, to become Socialists was burning their boats as far as any official promotion was concerned. A colleague, Sir Alexander Harris, has described the notable addition to the interest of official life in the Colonial Office that was caused by the foundation of the Fabian Society, and added that leading members of the Society looked in at the Office frequently. G.B.S. described Olivier as

> An extraordinarily attractive figure. He was handsome and strongly sexed, looking like a Spanish grandee in any sort of clothes, however unconventional. He was not interested in athletics, but his college chum, Graham Wallas, who stood six foot two (or was it four?) in his socks, told me that once when he alluded to Miss Margaret Cox, now Lady Olivier, as if she were no more than any other young lady, Olivier threw him across the room.

The Colonial Office did not profess to be open for public business before 11:00 A.M., but the clerks generally stayed until 7:00 or 7:30 P.M. Having a social conscience, Olivier worked "the earlier part of my mornings" for a Sanitary Aid Committee in a ghastly block of slums known as the Lisson

[24] Aiken, p. 140.

Grove district. "My duties were to inspect and report on the condition of the latrines, the stairs, floors and wallpapers." He would arrive, a tall, clean-shaven young man in a high top hat and black morning coat, knock at the door, and find the single women still in bed, in their single rented rooms, often with a client dressing. "On one occasion, when I was investigating the wallpaper and asked if bugs were troublesome, the young artillery man who was shaving himself at the window, had the wit to suggest that I might take a lodging there for a night and see for myself, which put us all at our ease." Elsewhere Olivier found the tenants smoking haddocks in the latrines by burning newspapers under them. His duties done, he would walk to his office, stopping off to call on G.B.S. in Fitzroy Street. G.B.S. was then dramatic critic on the *Star*, and Olivier wrote, "I used to share his vegetarian breakfast of luscious cocoa and Hill's whole meal bread and butter. I also enjoyed the delight of meeting his admirable and astonishing mother." Olivier notes that in due course he grew up and became secretary of the Fabian Society, from 1886 to 1890, being designed to pull the linchpin out of the capitalist system on which his class depended. He went from the Colonial Office to become Governor of Jamaica, and later Secretary of State for India. Many of his letters to H. G. Wells, who was also a great friend, survive. Wells described him as "a great success at charades, playing the infant Moses with touching realism, and also doing a mighty Samson with a sheepskin mat of hair." As a young Fabian, Olivier horrified Hubert Bland by his casual attire. Olivier liked to wear a brown velveteen jacket for dinner, and he arrived one night to dine at the Blands with one of its sleeves hanging by a thread. Edith Bland, meeting him at the door, sewed it back in place hastily, before her sartorially conventional husband could see it. Even at the Colonial Office, Olivier had trouble with clothes, dipping the white ostrich feather plumes on his court hat in ink when the Lord Chamberlain insisted black ones must now be worn. G.B.S. said of Olivier that he was a genius but of a kind quite different from Webb. He was an autocrat, who, had he not been a man of good will, would have been the greatest scoundrel alive, for he had no conscience. He was himself alone.

Olivier had come to Fabian Socialism directly from the Positivist philosophy of Auguste Comte, and G.B.S. declared him to be, as far as he knew, the only Fabian who came in through that gate. Auguste Comte had rejected Kant, Fichte, Hegel, and metaphysics generally, whether Aristotelian or idealistic. For Comte, only science was true: only what could be proved scientifically true was truth, and scientific investigation was the only approach to scientifically proven data, which were the only realities. Comte saw humanity—and each human being—as passing through a theological stage in which the human mind seeks analogies, animistic and anthropomorphic, in everything and everywhere; then through a second metaphysical stage when the anthropomorphic tendencies are etherealized into abstract concepts and reason is identified with cause. The proofs offered at this stage are concocted in the human brain, and result in deductions from so-called rationally self-evident truths which are prefabricated in the brain. This stage deteriorates into a struggle between "realists" and "nominalists" over the nature of universal concepts: did we make God because He is necessary to us, or did He make us because it is a necessity of His nature so to act? is an example. Such ratiocinations lead to the third, or positivist stage of human history, when the futility of the earlier theological and metaphysical stages is clearly seen, and positive science is accepted as "all we know and all we need to know." Genuine science finally emerges from the relationship of proven facts which are seen to be grouped in classes of phenomena coexisting with, or succeeding, other equally verifiable classes of phenomena. Coexisting patterns Comte calls static; succeeding patterns are dynamic laws.

Graham Wallas was the fourth member of the Fabian Junta—Olivier, Webb, and Shaw being the others. G.B.S. dubbed them the Three Musketeers and D'Artagnan, but for all other Fabians they were The Four. Wallas had quit the Highgate school where he was teaching, because he refused to lead the boys into chapel. Loving, gentle to everything else in the world, he was quite intemperate about religion. He described the difference between himself and his great friend Sidney Webb: "He is interested in town councils. I am interested in town councillors." Wallas was as devoted a disciple of Jeremy Bentham as Webb had been of John Stuart Mill or Olivier of Auguste Comte or Shaw of Henry George. In those days (as Robert Louis Stevenson noted in his *The Story of a Lie*) to be called a Benthamite was a term of opprobrium. Yet Jeremy Bentham, one of the creators of the British Civil Service, was in many ways a greater figure than any one of the Fabians who built so well on his foundations, for without him they never could have functioned at all, let alone succeeded. The Beveridge Plan, for example, the greatest of the pillars of the Welfare State, depended on Bentham's scaffolding: yet between Bentham and Beveridge stretched the whole of the long nineteenth century of laissez faire. Jeremy Bentham's grandfather and father were lawyers, and in his first book he attacked the great English jurist William Blackstone. He died at 85, leaving 9 large published books and 148 boxes of manuscripts. He was the founder of the *Westminster Review* and was responsible for the mitigation of the penal laws and the abolition of deportation to the colonies; he campaigned for Catholic emancipation, for the revocation of the laws against usury, and for Parliamentary reform. He also advocated secret ballots, annual Parliaments, manhood suffrage, and the establishment of an international court—in fact, he invented the term "international law," but cribbed his most famous phrase "the greatest happiness of the greatest number is the measure of right and wrong" from Priestley's *Essay on the First Principles of Government*. Essentially, the "utilitarianism" Bentham taught was the empirical creed of the rising British middle classes, who rejected Burke's aristocratic outlook as completely as they did the revolutionary theories of Paine and Godwin, based as they were on "foreign," French and American originals. For Bentham,[25]

Nature has placed mankind under the governance of two sovereign masters, pain and pleasure. It is for them to point out what we ought to do, as well as to determine what we shall do. On the one hand the standard of right and wrong, on the other the chain of causes and effects, are fastened to their throne. They govern us in all we say, in all we think; every effort we make to throw off our subjection, will serve but to demonstrate and confirm it . . . the principle of utility recognizes this subjection, and assumes it for the foundation of that system, the object of which is to rear the fabric of felicity by the hands of reason and of law.

Bentham had always thought that people in power only wanted to know what was good in order to embrace it, and when he discovered that they were against reform, he grew bitter and ever more radical. He developed a school which proved to be the most potent force in English reform for more than half a century. His best-known followers were James Mill, James's son John Stuart Mill, and David Ricardo. "I was the spiritual father of Mill, and Mill was the spiritual father of Ricardo so that Ricardo was my spiritual grandson," he wrote. Bentham died disappointed, and in his last memo he noted, "I have two minds, one of which is perpetually occupied in looking at and examining the other." Yet Sir Henry Maine said that he did not know "a single law reform effected since Bentham's day which cannot be traced to his influence." Personally, he was a delightfully prankish eccentric, who left his skeleton to London University, on condition an

[25] Opening sentences.

annual party be given for it—which still is done today. He also left a peculiarly unpleasant prison—the Millbank penitentiary—as a monument to his endeavors to increase human happiness. His disciple Graham Wallas was a splendid example of the absent-minded professor. Alys Pearsall Smith, the lovely, intelligent, and rich daughter of American evangelists —she later married Bertrand Russell—fell in love with Wallas and went to all his lectures. At one of these he asked a student what the latter had taken as his research project, and was somewhat discomforted when the student said, "You, sir." Another time, when someone pointed out to Wallas that he had come to class without a necktie, he gently asked, "Oh, would you mind getting me one?" Alys did over his rooms in Bloomsbury while he was away lecturing in the United States, but on his return he noticed nothing, and she did not like to point out the nice new chintz chair covers or the repainting job, for fear of being thought immodest.

Six feet, with a slouching figure—good features with a genial, open smile; utterly unselfconscious and lacking in vanity or personal ambition. Without convictions he would have lounged through life—with convictions he grinds; his natural sluggishness of nature, transformed by his social fervour into a slow grinding at anything that turns up to do. In spite of his moral fervour, he seems incapable of directing his own life, and tends to drift into anything that other people decide. . . . He preaches, too, a habit carried over from his life as usher and teacher of boys.

Thus Beatrice Webb[26] describes Graham Wallas, and she adds, "to his disciples he appears a brilliant man, a first-rate lecturer, a very genius for teaching, a great thinker and a conscientious writer." All comments on him agree on the rather slovenly, slightly pedantic, noble-spirited man.

"The Wallases, the Oliviers, and the Webbs," wrote L. S. Amery in his autobiography, "were quite the best of the leading Fabians—Shaw I refuse to count as a typical Fabian— they lived lives devoted to the *res publica,* right out to the end of their days. They took the idea of getting a living as something by the way . . . the real business of life began for them only after that had been settled and put to one side."

Sir Alfred Zimmern and Walter Lippmann were among Graham Wallas's devoted pupils, and there is scarcely a considerable figure in England among the younger generation of politicians and publicists, who does not owe something to Graham Wallas's slow, fussy manners, his penetrating and

[26] 1948, p. 37.

inspiring counsels. As an undergraduate, Wallas had been very influenced while at Oxford, at Corpus Christi College, by John Ruskin. "I heard his lectures," he wrote, "and for some time saw him almost every day. His mobile lips were not yet covered by a beard, and he always wore his precise costume, with an intensely blue neck-cloth. His face was that of a man who had seen, and was to see again, hell as well as Paradise." Ruskin's *Unto This Last* and his *Munera Pulveris* had been inspired by working with Charles Kingsley and other social reformers in the 1850's, but though eagerly read at the time, and although regarded as landmarks of Christian Socialism, Ruskin's works had little lasting effect on British Socialist thought, and, with the exception of Wallas, none at all on the Fabians, who preferred to read Edward Bellamy's American Utopia, *Looking Backward*, or William Morris's British sequel, *News From Nowhere*. As G.B.S. wrote,

> it is a curious fact that of the three great propagandist amateurs of political economy, Henry George, Marx, and Ruskin, Ruskin alone seems to have had no effect on the Fabians. Here and there in the Socialist movement workmen turned up who had read *Fors Clavigera* or *Unto This Last* and some of the more well-to-do had read the first chapter of *Munera Pulveris*. But Ruskin's name was hardly mentioned in the Fabian Society. My explanation is that, barring Olivier, the Fabians were inveterate Philistines. My efforts to induce them to publish . . . Oscar Wilde's *The Soul of Man Under Socialism* . . . fell so flat that I doubt whether my colleagues were even conscious of them.

Graham Wallas describes how

> Webb and Olivier were civil servants who had scored highly in political economy at the class one exam, owing to their ability to expound the Ricardian law of rent. On this point we definitely disagreed with Marx, and this led us to abandon "abstract Labour" as the basis of value, and to adopt Jevons's concept of value as fixed by the point where marginal effort coincides with marginal utility. It was this rejection of Marxism which made possible our partial permeation of Liberal and other non-social political organizations. During ten years of constant intimacy we learnt from Shaw's exacting passion for artistic perfection and Webb's almost incredible force and industry, that one could only get things done by steady and severe effort of will. The traditional Fabian attitude of mind and will was of course made by Webb and Shaw. Webb taught us to work. I remember Podmore complained that the strenuous life we were leading in 1887 left us no time for exercise

and amusement, and that Webb told him he should find
exercise in walking to lectures, amusement in delivering
them! The turning point in my own career was when I
explained to the Executive that I had been unavoidably
prevented from carrying out a promise to draft something,
and Webb said, "No doubt you had every excuse, but you
will observe that the thing has not been done."

G. D. H. Cole says that Wallas's great importance to the Fabians was that he was both a collectivist and a libertarian,
and Cole calls *Human Nature in Politics,* published by Wallas
in 1908, the promise of a really great book that Wallas spent
the rest of his life failing to write.

"The . . . chief reason for the success of the Society,"
wrote E. R. Pease, "was its good fortune in attaching to its
service a group of young men, then altogether unknown,
whose reputation has gradually spread . . . all over the
world, and who have always been in the main identified with
Fabianism. Very rarely in the history of voluntary organizations has a group of such exceptional people come together
almost accidentally and worked unitedly together for so many
years for the furtherance of the principles in which they
believed." Even those whose morals were outrageous, such as
Hubert Bland, and later, H. G. Wells, were hard-working
and impassioned Fabians whose political morality was far
superior to their sexual habits. Pease added, ". . . Sidney
Webb, Bernard Shaw, Graham Wallas and Sydney Olivier,
then and for many years afterwards may be said to have
worked and thought together in an intellectual partnership. Webb and Olivier were colleagues in the Colonial Office,
and it is said that for some time the Fabian records—they
were not very bulky—were stored in a table drawer in
Downing Street." For many years there were probably few
evenings of the week and few holidays which two or more of
them did not spend together. "As Webb, Olivier, and Wallas
were men of very exceptional character and attainments,
I was able to work with a four-man power equal to a four-
hundred ordinary manpower," Shaw[27] explained.

Frank Podmore was one of "Bland's group" among the
Fabians, and at the end of Fabian Society meetings he and
Hubert Bland and one or two others would go on to seances
—Podmore and Bland were both at the one at which the ex-
posure of Madame Blavatsky took place. Bland has been
described as a much more tawdry brain in the Fabian con-
stellation. The Blands lived at Lewisham, then almost in the
country, and often invited their fellow Fabians to dine. G.B.S.

[27] 1949, p. 112.

called Bland a Tory Democrat, and said his habit of black-
balling recruits on moral grounds, he himself being an incorrigible polygamist, irritated his fellow Fabians. Bland used to
wear very stiff, conformist clothes and a monocle; he was
very censorious about sex since, as Doris Langley Moore put
it, "His own position was fundamentally a little weak." He
had married Edith Nesbit when she was a lovely eighteen and
he was twenty-five: he had no job, and already a mistress
(probably his mother's companion), and an illegitimate child.
He never informed his mistress of his marriage: his wife discovered "Maggie" and the child only after three years of being Mrs. Bland. Later, his wife learned that one of her friends
was pregnant, and agreed to accept the baby and bring it up
with hers and as hers; when it was six months old she discovered it was her husband's child, and that he was still carrying on with its mother under their own roof. When Edith
proposed to turn the woman and baby out of the house, her
husband said he would go with them, and Edith weakly kept
the lot. Literally, too, for it was by her successful writing that
she supported her husband, their own three children, the ille-
gits, and the various lady friends.

Edith Nesbit's children's books were best-sellers in their
day, and some have become classics: *The Wonderful Garden*
and *The Would-Be Goods*, for example, found thousands of
admirers and are still read in England and reprinted in children's magazines in the U.S.A. Edith christened her own
eldest son Fabian. He died under an anesthetic at fifteen, just
a year after his father had produced yet another illegitimate
child by yet another lady, and had insisted upon again bringing mother and child home to live under his wife's roof.

Hubert Bland was on the Fabian Executive for twenty-six
years—until in 1911 he had become ailing and blind. He
wrote *After Bread, Education,* a Fabian tract, in 1905, and
edited *Socialism and Labour Policy* (1906). Some Fabians
took, and some did not take, a dim view of Hubert's goings on.
"Wallas made my blood run cold for a moment," Shaw wrote
to Bland after one meeting, "but he did not really mean it. He
was full of the meannesses of King and the profligacy of Bentinck. It was about *these* he was speaking when, by what
seemed an intentional stroke, he made it appear for a moment that he was talking about *you* in the most personal way.
This triumph of dialectics was quite unintentional. I attacked
him about it when he sat down, and he was unmistakably
taken aback and protested that I was giving an ingenious twist
to what he said . . . the bulk of the audience did not
catch the apparent innuendo."

What did Shaw see in Bland? They shared genuine Socialist convictions. As Edith Bland said, "There are two distinct elements in the Fabian Society, the practical and the visionary, the first being much stronger, but a perpetual war goes on which gives to the Fabian Society an excitement it might otherwise lack. We belong, needless to say—to the practical." G.B.S. also enjoyed staying with the Blands. He even used to put on boxing gloves and spar with Hubert, who was a big man and a competent boxer. J. F. Runciman, a young organist who was the music critic on the *Saturday Review* under Frank Harris, and drank himself to death, was a devoted Fabian. One day he came into the office and made an offensive remark implying some doubt of Bland's solvency as treasurer. Bland knocked him down to teach him better manners.

G.B.S. on one occasion almost seems to have condoned Bland's way of life, in a private letter to him. "Imagine," he wrote, "Mrs. Bland as the wife of a horrible city snob with a huge villa, a carriage and several thousands a year, which is exactly what, on moral principles, it was your duty to have made her. You and I have followed our original impulse and our reward is that we have been conscious of its existence and can rejoice therein." Shaw himself for nine years lived with his mother while supporting neither her nor his sisters, but letting them go out to work while he, as Mrs. Webb put it, "was a fellow with a crank for not making money, except he can make it exactly as he chooses."

Hubert Bland was useful in two ways to G.B.S. Bland became, in 1886, one of the editors of *Today*, which published one of Shaw's novels serially. This paper, under the editorship of Belfort Bax and J. L. Joynes, had not been doing too well. So Shaw told Joynes, "I'll tell you what you ought to do —run a serial. It doesn't matter a rap what it is—no one will read it. Now I have a pile of old novels that no one will publish. Take one and use it." Joynes hesitated, but Bland took the last—*The Unsocial Socialist*—which William Morris read, thus serialized, and liked. "This gave me the first idea I had," said Shaw, "that they [the novels] were not unreadable."

H. G. Wells[28] has well described the Blands, with whom he and his second wife, Jane, often stayed.

> She ran a great easy-going Bohemian household at Well Hall, Eltham, a moated house with a walled garden. Chesterton, J. C. Squire, Monsignor Hugh Benson, and many others came. Jane and I learnt to play badminton . . . at first it seemed to be a simple, agreeable multitudiness from which literary buds and flowers sprang abundantly, pre-

28 1934, II, p. 513 ff.

sided over by this tall, engaging, restless, moody, humorous woman. Then gradually the visitor began to perceive at first unsuspected trends and threads of relationship, and scented, as if from the moat, a more disturbing flavor. People came to Well Hall and went, and some of them went for good. There had been "misunderstandings" . . . Well Hall was a world of roles and not of realities. The Blands were the first people I met at all intimately who were fundamentally intricate. . . . The incongruity of Bland's costume with his Bohemian setting, the costume of a city swell, top-hat, tail-coat, grays and blacks, white slips, spatter-dashes and that black-ribboned monocle, might have told me of the general imagination at work in his *persona*, the myth of the Great Man of the World. . . . He presented himself as a Tory in grain . . . he became— I know of no confirmation—a man of a good old family, he entered the dear old Roman Catholic Church. . . . He was under an inner compulsion to be a seducer. . . . The astounded visitor came to realize that most of the children were not E. Nesbit's but the results of Bland's conquests, that the friend and companion who ran the household was the mother of one of these young people, that young Miss So-and-So who played badminton with a preoccupied air, was the last captive of Bland's accomplished sex-appeal. All this Edith Nesbit not only detested and mitigated and toler- ated but presided over . . . everywhere fantastic conceal- ment . . . had been arranged to adjust these irregulari- ties to Hubert's pose of ripe old gentility. You found after a time that Well Hall was not so much an atmosphere as a web.

Yet, during the Fabian heyday, when they were able to wirepull both sides of the House of Commons, Mrs. Cecil Chesterton declares Bernard Shaw and Hubert Bland to have been the Fabian star turns. Hubert was star turn, too, on the *Sunday Chronicle,* then a vast circulation paper, and his voracious public included bishops and stableboys. He had, it appears, a genius for interpreting current political, scientific, or economic problems and discoveries in easy, popular style.

But perhaps the most important Fabian of them all was E. R. Pease, the Society's secretary for twenty-five, and its member for almost seventy, years. Pease was the bête noire of H. G. Wells, and even Beatrice Webb wondered, in Decem- ber 1910, whether it would be possible to revivify the Fabian Society with E. R. Pease as secretary. But the Society's tre- mendous stability depended on Pease—one might almost say, it exuded from him. His utterances had none of the ap- proved Fabian crispness of form, and he would quell young members by describing their suggestions as futile and fatuous. He was so lavish with these two adjectives that some of the irreverent young Fabians nicknamed him "F. and F." Sidney Webb came to his rescue when the young and ribald overwhelmed him, by ruling that notice must be given of all questions, which effectively spoiled the fun. But it was largely thanks to Pease that Fabian debates kept to the point at issue.[29]

[29] Mrs. Cecil Chesterton, p. 34.

CHAPTER FOUR

ONE OF THE CHIEF problems any Socialist society had in the 1880's was its relationship with the refugee anarchists, nihilists, and other exiles who at that time were pouring in to England from Tsarist Russia and from Germany, after Bismarck's anti-Socialist decrees, from Austria, after the suppression of the Socialist paper *Zukunft,* from Italy, and from France. British radicals were indeed most hospitable, and enabled the various exiles not only to live, but to publish, and were continually getting up benefits for them and inviting them to stay in their homes. But the anarchists, nihilists, and others, true to form, repaid this hospitality by disrupting the various British Socialist organizations, and one of G.B.S.'s most forceful political papers is a long study of why it is impossible to work with anarchists, or to be one. Yet everyone tried to be kind to them, and anarchists were everywhere in the 1880's—they even tried to permeate the permeating Fabians. But the Fabians were as utterly opposed to anarchism as they were to revolution of any sort; they were mostly concerned with the ethical and evolutionary bases of society, and the British Labor Party owes to the Fabians its escape from the violence of the German Social Democrats and of the French Socialists, no less than from that of the Bolshevists.

But personally many of the Fabians' best friends were anarchists, and among these was the Russian Sergei Stepniak. A nihilist, he was as formidable in appearance as he was kindly at heart, a powerfully built man with a tremendous head, like a caricature of a Slav. E. L. Voynich says he was the gentlest of creatures, mystical and monumental, and that, of all the people she has ever known, only he and Charlotte Wilson were *perhaps* good enough to be anarchists. (For Mrs. Voynich, the reason it is impossible to be an anarchist is that no one is worthy.) Another view of Stepniak was less flattering. W. Earl Hodgson, describing a visit to a nihilist, said Stepniak was "fat, very fat, so fat, indeed, that you could not but wonder that his plump fingers could deign to attend to such a contemptible thing as the cigarette that two of them held. His countenance, devoid of wrinkles, or even of the slightest sign of care, beams upon you placidly . . . the small brown eyes were somewhat Japanese in shape." Stepniak had helped Kropotkin escape from a Russian prison and had killed Mezenzov, the brutal secret chief of the Tsarist secret police, in Russia, in 1878. Stepniak had escaped, and found his way, via Italy and Herzegovina, to London, after being sentenced to death *in absentia*, in Benevento. His house in London was the mecca of all Russian refugees and escapees. E. R. Pease's wife, Marjorie, was an enthusiastic worker for the Free Russia League, and personal contact between the Fabians and the Russian exiles was close.

When Stepniak fell to his death under an express train (it was not suicide) Eduard Bernstein complained that only about 1,000 mourners walked in his funeral procession, of whom a great many were the Russo-Jewish workers from London's East End. Both Bernstein and Kropotkin spoke at the funeral.

Sir Henry Slesser describes in *Judgment Reserved* a garden party of fellow Fabian Aylmer Maude's he attended at Chelmsford, which was full of Russian refugees living in tents. The drink was unfermented grapes, the food vegetarian, and sandals were worn—but not by G.B.S. The latter had once worn a pair, made by Edward Carpenter, while staying with the Henry Salts, but gave them up after he returned from his first walk in them with bleeding feet.

The trouble with the anarchists and the nihilists, too, apart from the way they disrupted Socialist societies, as they had done the Socialist League, was that any one of these mild-seeming men might at any moment be sitting on a dynamite bomb, as one actually was at a meeting in the Tottenham Court Road which G.B.S. addressed. Two days later, this anarchist in Greenwich Park blew himself to fragments with it—"unintentionally," Shaw[1] noted. To the Fabians, such behavior was unreasonable and un-English.

The crisis between the Fabians and the anarchists came to a head in 1886. The question, as G.B.S. put it, was how many followers had the one ascertained anarchist Fabian, Mrs. Charlotte Wilson, among the silent Fabians? The Fabian Executive determined to find out. At a meeting that fall in Alderton's Hotel, Annie Besant and Hubert Bland moved and seconded a resolution that Socialists should organize themselves into a political party—a suggestion that would bring

[1] *Christian Commonwealth*, Oct. 20, 1900.

any cowering or lurking anarchists into the open, as being complete anathema to them. William Morris dotted the *i*'s and crossed the *t*'s by adding a rider to the contrary: "because no Parliamentary party can exist without compromise and concession." The debate was so noisy that the Fabian secretary was subsequently told by the manager of Alderton's Hotel that the society could not be accommodated there for any further meetings. Everybody voted, whether Fabian or not, and Besant and Bland carried their resolution by 47 to 19, Morris's rider being rejected by 40 to 27.[2]

Edith Bland, with un-Fabian but feminine cattiness, described the redoubtable Charlotte Wilson in a letter:

> Charlotte Wilson, a Girton girl, is sometimes horribly rude and will never speak to a woman if she can get a man to talk to. I don't mean she is a flirt; she has a husband who is very nice and a perfect gentleman. He is a stockbroker and they used to live in Hampstead but she won't live on his earnings, so they have taken a quiet little cottage; she means to keep herself by keeping fowls. The kitchen is an idealized farm kitchen—where of course no cooking is ever done, with a cushioned settee, an open hearth, polished dresser and benches and all the household glass and china mixed up with aesthetic pots and pans.[3]

E. R. Pease said this cottage was where the Fabians held the most delectable of their social gatherings. But the Fabians could on occasion splurge also in town: Edith Bland writes of going on with others after a debate in the Temple, at which G.B.S. and Belfort Bax spoke, to a crab and cream supper, with Devonshire cream and strawberry jam washed down by wine and benedictine.

Charlotte Wilson was elected to the Fabian Executive of five in December 1884, but after some time devoted herself entirely to the anarchist movement, then led by Kropotkin, for whom she edited the paper *Freedom*. But she remained a faithful Fabian none the less. Lady Olivier, at that time still Margaret Cox, wrote of Charlotte Wilson, "She seemed to me a peaceful sort of anarchist and so did all the others who came to meetings, some of them Russians. Someone read a paper, and this was followed by a discussion, often very vigorous and exciting, lasting till Mrs. Wilson interrupted with sandwiches and drinks, after which we all turned out on the heath." [4]

[2] Shaw, 1892.
[3] Quoted in Moore, pp. 72-3.
[4] Hampstead Heath.

Charlotte Wilson is well portrayed as Gemma, the heroine of E. L. Voynich's *The Gadfly,* where her shining black hair, her courage, and her outspoken opinions are described. Ethel Voynich recalls how Charlotte Wilson had offered her either Kropotkin or Stepniak to teach her Russian, and she chose Stepniak because he lived in town. But she also met and made friends with Kropotkin, and was one day with him at the London Zoo when, looking at a supine, placid, bedraggled Russian wolf, Kropotkin began commiserating with it, in Russian, telling it that it was a victim, in exile among foreigners, and that no one appreciated its spacious Russian soul, until the wolf put up its head and howled with self-pity.

Kropotkin, who had been arrested and imprisoned in Russia in 1874, escaped in 1876. After being expelled from Switzerland, rearrested in France and imprisoned by the French government, and then released, he had settled in England in 1886. His appearance was what then was thought typically Russian: a bright, engaging face, lightly brushed long hair, with heavy beard and mustache. His doctrine was that each individual could be bound by nothing and nobody; and that no number of people could, in any circumstances, be overruled as to their individual rights, no matter how many thousands or even millions might be permanently injured or starved by their recusancy. His book, *An Appeal to the Young,* was translated by Hyndman. Sir R. C. K. Ensor, an early and distinguished Fabian, recalls that Kropotkin was universally distrusted. One day, when Ensor was sitting in an A.B.C. restaurant with two members of the British Executive of the Little Britain Society that helped Russian refugees, one of them told Ensor that of all these refugees only two, Wolkowski and Tsaikowski, were not supplying the Russian government with information. Kropotkin prophesied that with properly intensive agricultural methods, England could grow enough to feed a population ten times larger than she had in 1890.

Mrs. Bland did not disparage Annie Besant as much as she did Charlotte Wilson—perhaps partly because Annie Besant's sufferings, though dealt with far more competently, somewhat paralleled her own. Annie Besant was, like Shaw, raised in Anglo-Irish downstart gentility, lost her father young, and was farmed out by her impoverished mother with a rich Miss Marryat, who was a sister of Captain Marryat, the writer of boys' stories. Annie grew up in Clapham, a devoutly religious member of the Established Church, married a dull curate, and had two children by him, before losing her faith. When she refused to say the Creed or take the Sacrament, her husband turned her out of the house and the British courts removed her children from her, declaring her unfit to associate with them. Annie fell under the influence of Charles Bradlaugh, the professed atheist, whose refusal to take the oath on the Bible when elected to the House of Commons shook all England, and brought about one of the most discreditable quarrels in the history of Parliament. In January 1883, Annie Besant founded a liberal magazine, *Our Corner,* chiefly as an organ for her own and Bradlaugh's opinions. In 1885 she went one evening to hear G.B.S. lecture at the Dialectical Society. She came to scoff and stayed to worship. As Shaw describes it:

> . . . When the discussion began, everyone waited for Annie Besant to lead the opposition. She did not rise, and at last the opposition was taken by another member. When he had finished, to the great astonishment of the meeting, Annie Besant got up and utterly demolished him. There was nothing left for me to do but to gasp and triumph under her shield. At the end she asked me to nominate her for election to the Fabian Society, and invited me to dine.

Annie Besant's conversion to Socialism and, more specifically, to Fabianism, brought to the Society its first celebrity. For Annie Besant had already been recognized as an outstanding speaker, and the group of brilliant but unknown and rather callow young Fabians in the Executive were not at all sure how to deal with this phenomenon that had erupted in their midst. Her notoriety was such that Mr. St. John Ervine, in his life of G.B.S., very much doubts if any of the Fabians, except Shaw, welcomed the new recruit. "But," he adds, "she was meat and drink to G.B.S., whose liking for oddities was unlimited." She not only had then been stumping the country advocating atheism, but also birth control, and the generally staid Fabians, with their plain living and high thinking, were very reluctant to appreciate the glare of publicity that suddenly encompassed them. For, besides the young men of the Fabian Executive, there were also those Fabians who, as Mr. Pease gently put it, seemed to be at least elderly, and of these many were respectable. Mr. and Mrs. J. Glade Stapleton, for example, drove to meetings in their own brougham. Yet Annie Besant was so astounding a spellbinder that St. John Ervine[5] himself admits:

> I heard Mrs. Besant address the Fabian Society in her old age, when, clad entirely in white and looking very lovely, she uttered a flaming fire of eloquent words that seemed as if they must consume every man and woman who heard

[5] p. 138.

her. I came out of the Essex Hall, almost stunned by what she had said . . . my amazement at the speech . . . was slight, however, in comparison with my surprise . . . that I could not recall a single sentence she had spoken. I could recall only a sense of having been so beaten by burning words that my mind and body felt scorched.

Annie Besant serialized several of G.B.S.'s novels in *Our Corner* and paid him for his contributions until he discovered that her conversion to Socialism had lost her so many subscribers that the money was coming out of her own pocket.

Poor Annie Besant! She even learned to play duets to please G.B.S., for she was genuinely very much in love with him. But G.B.S. seems to have found her affection like that of the ass who climbed on its master's knee because it saw the little dog petted when it did so, for he noted nervously in his diary that their relations, although they never went further than a friendship, "threatened to become a vulgar intrigue." He portrayed her as Raina in *Arms and the Man,* and told Hesketh Pearson that she had absolutely no sex appeal. About this time Mrs. Besant was trying to present him with an umbrella, and Mrs. Bland was summoning him constantly to dine at Blackheath and keeping him so late he missed the last train and had to walk home (at least ten miles), several times a week, while a pupil of his mother's was working a pair of slippers for him. It was this latter, Jenny Patterson (not a Fabian), who finally succeeded in seducing G.B.S., on his twenty-ninth birthday.

The loss of his virginity was so heady in its effect upon him that almost immediately he found he had six affairs on his hands at once.[6] "My! You do warm both hands at the fire of life!" was Sidney Webb's comment.

Annie Besant poured all her dynamic energy into the Fabian cause, and G.B.S. describes her as

a sort of expeditionary force, always to the front where there was trouble and danger, carrying away audiences for us when the dissensions in the movement brought our policy into conflict with that of other societies, founding branches for us throughout the country, dashing into the great strikes and free-speech agitations of the time, forming on her own initiative such *ad hoc* organizations as were necessary to make them effective, and generally leaving the routine to us, and taking on the fighting herself.[7]

If all, or almost all, the Fabians disliked Annie Besant, not

[6] London *Times* Literary Supplement, July 27, 1956.
[7] Ervine, p. 223.

all loved G.B.S.: William Clarke, for example, could not stand him. Clarke was probably the ablest journalist among the early Fabians, but as they met in the evenings, when he had to be in his office, he worked very hard in order to get free from the bondage of his paper, the *Daily Chronicle*. He wrote a lot for the American papers, and also became a leader writer for the Conservative English *Spectator*. He was a close friend of C. P. Scott of the *Manchester Guardian*, and his daughter married Scott's third son, who was drowned while boating on Lake Windermere. Clarke had invested in the (U.S.) Liberator Companies, and when they folded and their fraudulent founder went to prison, William Clarke died, of overwork and disappointment. He had remained a devoted Fabian until the end.

Constance Black, elected to the Fabian Executive for 1894-95, regarded herself as rather a rival of Sidney Webb's wife, Beatrice Potter, though it is to be wondered whether Beatrice reciprocated. Constance and her elder sister Clementina cordially detested Beatrice, according to Constance's son, David Garnett. Constance was more than a little in love with Stepniak, and G.B.S. insisted he himself was more than a little in love with her, but he told her that though he would like to marry her, he just couldn't afford it. So Constance married Edward Garnett, six years her junior, and spent her life doing magnificent translations from the Russian. In 1938 David Garnett lunched with G.B.S. and his wife, and Shaw repeated to him, "I would have married your mother if I could have afforded it, but I was poor in those days."

Two other prominent early Fabians were Henry Salt and his wife Kate, and Kate's brother, James Leigh Joynes. Salt and Joynes were Eton masters, and Salt was responsible for William Morris and Henry George being invited to talk in the Eton Library. After Joynes was dismissed for having covered Henry George's Irish tour for the London *Times* (when he was also briefly arrested with George), Henry Salt resigned partly in protest at his brother-in-law's dismissal, and partly because he had been assured by Edward Carpenter, whom he and his friends called "The Noble Savage," that the simple life was feasible on one hundred pounds a year, which was exactly what Salt had saved. So Henry and Kate Salt retired to a workman's cottage in the wilds of Surrey, near Oxted, where G.B.S. and Olivier and other Fabians came for week ends. Edward Carpenter and G.B.S. both considered themselves Kate's "Sunday husbands" and used to "thunder duets for hours" with her on the "noisiest grand piano that ever descended from Eton to a Surrey cottage." Kate had dark hair, huge eyes, and a beautiful Dante-like profile, and she "spoilt and pampered" G.B.S. outrageously. After she died he wrote to her husband that the Surrey week ends were a most special part of his life: he had written several of his plays while staying with the Salts. He added that between himself and Kate there was a congeniality so complete that the mom seem ridiculous. Olivier wrote in even stronger terms: he admired Kate "this side of idolatry" and even suggested he wished he were dead, since she was, and envied the spirit world its gain. G.B.S. at the very end of his life wrote of Kate that she loved him as much as she could love any male creature. He had never met anyone in the least like her, though another friend, the Christian Socialist Stewart Headlam, also had a wife who was a homo. Salt's tragedy, according to G.B.S., was that Kate would not consummate their marriage because she thought she was an urning, a delusion she got from Edward Carpenter who said the urnings were a chosen race. What she really needed, Shaw thought, was children, so he told her to get a job in a factory, which to his amazement she did, but soon left it and worked for him as an unpaid secretary until his marriage. Finally, she went back to Salt, until she faded out mentally and died. Though the Salts were hard-working Fabians, Henry's chief interest was the Humanitarian League, which he founded. He was a lifelong vegetarian, and influenced G.B.S. to put his Shelleyan distaste for eating corpses into practice. In the 1880's new good, cheap vegetarian restaurants made such a course for the first time practicable in London. Not all the Fabians, however, were vegetarians, and Salt describes his horror when calling upon some Fabians in a rented villa. He found two Fabian women staining the floor with bullock's blood brought in a bucket from the shambles.

Joynes wore his red hair in long curls hanging down his neck, and became one of the editors of *Today*. He was one of the few Fabians of whom G.B.S.'s mother approved. She detested, for example, Sidney Webb, whom she describes as always "eating greedily, talking speedily and looking weedily." Joynes introduced G.B.S. to George Meredith, Watts, and William Morris. Joynes was, G.B.S. declared, murdered by his doctors who, when Joynes had a heart attack, immobilized him and fed him on whisky until he became a mere lump. When G.B.S. went down to see Joynes at West Hoathly, the dying Fabian said, "It doesn't matter if I go . . . We have achieved what we set out to do, we've started the world moving in the right direction at last. I'll be forgotten and you'll be forgotten, but the world will carry something of us . . . if a dozen of us could go on for 100 years, we'd change life beyond recognition." Actually, less than half a dozen Fabians went on for not quite one hundred years apiece—G.B.S., E. R. Pease, C. M. Lloyd, the Webbs, Sir Robert Ensor—while R. H. Tawney (b. 1880) is still alive, and all these certainly did some pretty effective world-changing; it is to be wondered if Joynes returned to earth today whether he would recognize the life his friends' children lead.

Among other then famous members of the Salt circle was Ernest Belfort Bax, a philosophic revolutionary, whose threatful attitude toward society was in somewhat strong contrast to his own personal apprehensiveness. He became fairly well known as a philosopher. He was a rabid Marxist, and induced William Morris to sign a manifesto declaring that all good Socialists were Marxists. Eduard Bernstein has a story of Bax and G.B.S. going together to the theater, and Bax immediately falling asleep. Shaw, at that time a drama critic, discussed the play on the way home, but Bax said, "How can you pretend to give an opinion when you were asleep the whole time?"

Henry Hyde Champion, another devout Fabian, resigned his commission in the Guards, after serving with conspicuous gallantry in the Afghan campaign of 1879, because he was disgusted by Gladstone's mismanagement of the Egyptian fiasco which culminated in General Gordon's death at Khartoum. Champion started a printing business, on the basis of an eight-hour day, and printed G.B.S.'s *Cashel Byron's Profession*. He joined the Social Democratic Federation and G.B.S. wrote of him that he was "so extraordinarily ready with a practicable plan in every emergency that if the plan could only have remained the same for half an hour he would have been the greatest general of his age." [8]

Shaw[9] describes the occasion when

> H. H. Champion delivered a blamelessly reasoned and documented lecture to a crowded audience. Suddenly he declared that if the entire capitalist class had only one throat, he would cut it without a minute's hesitation. While we were gasping . . . he rushed to the edge of the platform and, pointing down at the Press table, shouted: "Look! They are all scribbling as hard as they can, though they have not put pen to paper when I was talking sensibly."

Indeed, today this faked "outburst" is all that is remembered today of poor Champion, but alas! it is remembered as though it had been meant seriously.

On July 15, 1898, a mock Socialist government formed by

[8] Shaw, 1892.
[9] 1948, p. 112.

H. H. Champion took office. Champion was Prime Minister and First Lord of the Treasury; Annie Besant, Home Secretary; Shaw, President of the Local Government Board; Sidney Webb, Chancellor of the Exchequer; Hubert Bland, Secretary for Foreign Affairs; Graham Wallas, President of the Board of Trade; Sydney Olivier, Colonial Office. This Fabian ministry had to put its proposals into black-and-white in the shape of Parliamentary Bills. Champion really stood later as Socialist Parliamentary candidate for Aberdeen, in 1892, but when he was found to have accepted Tory help he was repudiated by the Fabians and retired to Australia, where his health broke down and he petered out.

Among the clashes of temperament among the Fabians was Hubert Bland and Sidney Webb's antipathy to each other, as strong as that between William Clarke and G.B.S. Clarke strove manfully to squabble with Shaw, but the latter always eluded battle; just as Webb's gentleness made Bland's bullying attacks sound hollow. As Shaw[10] put it, there was considerable strife of temperament in the Fabian Cabinet,

and in the other Socialist societies splits and schism were frequent; for the English are very quarrelsome. I believe that some of my own usefulness lay in smoothing out these frictions by an Irish sort of tact which in England seemed the most outrageous want of it. Whenever there was a quarrel I betrayed everybody's confidence by analyzing it and stating it lucidly in the most exaggerated terms. Result: both sides agreed it was all my fault. I was denounced on all hands as a reckless mischief maker, but forgiven as a privileged Irish lunatic. I flatter myself that the unique survival of the Fabian Society, among the forgotten wrecks of its rivals, all very contemptuous of it, was due not only to its policy, but in its early days to the one Irish element in its management . . .

Though the other Socialists despised the Fabians as bourgeois, they were, as G.B.S. pointed out

jolly glad to have us. We did not keep ourselves to ourselves. We aided the working class organizations in every possible way. In fact the main difference between us was that we worked for everybody (permeation) and they worked for their own societies only. The real reason that we segregated for purposes of thought and study was that the workers could not go our pace or stand our social habits. Hyndman and William Morris . . . and the other

[10] 1949, p. 112.

bourgeois in the Social Democratic Federation . . . were too old for us, they were between forty and fifty when we were between twenty and thirty.

A whole generation apart, in fact. It is not always easy, in view of the celebrity attained later by the founding Fabians, to realize how young they were at this time, nor how blithe and gay and full of physical as well as political vitality.

William Morris was, in the 1880's, the dean of British Socialists. He had never read Adam Smith, Ricardo, or Marx. "Why should I read Marx?" he said. "I can see the evils of society without going to him." But he seemed to believe that men could enjoy what G. K. Chesterton called a "perfectly flat felicity." Morris was quite unaware of the unexplored and explosive possibilities of human nature, of the unnamable terrors and yet more unnamable hopes. He hated the horror and ugliness of nineteenth-century industry. Yet as he shrank from that Beast, the fairy tale, that requires it to be kissed, had for him, alas, a different ending. He was in many ways an English Walt Whitman, stout, sturdy, stalwart, with a ruddy face and bright blue eyes; a handsome man with a beautiful wife. He disliked intellectuality, subtle metaphysical distinctions, and economic theory. He dreamed of a London "small and white and clean" and yet, at his best, in his *News from Nowhere* (one of the great Socialist romances), he distinguished clearly between the dream—be it behind mankind or before—and the reality. The dawn will be

> cold and grey and surly, and yet by its light shall men see things as they verily are, and no longer be enchanted by the gleam of the moon and the glamour of the dreamtide. By such grey light shall wise men and valiant souls see the remedy and deal with it, a real thing that may be touched and handled, and no glory of the heavens to be worshipped from afar off. And what shall it be . . . save that men shall be determined to be free.

Hyndman[11] said that at the back of Morris's mind, quite remote from the busy haunts of men, there lay a great lake of receptivity and imagination. Morris was terribly concerned over the divisiveness of Socialists, and after his Socialist League had split off from the Social Democratic Federation, he convened a series of meetings of delegates of the three groups—Shaw representing the Fabians, Hyndman the SDF and himself the Socialist League—at Kelmscott House, where he lived. Between them the three leaders concocted a mani-

[11] 1911, p. 252.

festo which both Morris and Shaw despised. Shaw wrote indeed that there was complete agreement among the three of them that the Manifesto was beneath contempt. They did not think it worth a penny, neither did the public. However, it was put out, on May 1, 1898, in a blood-red cover, as the *Manifesto of the English Socialists*. It was stillborn: Shaw described it as all over scraps of Hyndman, while Hyndman warned Morris it would fail as the Fabians would not keep faith. Later, G.B.S., in a long letter to Walter Crane, explained why a United Socialist Party would not work, because experience had shown it was not possible to carry union further than a supper club.

Yet they still all helped each other in many ways: William Morris spoke to the Fabians on *The Aims of Art*, and Shaw, his "long face like a ploughshare cutting its way everywhere to bedrock," as Frank Harris described him, often spoke for Morris, and, indeed, thought of marrying Morris's lovely daughter May. G.B.S. spoke too for that "trinity in unity, three persons and no God" of Annie Besant, Bradlaugh, and Edward Aveling, but he did not always say what they expected of him. Once, when addressing the secularists on *Progress in Freethought*, G.B.S. showed that "the Trinity and the Immaculate Conception were the merest common sense" (a view he touchingly reiterated at the very end of his life, when writing of "Sixty Years of Fabianism" in the Jubilee Edition of *Fabian Essays*). G.B.S. reduced G. F. Foote, his chairman, to speechless fury, and was asked to leave the meeting. Eduard Bernstein, after hearing G.B.S. speak in the Willis rooms (the seats fetched theater prices, he observes), said his chief defect as a speaker was that he knew his hearers expected paradoxes and produced them, conjurer-wise. Bernstein called Shaw a laughing Ibsen, and Hyndman said that Morris was a stopgap and G.B.S. a turn.

The Fabians, Socialist Leaguers, and SDF all contrived to see a lot of each other socially, however great their squabbles. Bernstein describes Eleanor Marx and Aveling, together with William Sanders, later a London County Council alderman and secretary of the Fabian Society, acting together in *By the Sea*, a play based on Tennyson's *Enoch Arden*. Hyndman recommended G.B.S. as book editor to the *Pall Mall Gazette*'s W. T. Stead, but the latter was shocked at the indifference of one of the characters in one of Shaw's novels to the death of his wife. Hyndman had more luck recommending Marx to the same editor, and Marx in turn introduced Engels. Marx himself seems to have been sociable enough: Sir Mountstuart Grant-Duff notes in his diary for 1881, "Lunched to meet

Karl Marx. He looks, not unreasonably, for a great and not distant crash in Russia, and thinks it will begin with reforms from above."

In 1883 the Social Democratic Federation's pamphlet *Socialism Made Plain* sold over 100,000 copies, and in January 1884 the Federation issued the first number of *Justice*, whose publication was paid for by Edward Carpenter. Hyndman, in his inevitable frock coat, and wearing good gloves, peddled the new penny magazine in the Strand, assisted by William Morris, more suitably clad in a blue suit and soft hat. But alas, by the end of the year, the Federation was irremediably split. William Morris, Walter Crane, Belfort Bax, Eleanor Marx, Edward Aveling, and the majority of the rank and file of the Socialist Democratic Federation left Hyndman to form the Socialist League.

Hyndman, whose lifelong devotion to Socialism acquits him of any onus of self-seeking, was a man who ardently wanted power, and had a strong tendency to order others about. G.B.S. described the exterior Hyndman as Tanner in *Man and Superman*. "His frock coat would befit a Prime Minister. A certain high-chested carriage of the shoulders, a lofty pose of the head, the Olympian majesty with which a mane, or rather a huge wisp of hazel-coloured hair is thrown back from an important brow . . . gave a Jovian effect." Hyndman had a "snorting nostril and restless blue eye, just a 32nd too wide open." Though his wives loved him (his second committed suicide after his death), he never was able to keep a friend.

Luckily for Hyndman, and for the Fabians, to the Socialist League gravitated most of the anarchists, who for a year or so had almost swamped the Fabian membership: these anarchists took over the direction of *Commonweal*, the Socialist League magazine, ably edited by William Morris, and Belfort Bax, and by 1887 they had turned Morris out and controlled both the League and *Commonweal*. Edward Aveling, still then living with the lovely Eleanor Marx, victimized everyone with whom he came in contact by his fraudulence in money matters, as Henry Salt wrote. G.B.S., who wrote Aveling into *The Doctor's Dilemma* as Dubedat, insisted Aveling was sincerely a Socialist, but when money was collected by subscription for a cable to be sent to the Governor of Illinois to pardon Parsons, Aveling kept the money and never sent the cable—hardly Socialist cricket! He seems to have been the Socialist League's equivalent of Hubert Bland: he had left his wife to live with, and on, Eleanor Marx. But in 1898, as soon as his wife died, this "almost totally amoral man" as St. John Ervine[12] called him, went off and married another woman, and Eleanor promptly committed suicide.

Eduard Bernstein described Eleanor as one who more than anyone had attacked the Fabian Socialists violently. But one day, while at the British Museum, she needed some books just issued to another applicant, and appealed to the Fabian, Graham Wallas, to look over his library. Wallas said he would be out but she could take any books she needed. Bernstein heartily applauded this cheek-turning behavior.

Eduard Bernstein, unable to return to Germany after the Socialists had been outlawed by Bismarck and obliged to settle in England, tried in his later years to minimize his Fabian past, but he admits that Friedrich Engels disapproved his "Fabian enthusiasm" (*Schwärmerei*), which Engels attributed to nervous illness. This did not prevent Bernstein, with Edward Aveling, Eleanor Marx, and Friedrich Lessner in 1895 from throwing Engels' ashes devoutly into the sea six miles off Beachy Head. Bernstein[13] writes of the early Fabians:

> If, in the final outcome, it was the reformist Fabians rather than the revolutionary Social Democratic Federation that made policy for the British Labor Party, this was due as much to specific circumstances as to the British tradition . . . The Fabian Society was willing to make common cause with anyone who appeared willing to further its aims. This policy rendered the Society suspect to many left-wingers who regarded Fabians as bourgeois opportunists . . . The majority of the Fabians belonged, by birth or by position, to the middle classes, and as they were accustomed to criticize the social doctrine of Marx (as then preached by Hyndman, Aveling and others), in a somewhat condescending tone, they were in bad repute with many representatives of proletarian Socialism as parlor Socialists, who thought of themselves as "superior persons." For a long time I had a prejudice against the Fabians and refrained from establishing personal relations with them."

Elsewhere Bernstein[14] states:

> The opinion which has gained wide currency that I was converted to my Revisionism by the model of the English Fabians is wholly erroneous. Upon closer acquaintance, I learned to value the Fabian Society and its outstanding

[12] p. 408.
[13] 1921, pp. 244-45.
[14] 1924.

leaders, but I was never ignorant of the fact that their special form of agitation was so closely fitted to English conditions that any attempt to imitate it on the Continent would be doomed to failure. That does not mean that I did not learn anything from the Fabians, for the work of the Webbs . . . widened my horizon.

One of the things Bernstein learned was a toleration for the marginalist as well as for the Marxist theory. "Peter and Paul stand before a box filled with minerals," he wrote. " 'These are parallel-planed hemihedral crystals,' says Peter. 'They are pyrites,' says Paul. And both are right. Peter's statement refers to form, Paul's to substance. The same is true of the value theory." He was thus kinder than some critics of Jevonian economics who penned a ditty about "the final futility of marginal utility."

But it was not only in Europe that the Fabians were now becoming well known. Their ideas were spreading, and their name was becoming known also in America.

William Clarke, writing for the American monthly, the *New England Magazine*, in March 1894, on the Fabian Society, noted that "No visitor to the British capital will mingle long in the political life of London before he will hear of the Fabian Society."

One of the Americans who heard of the Fabians and came to see them was Walter Rauschenbusch, a Baptist minister. In 1891, before going to Germany to pay visits in German Baptist circles, he came to London, where he met the Sidney Webbs and other Fabians, and studied industrial conditions. He also went to Birmingham. He met too the Salvation Army, to which he was much attracted. One of the results of this visit was his *How Rich Have I a Right To Be?*, published in the U.S.A. in 1894. Like G.B.S. he declared he owed his "social awakening" to Henry George, and supported him when he was running for mayor of New York. In 1907 his *Christianity and the Social Crisis* was published while he was Professor of Church History at the Rochester Theological Seminary, and was translated into seven languages. Woodrow Wilson and David Lloyd George are said to have consulted him. In 1907 he again visited the Webbs, and became even more influenced than before by Fabian Socialism. But he never joined the (American) Socialist Party. For this was at that time, and until 1939, wholly Marxian. Yet he influenced it greatly, and men like Norman Thomas claim that Rauschenbusch was the first man in America to Christianize and evolutionize Socialism, hitherto wholly and violently revolutionary.

Men as far apart as Kagawa, the founder of the Kingdom of God movement in Japan, and Harry Emerson Fosdick in New York, were influenced by Rauschenbusch. Walter Rauschenbusch once told Theodore Roosevelt that many thought Socialism was coming in the U.S.A. "Not so long as I am President," replied Roosevelt, "for I will sail the ship of State alongside the ship of Socialism and I will take over everything that is good, and leave the bad. What will Socialism do then?" Rauschenbusch replied, "I suppose the ship of Socialism will sink, but it will not matter, if you really save the valuable cargo. But do you propose to write into the nation's laws the social theories of Socialism?" "Precisely that," replied the President, "at least insofar as those theories are wise and practicable for the nation's well-being."

There was at this time a serious attempt to found an American Fabian Society. John W. Martin, who was a member of the Fabian Executive from 1884 to 1889 and who wrote Fabian Tract No. 52, *State Education at Home and Abroad,* in 1894 married the leading United States exponent of Fabianism, and settled in New York as editor of the *American Fabian,* which ran for several issues. Martin had considerable subsequent influence in local American educational and progressive politics. But he, too, failed in transplanting Fabianism to the U.S.A., although such intensely American figures as Jane Addams heartily endorsed it.

Meanwhile, in England the Fabians were now rapidly moving from the study-group and lecture-hall stage on to the wider political area. As Sister McCarran[15] notes:

Nothing more exciting than J. Ramsay MacDonald's demanding the recall of Tract No. 70 in which Shaw had talked of Fabians "throwing their weight" in elections (the I.L.P. wanted slower political action) than Olivier's going to Jamaica as Colonial Secretary, than Shaw's becoming Vestryman for St. Pancras and Wallas being elected to the School Board, occurred in the years 1894 to 1898. But each of these items had a far-reaching significance. . . .

[15] p. 21.

CHAPTER FIVE

O N JUNE 9, 1885, GLAD-
stone resigned as Prime Minister and Lord Salisbury formed
a minority government, which annexed Upper Burma and
passed Lord Ashbourne's act, "the first state-assisted scheme
of land purchase." [1] During the general election which followed in the fall, the Fabians, who had at that time only forty
members, tangled seriously with the Social Democratic Federation over what was called "Tory Gold." The Federation
had decided to run two candidates in London. Joseph Chamberlain, the M.P. for Birmingham, and its idol, was stumping
the country with a tremendous series of election speeches.
He declared, in these famous "Ransom" speeches that
harked back to the doctrines of natural law, that Liberals
must be refurbished by means of wide-sweeping social reforms: free and universal education, a graduated income tax,
land reform, an extension of municipal self-government and
local autonomy for Ireland. Lord Iddesleigh dubbed him
Jack Cade, and the SDF, particularly Hyndman and Champion, thought they would try and persuade Chamberlain to
back their candidates. He turned them down cold, whereupon H. H. Champion persuaded a personal friend of his, a
soap manufacturer named Hudson, to provide money to
finance the election expenses of John Burns. The Conservatives, afraid of Chamberlain, in order to split the Liberal
votes, then paid for the candidatures of two other SDF candidates. Mr. Williams, in Hampstead, got 27 votes, and Mr.
Fielding, in Kennington, got 32. As G.B.S. put it,

> They had presented the Tory party with 57 votes, at a
> cost of about eight pounds sterling apiece. What was
> worse, they had shocked London Radicalism, to which
> Tory money was utter abomination. It is hard to say which

[1] Ensor, p. 92.

cut the more foolish figure, the Tories who had spent their money for nothing, or the Socialists, who had sacrificed their reputation for worse than nothing.[2]

The result of this election almost proved fatal for the SDF, and G.B.S. noted that there was an immediate falling off from the Federation, on the one hand of the tacticians, on the other of those out-and-out insurrectionists who had repudiated political action altogether and who said, "I told you so." The Socialist League and the Fabian Society both passed very smug resolutions. That of the Fabians ran:

> That the conduct of the Council of the Social-Democratic Federation in accepting money from the Tory party in payment of the election expenses of Socialist candidates is calculated to disgrace the Socialist movement in England . . . December, 1885.

This was passed by 15 votes to 4, one of the minority against it being the first honorary secretary, Frederick Keddell, who thereupon resigned, his place being taken by E. R. Pease. "This," Pease[3] stated, "was the only occasion the Fabian Society ever interfered with the doings of its friendly rivals."

Also in 1885, G.B.S. and J. G. Stapleton represented the Fabian Society at the Industrial Remuneration Conference, which met in Prince's Hall, Piccadilly, to discuss whether "The increase of products of industry within the last hundred years tended most to the benefit of capitalists and employers or to that of the working classes, whether artisan, laborers or others?" Arthur Balfour, later Prime Minister, read a paper in which he declared:

> As will be readily believed, I am no socialist, but to compare the work of such men as Mr. Henry George with that of such men, for instance, as Karl Marx, either in respect of its intellectual force, its consistency, its command of reasoning in general, or of economic reasoning in particular, seems to be absurd.

This was the occasion when Shaw delighted the public with his suave comparison of landlords, burglars and shareholders, "all three of whom inflicted on the community an injury of precisely the same nature."

In 1886, as Kropotkin, newly returned from the Continent,

noted, the Socialist movement in England was in full swing. People flocked at night into Trafalgar Square to sleep there in the open air, in the wind and the rain, between two newspapers, so as to be present at the mass meetings held almost daily. There were more unemployed in England than ever before, and while the SDF-ers said it was all the fault of the capitalists, the protectionists said it was all the fault of free trade. At the end of January 1885 the SDF learnt that the protectionists were proposing to hold a big meeting in Trafalgar Square. The SDF at once decided to hold a counter-demonstration on the same day and in the same place. On "mad Monday," the 8th of February, both groups converged on the square. The police asked the leaders of the SDF to transfer their meeting to Hyde Park. John Burns seized a red flag and called on the crowds to follow him, while Hyndman, Champion, and a third man called Williams marched at the head of the crowd.

Four men later spoke from the plinth of the Nelson monument: Hyndman, in frock coat and silk hat; Jack Williams, a laborer, in corduroys and hobnailed shoes; Champion, trim and soldierly, nervously buttoning and unbuttoning his coat, and John Burns, holding the red flag. When the crowds surged into Pall Mall, the rich young clubmen lounging by their windows scoffed down at the demonstrators below, who thereupon, being hungry, threw a few stones and broke some august panes in the Carlton and other venerable clubs. As Keith Hutchison pointed out, the broken glass cut many purse strings, and the contributions poured into a relief fund opened by the Lord Mayor; the Mansion House fund for the relief of the unemployed went up with a bound from £30,000 to £79,000. The next day, Shaw[4] tells,

> Society, saved, came out of its hiding place, sold the fish from its baths and the hams from its larders at a sacrifice (the weather being very hot, and the hams in questionable condition), and voted gratefully for a government that had frightened it out of its senses with an imaginary revolution.

The four SDF leaders were arrested, but shortly after they were released on bail. When they were brought up for trial, John Burns delivered a fiercely revolutionary speech, but it was Hyndman who was the real counsel for the defense. Yet G.B.S. still had his doubts about Hyndman's willingness to die on the barricades. He would be quite willing to shoulder

[4] 1948, p. xxxii.

his pike and lead the SDF down the Edgeware Road, G.B.S. thought, but at the first sight of the machine guns at Marble Arch, he prophesied Hyndman would throw his pike down into the nearest area and return to his not uncomfortable residence in Sloane Square.

Later that spring the Fabians prepared their first Conference, held at South Place Chapel on the 9th, 10th, and 11th of June. Nonconformist chapels play a great role in early Fabian history. Barbara Ward has pointed out that John Wesley took the Gospel to the poor, and that his plans for reform led to a tremendous expansion of the Nonconformist, or free, churches. These in their turn decisively influenced the beginning of the trade-union and labor movements in Britain. Most of the early organizers of British labor were lay preachers, and Fabian meetings were constantly held in the chapels of various denominations. The Fabians attracted also many younger sons of peers or gentry, who traditionally entered the church or served in social work. Some of these were High Church and entered the Guild of St. Matthew. To this day there is nothing incongruous—indeed, it is only fitting—that the Labor Party's national conventions open with an evangelical prayer, and many a Socialist minister preaches from a Methodist pulpit. The early Socialists, like the early Protestants, mostly came from the same small tradesman class, and this strong and enduring religious connection is one of the forces that has kept English Socialism so simon-pure of Marxism.

The Fabians signalized their repudiation of political sectarianism by inviting the radicals, secularists, and anyone else who would come, to their Conference on the Nationalization of Land and Capital. Fifty-three societies sent delegates; the guarantee fund for expenses was one hundred pounds; the *Times* sent a reporter but did not publish his report. Eighteen papers were read, two by M.P.'s, others by William Morris and Edward Aveling, from the Socialist League; the National Secular Society sent Mr. Foote and Mr. John M. Robertson, the latter of whom read a paper on a scheme of taxation anticipating the later Fabian program on this subject; anarchism, as voiced in *A Plea for Liberty,* was preached by Wordsworth Donisthorpe; the Rev. Stuart Headlam spoke for Christian Socialism and the Guild of St. Matthew. Mrs. Besant, Sidney Webb, and Edward Carpenter also read papers (G.B.S. did not care for the latter's views or style, and wrote of "Carpenterings and illusions"). The prospectus for the conference had a design by Walter Crane at the top (he later drew the jacket also for the first edition of *Fabian Essays*).

A fellow artist has described Crane's art at that time as suffering from

> a mild attack of dilettante Socialism, which taught her to wag her finger and preach, to produce symbolic compositions in which God-like tho rickety British workmen appeared dressed in light suede shoes, knee breeches and liberty school shawls, and lounged about, presumably during the lunch hour, with female allegories, winged indeed, but otherwise attired with far stricter regard to economy.[5]

People sneered plentifully at the Fabians' stylish-looking, blood-red invitation cards, and other little smartnesses on which the Fabians prided themselves, and dubbed them fops. Shaw defended them with the plea that it was by no means the least of their merits, that they did their best to destroy the association between revolutionary literature and slovenly paper that is nasty without being cheap.

Concurrently with the conference, the Fabian Society prepared a report, written jointly by Messrs. Frank Podmore (the first half) and Sidney Webb (the last), on *The Government Organisation of Unemployed Labour*, which contained the germs of many ideas which more than twenty years later formed the leading features of the Minority Report of the Poor Law Commission. It was the first study of unemployment made in Britain.

The years 1886 to 1892 were years of spasmodic violence in London. Beginning with the dynamiting of the Junior Carlton and part of the War Office in 1884, there was a series of Fenian outrages, and the unemployed, huddling together, marching together, collided more and more with the police.

The General Election of 1885 had brought so near a balance between Liberals and Conservatives into Parliament that the Irish members, led by Parnell, held the balance. Early in 1886, after a defeat on an agrarian bill,[6] Lord Salisbury resigned, and Gladstone, newly converted to Home Rule, formed his third Cabinet. The very radical Joseph Chamberlain, already as a manufacturer committed to the imperialism that for most British businessmen was the only way out of the depression, resigned when he learned of his chief's conversion, and G. O. Trevelyan resigned with him. The Conservatives welcomed the rebellious Liberals, who

[5] Robertson, p. 41.

[6] "Three acres and a cow" moved by a follower of Chamberlain. Salisbury resigned the morning after the bill's defeat. *See* Ensor, p. 97.

thereafter were dubbed Liberal-Unionists. In June 1886, Gladstone resigned after his Home Rule bill had been thrown out, and in the following general election the Conservatives and dissident Liberals won a composite majority of 118.

Lord Randolph Churchill, whose spectacular rise in power seemed to have been crowned by his becoming Chancellor of the Exchequer at thirty-seven, abruptly resigned on the budget, and obliterated himself. He had been the great hope of the younger Conservatives, and was succeeded in this role (and much later also as Chancellor) by A. J. Balfour, Lord Salisbury's nephew, a lazy, brilliant philosophical Scot, who was to befriend the Fabians on many future occasions. While Balfour was coping with Ireland, William O'Brien, M.P., who had there been thrown in jail, refused to wear prison clothes, and insisted on being granted special privileges as a political prisoner.

The London radicals decided to stage a big joint demonstration in favor of O'Brien in defiance of a prohibition to use Trafalgar Square issued by the Commissioner of Police after "Mad Monday." Actually, ever since this prohibition, the Trafalgar Square meetings had been getting bigger and better—one was of more than 50,000 people. Sunday, November 13, 1887, was chosen, and the radicals began by getting Robert Bontine Cunninghame Graham, a Scottish Member of Parliament and a Socialist, to ask the Home Secretary for permission to use "the Square." When refused, the radicals determined to use the square anyway, and tried to confuse the police by approaching it in many small bodies from different sides. William Morris, Annie Besant, and G.B.S. were together at the start of the march. Cunninghame Graham and John Burns reached the side of the square, and G.B.S. describes how, in the Battle of the Square, Cunninghame Graham was personally and bodily assailed by the concerted military and constabulary forces of the capital of the world. Graham and John Burns chained themselves to the railings of Morley's Hotel, and John Burns, waving the red flag, resisted the police and was battered. Baton charges were made by the police in Holborn and the Strand, and finally the foot and horse guards were called out and charged the crowd. Graham was hit over the head with a truncheon and bled profusely; both he and Burns were arrested. G.B.S., after trying to persuade Annie Besant to "get out of here," as she was in danger of being knocked down by the front marchers who were being flailed from behind by police truncheons, left her. She reached the square alone; G.B.S. arrived later, separately. There were over 100 casualties among the demonstrators, and two men later died of their injuries. William Morris, who had written of Alfred Linnell's death in 1888 at the hands of the police:

> Not one, not one nor thousands must they slay
> But one and all if they would dusk the day

was himself witness of all that happened on Bloody Sunday. Henry Salt, who had been vociferous regarding the right of free assembly, had his watch stolen, and wrote sadly, "I couldn't protest the conduct of the police in the Square and then invoke them against the pickpockets." Cunninghame Graham and John Burns, arrested, were released on bail provided by Robert Burdon Haldane, the young Scottish Liberal who had been early butchered in debate by the Fabians and who as the result of many talks with Sidney Webb had in 1887 produced a monograph on Adam Smith. Cunninghame Graham and Burns, brought before a jury, were sentenced to six weeks' imprisonment: Haldane gave evidence on their behalf, and the brilliant young lawyer who eloquently defended them was H. H. Asquith, later Prime Minister of England. G.B.S.'s reaction to Bloody Sunday was to speak against Annie Besant when she made an impassioned appeal subsequently at a public meeting for another march on the square and he succeeded in having her motion voted down. Unarmed mobs, he had learned, seldom prevail over police and troops, and martyrdom, he noted acidly, is "the only way a man can become famous without ability."

Cunninghame Graham was the most spectacular Socialist of his time. When he bowed to G.B.S.'s mother on Regent Street, she asked her son, "Who is that *handsome* man?" and was told he was the well-known Socialist. She replied, "Nonsense. That man is a gentleman." Which indeed he was. He was often dubbed a "modern Don Quixote." His great friend Joseph Conrad said to him, "What you don't know from the outside of a snail to the inside of a prison, isn't knowledge." G.B.S. denied making him the hero of *Captain Brassbound's Conversion,* for such an incredible personage would have destroyed the play's likelihood—such as it was. And yet G.B.S. knew him to be real, and was one of the few living men who could decipher the curious alphabet in which he wrote his private letters. He was a fascinating mystery to a sedentary person like Shaw. The horse, a dangerous animal whom, when he could not avoid it, G.B.S. propitiated with apples and sugar, Cunninghame Graham bestrode and dominated fearlessly. He handled weapons as familiarly as the pen; the medieval sword and the modern Mauser were to him as umbrellas and Kodaks were to Shaw.

But G.B.S. never denied using, in *Arms and the Man,* Cunninghame Graham's remark in the House, "I never withdraw," when required to do so by the Speaker for saying "damn." Cunninghame Graham spent his six weeks at Pentonville doing hard labor, and, when he came out, was given a memorable welcome-home party by the Fabians. Lord Salisbury, meeting him in the House of Commons, quipped, "Well, Mr. Graham, are you thinking where to put your guillotine?" Though Graham was the hero of Shaw's *Arms and the Man,* Graham's own book, *Mogreb-el-Acksa,* is a far truer and more graphic autobiographical account of his adventures.

Cunninghame Graham wrote some thirty books in all and rode the whole length of the Americas on horseback. He also founded the Scottish Labor Party, and crusaded mightily for Socialism in its early, unpopular days. His great friend and fellow Scot, John Burns, was his complete antithesis.

Mrs. Sidney Webb has described Burns as unscrupulous, incurably suspicious, and rather mean in his methods, though she conceded his capacity, straightforwardness, and power of reason. A man of splendid physique, fine and strong intelligence, he stood absolutely alone. He was intensely jealous and acutely suspicious of all middle-class sympathizers. Yet she thought of him as a possible fifth in the Fabian junta, and indeed wished the junta "could be strengthened by his weight." She also noted that although uneducated he was essentially an intellectual man,[7] and that is borne out by Eduard Bernstein's description of meeting Burns on Fleet Street, a parcel of books under his arm. Burns told Bernstein: "Four editions of Sir Thomas More—I have upwards of a hundred. I got this one for 10 pence; this one cost me 4 guineas." And it is also implicit in Burns's retort in the House of Commons to the arrogant Lord Lowther, who had tried to snub him with "The Hon. Member is not at the London County Council." "And the Right Hon. gentleman is not on Newmarket Heath," replied Burns.

John Burns, in his straw hat, with his coal-black beard, had become the most powerful voice in England by the time of the Dockers' Strike, which he and Tom Mann led. The difference between the John Burns led off to jail in 1887 and the triumphant John Burns of 1889 was the difference between declining and reviving trade; as de Tocqueville has

[7] Beatrice Webb, 1948, p. 40.

remarked, revolutions only occur when conditions are improving. This improvement at the end of the century was largely due to the discovery of South African gold, which boosted sterling. Imperialism thereafter became the creed both of the Conservatives and of a section of the Liberals. Even the radicals fell for it: as G.B.S. put it, the world was going to be divided up among the great powers, whether anyone liked it or not, and England's rule was the only one that the Fabians could do anything about.

The series of strikes, which culminated in the great dock strike of 1889, had started in 1888 about conditions in the Bryant and May match factory. Annie Besant wrote an impassioned article about the seven hundred girls who came out on strike. Four hundred pounds was raised to help them, and they won important concessions. Engels' joke that this strike was the light jostle needed to make the entire avalanche move, was true enough; in 1888 the gas workers struck for an eight-hour day and won it.

Beatrice Webb,[8] then still Beatrice Potter, has described in her diary how, at the very time when she was meditating on the virtues and vices of trade unionism, there broke out the great London Dock Strike of 1889, which for the first time united in one solid phalanx the thousands of casual laborers she had watched, day after day, at the gates of the dock companies and in the tenement houses of East London. She describes the politicking during the strike itself as a battle royal at the Trades Union Congress (being held in Yorkshire) between the supporters of Broadhurst and old-fashioned methods, and the Socialists, led by John Burns and Mrs. Besant, two leaders who were absent in London. Broadhurst's supporters won, and Beatrice lunched with him after.

Next morning at breakfast, another clash, while Cunninghame Graham was poring over the *Labour Elector*.

. . . he is a cross between an aristocrat and a barber's block, but also an enthusiast and an unmitigated fool in politics. "I have a letter from Kropotkin," Cunninghame Graham whispers to me, "he says, and I agree with him, if Burns with 80,000 men behind him does not make a revolution, it is because he is afraid of having his hand cut off. Burns is a great fellow, different from these miserable slaves of bourgeois trade unionists,"—with a wave of a hand towards Broadhurst, a wave of a hand which gradually settles down upon a loaf of brown bread, which C.G. believes to be common property, but which, unfortunately, happens to be specially prepared for her great man's over-

[8] 1948, pp. 20 ff.

taxed digestion by Mrs. Broadhurst. The bourgeois slave watches with indignation the delicately tapering fingers of the anarchist clutch hold of his personal property, and with a large perspiring palm grasps the whole thing in his fingers. "No, sir, not that," he roars, "this is my *own* bread, made by my *own* wife, in my *own* house, and carried here in my *own* portmanteau. That you cannot have." C.B. withdraws with the apologies of a gentleman, "Not my bread. I'd rather he destroyed my reputation than took my bread," roars Broadhurst. C.B. looks unutterably disgusted, and wipes his aristocratic hand with soft cambric. . . .

In August 1889 the dockers struck for sixpence an hour instead of the average fivepence (at Tilbury they were only paid fourpence). Ben Tillett, who had run away from home to be a sailor, and Tom Mann, who had been a miner at eleven, with John Burns, masterminded this great strike. Ben Tillett had been organizing first warehousemen and then dockers from 1887 on, and the Fabian H. H. Champion placed at the strikers' disposal his military knowledge of "deploying and exercising large bodies of men and posting of sentries." [9] The dockers' work was hard and precarious, being "casual labour" and there being no guaranteed minimum. Public opinion favored the men, who, with their families, were the poorest and worst-housed in London (in 1931 in the dock area over 4.5 per cent of the population were still living three to a room—as a wit put it: "The earth may be the Lord's but the fullness thereof is the landlord's."). Sydney Buxton, the Liberal M.P. for Poplar, and his wife, distributed over 100,000 meals during the strike, and a fund raised for the strikers' families netted over two thousand pounds. Cardinal Manning, the eighty-two-year-old Catholic Archbishop of Westminster, favored both the strike and the stand taken by the trade unions. Shortly after "Bloody Sunday" he wrote: "The combination of socialism and the outcast population which is our rebuke, sin, shame, scandal and will be our scourge, is a misrepresentation of Law and Liberty and Justice. The appeal to physical forces is criminal and immoral, venial in men maddened by suffering but inexcusable in others." And he wrote to Tom Mann: "The public authorities ought to find work for those who want work, or relief for those who cannot." Before the men got their "tanner," as the sixpence was called, the troops were mobilized. It was August, and the Lord Mayor and the Home Secretary were both on vacation. The Archbishop of Canterbury, Temple, had spoken harshly against the hun-

9 Beer, II, p. 165.

gry men; the Catholic Cardinal waited hour-long, day-long at the Mansion House to negotiate, "a dying man went down to rescue a dead city." On September 12 the directors of the dock companies agreed to negotiate terms "if they came through Cardinal Manning" and on September 14 all parties signed "the Cardinal's peace." *Punch* celebrated the occasion with a poem:

> Hickory, Dickory, Dock,
> The Cardinal picked the dead lock
> The men struck then
> They worked again
> Dickory, Victory, Dock.

R. K. Ensor[10] wrote of the strike:

> The dockers' victory . . . gave trade unionism a decisive stimulus. . . . Even older societies like those of the miners were much affected. But its most striking feature was the organisation of unskilled labour. . . . The "New Unionism" as it was called, had two novelties, it organized men by the industries which employed them rather than by the crafts which they exercised; and it preached political as well as industrial action. Its leaders were conscious socialists; and they sowed much of the seed from which ten years later the Labour party germinated.

In the task of organizing the unskilled majorities, members of the older and skilled minorities in the more exclusive unions played a "missionary" role.

The Fabian Society held no meetings between July 19th and September 20th. The Fabians were, like the Lord Mayor and the Home Secretary, officially on holiday. But E. R. Pease[11] confirms that "many members as individuals lent their aid to the Dockers in their great struggle, which once for all put an end to the belief that hopeless disorganisation is a necessary characteristic of unskilled labour."

[10] p. 206.
[11] p. 83.

CHAPTER SIX

THE FABIAN SOCIETY'S first annual report appeared in 1889, when the Society had between 130 and 140 members; in 1891 the first issue of *Fabian News* was published. A general demand for the eight-hour day had arisen as the result of the dock strike, and the Fabian Society realized that thereafter one of its chief functions might be the putting into practicable form the blueprinting of any reform that was "in the air" and currently demanded, and the disseminating of all possible information about such reform, the need for such reform, the means of its achievement, the best means for circumventing, counteracting, or disarming and mitigating such opposition as it was likely to arouse. These were to be constant Fabian activities from now on. *Facts for Socialists,* a tract first published in 1887, was already in its second edition of 5,000: it is still today (1959) the second-best seller among Fabian publications, and is constantly revised and brought up to date, a hardy perennial necessary to Great Britain's political life. By 1889, 6,500 Fabian tracts had already been distributed, and 31 Fabian lecturers had in the course of one year delivered 721 lectures. Among these were the seven lectures first published in the fall of 1889, and never since out of print, the indestructible, seemingly immortal *Fabian Essays* for whose Jubilee Edition in 1948 their ninety-two-year-old original editor, George Bernard Shaw, wrote a triumphant preface. These *Essay* lectures were delivered in a room lent by King's College, Cambridge, and also at Leicester. Sidney Webb's lecture was delivered by Hubert Bland, for that fall Webb and Pease were touring the United States for three months. A Christian Socialist, the Rev. Stewart Headlam, was chairman throughout the essay lecture course, and members both of the Fabian Society and of the SDF attended.

Preparations for publishing *Fabian Essays* occupied almost a year, and with its appearance and instantaneous success, the Fabian Society's hidden years, its members' political apprenticeship and period of withdrawal and study, were over.

In the face of the extraordinary success of *Fabian Essays* —the first edition of 1,000, which was printed and published privately and not advertised in the press, nor taken round by travelers to the trade, was sold out in a month (at 6 shillings, then a substantial price), and by 1894, 30,000 copies had been sold—serious consideration must be given to this, the basic expression of Fabian philosophy. For *Fabian Essays* is not only still in print; it has become one of the classics of Socialism. Yet as Pease pointed out, it was— and is—important as much for what it left out as for what it contained. Possibly only the few remaining pioneers who lived through Socialism in its early days can fully realize the environment from which *Fabian Essays* showed a way of escape. The Socialism of the Social Democratic Federation and that of the Socialist League was entirely revolutionary; that of the Christian Democrats, Utopian. *Fabian Essays,* on the other hand, squarely based Socialism not on philosophical speculations but on the self-evident evolution of society. It accepted accredited economic science as taught by the professors; it constructed the edifice of Socialism on the firm foundations of existing political and social institutions. Even its genealogy was thoroughly British and very sound.

The Latin tag *post hoc, propter hoc* better describes the relationship of Fabian theory to Sidney Webb's beloved Jeremy Bentham and to Graham Wallas's mentor John Stuart Mill, than do the studbook terms "by" and "out of." For the relationship is temporal rather than genetic. Without Bentham and Mill, the Fabians could not have thought as they did, indeed, could not have happened at all. But the descent was sequential, not filial. What had turned Mill into a Socialist at the end of his life was the horde of semibarbarians living in the slums of great cities, whose unskilled labor is neither required in our present complex industrial organization nor capable of earning a maintenance there.[1]

With the publication of *Fabian Essays,* projected and coordinated and most carefully edited by G.B.S., but the work of no one individual, the seven essayists, who made no claim to be more than communicative students of Socialism, since there were at the time no authoritative teachers, went forward from Mill to designate the Welfare State as the in-

[1] Sidney Webb, 1896, p. 12.

evitable imminent guardian of, and guide to, the greatest good of the greatest number. In his essay on the history of Socialism, Sidney Webb remarked:

> Though the social organism has itself evolved from the union of individual men, the individual is now created by the social organism of which he forms a part: his life is born of the larger life; his attributes are moulded by the social pressure; his activities, inextricably interwoven with others, belong to the activity of the whole. Without the continuance and sound health of the social organism, no man can now live or thrive; and its persistence is accordingly his paramount end. His conscious motive for action may be, nay always must be, individual to himself; but where such action proves inimical to the social welfare, it must sooner or later be checked by the whole, lest the whole perish through the error of its member. There is, at any moment, one particular arrangement of social relations which involves the minimum of human misery then and there possible. . . . Fifty years ago it would have been assumed that absolute freedom in the sense of individual or "manly" independence, plus a criminal code, would spontaneously result in such an arrangement for each particular nation; and the effect was the philosophic apotheosis of *laissez-faire*. Today every student is aware that no such optimistic assumption is warranted by the facts of life.[2]

Delicately Webb thus points to the fallacy Socialists see in Mill's *On Liberty*. For Mill, the widespread interference of institutions, formal and informal, with individual self-development blocked the way to individual and collective wellbeing. The greatest good society could bestow was to make itself as scarce as possible; that the state should "wither away" was his hope, as it was Karl Marx's faith.

The doctrine of Fabianism as expressed in the *Essays* began with the conviction of the value of the human person, and a belief that all men and women have an equal right to live their lives in a manner that seems to them morally good. The essayists agreed with Bentham in their insistence that the state exists for the individual and the maintenance of his rights is its first duty. These rights are the conditions which the individual feels necessary to the fulfillment of his best self, and these rights cannot be equal unless the freedom is equal, and for individuals to have equal freedom their economic opportunity must be equal. Where the Fabians broke away from Bentham was in declaring that economic equality could only be imposed by collective control. Nor

2 Shaw, 1948, p. 53.

could this collective control be effective without collective ownership of the means of production. Thus, from the outset, the Fabians recommended nationalization, first of utilities: thus it was that they were—and still are—called "gas and water Socialists"; then of other national assets, such as coal, electricity, railroads, transport, cables and communication, medical services, iron and steel, and banks. Each citizen, the *Fabian Essays* declare, has an equal claim to the common good in respect of his equal needs.

The Fabian view of collectivism from the first took great pains to insist on the absolute value of private property. In *Fabian Essays*, discussing the moral basis of socialism, Sydney (Lord) Olivier wrote:

The institution of private property in certain things is in many respects so reasonable and convenient for the majority of mankind, and was so conspicuously advantageous for those stronger individuals under whose leadership the beginnings of tribal civilisations were developed, that very early in their history it received the sanction of moral convention, religion and law. It was obviously necessary for the establishment of industrial society that each man should own the product of his labour and the tools necessary for them to labour effectually. But the Industrial Revolution so entirely changed the conditions under which men produce wealth, and the character of the tools with which they work, while the sanctions of law and conventional morality still cling to all that has been imported under the old definition of property. If the idea so constantly appealed to in justification of property law is to be realised; if the fruits of each man's labour are to be guaranteed to him and he is to own the instruments with which he works; if the laws of property are not to establish a parasitic class taking tribute from the labour of others in the forms of Rent and Interest, then we must modify our administration of property. We must admit that as the agricultural labourer cannot individually own the farm he works on and its stock, as the factory hand cannot individually own the mill, land and industrial capital are things in which private property is impossible except on condition of a small minority owning all such property and the great majority none at all. . . . The Catholic Church has always insisted on the duty of helping the poor, not on the ground of the social danger of a "residuum," but by the nobler appeal to the instinct of human benevolence. The Catholic Church developed, relatively to the enlightenment of its age, the widest and freest system of education the world has ever seen before this century. Catholic Christianity, by its revolutionary conception that God was incarnated in Man, exploding the hideous superstition that the imagination of the thoughts of man's heart was only to do evil continually, and substituting the faith in the perfectibility of each individual soul; by its brilliant powerful generalisation that God must be Love, because there is nothing better, and that man is freed from the law by the inward guidance of grace, has done more for social morality than any other religion of the world.

Protestant Individualism in England shattered the Catholic Church; founded the modern land system upon its confiscated estates; destroyed the medieval machinery of charity and education, and in religion rehabilitated the devil. . . .

Out of the wreckage of the Catholic Church, and amid the dissolution of the Protestant religion, there successively emerged, at an interval of some three hundred years, the two great socialistic institutions of the Poor Law and the People's Schools. . . .

Not for many centuries has there been such a compulsion as now for the individual to acknowledge a social ethic. For now, for the first time since the dissolution of the early tribal communism, the individual worker earns his living, fulfils his elementary desire, not by direct personal production, but by intricate co-operation in which the effect and value of his personal effort are almost indistinguishable. . . . The factory system, the machine industry, the world commerce, have abolished individualist production; and the completion of the co-operative form towards which the transition stage of individualist capitalism is hurrying us will render a conformity with social ethics a universal condition of tolerable existence for the individual. . . .

But the right to ownership remains, however co-operative the form:

Whatever things . . . we allow a man to possess, we must allow him to exchange, for exchange never takes place unless both parties believe themselves to benefit by it. Further, bequest must be allowed, since any but a moderate probate duty or personalty would, unless supported by a strong and searching public opinion, certainly be evaded. Moreover, if we desire the personal independence of women and children, then their property . . . must for a long time to come be most carefully guarded . . . Voluntary associations of all kinds, whether joint stock companies, religious corporations or communistic groups would in the eyes of the Social Democratic State, consist simply of so many individuals possessing those rights of property which are allowed to individuals.

The Essayists saw the intricacy of industrial co-operation as exploding any possible apologia for individualist appropriation. "No man," wrote Olivier,

> can pretend to claim the fruits of his own labour, for his whole ability and opportunity for working are plainly a vast inheritance and contribution, of which he is but a transient and accidental beneficiary and steward and his power of turning them to his own account depends entirely upon the desires and needs of other people for his services. . . . Socialist morality, like that of all preceding systems, is only that morality which the conditions of human existence have made necessary. . . . Socialism is but a stage in the unending progression out of the weakness and the ignorance in which society and the individual alike are born towards the strength and the enlightenment in which they can see and choose their own way forward—from the chaos where morality is not to the consciousness which sees that morality is reason.[3]

Sidney Webb based his essay on Mill's theory of social reform by means of the Ricardian law of rent, but took it much further. Mill, though he died a confessed Socialist,[4] had stopped at land reform, but Webb noted that as soon as production was sufficiently advanced to furnish more than the barest necessities, a struggle for the surplus began. Whatever individuals or classes were in power used it to get hold of that surplus product, leaving the rest of society

> practically nothing beyond the means of subsistence according to the current local standard. . . .
>
> This surplus produce possessed the character of rent. In relation to agriculture it was fertility, mineral contents, position, or even the mere presence of human beings (labour) that combined to make the net advantages of one piece of land very different from that of another. This differential advantageousness, rising in scale . . . accounted for the phenomenon of economic rent. . . . Under unrestricted private ownership and free competition, with the motive of pecuniary self-interest in full play, the man in possession of any position economically superior to the very margin of cultivation . . . was able to retain for himself the whole differential advantage of that position.

[3] Shaw, 1948, pp. 125-28.

[4] "If therefore, the choice were to be made between communism with all its chances, and the present state of society with all its sufferings and injustices . . . if this or communism were the alternative, all the difficulties great or small, of communism, would be but as dust in the balance."

This law of rent held good not of land only. . . . Alike in all capitalist enterprise—in manufacture, in transport, in distribution, as well as in agriculture—the factors of production were different from one another in net advantageousness no less than the land itself.

But the product, whatever its cost to produce, is worth only what the market will bear, and the exchange value of the least useful part of the supply fixes the exchange value of all the rest. Technically this occurs by the "law of indifference" and since the least useful unit of the supply is generally that which is last produced, its utility is called the final utility of the commodity. The utility of the first or most useful unit is called the total utility.

Final utility is sometimes called "marginal utility." . . . The main point to be grasped is that however useful any commodity may be, its exchange value can be run down to nothing by increasing the supply until there is more of it than is wanted. The excess being useless and valueless, is to be had for nothing, and nobody will pay anything for a commodity as long as plenty of it is to be had for nothing.

On the other hand, of course, by withholding necessary things, private owners of them can send the price up: thus if gas, electricity, water, transportation, sewers, mail delivery, etc., are privately owned, the owners can make people pay much more for them than if the State—that is, all the people—own them and pay for them in proportion to their use of them.

Thus for Webb, the struggle is not between the capitalist class and the working class, but between the great mass of the people and the appropriators of differential rent, between producers—those who organize industries, design machinery, make inventions or discoveries, or perform bodily labor—and those who fatten on the results merely because they invest capital. Since differential rent is the result of improvement performed by or belonging to, the whole community ("social labor and general development"), it should belong to, and be utilized by and for, the good of the whole of society: this is to be done by municipalization, nationalization, and taxation.

The seven essayists were thus totally unconvinced of the relevance of the class theory, or of class distinctions, and they had no belief in the class struggle as the instrument of social change. Nor did they have any *mystique* about the proletariat: the early Fabians ignored the trade unions and the co-operatives, at that time the two leading working-class organizations.

"Socialism is nothing else but common sense," Olivier had declared, and Webb said, "We must frankly accept the changes brought about by the Industrial Revolution, the factory system, the massing of population in great cities, the elaborate differentiation and complication of modern civilisation, the subordination of the worker to the citizen and of the individual to the community."

The Fabian Society from its beginning opposed all pretensions to hamper the socialization of industry with equal wages, equal hours of labor, equal official status, or equal authority for everyone. Such conditions they considered not only impracticable, but incompatible with equality of subordination to the common interests. They recognized that wealth was "social in its origin and must be social in its distribution," since the evolution of industry had made it impossible to distinguish the particular contribution that each person made to the common product or to ascertain its value.

And the essayists dismissed alike Utopians and revolutionaries. As Sidney Webb put it:

> Wise prophets nowadays do not found a partial community which adopts the whole faith; they cause rather the partial adoption of their faith by the whole community. Incomplete reform is effected in the world of ordinary citizens, instead of complete reform outside of it. Genuine Socialism grows by vertical instead of horizontal expansion; we must make ever more Socialistic the institutions amid which we live . . . by this method progress may be slow, but failure is impossible. No nation having once nationalized or municipalized any industry has ever retraced its steps or reversed its action.

The first fifty years of the twentieth century have proven how truly prophetic were these words.

Here is expressed the heart and core of Fabian philosophy, that expectation of "the inevitability of gradualness" to quote Webb's most famous phrase, which does not seek to find work or even dole for the unemployed, but rather seeks so to reorganize the public services that unemployment simply cannot happen; seeks so to administer, for example, the docks and gasworks that there can be no constant fringe of casual labor. For over half a century, as Henry Pelling[5] has remarked, the Fabian essays formed the basis of British Socialist thought.

[5] p. 66.

After the publication of the *Fabian Essays* in 1889, the next most important statement of Fabian purpose was Shaw's *Report on Fabian Policy* published in 1896 as Fabian Tract 70. The Fabian aim, G.B.S. anonymously declared in this tract, was

> to persuade the English people to make their political constitution thoroughly democratic and so to socialize their industries as to make the livelihood of the people entirely independent of private Capitalism . . . it has no distinctive opinions on the Marriage Question, Religion, Art, abstract Economics, historic Evolution, Currency, or any other subject than its own special business of practical Democracy and Socialism.

And he goes on:

> Socialism, as understood by the Fabian Society, means the organization and conduct of the necessary industries of the country, and the appropriation of all forms of economic rent of land and capital, by the nation as a whole, through the most suitable public authorities, parochial, municipal, provincial or central. . . . The Socialism advocated by the Fabian Society is State Socialism exclusively.

Tract 70 goes on to explain to "the foreign friends of the Fabian Society" that as England now possesses an elaborate democratic state machinery, graduated from the parish council or vestry up to the central Parliament, and elected under a franchise which enables the working-class vote to overwhelm all others, Continental distinctions between state and people do not

> hamper English Socialists. For example, the distinction between State Socialism and Social-Democracy in Germany, where municipalities and other local bodies are closed against the working classes, has no meaning in England. The difficulty in England is not to secure more political power for the people, but to persuade them to make any sensible use of the power they already have.

One of the aspects of Fabian philosophy too often ignored is its realistic concern for the individual. In this same Fabian Tract 70, *Report on Fabian Policy,* published in July 1896, Rubric VIII is headed, "Fabian Individualism." This rubric makes it abundantly clear that "the State should not monopolize industry as against private enterprise or individual initiative further than may be necessary to make the livelihood of the people and their access to the sources of production completely independent of both." It goes on,

> The freedom of individuals to test the social values of new inventions, to initiate improved methods of production; to anticipate and lead public enterprise in catering for the new social wants; to practise all arts, crafts and professions independently; in short to complete the social organisation by adding the resources of private activity and judgment to those of public routine, is as highly valued by the Fabian Society as freedom of Speech, freedom of the Press, or any other article in the charter of popular liberties.

Sidney Webb dotted the *i*'s and crossed the *t*'s of this concern of Fabianism for the individual in his *The Necessary Basis of Society,* an address given to the Social and Political League in London, on May 14, 1908. "We are apt to forget," he admitted,

> that the average citizen or the normal human being is a mere abstraction, who does not exist. You and I have never seen him in the flesh. So varied is our individuality that whatever is handed out to all alike must necessarily fail to meet our requirements with any exactness. . . . A regiment of naked men needs clothing too urgently to allow us to grumble that the standard sizes of the regimental contractor make all the uniforms, if closely scrutinized, nothing better than misfits. The early Victorian community, bare of schools, or drains, or Factory Acts, had to get itself supplied with the common article of standard pattern, so to speak, by wholesale, in order to be able to survive at all. But this necessity ought not to blind us to the fact that . . . all these governmental products . . . are . . . one and all, like the contractor's uniforms, nothing better than misfits. My first proposition is, therefore, the paradoxical one that, whilst it may have been the most pressing business of nineteenth century governments to deal with the whole people, far the most important business of twentieth century governments must be to provide not only for minorities, but even for quite small minorities, and actually for individuals. We are no longer content with the army contractor's standard sizes. . . . Every minority, every citizen, in fact, has to be supplied . . . just as every soldier in the regiment has to have . . . his pair of marching boots.

And Sidney Webb used education as his actual example of progressive government action. In a hundred years, the provision of schools by the State had changed from no provision of any schools at all, to many different types of schools—for the precocious, for the backward and feeble-minded, for the blind, deaf and crippled; truant and industrial, vocational and art schools. And the ideal is to provide "each individual child with exactly the kind and grade and amount of education that its individuality requires." [6] In this, perhaps the most thought-through statement of Fabian philosophy, Sidney Webb proposes a National Minimum of Health, of Wages, of Leisure, of Sanitation, of Education; in fact, the formulation and rigid enforcement, in all spheres of social activity, of a National Minimum below which the individual, whether he likes it or not, cannot, in the interests of the well-being of the whole, ever be allowed to fall. And Webb prophesied that this National Minimum would inspire and guide and explain the statesmanship and the politics of the twentieth century. Thus, by "fencing off the downward way, we divert the forces of competition along the upward way." And the most rugged individualist need never fear, for this National Minimum "will not interfere either with the pecuniary profits or with the power or the personal development of the exceptional man. The illimitable realm of the upward remains, without restriction, open to him."

Thus, while the Fabian Society reversed the repudiation of existing economic and constitutional methods required by the older Socialists, it did not present Socialism as a panacea for all the ills of human society, only for those which were produced by defective organization by the individual of the individual, and by a radically uneconomic distribution of wealth. In the Fabian Society's report to the Trades Union Council (1896) the Society declared that it brought:

> . . . all the pressure and persuasion in its power to bear on existing forces, caring nothing for what name any party calls itself by, or what principles, socialist or other, it professes, but having regard solely to the tendency of its actions. The Society is pledged to support those which make for Socialism and Democracy, and to oppose those which are reactionary. It does not ask the English people to join the Fabian Society. It urges its members to join other Societies, Socialist or non-Socialist, in which Fabian work can be done.

At the Fabian Society's first annual conference (the second was not until twenty years later), in London on February 6 and 7, 1892, a resolution to expel from the Society any member "becoming an official of the Conservative, Liberal, Liberal Unionist or National League parties" was rejected by

[6] Sidney Webb, 1911, p. 4.

a large majority. For as Shaw[7] put it: "Though the [Fabian] Society may be officially affiliated to the Labor Party, the true Fabian is not, and never can be, a party man or woman. My Party, right or wrong, is not our slogan. All Fabians have their price, which is always the adoption of Fabian measures, no matter by what party."

The final word on the success of the *Fabian Essays* was perhaps written by Graham Wallas. He tells how nearly forty years ago he was one of the Fabian Society who had just written their drafts and had appointed G.B.S. to edit the published volume. He was a schoolmaster and Shaw was already a professor, though not yet a successful writer. One of their difficulties was that the seven essayists included minds of very different types, especially, perhaps, those of Mr. Sidney Webb and Mr. Hubert Bland. Wallas, with his schoolmaster's outlook, was greatly struck by the fact that Shaw, when discussing the kind of revision which he would urge on the essayists, said, "I'm not going to Webbulize Bland or Blandulate Webb."

[7] 1892.

CHAPTER SEVEN

GRADUALLY THE FA-
bian permeation was becoming widespread. With the tremendous success of the *Essays*, the enormous distribution
of tracts, the proliferation of lectures, went the success of
Fabians in local and municipal elections, county councils,
school boards, and vestries. Mrs. Besant and the Rev.
Stewart Headlam, standing as Progressives, were elected to
the school board of the brand new London County Council
(LCC) in 1888. In 1892 the LCC Progressive Party won
an unexpected victory with a program which G.B.S. said
was imposed on it by Webb's *Questions for Candidates*,
published by the Society. These, printed and widely distributed before the election, launched the Fabian Progressive
Party in municipal London. Webb's *Questions*, Pease pointed
out, gave definiteness and point to the vague ideas floating
around.

Facts for Londoners, Fabian Tract 8 (fifty-five pages of
statistics for sixpence), published in July 1889, was a timely
birthday present for London's County Council, then only a
few months old. Sidney Webb also circulated a pamphlet
called *Wanted, a Programme*. Privately printed, it appeared
just in time for the meeting of the National Liberal Federation at Birmingham, together with *The Progress of Socialism*
by the same author. (Sidney Webb later lectured on Charles
Booth's *Life and Labour of the People of London*, which
upped to 30 per cent the SDF's figure that 25 per cent of London workers' wages were inadequate. Booth's original inquiry
had been undertaken to prove the SDF figure "grossly over-
stated" and had ended by admitting it fell short of the mark.
Pease points out with regard to *Facts for Londoners* that
it served to expose the legend of the wide extension of

municipal ownership in Britain being due to the Fabian Society as a myth: Birmingham in the seventies was, he declares, the Mecca of municipalization. Indeed, Mr. Joseph Chamberlain's Electric Lighting Act of 1882 was so careful of the interests of the public, so strict in the limitations it put upon the possible profits to the investor, that electric lighting was blocked in England for some years, and the act had to be modified in order that capital might be attracted to it.[1]

Sir Robert Ensor[2] has pointed out the importance for London's new County Council in successfully avoiding at the outset a mechanical party division as between Conservatives and Liberals. The special municipal parties which were created instead—the "moderates" and "progressives" —succeeded almost until 1906 in excluding the irrelevancies of national politics. "Now we have the machinery of social democracy," Annie Besant exclaimed triumphantly at the birth of the LCC, and the new body also included men like James Ramsay MacDonald and John Burns, who at that time had still, perhaps, the largest working-class following in London.

Very much heartened by its successful capture in 1892 of the still infant London County Council—by the election of an unconscionable crowd of Fabians—the Fabian Society cast its nets further afield. One Henry H. Hutchinson of Derby had been elected a member of the Society in June 1890, and upon his election offered the Society the sum of 200 pounds sterling, approving the suggestion that it should be used chiefly for lectures in country centers. The thoroughly organized "Lancashire campaign" was the result.

All the essayists except Sydney Olivier took part, and several other prominent Fabians, including the Rev. Stewart Headlam. The campaign, during which sixty lectures were delivered, was of only five weeks' duration (September 20 to October 27), but it was concentrated. The Dukeries and the strongholds of the old unionism and new Toryism— Lancashire, Lanchester, Liverpool, Rochdale, Sheffield, and Barnsley were invaded, and vigorous propaganda in the manufacturing districts was carried on chiefly by extremely well-attended outdoor meetings. The lectures were given in sets of four, consecutively, mostly at Liberal and Radical clubs and some were even sponsored by Co-operative societies. This campaign was so successful that the series of lectures was continued for several years, and the results were

[1] Pease, p. 82.

[2] p. 296.

important not only for the Fabian Society and Socialism, but
for English political history.

> Hitherto the Socialism presented to the industrial districts
> of England, which are the backbone of Trade Unionism
> and Co-operation, was revolutionary and destructive, ill-
> tempered and ungenerous. It had perhaps alarmed, but it had
> failed to attract them. It had made no real impression on
> the opinion of the people. From this point a new move-
> ment began. It first took the form of local Fabian Socie-
> ties. They were succeeded by, and merged into, branches
> of the Independent Labor Party. They adopted everything
> Fabian except the Society's peculiar political tactics. No
> doubt something of the sort would have happened had
> there never been a Lancashire campaign, but this campaign
> may be fairly described as the first step in an evolution, the
> end of which is not yet in sight.[3]

The Fabians now also stepped up their lecturing. During
1891-2, 3,339 lectures were given by 117 Fabian Society
members, of which 300 were delivered in the provinces. In
addition, Fabian Society membership rose in 1891 from
178 to 361, while the Society's income rose from £126
($500) to £520. This income was chiefly devoted to the
distribution of tracts. In 1891 ten new tracts, four pamphlets, and six leaflets, as well as reissues of all the old ones,
were published, 333,500 printed, and 98,349 distributed. In
1891-2, 378,281 tracts were distributed. This was the largest
number ever, and can be accounted for, Pease[4] suggests, by
the fact that at this period the Society had a virtual monopoly in the production of political pamphlets in which
facts and figures were marshaled in support of propositions
of reform in the direction of Socialism.

New branch Fabian Societies were meanwhile mushroom-
ing all over the place, one even as far afield as Bombay
(listed laconically between Birmingham and Bristol), and by
1892 the over-all branch membership was 400; by 1894,
681. In 1898 there were 74 local societies, an all-time high.
Yet the Fabian Society was not maternal. Although membership was as carefully screened and as much a privilege in the
local societies as in the parent, the groups of earnest workingmen influenced in the provinces by Fabian teaching were
hardly the matrix from which the highly educated speakers,
writers, and active political workers required to spread the
Fabian gospel could be drawn. In fact, Pease notes, from the

[3] Pease, p. 97.
[4] p. 99.

first the local Fabian Societies were Independent Labor Parties in personnel and policy, and Fabian only in name. They folded silently, until by 1900 only four local and four university societies remained.

The Fabians at this time also were able to permeate the press very successfully. Webb's *London Programme* published in book form, in Sonnenschein's Social Science Series, first appeared as a series of articles in the *Speaker,* a Liberal weekly. (As a result of the fact that the *Pall Mall Gazette* had been "held aloft" in Trafalgar Square on Red Sunday, the owner, Henry Yates Thompson, Gladstone's private secretary, dismissed W. T. Stead as editor, and in his place hired John Morley.) The *Star,* founded in 1888, had G.B.S. as its music critic and H. M. Massingham, then a Fabian, as its assistant editor. When the latter left to join the staff of the *Daily Chronicle,* its editor, though not a Fabian, proved sympathetic.

In 1892 Sidney Webb was elected to the London County Council for Deptford, and resigned from the Colonial Office to become chairman of the LCC's Technical Education Board, which controlled all the education in London except Greek and theology. Working here, he was able, during the eight years of his chairmanship, to increase secondary education and immeasurably to widen the scope of the University of London, hitherto merely a degree-giving institution with no pretensions at university curriculum or life.

But the crowning achievement of the Fabians during the nineties was their foisting onto the Liberals of the Newcastle Program, "reluctantly blessed by Mr. Gladstone" and adopted by the National Liberal Federation in 1891. Shaw[5] has described the "exact facts of the launching of the Newcastle Program."

> Webb gave me the Program in his own handwriting as a string of resolutions. I being then a permeative Fabian on the Executive of the South St. Pancras Liberal and Radical Association (I had coolly walked in and demanded to be elected to the Association and Executive, which was done on the spot by the astonished Association—ten strong) . . . I took them down to a meeting in Percy Hall . . . where the late Mr. Beale, then Liberal candidate and subscription milch cow of the constituency (without the ghost of a chance) was to address as many of the ten as might turn up, under the impression that he was addressing a public meeting. There were certainly not twenty people present, perhaps not ten. I asked him to

[5] 1948, Preface.

move the resolutions. He said they looked complicated, and if I would move them he would second them. I moved them, turning over Webb's pages by batches, and not reading most of them. Mr. Beale seconded. Passed unanimously. That night they went down to *The Star* with the report of an admirable speech which Mr. Beale was supposed to have delivered. Next day he found the National Liberal Club in an uproar at his revolutionary break-away. But he played up; buttoned his coat determinedly, said we lived in progressive times and must move with them; and carried it off.

The Liberals were then facing a general election with only Home Rule to distinguish their program from that of the Conservatives, and the Newcastle Program caught on. G.B.S. describes candidates scrapping their Home Rule literature and frantically sending for Fabian tracts. G.B.S. issued an election manifesto, telling the working classes that until they cared as much about politics as they did about horse racing and provided themselves with a genuine working-class party, they should only vote for the better (or against the worse) man. Six Fabians were candidates, and only J. Keir Hardie got in, for West Ham, though Ben Tillett did well at West Bradford, to which the Fabian Society sent speakers and for which they collected £152. The Liberals won the election of 1892 by a narrow margin.

Gladstone's fourth Cabinet was rickety from the start. Its chief importance was as a Liberal hiatus in an otherwise solid Conservative rule of nineteen years. The Liberals began by shelving the Newcastle Program, but in March 1893 Sir Henry Campbell-Bannerman pledged the government to "show themselves to be the best employers of labour in the country," adding, "We have ceased to believe in what are known as competition or starvation wages." But, as E. R. Pease[6] put it,

enunciating a principle is one thing and carrying it into effect in scores of departments is another. . . . Permanent officials doubtless obstructed, as they always do; and but a few members of the Cabinet accepted or understood the new obligation. . . . At that time legislative reforms were difficult because the Government majority was both small and uncertain. . . . But administrative reforms were subject to no such limitation; wages and conditions of Labour were determined by the department concerned, and each minister could do what he chose for the workmen virtually in his employment.

[6] p. 115.

But the Cabinet did not care, and its apathy cost it dear. For it was this administrative refusal to implement the promises explicitly stated in the Newcastle Program, rather than the Liberal Party's failure to do so on a national scale, that caused the Fabian Society to reverse its own policy completely.

During the Bradford campaign in 1892, Shaw had explicitly and repeatedly stated that the Fabians would *not* form a party of their own, but before a year had elapsed, Webb and Shaw drafted and launched a magazine article, sanctioned by the Fabian Society and accepted by the *Fortnightly Review*, attacking the Cabinet "with all the Fabian guns in action." The article, "To Your Tents, O Israel," examined each of the government departments in detail, and described what should be done in each before Sir Henry could be said to have kept his word. "So far there was little to show as results from the Liberal victory of the previous year," declares Pease.[7] The Fabian Society therefore "called on the working classes to abandon Liberalism, to form a Trade Union party of their own, to raise £30,000 and finance fifty candidations for Parliament." Thirteen years later, in 1906, the Labor Party, formed as suggested by the big trade Unions, "financed precisely fifty candidates and succeeded in electing thirty."

This article, then, marked a real change in Fabian policy, and, hereafter, although the Fabians continued to permeate as individuals, the simple permeation of the Liberal Party hitherto indulged in by them as a society ended. H. W. Massingham, disapproving the new policy, left the Fabians, and, indeed, his *Daily Chronicle* became hostile to them. When the Liberals were defeated in 1895 the Fabians felt they had done well to leave a sinking ship which, in effect, they had helped founder; but few Fabians thought the Liberal Party would be so unconscionably long a-dying, and none foresaw, after Joseph Chamberlain's defection, the advent of the black-haired, blue-eyed Welshman, who spoke English as though it were a foreign language, David Lloyd George. His personality was to split the Liberal Party, but his policy was to delay the advent of the Labor Party into power until after the end of World War I, and was further to delay the disappearance of the Liberals until the depression of 1929.

[7] p. 116.

CHAPTER EIGHT

T HE EVIDENCES OF LIFE
are warmth and growth, and the Fabian Society certainly owes
much of its perennial vitality to the warm bonds between its
members, and to its capacity for using whatever adaptations
to circumstances might be necessary as adjuncts to growth.
With the defeat of the Liberals in 1895 Fabian emphasis
had to change its entire orientation. After the Liberal government let down the Fabian side in 1893 by its refusal to implement the Fabian promises it (albeit somewhat unwittingly
and involuntarily) had made, the Fabians had swept the Liberal dust from their shoes with the article, "To Your Tents, O
Israel," and suggested the formation of a strictly working-
class Labor Party. The foundation of the Independent
Labor Party was the immediate result, but it could not be a
final nor even a complete one, for the trade unions held
back from the ILP, feeling that political commitment might
divert their resources from what was the main purpose of
their existence, the improvement of working-class conditions.

It was in January of 1893 that J. Keir Hardie, who had
been elected to Parliament as an independent Socialist
with Fabian help for West Ham in 1892, was chairman of
the first Independent Labor Party Conference at Bradford; at that time he was also treasurer of the York Fabian
Society. Lord Snowden hailed the birth of the Independent
Labor Party registered by this conference as "the most important political event of the nineteenth century." Also at
this conference, Ben Turner voted against G.B.S. and W. De
Mattos, two of the twelve Fabian delegates, because, he declared, they were Liberals.

There remains the question which Margaret Cole asked
G.B.S.: Why had he and Sidney Webb turned back to permeation and continued with it as a policy for so many years
after their joint manifesto, "To Your Tents, O Israel," had
proclaimed the existing parties useless? G.B.S. replied:

"There was no turning back. The organization of the labor interest as a political party in no way suspended nor reversed the necessity for permeating all parties with the Socialist outlook. . . . At the initial I.L.P. Conference in Bradford I defeated Blatchford on this question [The exclusion of all Conservatives and Liberals]." [1] Furthermore, in a reply by the Fabian Executive to H. G. Wells in 1906, also written by Shaw, the Fabian position is even more explicitly stated:

> Permeation as applied to Parliament means wire-pulling the Government in order to get Socialistic measures passed, and stimulating the opposition to denounce the Government for neglecting the grievances of the people. . . . Thus in the 1885-92 Parliament our Permeation of the Government was represented by the County Government Act, in which our hand was not seen, whereas our Permeation of the Opposition was represented by the Newcastle Programme.
> Now it was perfectly well known to us that the Liberal leaders resisted . . . the foisting of this programme on the National Liberal Federation by Fabians who had joined the Liberal Federations in all directions with this object. But without the Newcastle Programme they would have been defeated: as it was, they scraped through with a very small majority. Having scraped through, they promptly threw over the Programme. We had foreseen they would do this. Our plan was to use their disregard of the Programme and their breach of its pledges to Labour, as a proof of the need for an Independent Labour Party. Accordingly, we unmasked our battery and delivered the most smashing attack on the Liberal party that has ever come from the Labour side.[2]

A section of the delegates at Bradford wished to include the word "Socialist" in the title of the new party. G. D. H. Cole noted that the proposal was defeated on tactical grounds, but there was never any doubt that the ILP regarded itself as a Socialist Party. The object of the party was defined at Bradford as "the collective ownership of all the means of production, distribution and exchange." But "although socialization was made the criterion of the Socialist nature of the new party, the inspiration that lay behind it was ethical rather than economic." [3]

Then, too, though the 120 delegates gathered at Brad-

[1] Margaret I. Cole (ed.), 1949, p. 11.
[2] *Ibid.*
[3] G. D. H. Cole, 1956, p. 157.

ford under Keir Hardie's chairmanship were all Socialists, and included five from the Social Democratic Federation, yet they were engaged in forming a rival organization to the SDF and would not give their organization a Socialist name, because they realized how the land lay. The working classes were not yet ready to be tagged "Socialist." [4] Yet now "for the first time a popular socialist party was founded in England on thoroughly English lines, deriving from, and appealing to, what were then the natural channels of working-class expression in the industrial areas, *viz.* the trade unions and the non-conformist chapels. Compared with the incurable exoticism of the S.D.F. or even the middle-class astuteness of the Fabian Society, the I.L.P. represented an enormous advance towards making practical socialism a genuine popular issue." [5] At this time membership in the Fabian Society, including the branches, had risen to over 1,100. In 1894 the newly formed ILP contested three Parliamentary by-elections, and polled over 9,000 votes. It now had a paid membership of over 5,000. The Webbs lost no time in having Keir Hardie to dinner to meet their fellow Fabians J. Ramsay MacDonald and Frank Smith, on January 23, 1895. Beatrice Webb confesses she found Keir Hardie's insistence on wearing working-men's clothes and a cloth cap in the House of Commons a pose, and Keir Hardie had said the Webbs were the worst enemies of the social revolution, because in Beatrice's view "no great transformation is possible in a free democratic state like England *unless you alter the opinions of all classes of the community,* and even if it were possible, it would not be desirable. That is the crux between us." [6] At this dinner party, the Webbs made the Fabian position quite plain: the Fabians in no way competed with the ILP, for they were purely an educational body, nor did they wish to become a political party. "We should continue our policy of inoculation—of giving to each class, to each person coming under our influence, the exact dose of collectivism that they were prepared to assimilate. And we should continue to improve and enlarge such machinery of Government that came into our hands." [7]

With the Liberal government which had, at its inception, aroused high hopes, the Fabians had become very disappointed. "None of the Ministers are doing any work," complained Beatrice to her diary on January 20, 1895. Rose-

---

[4] Beer, II, p. 302.

[5] Ensor, p. 122.

[6] Beatrice Webb, 1948, p. 123.

[7] *Ibid.,* p. 122.

bery saw no one but Eddy Hamilton, a flashy fast Treasury clerk, his stud groom, and various nonpolitical socialites. "Asquith, under the dominance of his brilliant and silly wife, has given up attending to his department and occupies his time by visiting rich country houses and learning to ride."

The official Liberals had, as she put it, "rucked up." So the 1895 election, necessitated by the Liberal government being censured because Campbell-Bannerman, as War Minister, had not purchased enough cordite, caused the Fabians no surprise. Lord Rosebery decided to resign, and Lord Salisbury took office. In the general election following in July, the ILP set up 28 candidates, but they and the Liberals were trounced: Lord Harcourt and John Morley lost their seats; so did Keir Hardie and Cunninghame Graham. Every one of the 28 ILP contestants was unsuccessful: the Conservative majority of 152 enabled Lord Salisbury to make his third Cabinet one of the strongest that ever held office in Great Britain.

Yet the precarious and short-lived Liberal Government of 1892-5 had brought in two measures much approved by the Fabians. The Local Government Act of 1894, better known as the Parish Councils Act, democratized parish administration, and constituted out of chaos a system of local government for rural England. Herbert Samuel (later Lord), then Liberal Member for South Oxfordshire, though never a Fabian, not only prepared for the Society an explanation of this act, but also wrote for it *Questions for Parish, Rural, and Urban District Council Candidates* (Fabian Tracts 56, 57, and 59). "Probably," notes Pease, "this was the first time that an analysis of a new Act of Parliament had been published at a penny . . . 30,000 copies were sold in five months." The other measure that brought unalloyed joy to Fabian hearts was the imposition of death duties, which, they felt, was a substantial blow at the social and economic inequalities inherent in succession by inheritance, and particularly so in a society based, as is the English, on primogeniture. From 1895 on, with the Conservatives securely in the saddle, and likely to remain so in the foreseeable future, the Fabian Society ostensibly returned to its most permanent function, the political, economic, and social education in Socialism of the English people, from the working classes on up to the highest in the land. (G.B.S. was later to find he had no more devoted a fan of his political plays than King Edward VII.) The Fabians had at first circulated their now famous "book boxes" among their local societies; as these folded, they offered the book boxes to any working-class organization, and, indeed, to any organization of readers or students. A collection of around 5,000 volumes was formed, and some 200 boxes of books on Socialism, economics, history, and social problems were kept in circulation. The books were intended to be educational rather than directly propagandist; each box was made up to suit the taste, expressed or inferred, of the subscriber. Quarterly exchanges were allowed, but the twenty or thirty books in a box usually lasted a society for a year. It was a remarkable fact that, although boxes were lent freely to such slight organizations as reading classes, and even sent to the remote mining villages of Wales or Scotland, not a single box was ever lost.[8] Lists were also prepared of books on social subjects, and were kept up to date: these were sent to each Fabian, who then was expected to report on how many were in the public library in his district and to apply for the inclusion of those missing.

That the work of the Fabian Society is the sum of the work of individual Fabians was, and is, a Fabian article of faith, and members of the Executive were expected to attend the two Fabian committee meetings held every week. G.B.S. never missed a single meeting in all the years he was on the Executive.

[8] Pease, p. 21.

CHAPTER NINE

ANNIE BESANT'S DE-
parture from the Society was almost as abrupt as her arrival
had been. But luckily the Fabians were blessed, each decade
of their existence, with the advent of new and impressive personalities. As the Society lost, by death or defection, dominant (and sometimes dominating) members, others of at least
comparable caliber and stature have always appeared to take
the vacant places. Thus in the 1890's, the loss of Annie
Besant, generally admitted to have been the most brilliant
speaker of her generation, was more than compensated by
the arrival of Beatrice Potter, who became Mrs. Sidney
Webb on July 23, 1892. She was to prove one of the most
distinguished among the Fabians, both as writer, thinker, and
organizer.

One day, when G.B.S. was in the editorial office of the
Star chatting with H. W. Massingham, he looked instinctively
down to the signature on the proof of an article entitled
"How I Became a Theosophist" and saw it was Annie
Besant's. "I was staggered by this unprepared blow," he
wrote, "which meant to me the loss of a powerful colleague
and of a friendship which had become part of my daily
life." Also he felt a trifle guilty, for it was he who had suggested that Annie Besant should review H. P. Blavatsky's
book, the reading of which had converted the reviewer.

I instantly rushed around to her near-by office at Fleet
Street, and there delivered myself of an unbounded de-
nunciation of theosophy in general, of female inconsistency, and in particular of H. P. Blavatsky. This time I
met my match. She listened to me with complete kindness
and genuine amusement and then said she had become a
vegetarian (as I was) and that perhaps it had enfeebled her
mind. In short, she was for the first time able to play with
me; she was no longer in the grip of her pride; she had,
after many explorations, found her path, and had come to
see the universe and herself in their real perspective.

G.B.S., though he continued to feel as he always had done about theosophy, always also recognized the reality of religion, the thing which binds, and wherever he met it, reverenced it. He was probably the only Fabian who mourned Annie Besant. "Annie Besant left the Fabian Society because she became a Theosophist and regarded poverty and misfortune as punishment for sin in a former incarnation," commented a less kindly spectator, E. R. Pease.

Beatrice Potter was already a well-known figure before she married Sidney Webb at the age of thirty-four (he was thirty-three). Born in 1858, the ninth child and eighth daughter (her only brother died in infancy) of Richard Potter, a wealthy businessman, and his beautiful wife, Beatrice grew up a voracious reader, admirably tutored and guided by a father who treated all his daughters in a remarkably un-Victorian way, as friends and equals—rare in England, where the birth of a daughter is generally rewarded by the wish, expressed by parents, relatives, and friends alike, for better luck next time. John Stuart Mill was a frequent visitor at the Potters' home and Beatrice's mother had even, discreetly, suggested matrimony to him as a cure for rationalism. "I am perfectly willing to try your remedy," he wrote Mrs. Potter. "Indeed, marriage has been prescribed as a means of setting my brain right in another sense." But, alas, it wasn't so simple, for Mill was hardly an extrovert. He describes himself as, on one occasion, going upstairs to his hotel room during a fair and finding "my bedroom to my dismay full of men smoking and drinking. Had I been prone to study human nature in the concrete as well as in the abstract, I might have utilised the occasion. But a retreat and a protest . . . came much more naturally." Mill thought the Potters the most admirable pair he had ever seen. But among her parents' visitors it was not Mill but Herbert Spencer who spent most time with young Beatrice, and became her "respected and rejected mentor," in Margaret Cole's phrase. "How we teased Mr. Spencer into kissing B. under a bit of mistletoe and put a fool's cap out of a cracker on his philosophical head!" So Lord Courtenay, who married Beatrice's elder sister, Katherine, wrote nostalgically of Christmas 1881 at Standish, one of the many country houses rented in turn by the Potters.

Herbert Spencer had invented the phrase "the survival of the fittest." His synthetic philosophy was naturalistic and materialistic rather than positivistic. He agreed with Kant in regarding knowledge as limited to phenomena appearing in space and time, and he regarded God as "a power outside ourselves which makes for righteousness." He followed Schelling in believing that organic life shows a tendency toward increasing differentiation, organization, and individualization. Counterbalancing this process, there is another tendency towards integration, expressed in human life by the progressive integration of individuals within more comprehensive and more organically related associations.

"Like Comte . . . Spencer proposes three stages of social development. In the first stage, societies are still small . . . each individual or family doing everything for itself." The second is "militaristic." In the third stage "there is an increased differentiation of labor, an emphasis upon commerce and production, a lessening of centralized governmental control, and a gradual weakening of the old authoritarian social forms." [1] Socialism was for Spencer a by-product of the militaristic second stage, and one that could lead only to a society like that of the ants or bees, where regimentation would be complete. "He predicted, prophetically, that in a socialized society, the bureaucracy would give rise to a new form of aristocracy, more powerful than any that had gone before, for whose support the masses would be obliged to labor unceasingly and without effective recourse." [2]

As Beatrice Webb grew older, and discovered her vocation as a social researcher, she became gradually converted from her mentor's rugged individualism to the collectivism that was its direct opposite. "At last I am a Socialist," she wrote on February 14, 1890. The process had taken years. G.B.S. wrote that when he first knew her Beatrice had an intense contempt for the Fabian Society as a rabble of silly suburban faddists. Beatrice Potter's Socialist education had begun, when, under an assumed name, she went to stay with humble relatives in the north of England—working-class folk, linked to her by her beloved nanny, a poor relation. The result of her incognito visit was the first of many publications on the conditions of the working classes, and Beatrice's articles soon appeared in the great monthlies such as the *Nineteenth Century* and she became something of a celebrity in this hitherto little-worked field.

Beatrice, pretty as a girl, grew into a very beautiful woman. Desmond MacCarthy has described her "pale, emphatic face, her dark hair, aquiline features, fine eyebrows and bright brown eyes like a benevolent hawk." Even her bitterest enemies granted Beatrice's striking, rather Jewish, good looks. With these, and with one thousand pounds annually of her own—a much larger sum then than now—Beatrice had many suitors, in spite of her formidable brains.

[1] Aiken, p. 167.
[2] *Ibid.*, p. 168.

The one she most favored was Joseph Chamberlain, and she nearly became his third wife. (His second had died in 1875 when he was only thirty-nine.) In her diaries she tells how the "great man" came to stay at Standish in January 1884. On January 12 she notes, "another small episode in my life over." The great man's son and daughter were among the houseful of young people staying on after a ball party. Richard Potter retired to play patience with an absent and distressed look, utterly disgusted at the supposed intentions of his guest. The opposition between Beatrice's views and those of her suitor broke out over a discussion of state education. "It is a question of authority with women: if you believe in Herbert Spencer, you won't believe in me," said Chamberlain. Herbert Spencer had said to Beatrice of her distinguished beau, "A man who may mean well, but who does, and will do, an incalculable amount of mischief." Chamberlain returned the compliment in kind: "Happily, for the majority of the world, Spencer's writing is unintelligible, otherwise his life would have been spent in doing harm." Beatrice remained modestly silent. Chamberlain, noticing this, remarked that he required "intelligent sympathy" from women. "Servility, Mr. Chamberlain, think I, not sympathy but intelligent servility."

During the garden walk with her that followed, Chamberlain's expression became every moment more gloomy and determined. "My aim in life is to make life pleasanter for the great majority. I do not care if it becomes in the process less pleasant for the well-to-do minority," he told Beatrice, but he did not show a "suspicion of feeling" toward her. "I felt his curious scrutinising eyes noting each movement as if he were anxious to ascertain whether I yielded to his absolute supremacy." Beatrice ventured to say, "You don't allow division of opinion in your household, Mr. Chamberlain?" "I can't help people thinking differently from me." "But you don't allow the expression of the difference?" "No." "And that little word ended our intercourse." [3]

Family legend has it that he actually proposed later. My great-uncle, Daniel Meinertzhagen, married to Beatrice's sister, Georgina, crossing from his house in Rutland Gate to that of his father-in-law, Richard Potter, almost collided with Joseph Chamberlain rushing down the steps, looking miserable. Daniel went on upstairs to the drawing room, where he found Beatrice alone. "Bee, whatever have you done to make Joe Chamberlain look so wretched?" he asked. "Refused him," Beatrice said, and left the room, sob-

[3] Beatrice Webb, 1956, p. 315.

bing. She never mentioned Chamberlain without emotion, and years later wept when she told Bertrand Russell how she had refused Chamberlain out of principle. She could not, she said, marry a man with his opinions. But she never ceased to care for him.

The following year—1885—Beatrice accepted the offer of her cousin, Charles Booth, to help him on his monumental eighteen-volume survey, *The Life and Labour of the People of London*.

It certainly proved, as William Clarke wrote, that when Shelley had said Hell was like London he was being unfair to Hell—for in London half the population earned less than the twenty-five shillings a week then necessary for a family of five to earn in order to exist even marginally. Beatrice Potter's investigations into the industries of East London had convinced her that capitalist enterprise had to be controlled "not exceptionally nor spasmodically but universally, so as to secure to every worker prescribed minimum conditions of employment." [4] Gathering the material for her first epoch-making little book on the co-operative movement had taught Beatrice that even the co-operative movement needed some control. But it is quite possible that her lifelong underestimation of, and marked distaste for, trade-union personalities and politics stemmed from her background and upbringing. As she herself admitted:

> Brought up as I had been in a stronghold of capitalism, under the tutelage of the great apostle of *laissez-faire*, Herbert Spencer, I was fully aware of the various objections to trade unionism: how it prevented, or at least hindered, the introduction of new inventions and the better organisation of the workshop; how it had fomented strikes and compelled employers to resort to lockouts; how it had restricted output, either by rule or indirectly by limiting the number of apprentices; and how it had thus checked the mobility of Labour from place to place and industry to industry and damaged Great Britain's capacity to compete in the markets of the world. [5]

Beatrice quite deliberately sampled the Fabians as possible husbands, G.B.S. declared, by inviting them down to her bedridden father's house in Gloucestershire for week ends one after another. Shaw resolutely refused to come, pleading he hadn't got the fare. But the real reason, he declared, was because he had discovered that Sidney was in love with her, and

[4] Beatrice Webb, 1948, p. 19.
[5] *Ibid.*

he would not take a chance of cutting him out.[6] G.B.S. had learned of Sidney's infatuation because he always came out in spots when he fell in love. It had happened once before, with a girl who preferred to marry a politician called Corrie Grant. Their daughter became a Fabian, and Sidney was always particularly nice to her for her mother's sake.

It was at the Glasgow Co-operative Congress in 1891 that, as Beatrice put it, "with glory (at sunset) in the sky and hideous bestiality on the earth," wandering through the mean Glasgow streets "two socialists came to a working compact." "One and one placed close together, in a sufficiently integrated relationship, make not two but eleven," Sidney told Beatrice, who admitted, "we are both second-class minds, but we are curiously combined. I am the investigator, and he the executant." G.B.S., who loved them devotedly, and spent a great deal of the next five years, until his own marriage, staying with them, said, "Beatrice was, perhaps, the sparkplug, but Sidney was the engine."

Alys Pearsall Smith, an admirer of Beatrice's, found her and Sidney together one day at the National Gallery, and sensed romance was in the air for she knew they could not possibly be looking at pictures since such aestheticism was impossible in either of them.[7] But Beatrice did not dare break the news to her dying father of her engagement to the "Fabian leader" as her sisters called him, and even waited for six months after his death before marrying. Her sisters began by despising their low-class brother-in-law, nicknaming him "the gnome." One nephew even declared Sidney to be a Cockney seditionist. But they all became devoted to him, and he eclipsed them all in distinction.

The Webbs' marriage was one of the most successful and fruitful in history, although they had no children. They often spoke longingly of a "Sunday baby"—a baby they would play with on Sundays—but it never arrived. The stone on the floor of Westminster Abbey which covers them both also commemorates their perfect partnership of more than fifty years in complete harmony, a partnership which laid the foundation of many of the great social changes of the twentieth century, and also produced an enormous number of invaluable books. The Webbs associated their personalities so closely that when one of them spoke, it was always in the royal, or editorial, plural: "We think." Yet no wife has ever so objec-

---

[6] Lord Haldane used to accompany Sidney to Beatrice's home, as a decoy, to prevent her father and sisters guessing it was Sidney she favored.

[7] Note supplied by Mr. Robert Parker.

tively analyzed her beloved husband as Beatrice did in the opening pages of her *Our Partnership*.

G. D. H. Cole,[8] who had some spectacular fights with the Webbs, thus comments on them:

> In some respects, Beatrice Webb was less amiable than Sidney. Coming out of the top layer of capitalist business, she had a considerable amount of inborn arrogance, and was apt to be disconcertingly rude to those whom she dismissed as stupid. Sidney had no arrogance at all, and could bear with fools more easily. Beatrice in practice schooled herself to bear with them, subject to occasional lapses, but the strain was often visible.

"Her work," E. M. Forster[9] wrote, "was the investigation of society . . . a full and interesting life, based economically upon capitalism politically on liberalism and philosophically upon individualism."

Bertrand Russell once asked Beatrice whether she had ever felt shy, and she replied, "Oh, no. If I ever felt inclined to be scared going into a room full of people I would say to myself, 'You're the cleverest member of one of the cleverest families in the cleverest class of the cleverest nation in the world, so what have you got to be frightened of?' "

H. G. Wells, whose fight with the Webbs nearly split the Fabians—and would have done so but for G.B.S.—began by admiring both the Webbs, of whom he wrote: "I found them very good, if antagonistic, stuff. She fights with unscrupulous candour and invincible good temper. . . . Sidney is not nearly so exploratory, his convictions are less vigored and plastic, his aim is rather persuasion than truth, he is politic rather than philosophical." [10] But Wells concedes to both "the pervading sense of the importance of social service as the frame of life." And for E. M. Forster, when he met them, the firm of Webb and Webb was "augustness radiating." But even their best friends did not think of them as democrats. Mary Agnes Hamilton,[11] who wrote their biography during their lifetime, says of them: "Neither of them was by temper, instinct or training, democratic: Sidney was a born bureaucrat, Beatrice a born aristocrat." And how they both came to be hated, too!

> Among the acolytes of the Fabian order there is constant controversy as to which of the two [Webbs] is before or after the other. . . . Between them, they have an un-

[8] 1956, p. 211.
[9] p. 218.
[10] Wells, 1934, II, pp. 600-01.
[11] 1944, p. 260.

canny power of persuasion. Their knowledge overwhelms you, their sweet reasonableness disarms you. You are led captive in the chains of their silken logic. . . . It is this sleuthlike pursuit of their purpose that makes them so powerful and so often distrusted. They sit behind the scenes touching buttons, pulling wires, making the figures on the stage dance to their rhythms. To their modest table come the great and the powerful to learn their lessons, and to be coached up in their facts. Some fear to enter that parlour of incantations, and watch the Webbs with unsleeping hostility. . . . "To dish the Webbs" became the aim not only of certain Liberals or Conservatives, but later also of many members of the Labour Party.[12]

The Webbs inspired many cartoons—one of the most famous being Max Beerbohm's one of Sidney manipulating a cabinet of toy soldiers. Another was of Sidney walking casually in front of the path of an express train; this was captioned "the inevitability of gradualness." The Webbs also moved their enemies to verse; one of the most piquant, for example, the couplet:

> The world is so full of a number of plebs
> I am sure we should all be as happy as Webbs

was quoted to me by Aldous Huxley. The following poem, published in the *Spectator* on March 18, 1953, and written by Sir William James, is remarkable for its departure from what is generally regarded by the British as the eleventh commandment, *de mortuis nil nisi bonum*. It is simply entitled: "The Webbs."

> How beautiful it was to see
> Those two soul mates cohabit
> For no such mundane purposes
> As activate a rabbit
> But for the nobler, purer aim
> Of hatching out statistics
> The life blood of enchanting tomes
> On humble-life logistics
> How wise it was of Mrs. Webb
> To mate with little Sidney
> A man of slightly lower class
> But one of her own kidney
> What fun that happy couple had
> As with a gentle laugh
> They added and subtracted
> Then drew another graph.

[12] Gardiner, pp. 204-05.

Shaw[13] described their way of working, how

Beatrice every now and then when she felt she needed a refresher (Sidney was tireless) would rise from her chair, throw away her pen and hurl herself on her husband in a shower of caresses which lasted until the passion for work resumed its sway; then they wrote and read authorities for their footnotes until it was time for another refresher. Meanwhile I placidly wrote plays, but was confirmed in my peculiar doctrine that a point will be reached in human mental development when the pleasure taken in brain work by St. Thomas Aquinas and the Webbs (and saints and philosophers generally) will intensify to a chronic ecstasy surpassing that now induced momentarily by the sexual orgasm and produce a normal enjoyment of life . . . the census most needed at present is of the few people who would not prefer unlimited champagne and expensive cigars, ropes of pearls or a box at the opera . . . to the Webb-Aquinas routine.

Some other Fabians might have been included in that census, notably Alys and Bertrand Russell, with whom the Webbs often stayed for two or three months at a time. "The Russells are the most attractive married couple I know," Beatrice wrote in her diary for July 1, 1901.[14]

Young and virtuous, they combine in the pair personal charm, unique intelligence, the woman having the one, the man the other, in the superlative degree. Romantically attached to each other, they have diverse interests; Alys concerns herself with social reform, Bertrand with the higher mathematics. . . . The routine of their daily existence is as carefully planned and executed as our own. They breakfast together in their study at nine o'clock (we breakfast at 8!). Bertrand works at mathematics until 12:30, then three-quarters-of-an-hour reading together, a quarter-of-an-hour strolling in the garden together. Lunch with us, 1:30; chat in our sitting room or out of doors, over cigarettes and coffee. Then Bertrand plays croquet . . . until tea at 4:40. After that mathematics until 6, reading with Alys until 7:30, dine at 8 o'clock, chat and smoke with us until 9:30, another hour's reading aloud with Alys until 10:30. They sleep and dress in the same room, and they have no children. . . .

But, while the Russells soon divorced (and he married another three wives), the Webbs grew happier with every year. "I am

[13] "The Webbs and Social Evolution," New York *Times* magazine, Nov. 18, 1945.
[14] Beatrice Webb, 1948, p. 215.

so happy I am sometimes frightened," Sidney declared later
in life, and Beatrice after twenty years of marriage wrote of
Sidney: "He is the most perfect of lovers, by night and by
day, in work and in play, in health and in sickness!" Still
later, in 1926, after more than thirty years together, Beatrice
finished a sketch of Sidney, briefly absent, with these words:
"the days of his absence are weary to get through; and the
sleepless hours of the night are haunted, not by the fear of
death, but the dread of life without him."

Little wonder that the younger Fabians often complained
that the chief fact about the Webbs was that they were married. For example, Arnold Bennett, in his journal for January 28, 1913, wrote: "G.B.S. and H. Belloc discussed the
connection between private property and servitude at the
Queen's Hall. Crammed at concert prices, not a seat unsold.
Shaw very pale with white hair, his wife beside him. Effect
too conjugal for a man at work. Sidney and Beatrice Webb
next to them. Effect also too conjugal here." And Charles
Sorley, a young Scottish poet soon to be killed at the front,
wrote in the same year: "Sidney Webb, besides being Fabian
is beyond all other things a Husband. At the Fabian Summer
School, the same sweet conjugality hovers around. The
Webbs live in a perfect halo of mutual admiration and put
their trust in figures." [15]

The volumes of Beatrice's journal, *My Apprenticeship,*
published in 1926, followed by *Our Partnership,* published
posthumously in 1948, and the subsequent posthumous two
volumes, all became best-sellers, and have entirely altered
most people's view of the Webbs. Hitherto, the best known
description of them had been H. G. Wells's in *The New
Machiavelli.*[16]

   The Baileys [Webbs] were specialized, concentrated,
accurate. . . . The Baileys loved a world as flat and metallic as Sidney Cooper's cows. Altiora [Beatrice] thought
trees hopelessly irregular and sea cliffs a great mistake
. . . her soul was bony, and at the base of her was a
vanity gaunt and greedy . . . her marriage . . . was a
stroke of genius, and forthwith they proceeded to make
themselves the most formidable and distinguished couple
conceivable. P.B.P., she boasted, was engraved inside their
wedding rings, *Pro Bono Publico,* and she meant it to be
no idle threat . . . she saw men as samples moving . . .
two people . . . who've planned to be a power . . . and
by Jove, they've done it.

[15] Sorley, p. 113.
[16] pp. 193 ff.

But even H. G. Wells grants Altiora her looks:

> the tall, commanding figure, splendid but a little untidy
> in black silk and red beads, with dark eyes that had no
> depth, with a clear hard voice that had almost visible
> prominence. Aquiline features and straight black hair that
> was apt to get astray, that was now astray like the head
> feathers of an eagle in a gale.[17]

How different is the woman the diaries reveal: puzzled,
perplexed, constantly searching, asking, arguing, hankering
after a Church "with its communion of the faithful, with its
religious rites and its religious discipline, and above all with
its definite code of conduct . . . somehow or other we must
have the habit of prayer, the opportunity for the confession
of sin and for the worship of goodness if we are to attain personal holiness." She is continually aware of the "good that I
would I do not" and chides herself for an evening dress
bought, indulgence in drinking one glass of wine or smoking
an extra cigarette;

> like so many other poor souls I have the consciousness
> of being a spiritual outcast . . . I have failed to solve
> the problem of life . . . of man's relation to the universe,
> and, therefore, to his fellow men. But I have a growing
> faith that it will be solved by a combination of truth-
> seeking and personal holiness—of the scientific mind with
> the religious life.[18]

The Webbs spent their honeymoon investigating Dublin
trade societies and attending the Trades Union Congress at
Glasgow; they had two days off; one was spent with Auberon
Herbert, a dreamy widower who had wanted to marry Beatrice, and who with vague blue eyes, a soft high voice, flow-
ing white beard, gave them his final blessing: "You will do a
lot of mischief, and be very happy doing it." (He later got
into a row with G.B.S. in the columns of the magazine *Free
Life:* "You have not the slightest warrant for assuming that
I worship physical force a bit more than you do," complained
G.B.S. "As a matter of fact, my objection to what you call a
free life is that it offers no solution whatever to economic
problems, which, if left unsolved, would produce not a free
life but a free fight, ending in the enslavement of the vanquished.") The Webbs spent their second free day with
R. B. Haldane, who had helped them to their romance and
who became Sidney's second closest friend, G.B.S. remaining
always his first. Then they settled down at 41 Grosvenor

---

[17] *Ibid.*, p. 199.
[18] Beatrice Webb, 1948, p. viii.

Road, a ten-room house renting for 110 pounds for a year, which they leased for nearly forty years, and were served by two maids. During their joint lifetime they only had five separate servants, one of whom remained with them over thirty years. "A hard little house," H. G. Wells had called 41 Grosvenor Road.

> Almost pretentiously matter-of-fact and unassuming . . . the room was one of those long apartments once divided by folding doors, and reaching from back to front . . . its walls were hung with two or three indifferent water colours, there was scarcely any furniture but a sofa or so and a chair, and the floor, severely carpeted with matting, was crowded with a curious medley of people, men predominating.[19]

Wells goes on to describe the guests, the evening, the feeling that here play was at the top table, "one always seemed to be getting one's hands on the very strings that guided the world." But he resented it all and described the relief of getting out from this administrative fizzle, this pseudo-scientific administrative chatter into the "limitless grimy chaos of London streets and squares," where "wanton crimes and accidents bawled at you from the placards . . . you saw shy youths conversing with prostitutes."

Beatrice gives much the same picture of the drawing room, with the "three easy-chairs but no sofa; all designed to accommodate the largest number of guests standing or sitting." But this "harsh exterior" as she calls it,

> was redeemed by the unique interest and beauty of the outlook. To spring out of bed on a summer morning and see spread out before you, the sun rising behind Lambeth Palace, on clear days, the Dome of St. Paul's and the spires of the City churches, its rays lighting up the tiny waves breaking the surface of the swift-flowing river, whilst oar-steered barges, some with red or yellow sails, drifting rafts of timber, and steaming colliers, was a joyful greeting to another day. Other scenes from the balcony of the sitting room I remember; on still autumn days the river, in ebbing tide, sulking among the mud banks and lapping the anchored river-craft; or, in full tide, losing itself in fog, yellow or black. . . .

And Beatrice confesses herself faced with always the

> same old problem, how much sacrifice of personal efficiency to personal influence? In England, all power to establish new undertakings rests on your influence over

[19] Wells, 1911, p. 190.

the various ruling cliques. The more cliques you are in
touch with, the easier it is to lay broad foundations. On
the other hand your power for good depends . . . on
the quality of your special product, and this last depends
on whole-hearted devotion to your subject.

Beatrice resolved her dilemma by a compromise: the time
spent in London, entertaining, she regarded as holidaying:
her work was achieved during the months she and Sidney
"holed up" in the country, either with the Bertrand Russells
or in some rented house. When in such a house in the country, the Webbs often had G.B.S., Wallas, and Bertrand Russell to stay with them, singly or together. They all worked,
argued, and bicycled endlessly (Beatrice stopped Sidney bicycling only after he had fainted and fallen off once; after that
she took him instead for long walks). Once, Bertrand Russell
nearly killed G.B.S.; Russell had stopped to look at a signpost,
and held his bicycle in Shaw's way: Shaw flew straight over
the handlebars into the road, a terrible crash. On another occasion, Mrs. J. G. Green, "the widder Green" [20] as she was
known, came for the night, and was so surprised by the after-
dinner arguments that she could not believe the Webbs and
G.B.S. could remain on speaking terms after. She was delighted to discover at breakfast "that it had made not the
smallest change in our personal relations and was part of the
daily routine." For G.B.S., though not "a complete apriorist"
started always from a simple fact that struck him as significant. Only one. "One is enough," he declared, while the
Webbs would not form any conclusion until "they had with
inexhaustible industry investigated all the available evidence"
and had collected voluminous data. But country life suited
them all. As G.B.S. wrote to Ellen Terry,

Four hours writing in the morning; four hours bicycling
in the afternoon every day . . . I have to spend a lot of
time mending punctures in female bicycle tyres . . . I
wonder what you would think of our life—our eternal
political shop, our mornings of dogged writing, all in our
separate rooms, our ravenous plain meals, our bicycling.

What energy sustained the Webbs and G.B.S. in this gruel-
ing life, that G.B.S. dubbed Trappist? Beatrice described
clearly what made her Sidney tick:

By religion, I mean the communion of the soul with
some righteousness *felt to be outside and above itself*.
This may take the conscious form of prayer, or the

[20] Widow of the historian.

unconscious form of ever-present and persisting aspirations—a faith, a hope and a devotion to a wholly disinterested purpose. It is this unconscious form of religion which lies at the base of all Sidney's activity. He does not pray, as I often do, because he has not acquired so self-conscious a habit. But there is a look in his eyes when he patiently plods on through his own and other people's work, when he unwittingly gives up what other people prize, or when he quietly ignores the spite or prejudice of opponents, that tells of a faith and a hope in the *eventual* meaning of human life—if not for us, then, for those who come after us. He refuses to put his aspiration into words, because he would fear the untruth that might be expressed in those words—he has a dread of being even remotely irrational or superstitious. But for all that, he believes.

Beatrice herself was more consciously a mystic:

If you are conscious of a great reality, this consciousness may be as valid as any other part of your consciousness? But this validity remains your own secret not communicable to those who are not already in possession of it. Possibly, by attempting to put it into words, you rouse in other minds the knowledge that they do possess the secret somewhere—in the recesses of their souls. . . .[21]

Beatrice gave her own recipe for

the best intellectual effort of which a given brain is capable, I suggest two habits of body are needful—abstinence in indulging appetites and the trick of complete relaxation of muscle and obliviousness of mind. With these two, you can get the greatest output of mental energy of which your particular brain is capable. And, with John Stuart Mill, I am inclined to think that the exercise of the intellect—perhaps suffused with love—is the highest happiness of which we poor mortals are capable.[22]

"What I fear," she admitted, "is weakness in my own nature: incapacity to keep my intellect and heart set on our own work undistracted by personal vanity or love of admiration."

Both Lord Haldane and his sister scoffed unkindly when, at dinner one evening, in a moment of intimacy Beatrice unwisely divulged the large part prayer occupied in her life. To whom do you pray, quizzed Haldane, and what form does your prayer take? Bertrand Russell called her, "full of superstition" and said she preferred the Church of England to any

21 Beatrice Webb, 1948, p. 258.
22 *Ibid.*, p. 344.

other because it was a state church. She walked along the embankment from her house almost daily to St. Paul's for evensong and there knelt, listening to the music of the psalms and repeating, with childlike fervor, the words of the old Elizabethan prayers. She had felt the pull of the Catholic Church strongly as a girl, and in 1900 found refreshment in theological reading,

Specially interested in the Catholic religion as mental hygiene and discipline of the emotions, an authoritative guidance to the motives of conduct. . . . The Catholic discipline has a traditional—and no doubt empirical—wisdom in the training of character and the direction of the emotions. I have no special sympathy with the ascetic saint, yet the world could do with a good deal more physical self-control, humility and disinterested love. All this experience was, it seems to me, thrown clean away with the Protestant Reformation. Perhaps other qualities were gained: but it is easier for me to see the loss than the gain.[23]

She felt, personally, that

Sidney and I can hardly repay by our work the happiness and joy of our life . . . we are responsible for the single-hearted devotion of our talent, whether of capacity, means or position, to the work one believes in . . . with me it is always a struggle to keep my mind from wandering off into foolish romancings. It is in this self-discipline that I find the need and the truth of prayer.

But, although she rose daily at 6:30, and spent an hour in prayer, this was never addressed to Jesus Christ, who, she wrote,

seems to me only one, and, perhaps, not the most perfect embodiment of the ideal of faith. It is, in fact, more difficult for me to accept the *Person* than the *Institution*—the person is limited by circumstances, temperament and capacity for expression, and even by the day in which he lived—the institution is indefinite in its power of experience, of expression, comprehension and growth.

And elsewhere she wrote: "The character of Jesus of Nazareth has never appealed to me." [24]
The growth Beatrice found in the mystical body, the Church, G.B.S. found in God Himself, Whom he saw as the

[23] *Ibid.*, p. 170.
[24] Beatrice Webb, 1952, p. 148.

Life Force, life everlastingly evolving. St. John Ervine[25] described G.B.S. as a preacher not less determined than Savonarola to call sinners to repentance, who gave to all his plays a highly charged religious significance. In *Major Barbara* the heroine says: "Let God's work be done for its own sake: the work he had to create us, to do because it cannot be done except by living men and women." G.B.S. saw the true joy of life as "the being used for a purpose recognised by yourself as a mighty one, the being thoroughly worn out before you are thrown on the scrap heap, the being a force of Nature instead of a feverish, selfish little clod of ailments complaining that the world has not devoted itself to making you happy." And he declared, "Conscience is the most powerful of all instincts, and the love of God the most powerful of all passions." [26] In 1910 he wrote Tolstoi that his theology and his explanation of the existence of evil were roughly expressed by Blanco Posnet, who declares, "there's no good and bad, but by Jiminy, gents, there's a rotten game, and there's a great game. I played the rotten game; but the great game was played on me; and now I'm for the great game every time."

As Walter Eaton wrote of G.B.S. in the New York *Times*: Shaw was one of the most religious of men. Like Beatrice Webb, he used contemplative prayer and for the same purpose as she did, "to produce the feeling usually produced by the teapot, the bottle and the hypodermic syringe." Living, as Shaw explained,

by the sweat of my brain in a world unable to live by bread alone . . . that lives spiritually on alcohol and morphia. I go to church. If you should chance to see in a country churchyard a bicycle leaning against a tombstone, you are not unlikely to find me inside the church if it is old enough or new enough to fit its purpose. There I find rest without languor and recreation without excitement . . . any place where men dwell, village or city, is a reflection of the consciousness of every single man. In my city there is a market garden, a workshop, a lovers' walk, and, above all, a cathedral . . . showing me where, within the cathedral, I may find my way to the cathedral within me . . . at all events, the godhead in me, certified by the 10th. chapter of St. John, refuses to enter barren places.

Elsewhere, after visiting Italy, he wrote, "Let a man go and renew himself for half an hour occasionally in San Zeno (the cathedral of Verona) and he need eat not corpses, nor drink

[25] p. 250.
[26] *The Christian Commonwealth,* July 20, 1910.

any drugs or drams to sustain him." As a child, G.B.S. had hated the Protestant churches to which he was forced to go, but twenty years later, and in foreign lands, he became, he said, once more a churchgoer.

Their truly religious lives of dedication were what made the great Fabians so effective, but it was their social life which sometimes caused the greatest surprise. It was not only the long underwear or the bicycling, or even the short hair and smoking, but the complete outspokenness that astonished their contemporaries. In the Edwardian age of elegance, Beatrice Webb, for example, suggested to Oscar Wilde at tea that colonic irrigation might help his flatulence, as it had helped Sidney so. Their friends reacted variously to this outspokenness. Bertrand Russell describes how during the first ten years of their marriage, Mrs. Webb would remark at intervals, "As Sidney always says, marriage is the wastepaper basket of the emotions." In later years, there was a slight change. They would generally have a couple to stay with them for the week end, and on Sunday afternoon they would go for a brisk walk, Sidney with the lady and Beatrice with the gentleman. At a certain point Sidney would remark, "I know just what Beatrice is saying at this moment. She is saying, 'As Sidney always says, marriage is the wastepaper basket of the emotions.'" Desmond MacCarthy, who related the same incident, was not amused, as Bertrand Russell had been. And Lowes Dickinson, to whom the remark also was made, said it determined him never to become a Fabian.

There were whole categories of people whom the Webbs dismissed as what André Maurois called *chronophages*—time wasters. Beatrice divided her friends into (a) aristocratic, anarchistic, and artistic and (b) bourgeois, bureaucratic, and benevolent. To her diary, Beatrice purred, "March 22, a brilliant little luncheon, typical of the 'Webb' set. Dr. Nansen, Gerald and Lady Betty Balfour, the Bernard Shaws, Bertrand Russells, Masterman and Lady Desborough, typical in its mixture of opinions, classes, interests—all as jolly as jolly could be—a rapid rush of talk." [27] The Webbs used every occasion to further their schemes. For example, when they went one Good Friday to hear *Parsifal* at Covent Garden, they met Lloyd George and Herbert Samuel during the long intermission. Asked next day how he had enjoyed the opera, Sidney said, "We had a most enjoyable time. Our discussion with Samuel was enlightening on the striking incidence of sickness in pregnancy."

Beatrice had begun by being suspicious of G.B.S., calling

[27] Beatrice Webb, 1948, p. 375.

him a "sprite" because he would not fit into any of her categories and Sidney insisted Shaw was so completely a sprite no one could ever know which way he would jump. But they quickly grew fond of each other, and Shaw's letters to her are as intimate and affectionate as his to Sidney. On July 20, 1894, G.B.S. writes to Beatrice from Bayreuth and tells her how much he misses the Fabians. "I will include your satellite Wallas, and your sun Webb, I being a mere comet." [28] After G.B.S.'s marriage, the Shaws always dined with the Webbs on Thursdays. In 1903 Beatrice writes: "For the first time for many years the three old friends!—Sidney, Bernard Shaw and Graham Wallas—spent a week together with their wives as chorus." But if the visits were less frequent, the intimacy was undiminished: Charlotte Shaw provided the Webbs with the money to run their Minority Report campaign efficiently, and the Shaws often lent the Webbs their country house, or Webbs and Shaws would stay together at some hotel. Once, when Beatrice had taken a house near him, R. B. Haldane brought over a bevy of "Souls," to the Webbs, as he prided himself on hovering "between the fashionable paradise presented by the 'Souls' and the collectivist state represented by the Fabians." Beatrice comments that their "Souls" were "good to look at; pushing and anxious to strike up acquaintanceship . . . to me the 'Souls' would not bring the 'peace which passeth understanding' but a vain restlessness of tickled vanity. One would quickly become satiated." [29]

Haldane[30] explains who the "Souls" were: "There was a group of well-known people nicknamed the 'Souls.' They sometimes took themselves much too seriously and on the whole it is doubtful whether their influence was on balance good." But he and many others liked the Souls' society for its brilliance. Among the women Souls were Margot Tennant (afterwards Lady Asquith), whom Beatrice detested, and Lady Elcho, who brought Mrs. Pat Campbell, the actress, to see Sidney, who couldn't abide her, and thought G.B.S.'s infatuation for her was "a clear case of sexual senility."

In London, Beatrice continued to invite everyone who was anyone, and they all came: Conservative Prime Ministers, Liberal Prime Ministers, Foreign Secretaries, Archbishops of Canterbury, Chancellors of the Exchequer, dons, peers, and trade-union leaders. They certainly roughed it at 41 Grosvenor Road, in the days when a dozen-course dinner was bogey. Beatrice served only a clear soup, fish, a roast, and a pudding. No wine—only whisky and beer. (Good Scotch then

28 Quoted in Henderson, p. 363.
29 Beatrice Webb, 1948, p. 33.
30 pp. 120-21.

was 4 shillings—under $1.00—a bottle, and a maid cost $2.00 a month.) She longed to do without napkins, but decided, regretfully, that would be asking too much of her guests. Then, too, after dinner, no one (except Kingsley Martin, once), ever dared use the lavatory: Harold Laski and J. Ramsay MacDonald used a timber yard on their way home —others just suffered. "Yet my little parties are said to be successful," Beatrice notes in 1892, "but they don't please me. Directly you entertain for entertaining's sake, then they become hollow and unpleasant."

No time was wasted at a Webb dinner. Sir Robert Ensor has made notes of some evenings he spent at the Webbs. For example, on January 8, 1904, Ensor and Sidney began by discussing the development of a scheme of local government, whose principles Sidney said would be a great remodeling of areas and powers, and a staff of paid, elected persons, not departmental experts, but experts in local government.

These should stand above the bureaucracy of skilled paid specialists, but should receive enough pay to take their work as a profession. Their profession would be to represent the electors. Although themselves elected, they would be in the business for life. If the views of one such caused his rejection at one place, he would at once be in the market as an expert holding those views at the disposal of constituencies approving them. I pointed out that a caucus of professional politicians would thus be formed over the country. Webb was not impressed by the danger. His main idea seemed to be to enable the elector to control the bureaucracy. This he does at the present time through unpaid elected persons, who being unpaid are inefficient— i.e., bad tools for the elector's need. He was very emphatic as to the unwisdom of combining your paid elected person and your paid bureaucratic head in a single man. Such a combination inevitably produces a tyrant: the function of the people simply goes by default. Mrs. Webb shared the last view strongly: quoted the disaster of the paid LCC chairman. I asked if it would have been so, if besides the paid chairman there had been a whole college of paid heads with seats on the council: then, surely, they would not all have been so abashed into nonentity? Mrs. Webb illustrated the case from the new London Education Committee, which has kept Webb out of the chair "from a healthy instinct." Another evening, they discussed the Labour Party. Beatrice thought it would never come to anything. No working man is any good at committee-work. To be good you must always be 6 months ahead with your subject, and at a committee must have your resolu-

tions drafted the instant they are needed. No workmen
have intellectual initiative enough for the former, nor
facility for the latter. For the same reason they could
never triumph over permanent officials—she thought this
would render Burns impotent if he took office in a
Liberal Government. Nor did she believe in a Labour
Party with some middle class leaders to fill up these
lacunae. She quotes with approval a remark by an ILP-er
re such, "No, they always want to come in at the top and
expect to stay there. We don't want them." [31]

The Webb view expressed that evening was also prophetic.
For one of the reasons for the twentieth-century dictator-
ships, whether of Hitler or of Stalin, was the inability of the
democracy to remove, or, indeed, to contact, the bureaucracy: appointed, it is immovable and, naturally, is on the side
of the powers that appointed it and keep it in being. Simi-
larly, one of the main causes for Labor failure to rule in the
twenties was the fact that Labor Cabinet ministers were at the
mercy of their permanent officials, who despised them. But
the Webbs, who so early saw the problem, also provided the
remedy, which obviously would be to train up members of
the working classes or of the radical intelligentsia to become
permanent officials, so that, eventually, England would have a
Socialist civil service.

[31] Notes sent me by Sir Robert Ensor.

CHAPTER TEN

FORGING THE TOOLS— that is, training the personnel who, through their knowledge of the new disciplines of the social sciences, could achieve the reforms all parties wished, was perhaps the greatest of all Fabian achievements, and it was a Webb brainstorm that produced the plant wherein were forged these tools.

In 1894 Henry Hutchinson, who had provided the funds for the successful "Lancashire campaign," died and left nearly 10,000 pounds to five Fabian trustees, appointing Sidney Webb chairman and administrator with the instruction that "all the money be spent in ten years." The old man, whom Sidney had never seen, had alternately sent to the Society considerable checks and querulous letters about Shaw's rudeness, then blew his brains out, leaving his wife and children badly off. But, though Sidney tried to break the will so these could benefit, they refused to take a penny and joined the Fabians themselves. The unmarried Hutchinson daughter made a will leaving her tiny portion also to the Fabians, and then within a few months herself died. Now the question was, what to do with the money? The Fabian Society might just spend it on better and bigger propaganda. Or the whole Fabian Executive might stand for Parliament. Or ILP candidates might be subsidized. But none of these seemed sufficiently dramatic or even immediately necessary. What *was* needed, the Webbs knew, was hard thinking—not the sending of "nondescript socialists" to Parliament. Sidney's inspiration was to found "slowly and quietly a London School of Economics and Political Science. . . . Above all, we want the ordinary citizen to feel that reforming society is no light matter, and must be undertaken by experts specially trained for the purpose." Graham Wallas, G.B.S., and the Webbs were staying together at a little farm, a couple of miles southwest of Godalming in Surrey, when at breakfast one morning in August 1894 the Webbs proposed to Wallas and Shaw that the deeded money should be used to found a school in London on the lines of the École Libre des Sciences Politiques in Paris.

The Webbs considered themselves at that time to be relatively unknown and without academic distinction. The total capital to hand was the few thousand pounds of the Hutchinson bequest. The first problem was to find a young economist sufficiently disinterested to devote himself wholeheartedly to the creation of the proposed institution in return for a small and possibly uncertain salary. And the young man must preferably *not* be a Fabian, for the school's purpose was to educate, not to indoctrinate. The Webbs, quite by chance, discovered their man, W. A. S. Hewins, working in the Bodleian Library at Oxford—whose librarian had just, Beatrice noted, repelled the Webbs with downright rudeness.

Hewins had already published a book on *English Trade and Finance Chiefly in the 17th Century*. His views were almost diametrically opposite to those of the Webbs; he was, spiritually, a medievalist, and he became a Catholic; politically, he was a lifelong advocate of a scientific tariff. But the Webbs and Hewins agreed in their dislike of the Manchester School, its unverified deductive reasoning and abstract generalization, its apotheosis of the "economic man" exclusively inspired by the motive of pecuniary self-interest, and its passionate stand for the rights of property against the needs of humanity. A threefold back was thus, indeed, mostly firmly turned on Herbert Spencer.

On March 29, 1895, Hewins was formally invited to undertake the organization of the proposed school, and accepted. For eight years he was responsible for the "sickly infant, of doubtful parentage, born into an indifferent if not hostile world,"[1] which throve lustily under his devoted care and by 1931 had 3,000 students.

Hewins and the Webbs met daily for years and never had a dispute. With the ludicrously small capital of 5,000 pounds the London School of Economics (LSE) set out to remedy the economic ignorance of five million Londoners. Founded in two rooms, LSE grew so steadily that Margaret Cole quipped, "On the building of the London School of Economics the concrete never sets."

"We desired," Hewins[2] wrote, "that the lectures and investigations held at the School should be representative of all branches of economics and political science, and no differentiation against persons was to be allowed on the grounds of sex, religion, or economic or political views. Full provision was to be made for training for business administration, and

[1] Beatrice Webb, 1948, p. 88.
[2] pp. 24-28.

for the central or local governments; for library work; for the higher forms of research."

The London School of Economics has never had any organic connection with the Fabian Society, although its founder, Sidney Webb, was instrumental in the reorganization of London University, and also in adding LSE to London University as an organic part. Lord Beveridge, who became head of LSE, describes how Webb felt scruples about using Hutchinson's money for a purpose not clearly Fabian. So he consulted R. B. Haldane. Haldane asked Webb whether he remained a convinced Socialist. "Yes," replied Webb. "Do you then believe," asked Haldane, "that the more social conditions are studied scientifically and impartially, the stronger does the case for Socialism become?" "Yes," replied Webb. "Very well, if you believe that, you are entitled to use the bequest for the starting of a school for scientific, impartial study and teaching." Beginning with no endowment at all, the school has become one of the most heavily endowed of modern academic institutions in Britain. Lord Beveridge has declared, "The School of Economics was the Webbs embodied in an institution. In his dealings with it, Sidney's qualities of superhuman industry, breadth of view, ingenuity and absence of personal egotism were illustrated again and again." [3]

To many, W. A. S. Hewins, director of LSE, was "a remote and shadowy figure who counted for little in the life of the students. The dominant influence, amounting almost to a spiritual dictatorship, was that of these two great leaders of the middle-class revolt against itself, Mr. and Mrs. Sidney Webb." [4] Their portrait, painted of them by Sir William Nicholson in Passfield Corner, their country house, before their fire, at which Beatrice is warming her hands, for she certainly fulfilled the French description of the perfect hostess ("always a little hungry, a trifle cold, and easily bored"), is the most alive thing, still today, in LSE, that institutionalized concrete municipal-Doric box stuck cornerwise on to Aldwych, home of farces. But not even the Webbs commanded such blind devotion at LSE as G.B.S., "whose lightest utterances were quoted as a field preacher quotes the Bible, even when he came down to the school for the express purpose of denouncing reverence." [5]

Just before the opening of the second session of LSE, Hewins fell ill, and the Webbs had to take over. "Poor Sid-

[3] Margaret I. Cole (ed.), 1949, p. 48.

[4] Wingfield-Stratford, 1930, p. 185.

[5] *Ibid.*, p. 186.

ney trudges over there directly after breakfast and spends his mornings with painters, plumbers and locksmiths," Beatrice wrote, while she did the housekeeping for the new school and its students. At first the school was housed in St. John Street, then moved to 10 Adelphi Terrace.

LSE illustrated its founders' lack of concern for the aesthetic. To Desmond MacCarthy at dinner Sidney Webb had said, "We are interested in the drains, in stopping dry rot in the house; you in its decoration." A. J. Penty, an architect, first determined to oppose the Fabians when he discovered the way in which the judges chose the winning design in an architectural competition to build LSE's permanent home. They simply measured the floor space of all the designs submitted, and awarded the prize to the architect whose classrooms added up to the highest total of superficial square feet. This was called decision by the statistical method.

Sidney, Lord Beveridge notes, for many years did all the important things: chose the successive directors (the first two became Conservative Members of Parliament), got the Army class to the school in 1906 through his friendship with R. B. Haldane; got the present site of the school from the London County Council (for free), and got 260,000 pounds from Sir Ernest Cassell after World War I. Lord Beveridge concludes: "The School of Economics was the Webbs' favorite child, dearer even than Fabian Socialism." Yet, dearest, perhaps, because it was the matrix as well as the alma mater of so many great Fabians, of S. G. Hobson, of Lord Beveridge, not himself a Fabian, but whose Beveridge Plan is pure distilled Fabianism; of Harold Laski; of the Coles; of R. H. Tawney; of Kingsley Martin, and of so many others.

Among the by-products of Hutchinson's legacy were regular courses of Fabian educational lectures on social and political subjects; among the first lecturers appointed were James Ramsay MacDonald and a brilliant woman, Enid Stacy. At this time, Ramsay MacDonald was very much in love with Miss Stacy, and his letters to her give a vivid picture of the early days of the ILP and of the role played by members of the Fabian Society in ILP affairs. Enid Stacy wrote for the *Clarion*, a Socialist weekly, and toured the country in the *Clarion*'s van (which looked exactly like a gypsy caravan) giving Socialist lectures.

Early in their friendship MacDonald discusses the ILP in his letters to her[6] and comments at some length on its rela-

---

[6] I am most grateful to Mr. Gerald Widdrington for his kind permission to quote from James Ramsay MacDonald's unpublished letters to his mother, and for permission to quote G.B.S.'s letter to her *in toto*.

tionship to the Fabians. On July 9, 1894 he told Enid Stacy
that

> I have done my level best to get at the "metaphysic"
> (hem!) of the I.L.P. and after going carefully over the his-
> tory of its ideas, have come to the conclusion that, whatever
> the leaders may preach, the growth of the party was from a
> desire for Labour representation among Liberals. I admit,
> and state, that it is finding a distinctive position on other
> grounds, e.g. that it has attached itself to Socialism and is
> not the child of Socialism. Even yet, I am convinced, if a
> strong man with genuine insight arose in Parliament St.,
> the I.L.P. might be "squenched." Your instincts are right
> when you in an involuntary way insist more on "Independ-
> ent" than on "Labour." But perhaps this will inspire your
> pen of contention. My own opinion is that if you can
> only manage to take that hilly ground ahead of the Liberal
> Army nothing can save the defeat of the Liberals.

On July 14, 1894 he wrote to her again on the same subject:

> I cannot argue with you on the I.L.P. because you be-
> lieve in my position. The order of the infall of the many
> tributaries which make up the I.L.P. is more important than
> an enumeration of those tributaries, and you will find, it
> seems, that the socialist conversion was not primary—e.g.
> Keir Hardie in 1888 saying he was not a Socialist—but
> secondary, as a necessity imposed upon the new party to
> find a sufficiently ample basis for independent existence. Do
> you remember Matthew Arnold's observations in *"St. Paul
> and Protestantism"* on the growth of the creed of the non-
> conformist churches? Apply it to the I.L.P., and you will
> have peace and comfort and salvation and clearness of
> ideas. (Don't toss your head and mentally note another
> evidence of Fabian impudence.)
>
> Apropos my figures re. the Attercliffe polling, and which
> you do not quite accept (being a Fabian I am awfully cut
> up at my failure to carry conviction to every heart) you
> must not think that I dispute the contentions that Hardie
> and the others are so fond of making, that the benches of
> the I.L.P. assemblies are being overcrowded by Tories. In
> a mild way they are right. But we did not get these people
> in Sheffield. My estimates are formed from the impressions
> I had whilst the votes were being counted. It was quite
> plain then that we were polling well *only* in the two Liberal
> wards; and Hill Smith lost his support from the Park dis-
> trict. So take more heart than ever, my champion of la-
> bour! We start with 1249 votes, and we have not yet had
> time to do the usual trick. That means that ordinarily

speaking, some 800 to 1000 votes are waiting to hear us whistle—you, perhaps in October. You ought to have seen me on Wednesday night at the Club hastening the death of two or three Liberal members by harping on exactly those strings which you touch. Still, still, be patient with a cautious man. You are old in your admiration for the young political giant. You were blessed by being privileged to see its star, before many of us even saw it in flesh and blood, and you hailed it as king when many a mundane soul put their fingers in their ears to shut out its squeals. The dear little thing has outlived the feeding bottle. I have stuck pins in it and it has kicked me. Consequently I respect the cuss.—I am in Bradford in September, and they will probably serve Labour tories for breakfast, lunch, tea and dinner. My robustness ought to be assured. In my topics in this week's *Dispatch* you will find two croaks on Lord Tweedmouth's wisdom. . . . Has Nunquam described the great meeting in the *Clarion*?

In this same letter something of the social schizophrenia of the enigmatic MacDonald comes through.

Though I have dated this from London, I am writing in Canterbury. I am not at all well somehow and there is a friend of mine here who is always willing to take me in. I am alone in the house except for the servants—who are nothing. . . . But I have only come down today and tomorrow I am back amongst mine own people. It will be a kind of a holiday. These five days and the election struck a spring in me and I am moved to go away into the country. So I must home whatever happens. I have a house which I have taken for my mother in a place called Lossiemouth by the sea, and there, there is always a bed and bread and cheese for broken-down Labour 'osses. Last year I had some up with me. And if you were going that way, or cared to go up for a rest and complete change, the door is open. I shall be up there, probably from the middle of August to the middle of September. The country is very fine and very interesting. That is why I asked if you were going.

The towns on the South Coast that might be induced to have a paid speaker are Devonport, Plymouth, Southampton, Brighton, Folkestone and Dover. If your agent cannot manage to fix you up, he might let me know. It is very important that something should be done in the South. The North and Midlands are very selfish keeping all the good speakers for themselves. Why don't they have a whip-up for the poor maimed South?

In another letter he describes himself on a Fabian tour.

How chaste one feels in starting on a Fabian tour! How you screw up to sticking point your faith in humanity, hotels and the weakness of commercialism in argument; and how you go forth with an express train as your steed, a black bag as your equerry, a Fabian tract as your armour of offence and defence! Your moral nature is at its best. At no other time would Caroline D. Martyn bow down so readily and worship you unless it be if your first meeting is a dead failure. Then in order to live you summon more angels from heaven who come with advanced copies of the history of human evolution in the pages of which you read of the doom of John Burns and the *Daily Chronicle* and the divine calling of yourself and Fabian Questions for Poor Law Guardians. Oxford is noted for colleges and bag carriers. Night had fallen when I got there. I could not see the first and I pretended not to see the second. But alas in this freeborn country if a man stands in your way you cannot knock him down unless you are sure of your magistrate, and one human being cannot walk through another. I was the only traveller by the train who apparently had provided himself with a night shirt and a change of linen. At least if any of my fellow passengers were so provided they had put them in their pockets. So a crowd of ragamuffins surrounded me and a Dutch bargain immediately began. Said I: "Bag-carriers and fellow citizens, read the *Clarion* and the *Labour Leader*. Having given that general advice let me come to particulars. My bowels yearn with the thought of your degradation, but until the means of prod: dist: & exch: are nationalised—well gentlemen, I can but address meetings and split the Liberal vote. Fellow workers, I am a Labour candidate, and I am shocked at this unseemly wrangle. I was born to be sacrificed for Democ. My clothes hang loosely upon me. Distribute them amongst you, and when you have relieved me of all my exterior impedimenta conduct me please to a respectable inn." Of course when brought to the scratch the loafers would not work and I marched to the Wilberforce. There is nothing at the Wilberforce except hops ale and Ginger Beer—unless it be aggressive nonconformity. The Travellers' Asstn. has sent a box of books, selected so that they are only looked at in cases of great emergency. There was a young man there—my only companion—with a somewhat low cast of face, so I took down the Bible, laid it on my knee, and enjoyed my tea and toast without having to give my opinion on things in general. There is an air of sad sanctity about Oxford. When I bury my mother-in-law I shall go to Oxford to do justice to my sorrow. I remembered your reprimands and looked at the waitresses. They did not strike me as being very pretty and the lace at their necks was rather dirty. However I observed that one had a sweetheart, and I told her so. She denied it. "I can prove it" said I, and drew her attention to a dirty expanse on the right side of the waist of her light frock. "His hand passed round your back rests there. You lean to the left. His shoulder is on your left. From that I conclude you have been engaged or courting a long time." She fled. That girl will never look me in the face again. There is one man more important in Oxford than the Master of Balliol. It is Hynes, chimney sweep, Fabian, Land lecturer, verbalist, maker of pills, and member of the Independent Haspirate Party. He wears a wig, knows everybody and is the possessor of very pretty daughters. He took me to see Oxford and its men in the morning beginning with one of the college kitchens with its masses of rump steak, mutton cutlets, gorgonzola and smells of mock turtle. Hynes on the Dons is like a young genius on his father. Two things he honours and no third—a Fabian and the grasp of a professor's fingers. Well, I distributed my smoking capacity over some three or four rooms finishing up with Yorke Powell with whom I stay when I go down next: He showed me my room after the manner of the Don who wishes to make an old friend comfortable. It contains a broken chair, an iron bed with Mont Blancs and Himalayas under the blankets, a fireplace, bath, and outlook upon the back of the Cathedral.

From Bradford J.R.M. wrote Enid signing himself "Jim with the lip or the traitor in the Labour Movement, a warning to the young and rising generation to be just and foolish." The social-climbing that blighted MacDonald's later years rears its ugly head in a letter about a dance he attended:

Met young Fowler, son of Rt. Hon. He is a cad and an ass to boot. After dance was over and three or four of the special folks (myself included of course) were having a smoke and refreshments in the library (2 a.m.) he spoke of the faddists who split the Liberal vote. But no Donnybrook fair for me. I gently lifted the ends of his coat tail from the gutter and stuck them in his pocket. But the silly fool told stories that if I cared to use would bring a load of bricks about his father's ears. But this was what my vanity was leading me to:

Distinguished looking woman whispering: "Oh, Lady Montagu, who is that gentleman immediately behind us talking to the lady in white?"
Lady M.: A Mr. MacDonald. He is a Labour candidate for Parliament.

D.L.W.: I mean the dark gentleman.
L.M.: Yes! That is Mr. MacDonald.
D.L.W.: A Labour candidate?
L.M.: Yes! But nothing like the ordinary sort you know
&c., &c.
Presently:
L.M.: I should like to introduce you to Mr. MacD. to
M. deBlouet—Mrs.

Woman! Can your vanity exceed that? Got home at three
now awfully sleepy.

Enid Stacy's replies have not survived, but their tenor may
be gauged from the reams of electioneering and canvassing
advice MacDonald gave her, and from his urging her to become a Fabian. "Why not?" he asks her, boasting that in the
election to the Fabian Executive "I am in 6th or 7th place,
and am only twenty or thirty votes under the highest." Elsewhere he tells her he is "the most modest man on the Fabian
Executive" and that "my biography goes into the Labour Annual among the Fabians." He is never very happy about the
ILP, noting in one letter that in Hackney it has been taken
over by the SDF who are openly boasting of their control of
it, and elsewhere saying "Our very virtue—independence—
in that it has become a dogma has become dangerous." He
warns Enid "not to mistake my Fabian sneers for my own
thoughts" and again "disappears on a Fabian tour for a week."
But he admits that "God planted me on the borders of socialism. Only noble souls . . . may enter the shadows, may grip
the brawny arm of the pioneer and may say 'Comrade.' " In
another letter (June 18, 1894) he records that "My own position was given me with tolerable accuracy by a politician the
other day when he said that I was a Scotch attempt at making
a Machiavelli, and, I would add, a muddled attempt." Starvation, he glooms, is "constantly staring me in the face" and he
longs to retire from the political arena. Life is going downhill
for him, and it is in this gloomy tone that he congratulates
Enid on her thirtieth—or, he asks, is it her thirty-first?—birthday.

Before she actually came to stay with him in Lossiemouth—
from September 6 to 12, 1894—there are several letters telling
her what shoes and other clothes to wear. Her attendance at
Kirk is insisted upon and MacDonald explains that he often
preaches, and also "am quite Jewish in my customs, holding a
Sunday School class on Saturday morning." He warns Enid
that his mother "is a kind of rough diamond"; she will not be
likely to quote Swinburne "for she was a day labourer on a
farm and then made frocks for the village girls. When a raw

animal on a farm she trusted my scoundrel of a father too much, but, poor soul, she has done her best for me and I am now trying to repay her. Already she is one of the most respected people hereabouts."

Evidently Enid's brief visit was a great success, for the letters, hitherto to "Dear Miss Stacy" now begin "My dear." And J.R.M. admits his poverty to her by announcing in one letter in capitals: TOMMORROW I HAVE A NEW NAVY BLUE SERGE SUIT. One letter, in pencil, tells Enid he has "acute Bright" and if it proves chronic "I shall be dead in a month or two." He goes into hospital next day for an operation.

In 1895 the Rev. Percy Widdrington appears, staying with MacDonald at Lossiemouth. He was born in 1873, and, while at Oxford, was secretary of the Fabian Society there, and, once, when G. B. Shaw was his guest at St. Edmund's Hall, engineered an escape when G.B.S. was besieged by a mob of clamant undergraduates. Legend has it the escape was by way of a drain-pipe. J.R.M. calls Percy "Widder" in his letters to Enid, and the two men write her jointly about the stupidities of a candidate defeated in a by-election, and evidently a pain in the neck. As a result of this *contretemps,* J.R.M. tells Enid, "Widder is in quite a perturbed state," which "makes it easy for a man to enter upon all sorts of extravagances—propose, invent flying machines, study the mystery of perpetual motion." Enid is to give him good advice "persuade him that drink leads to death and matrimony to hell—that the first is bad for the Church and the second for the movement."

But Enid herself got engaged to "Widder" and both James Ramsay MacDonald and George Bernard Shaw wrote her at length on the subject of matrimony. G.B.S. wrote from Beatrice Webb's house in Wales where he was staying:

> The Argoed. Monmouth. (until Saturday
> morning: then 29 Fitzroy Square W.)

My dear Miss Stacy

I redeemed my promise to write to you in the noblest manner by doing it that very evening before I went to bed. But I did not finish the letter, and never had a moment of the sort of leisure I wanted for it until this evening, when I read it over and promptly tore it up. After all, your letter writing energy must be fully absorbed at present by Widdrington.

You probably have considerable misgivings as to the

wisdom of getting married; but you might as well concern yourself about the wisdom of growing old. At the worst you will only regret having married W. (though I see no reason to anticipate that, as I can see nothing wrong with him): you will not regret having got married. And you would most certainly regret not having got married. You cannot have a better reason for marrying W. than that he has asked you to. He must have wanted you a great deal—wanted you *always*—to do that; for, after all, he might have enjoyed a very considerable acquaintanceship, and even friendly intimacy, with you without committing himself any farther. And although a woman has to belong primarily to herself, and to defend herself against even the most affectionate claims to possess her altogether, yet, however much or little she intends to grant, she is right to exact from the man that he shall *want* her altogether before she marries him. Now clearly W.'s need for you must have risen to that point to have moved him to ask you to marry him without his feeling any hesitation, any caution, any sense of running a risk about it. You can never have a better reason for marrying than that. Any possible marriage you could ever make in your lifetime would be just as risky; and no possible marriage would be likely to be any happier. So you may dismiss all doubt from your mind if you feel kindly towards him & would like to help him and protect him & satisfy his love for you and take care of him generally as it is woman's function to take care of that helpless little baby, man. Don't be prudent and wait: long engagements are the devil: marry him as soon as he gets his degree. The poorer you start the better; so that every success, every advance, every new interest & outlook will come to you both together—otherwise they will tend to separate you. And that is all the practical wisdom I can offer you in the matter. I hope your life will be too active and completely fulfilled to leave you either time or inclination to trouble yourself about happiness or unhappiness or any other morbid development of self consciousness; for I really have always had a greater regard for you than ever I told you of. When I first met you at Bristol, I was charmed and touched somehow; and I was greatly refreshed and recreated by that sensation. The feeling was of no value to you: I was satisfied, and wanted nothing: what you touched in me is what people often mistake for my heart (which hardly exists), that is to say, a sensitive imagination. I shall probably never marry; for nobody can help me in my work, no woman can make any real difference to it; and therefore, though I can appreciate women, understand them sometimes, and often fall in love with them with all the customary infatuation, yet I don't *need* them, don't want them except for a few rare moments which are really only my playtime, should not know what to do with them if I had them always, and therefore cannot make the one appeal to them that W. has made to you. If ever I am able to say to a woman, "I can't do without you"—meaning that I cannot reach some point without her that I could reach with her, then she will marry me. But I am afraid that will never happen, because I have felt all sorts of things for women, from the commonest sort of passion to an entirely noble tenderness; but I never felt *that*.

I tell you this about myself to elucidate my point about W.'s claim on you. He has asked you to marry him. That means that he cannot do without you. So strike up the wedding march.

I also say it all to amuse you; for no doubt it is the greatest nonsense.

Yours sincerely
G. Bernard Shaw.

MacDonald wrote to Enid in pencil, from Inverness, on a Sabbath, after "making sermons." He divides his letter into a firstly, about politics, a secondly, "about matrimony and booze" telling her she will make a "very good wife, don't you fear" and assuring her that "Widder is a good feller. In my heart of hearts (rather a dusty chamber with very creaky hinges to its old worm-eaten door) he has a shrine. Would he was less priestly, but that is not my business." Then he writes about himself:

Sister I shall now take the third heading and descend to hell. And so you still think that politics, ambition and work engage me, and that I dream of no conspiracies for forcing the gates that guard the kingdom of Fife? Perhaps if I allowed myself to think much I might contradict you on that specific point, but I suppose I am doomed to live outwardly in proof of your idea. Soon in my thirties, with claims on time and cash on the increase, my day is well nigh over. The withered leaf of a fragrant flower or two will be found in the diary pages of my twenties but that I suppose will be all, and when the pages are opened the leaves will not be recognised. But when you think of me as a politician, remember that I am that by accident, not choice, and that I would be a better man if I allowed my natural lack of keen political interest to sway with me; that that absorbing ambition is such that I am prepared to give up everything tomorrow of that kind, except misty literary dreams that seem to become more misty every day I rise now; that my work has always been done (except writing) for somebody's sake. But the fact is that I am getting very tired. You want to do better work and you marry. I am yawning and I don't see why I should rise from my chair. Socialism might inspire me were it not for Socialists; literature might receive me into its arms were it not for the arms of the demimonde Politics; in both cases the fault is very likely my own. Now my sermon is ended. My soul retires within the shell of my will, and I am just as of old a politician, ambitious, full with work—enjoying my heaven, with its spotlights, proscenium and "lavley" scenery. To that glory Widder has added an altar and a cross, and to these you will add white lilies and red geraniums. These will make your heaven undoubtedly better than mine.

This was his last letter to Enid. She died soon after her marriage, leaving a son, but Percy Widdrington died only in 1958, aged eighty-five, having become a rural dean and a canon.

Shortly after writing such rather melancholy farewell bachelor letters to Enid Stacy, both George Bernard Shaw and James Ramsay MacDonald themselves married, both very happily indeed.

Charlotte Payne Townshend, "a large, graceful woman with masses of chocolate-brown hair, pleasant grey eyes (they are green, she observed, on reading this entry) *matte* complexion that sometimes looks muddy, at other times forms a picturesquely pale background to her brilliant hair and bright eyes," [7] was introduced to the Webbs in the fall of 1895. Hearing she was Socialistic, they interested her in the London School of Economics. She subscribed 1,000 pounds to the library, endowed a woman's scholarship, and paid the Webbs 300 pounds a year for the rooms over the school. Beatrice suggested they take a house together in the country and entertain their mutual friends. "She is fond of men and impatient of most women; bitterly resents her enforced celibacy but thinks she could not tolerate the matter-of-fact side of marriage," Beatrice wrote in her diary, and thought Charlotte would do for Graham Wallas. But he bored her to death with his morality and learning. In a few days Charlotte and G.B.S. were constant companions. The house party was reduced to the Webbs and Shaw, and to cut a long story short, as Beatrice put it, Charlotte and Shaw were married on June 1, 1898, while the Webbs were journeying round the world,

[7] Beatrice Webb, 1948, p. 90.

studying Anglo-Saxon democracy. Arnold Bennett[8] commented in his journal:

> Nolan told me that every few years some promising member of the Fabian Society contrived to marry an heiress, whose wealth and energies were subsequently devoted to the cause. Thus Sidney Webb married Beatrice Potter, B. G. Costelloe married Miss Pearsall Smith, and J. Ramsay MacDonald married Miss M. E. Gladstone. Nolan assured me as a fact that G.B.S. some months ago discussed with certain other Fabian Society members as to whose "duty it was to marry an heiress."

The Shaws were married at Caxton Hall, Westminster. Henry Salt and Graham Wallas, invited to be G.B.S.'s witnesses, found the bridegroom had arrived on crutches. He was suffering from what had proved to be a nearly fatal leg infection, necrosis of the bone. Putting his hand out playfully, he was taken for a beggar, and almost bidden move on from his own wedding. The marriage, in which "sex had no part . . . it ended all of the old gallantries, flirtations and philanderings for both of us," as G.B.S. wrote, was very happy. But Shaw disclaimed any knowledge of what marriage really meant—he had no illusions about the unconsummated relationship between himself and Charlotte. "What do you call married life? Real married life is the life of the youth and maiden who pluck a flower and bring down an avalanche on their shoulders. Thirty years of the work of Atlas, and then rest as pater and mater familias. What can childless people with independent incomes, marrying at forty as I did, tell you about marriage? I know nothing about it except as a looker-on," [9] he said.

Charlotte had, G.B.S. said, a face like a muffin. "I remember," he told Hesketh Pearson after her death, "how when we went to the first Fabian summer school, she was dressed in a very masculine costume, tailormade, and I said, not to her, but to the associated gathering, how much I disliked the way women had of dressing like men. That evening she appeared in a lovely dress with a low-cut chiffon bodice, through which her skin showed very attractively, and she never reverted to the masculine garb again."

Shaw's nearly two years of illness due to his leg resulted in his working less hard at his Fabianism after his marriage. For twelve years he had given it all he had: "My hours that make my days, my days that make my years follow one another

[8] I, entry for Wednesday, July 8, 1898.
[9] Shaw, 1949, p. 89.

into the maw of socialism, and I am left ageing and out of breath, without a moment to rest my tired soul," he had written. And what heavy work much of it was: for six years, for example, as a vestryman at St. Pancras, he never missed a meeting, and there was one every two weeks. All the other vestrymen and women delighted in the fireworks he produced. There were 120 members of the Vestry, and it must be confessed that G.B.S. was the only one with exquisite personal distinction and lovely speaking voice. Yet "he did not take more than his fair share of time. His services on the committees (Electric Lighting, Health, Parliamentary, Housing and Drainage) were so valuable that the unique step was taken of extending him a vote of thanks . . . it has been said that he contributed wit, vigor and good by-laws to St. Pancras." [10]

However, Beatrice Webb could get quite cross with G.B.S.'s unorthodox methods of canvassing. In 1904 she gloomed in *Our Partnership* how hopelessly intractable G.B.S. was. He refused to adopt any orthodox electioneering devices and was continually inventing ones only suitable to Fabians or Souls. He insisted he was an atheist, and, though he was a teetotaler, insisted too that he would force everyone to imbibe a quart of rum. He laughed at the Nonconformist conscience, and chaffed the Catholics about transubstantiation. "We did our best for him," she says smugly, "Sidney even puffing him in the *Daily Mail.*" But it was no use; he lost, and "he will never be selected again by any constituency that any wire-puller thinks can be won."

He even crossed swords with his friend Sidney Webb at St. Pancras when there was a smallpox outbreak. For G.B.S. made Socialism ridiculous, said Webb, by putting forward trivial and controversial opposition to inoculation. But Shaw said inoculation did not deal with the causes of disease, which are dirt, poverty, and overcrowding. These should be tackled and removed to prevent another occurrence. And again, when in charge of Labor Committee rooms in Old Street, New Cross, where Sidney was seeking re-election to the LCC, Shaw spent days upon days addressing envelopes in a dismantled shop, with no fire. He had almost been arrested, too, in the Dod Street dock area, being one of the volunteers "to do the Dod Street trick." This, he explained, was simply to find a dozen or more persons (a gathering of rather debauched-looking persons around the pump at Clerkenwell Green, H. M. Hyndman, who had often been one, called them), who were willing to get arrested at the rate of one per week by speaking in defiance of the police. In a month or two, the re-

[10] Henderson, p. 262.

peated arrests, the crowds which they attracted, the scenes which they provoked, the sentences passed by the magistrates, and the consequent newspaper descriptions, forced the Home Secretary to give way whenever the police were clearly in the wrong. When it was G.B.S.'s turn to be arrested was one of the occasions when the police had been told to let well enough alone—rather luckily for him, as his mother had just managed to get a job teaching at a girl's school, and a jailed son would have been a likely cause of her instant dismissal.

Even when illness caused a slackening of his political work, G.B.S. kept writing strictly political plays: "I am a specialist in immoral and heretical plays . . . I write plays with the deliberate object of converting the nation to my opinion on sexual and social matters. I have no other incentive to write plays as I am not dependent on it for my livelihood," he explained.

Perhaps even a more permanent landmark of Fabian permeation than LSE was the Education Act of 1902. According to Sir Robert Ensor, it

> ranks for England and Wales among the two or three greatest constructive measures of the twentieth century. Balfour did not devise it; that was done by R. L. Morant, an official of the board of education. But no statesman less dominated than Balfour was by the concept of national efficiency would have taken it up and carried it through, since its costs on the side of votes was obvious and deterrent.

At the time of the act's drafting the Webbs had settled down again for their annual nine weeks' sojourn with the Russells, at Friday's Hill. Beatrice wrote in May: "Sidney asked Morant to stay here. Morant is the principal person at the Education Department . . . he has been exclusively engaged by the Cabinet Committee to draft this present bill and is trying to get some sort of bill through the Cabinet." [11] Beatrice notes that

> all our radical friends bitter or sullen with us over Sidney's support of the Education Bill. Certainly, if he had political ambitions, it would have been a suicidal policy on his part. . . . The Liberal League, notably Haldane and Rosebery, have been good friends to us, and we feel bound to return in kind. Haldane and Sidney are constantly cooperating in educational matters.

[11] Beatrice Webb, 1948, pp. 239-40.

But other Fabians disliked Haldane. H. G. Wells described him as a pasty-faced butler serving the Absolute on a silver salver; Sir Robert Ensor thought he was the evil genius of the Webbs.

Meantime, Alfred Cripps (Beatrice's brother-in-law) had been in close communication with Balfour and Chamberlain, trying to arrange some sort of compromise between them with regard to the Education Bill. In the end it was the Fabian plan, drafted by Sidney Webb, and fiercely criticized by Stewart Headlam, as a churchman, and by Graham Wallas, as a secularist, that substantially became

> the system of administration . . . under which present-day education is organized . . . how far the draughtsmen of the Bill were influenced by the Fabian scheme cannot here be estimated, but the authorities at Whitehall were so anxious to see it that they were supplied with proofs before publication; and the tract when published was greedily devoured by perplexed Members of Parliament.[12]

In May 1902, the Fabians welcomed the bill itself but advocated amendments on eighteen different points, nearly all of which—the chief being directed to making the bill compulsory where it was drafted as optional—were embodied in the act.[13]

The Fabians really stuck their necks out supporting the Education Act, for at the time it was considered a most reactionary measure. Liberals and Labor were united in denouncing it as an entirely Tory concoction. Yet the act made possible great advances in public elementary, secondary, and technical education. It abolished the school boards, transferred control of all elementary education to the local authorities (this made the public feeding of schoolchildren, strenuously advocated some time earlier by Graham Wallas, at last possible), made "county and country borough councils the local authorities for all secondary and technical education . . . and brought under the new authorities not only the board schools but also the voluntary schools." [14] The current expenses of these voluntary schools (Church of England and Catholic) were to be thereafter provided for out of local rates. In the board schools undenominational teaching was retained to please the Nonconformists, and all local education authorities were to discharge their functions through a statu-

12 Pease, p. 144.
13 *Ibid.*, p. 145.
14 Ensor, p. 356.

tory education committee, which included members co-opted from outside the council.

Catholics and members of the Church of England were delighted with the bill, which saved their schools from bankruptcy. But the Nonconformists were furious, since the sectarian schools were thus financed from the rates. Moreover, since in many areas the only school was the church school, Nonconformist children had to attend it. Their parents had hoped the church schools would go broke, and board schools be substituted. Their agitation affected the Fabians, too: Graham Wallas resigned from the Society on this issue, and, as G.B.S. put it, a blameless clerical member of the Fabian Executive (the Rev. Stewart Headlam) lost his seat. He added:

> Half the children in the country were in church schools which very urgently needed the State inspection and control their endowment involved. The Fabian Society leaders had to support the Bill . . . the Act passed . . . it had proved that the Socialist movement was confused and divided by the Radical superstition that Progressives must always vote against the Government, against the Church, and in fact against all collective as opposed to individualist legislation except such as had been demanded by the trade unions and opposed by the Conservatives. The Fabian policy was to support and take advantage of every legislative step towards Collectivism no matter what quarter it came from.[15]

15 Shaw, 1948, p. 211.

CHAPTER ELEVEN

COMING OF AGE OFTEN requires, in human beings, a radical reorientation, and the Fabian Society on reaching its twenties seems to have changed somewhat its course and its character. For circumstances alter cases, and the Liberal Party's reneging on the Newcastle Program that had been stuffed down their rather unwilling throats by the Fabians marked the first Fabian *volte-face*. The Shaw-Webb article "To Your Tents, O Israel" ended the permeation of the Liberal Party as a Fabian policy and adumbrated the infant ILP. The second most notable surprise caused by the Fabians was their advocacy of, indeed their single-minded lobbying for, the Education Act—a Conservative measure that nevertheless proved a great step in the collectivist direction.

But it was the South African War that brought out the Fabians for a third time in an even stranger new color. All the other radicals, from the old-fashioned Liberals to the ILP and the Social Democratic Federationists, were anti-imperialists, solidly against the war. The Fabians proved to be personally widely divided on this issue, but some of the greatest among them—for example, G.B.S. and Graham Wallas—were for the war; Sydney Olivier, Bertrand Russell, and J. Ramsay MacDonald were desperately against it, and Sidney and Beatrice Webb occupied a middle position.

The South African issue was extremely complicated. It was South African gold that had saved England from the serious depression of the eighties, when the American Henry Adams had written to his brother: "British industry is quite ruined, and its decline has at last become a debacle." This discovery of gold and the new imperialism which it financed, raised wages at home, and so improved the condition of the working classes that the labor movement became a possibility. This was certainly one reason why social historians, such as the Webbs, approved in principle so obviously a socially amelio-

rating factor as South African gold, and the colonies whose
conquest it paid for, proved to be.

When Mr. Gladstone finally resigned in 1894, after his
Second Home Rule Bill had been thrown out, it was at least
partly from a moral refusal to share the spoils—particularly
of Africa, over which in the South the two occupying white
races, the British *Uitlanders* and the Boers, rapidly came to
loggerheads.

The new imperialism, that Élie Halévy so brilliantly desig-
nated as a species of Darwinish philosophy, was the law of the
jungle, which maintains the balance of species at the cost of a
never-ending struggle, a truceless war. "This became for the
British the foundation of a moral code, chaste, brutal, heroic,
and childlike." [1] In the name of this code, the Arab slavers
were banished from Africa, to be replaced by European over-
seers, and white settlers sequestrated the fertile areas of Cape
Colony, Rhodesia, and Kenya, leaving to the natives land so
unusable that their only hope of staying alive was to enter the
mines as indentured labor. Liberals like Lord Morley, Sir William Harcourt, Lord Courtenay, and the young Lloyd George,
were dubbed pro-Boer after the war began on October 11,
1899. Asquith, Grey, and, of course, the arch-imperialist
Joseph Chamberlain (who with his brother and son had so
profited by the war that, as Halévy said, "though their critics
did not accuse them in so many words of making the war to
fill their pockets, yet the fact remained that the war had filled
them" [2]) were, with their leader, Lord Rosebery, the chief Liberal imperialists, or "Limps."

It is hardly surprising that imperialism should split the
Socialists, since it so split the Liberals as almost fatally to
sever them. Mrs. Sidney Webb noted: "The cleavage goes
right through the Liberal Party into the Fabian Society." [3]
Shaw, too, notes how real dissension arose for the first
time within the Fabian Society as the result of the South
African War.

This war was an imperialist war, and Shaw noted that
anti-imperialism was so strong a habit in democratic van-
guards that a section of the Fabians broke off from the
Society on this issue. J. Ramsay MacDonald and his wife,
Bertrand Russell and his, G. K. Chesterton, Walter Crane,
G. N. Barnes, Henry Scott, and S. G. Hobson, all left. Some,
like Bertrand Russell, were to return. "I joined the Fabians

---

[1] Halévy, p. 21.

[2] *Ibid.,* p. 97.

[3] Beatrice Webb, 1948, p. 188.

several times," he said. (Since this appeared to me redundant: "Was it not like rebaptism to rejoin?" I asked him, and he replied: "Not unlike.") G.B.S. minimized the loss to the Society with his boast: "I managed to pull the Fabian Society through this convulsion with the loss of less than two dozen members, by drafting a tract called *Fabianism and the Empire.*" [4]

The Boer War actually split the Fabians four ways. There were the out-and-out pacifists, generally dubbed pro-Boer; there were those who opposed this particular war as imperialist; there were the bitter-enders, who had been against getting involved, but once in, felt England must go on; and there were the blood-letters, who, with a moral fervor, approved of the war as salutary, and of these, G.B.S. was passionately one.

> In this matter the left and right wings of the Fabians joined hands in opposition to the centre, while the older leaders took the view that the members had come together for the purpose of promoting Socialism, and that the question at issue was one which Socialism cannot solve and does not touch, and that whilst each member was entitled to hold and work for his own opinion, it was not necessary for the Society in its corporate capacity to adopt a formal policy. . . . [5]

At a meeting on December 8, 1899, S. G. Hobson moved a resolution which concluded: "The Fabian Society therefore formally dissociates itself from the imperialism of Capitalism and vainglorious Nationalism and pledges itself to support the expansion of the Empire only in so far as it may be compatible with the expansion of that higher social organisation which this Society was founded to promote." This was carried 59 to 50, and thereafter the Executive submitted a postal referendum in February 1900 to all members: "Are you in favour of an official pronouncement being made by the Fabian Society on imperialism in relation to the War?" The membership of the time was about 800: 476 votes were cast, 217 in favor of a pronouncement and 259 against. E. R. Pease indignantly denies that the Society voted its approval of the South African War. A vote on government policy would have given an overwhelming adverse majority, but it would have destroyed the Society, he averred. The Fabians had already refused to take sides on Home Rule or Church Disestablishment, for example, because these were red her-

[4] Shaw, 1948, Preface.
[5] Pease, p. 130.

rings and matters of no importance in comparison with the
economic enfranchisement advocated by the Fabians.

Pease insisted that Socialism was an economic doctrine,
and had nothing to do with other problems. "Later," he admitted, "we realised that the form of government is scarcely
less important than its content: that the unit of administration, whether imperial, national, or local, is germane to the
question of the services administered." [6] But at that time,
what mattered to the Fabians above all was simply to survive:

> The instinct of self-preservation actuated us; it is certain
> that any other decision would have destroyed the Society.
> Passions were high; pro-Boers were guilty of anti-patriotic
> excesses; all, or nearly all of the "old gang" on whom from
> first to last the initiative and ability of the Society de-
> pended, would have resigned their membership or at any
> rate their official positions in the Society, had it adopted at
> that time the same policy as the I.L.P.[7]

At the annual meeting, in May, G.B.S. undertook the
writing of a tract on imperialism, for at this period all the
official pronouncements of the Executive were drafted by
him. It was sent to the members in September, and 134 returned amended proofs or wrote letters of criticism. G.B.S.
"gave every criticism its proper weight and accepted every
useful amendment." At the subsequent meeting about 140
members were present, and only 14 were against publication
of the 20,000-word tract, *Fabianism and the Empire,* which,
offered at a shilling, sold only a bare 2,000 copies during
1900.

G.B.S. indeed was an enthusiastic blood-letter. To Henry
Salt, who could not have disagreed with him more, he
wrote: "I delight in the war more and more. It has waked the
country out of its filthy wallowing in money; blood is a far
superior bath; and it has put 4d on the income tax which
will never come off it if the Fabians can help it; so that old
age pensions will be within reach at the end of ten years re-
payment period."

In a speech delivered on February 23, 1900, he declared:
"The more governed state over the largest area is preferable
to a number of warring units with undisciplined ideals. . . .
The world is to the big and powerful states by necessity; and
the little ones must come within their borders or be crushed
out of existence." His overriding claim was for efficiency,
"not only in our own government, and in our empire, but

6 *Ibid.,* p. 132.
7 *Ibid.,* p. 133.

throughout the world." The earth belongs to mankind, and the only valid moral right to national as well as individual possession is that the occupier is making adequate use of it for the benefit of the world community, he averred.

G.B.S. foresaw the whole world partitioned, and hoped it would be by Great Powers of practically international scope. This attitude was partly a general Fabian one, because the Fabians wanted to get things done, and were sometimes rather casual about the means and the personalities by which things got done. Partly, however, it came from the truly majestic scale of Shaw's policy for the British Empire. In Fabian Tract 127, published anonymously, he wrote in 1908: "The Labour Party is against the landlord. It is also a trustee of the internationalization of a great and historic Empire, an Empire which, if it is worthily to develop, must be transformed into a great democratic commonwealth." The Fabian Society actually also invented a sort of mandate or trusteeship system, not unlike the form developed under League auspices after World War I. As early as 1900 G.B.S. wrote:

> The notion that a nation has a right to do what it pleases with its own territory, without reference to the rest of the world, is no more tenable from the internationalist socialist point of view . . . than the notion that a landlord has a right to do what he likes with his estate without reference to the interests of his neighbours. The value of a State to the world lies in the quality of its civilization, not in the magnitude of its armaments. . . . There is therefore no question of the steam-rollering of little States because they are little, any more than of their maintenance in deference to romantic nationalism. The State which obstructs international civilisation will have to go, be it big or little. That which advances it should be defended by all the Western Powers. Thus huge China and little Monaco may share the same fate, little Switzerland and the vast United States the same fortune.[8]

G. K. Chesterton very effectively attacked these views in his *Autobiography*.[9]

> Those who do not understand what the Fabian political philosophy was may not realise that the leading Fabians were nearly all Imperialists. Mr. and Mrs. Sidney Webb were in that matter strong Imperialists;[10] Hubert Bland

[8] Shaw, 1900, pp. 44-45.

[9] pp. 229-30.

[10] Sidney Webb later horrified Bertrand Russell in World War I, when there was a chance of England's making a separate peace, by saying, "Soldiers' noses must be kept to the grindstone."

was a still stronger Imperialist. It was the same, for that matter, with Mr. H. G. Wells, then a sort of semi-detached Fabian . . . I say this as a compliment to the Fabians. I say it as a compliment to their consistency, as well as in contradiction to their controversial views. They were, and are, quite right holding their views about centralisation, to be on the side of the Big Battalions and the Big Businesses. It is the sentimental Socialists who are inconsistent, in saying that a peasant has no right to a cornfield, but a peasantry has a right to an oil-field. It is they who are the more nebulous thinkers when they defend small nationalities and not small properties. There is only a thin sheet of paper between the Imperialist and the Internationalist; and the first Fabians had the lucidity to see the fact.

That this imperialism was generally considered Fabian policy is further proved by Sidney Webb's article "Lord Rosebery's Escape from Houndsditch," published in the *Nineteenth Century* in September 1901, and subsequently as Fabian Tract 108: *Twentieth Century Politics: A Policy of National Efficiency.* Houndsditch was the birthplace of Jeremy Bentham: in his article Webb congratulated the Liberal leader on his escape from Bentham's principles, an escape he himself had also found it necessary to make. Lord Rosebery, according to Sir Henry Campbell-Bannerman, was very much under Sidney Webb's influence, as even more were R. B. Haldane and A. J. Balfour, both of whom were habitués of Beatrice's *salon.* Campbell-Bannerman, on the other hand, was anti-Webb. "We have had the benefit of instruction by Mr. Sidney Webb and have survived it," he sneered in a letter to Herbert Gladstone (September 12, 1901).[11]

Most Socialists disagreed violently with the Fabians about the war. However, generally speaking, the Boer War was very popular in England: An old music-hall ditty of 1877 was revived and widely sung:

> We don't want to fight
> But by jingo, if we do
> We've got the men, we've got the ships
> We've got the money, too.

Yet at this very time Keir Hardie was elected to Parliament in the "khaki election" of 1900 by the South Wales miners for Merthyr Tydfil, although the Conservatives had said that every vote against the government was a vote for the Boers. "The recognised Labour leaders have one and all gone pro-

11 Quoted in Spender, 1923, II, p. 4.

Boer. The Fabian Society, it must be admitted is completely out of it, the majority believing in the inevitability of the war, while the minority regard the majority as being the worst of traitors." [12]

The ILP was solidly anti-war. Keir Hardie's great work in the ILP had been converting the leaders of trade unionism to Socialism. Up until 1899 the secretary of "one trade union might be a Conservative, the secretary of another a Liberal, and in consequence the unions were in a position to direct pressure on both parties." [13] Both parties, indeed, flirting with the unions, dangled social legislative programs, constantly upping the ante, with insurance schemes, such as that advocated by Joe Chamberlain in the wake of Bismarck, or old-age-pension schemes, such as that then recently passed in New Zealand, and put before the British public by the Fabian New Zealand Agent-General, A. Pember Reeves.

At the Trades Union Congress of 1899, held in London in February, representing 353,070 trade unionists and 22,861 members of the three Socialist societies, the ILP offered an amendment to a SDF proposal to establish a "distinct party" in the House of Commons, of representatives of the working class. This ILP amendment, passed by 53 votes to 39, resulted a year later in the formation of the Labor Representation Committee, with a combined membership of 375,931, composed of the trade unions, the ILP, the SDF, and the Fabians. A year later, the SDF withdrew. This left the trade unions, which "supplied a rather inert bulk membership and most of what little money was available. They were still so unwilling to pay for the benefits of political representation that the Committee's income was only £243 the first year and £343 the next." [14]

The Fabian Society was entitled to send only one delegate to the Labor Representation Committee, but that delegate was included on the executive of twelve. For several years, E. R. Pease, as the only Fabian delegate, appointed himself to the executive, which duly confirmed his appointment. Gradually the long, clumsy word "representation" was dropped, and in 1906 the Labor Committee blossomed into the Labor Party.

For several years after this, the Fabian Society did not greatly concern itself with the Labour Party . . . my colleagues . . . as a whole showed little interest in the new body. In a sense, it was not in our line. Its object was to promote Labour representation in Parliament, and the

---

[12] Beatrice Webb, 1948, p. 200.
[13] Halévy, p. 240.
[14] Hutchison, p. 93.

Fabian Society had never run, and had never intended to run, candidates for Parliament or for any local authority.[15]

But the Fabians were deeply concerned, at least individually, with the trade unions and with their conversion to collectivism. As early as 1897, the Webbs had been concerned by several legal judgments given against trade unions. "Collective bargaining will become impossible if, whenever trade unionists are warned not to accept employment from a particular firm . . . the trade union officials can be harassed by writs, costs in damages and driven into bankruptcy." [16]

In 1900 a strike broke out on a small railway line, the Taff Vale, carrying coal in South Wales. Hours were twelve a day, wages under a pound a week. The management of the line, bitterly opposed to the Amalgamated Society of Railway Servants, imported strikebreakers to counter this society's successful picketing. The strikers damaged some railroad property, and the company sued. The House of Lords held the society responsible, and condemned it to pay £28,000 in damages, with total costs £32,000. Such a sum completely ruined a then relatively small union, and "The effect on the trade unions was frankly disabling." [17] "The Taff Vale Case seemed to cancel most of the gains made by the trade unions in a hundred years of struggle. Theoretically, the right to strike remained, but it could only be exercised at the risk of exposing . . . union funds. . . ." [18]

Élie Halévy has declared that the working class became panic-stricken as a result of this decision. But the Labor Representation Committee profited by the general alarm. In fact, some labor historians, among them S. F. Markham,[19] think the Labor Party largely to have been created by the indignation of trade unionists at the Taff Vale judgment, which deprived the trade unions of the immunity they had held for a generation from actions for damages by employers injured by strikes. "The Taff Vale case and the *Times* attacks were the deciding factors in bringing the trade unions to the support of the Labor Representation Committee," wrote Henry Pelling.[20]

The Labor movement was united in demanding the reversal of this judgment by Parliament, and this was the first

[15] Pease, p. 151.
[16] Sidney and Beatrice Webb, 1920, I, p. 858, n.
[17] Ensor, p. 378.
[18] Hutchison, p. 91.
[19] p. 125.
[20] p. 87.

plank in its program. In the election campaign of 1906—the first after the restoration of peace, and the first in the new reign—the Labor Party put fifty candidates into the field; twenty-nine were elected, of whom four were Fabians. Another three Fabians were elected as Liberals, including one member of the Fabian Executive. This situation, in which the Fabian Society as a whole was affiliated with the Labor Party, while some of its members were Liberal Members of Parliament, seems today schizophrenic. But the Labor Party never complained of the anomaly, nor did the Fabian liberals ever take action hostile to the Labor Party, which for its part never questioned the Fabians' collective loyalty.

Arthur Henderson, triumphantly elected, pointed firmly to the fact that Labor's social salvation was now in its own hands: "Upon our party rests the responsibility of keeping this government up to the scratch of their own professions." R. B. Haldane[21] was not taken in by the apparent Liberal triumph:

The Liberals got 379 as against 155 Unionist seats. But Labour returned 51 members . . . enough to form a permeating influence on Parliament. It is a common delusion to think that a party is to be estimated merely by its numbers. The real question is whether it stands for a permeating power in the country. This was well illustrated early in our career as a new Government. One of the things democracy had pledged itself to get rid of was the result of the Judgment of the House of Lords in the Taff Vale case . . . I had been the leading counsel of the Trade Union in the Taff Vale case. But we considered it too violent a proposition to say that a Trade Union should under no circumstances be capable of being sued in tort. We therefore prepared a bill . . . leaving those who had actually behaved illegally to bear the brunt of having done so. . . . But when the House of Commons met, a Bill, of which Keir Hardie was the real protagonist, was introduced, and it became plain . . . that it was going to be carried against the Government by a huge majority. It passed easily indeed, and later on the House of Lords, like the Conservative Party in the Commons, showed that they too dared not throw it out. That was how the Trades Disputes Act of 1906 came to be passed.

The Webbs rejoiced. "Two of the new Cabinet have already come to talk over their new life," wrote Beatrice Webb.[22]

[21] p. 211.
[22] 1948, p. 325.

"John Burns . . . for one solid hour paced the room expand-
ing his soul before me. 'Don't be too doctrinaire about the unemployed, Mr. Burns,' I suggested mildly. 'Economise your
great force of honesty, Mrs. Webb,' he said." Haldane was of
course the other Cabinet member. He was also exuberant.
"I chose the War Office out of three offices," he told Beatrice.
On February 9th Burns appeared

> about nine o'clock in the evening, and described the three
> committees of the Cabinet upon which he had that day
> sat—one on the Trades Dispute Bill—"They are all so
> kind to me," he said, "especially the great employers,
> just the men who might have objected to my appoint-
> ment." Oh! the wisdom of England's governing class. . . .
> Altogether Sidney and I are in better spirits as to the
> course of political affairs than we have been for many
> years.[23]

Things were going almost too well for the Webbs:
"We can now feel assured that with the School [LSE] as
a teaching body, the Fabian Society as a propagandist organisation, the LCC Progressives as an object lesson in electoral
success, our books as the only elaborate and original work
in economic fact and theory, no young man or woman who is
anxious to study or work in public affairs can fail to come
under our influence," [24] Beatrice confided to her diary.
She admits such sentiments to be hubristic. Certainly, the
London Education Act of 1908, which followed upon and
completed the Education Act of 1902, "proved to be a landmark . . . a successful achievement . . . which entailed
some consequences that were unpleasant . . ." one of which was
being accused of putting Rome on the rates.
In 1907 the Progressives were routed on the LCC. As
G.B.S. put it, "The Fabian conquest of the L.C.C. lasted only
twenty years. Then the capitalists woke up and plastered the
walls with a picture of a very ugly stage villain glaring at
the ratepayers and growling, 'It's your money we want.' The
Fabians had no funds to combat this expensive weapon.
. . ." [25]
The Webbs themselves escaped with their bare lives in
the general rout: "On Wednesday the seats were, I am
convinced, lost. But we poured some three hundred Fabians
into the constituency on polling day, admirably marshalled

[23] Ibid., p. 330.
[24] Ibid., p. 145.
[25] Shaw, 1948, p. 209.

under eleven captains in eleven committee rooms, and by their dogged work we won the constituency back again." [26]

For the Fabians, there was another major fight ahead—the war with Wells.

[26] Beatrice Webb, 1948, p. 373.

CHAPTER TWELVE

Ɪᴛ ᴡᴀѕ ɪɴ 1902 ᴛʜᴀᴛ Beatrice noted in her diary,

> We have seen something lately of H. G. Wells and his wife. Wells is an interesting though somewhat unattractive personality except for his agreeable disposition and intellectual vivacity. His mother was the housekeeper to a great establishment of 40 servants; his father the professional cricketer attached to the place. The early association with the menial side of a great man's establishment has left Wells with a hatred of that class and of its attitude towards the lower orders.[1]

Wells, on his side, has described, in *The New Machiavelli*,[2] how the Baileys (Webbs) took him up and how he became an habitué at their dinner parties, arriving a little early, "for a preliminary gossip with Altiora, in front of her drawing room fire. One got her alone, and that early arrival was a little sign of appreciation she valued. She had every woman's need of followers and servants." He noted of the Webbs,

> Their effect upon me from the first was very considerable. Both of them found occasion on that first visit of mine to talk to me about my published writings. [Wells had already written nineteen novels], and particularly about my then just published book, *The New Ruler* [*A Modern Utopia*] . . . it fell indeed so closely with their own way of thinking that I doubt if they ever understood how independently I had arrived at my conclusions. It was their weakness to claim excessively.[3]

In this book Wells had developed his idea of the Samurai, a new class, somewhat like Plato's guardians, with a deeper consciousness of, and a new relationship to, the state. The

[1] Beatrice Webb, 1948, p. 230.
[2] p. 204.
[3] *Ibid.*, p. 198.

Webbs explained to Wells at their first meeting in a sort of chorus "the cardinal idea of their lives . . . the inevitable development of an official administrative class in the modern state." They wanted to suggest that these expert officials must necessarily develop into a new class and a very powerful class. They wanted to organize that. It may be *the* power of the future. "We consider ourselves as unpaid precursors of such a class. The vision they displayed for my consideration as the aim of public-spirited endeavour, seemed like a harder, narrower, more specialised version of the idea of a trained and disciplined state . . . I had worked out . . . it wasn't clear at first how we differed," wrote H. G. Wells.

Beatrice and Sidney stayed with the Wells at their Sandgate house for a couple of days in 1904, and her analysis of H. G. Wells may suggest some part of the difference between them.

> We like him much—he is absolutely genuine and full of inventiveness—a "speculator" in ideas—somewhat of a gambler but perfectly aware that his hypotheses are not verified. In one sense, he is a romancer spoiled by romancing—but, in the present stage of sociology, he is useful to gradgrinds like ourselves in supplying us with loose generalisations which we can use as instruments of research.

Beatrice asked him why Wallas and some others in the Fabian Society were "so intensely suspicious of us, and seem bent on obstructing every proposal of Sidney?" [4] Wells suggested in reply that Sidney gave a foxy impression and that no one liked to feel they were being managed, and told her she and Sidney were regarded as a "combination" working into each other's hands.

Wells's whole incursion into the Fabian Society must be seen, on his part, as a sincere and dedicated attempt to forge the Fabians into his Samurai. On the Webbs' part their "adoption" of Wells was no less as sincere and dedicated a plan to use his immense popularity, his imaginative gifts and journalistic flair, for popularizing their visions and his. These visions became, in an incredibly short time, the most concrete of nightmares, as later prophets—beside whom Wells seems a huckster—such as Franz Kafka in *The Castle* and George Orwell in *1984,* foresaw they would. Perhaps the clearest outline, written as a blueprint, not foretold as fiction, of the collective Frankenstein into which the Webb-Wells dream materialized can be studied in James Burnham's *The Managerial Revolution.*

[4] Beatrice Webb, 1948, p. 299.

Corruptio optimi pessima—the corruption of the best stinks the worst, and because the Webb-Wells vision has landed so many people flat on their faces is no reason to belittle that vision, nor to avoid others. While it is true that without vision the people perish, yet the Scriptures have never denied that they perish with it, too, though usually more spectacularly and certainly more contentedly. Wells himself saw this very clearly: after his Fabian fiasco he described how his theory of revolution by Samurai hung in the air, and he could not discover any way of bringing it down to the level of reality. At the very time when he was failing, Lenin, under the stresses of a more pressing reality, was steadily evolving an extraordinarily similar scheme, the reconstituted Communist party. Sir Henry Slesser, a devoted, pious Christian convert and Fabian, put his finger in his autobiography on the fatal flaw—the real Fabian fault. The Fabians were trying to achieve a Socialist society without the abrogation of existing conventions, he explained. The world in which they believed was one potentially good. Of sin and the fall they reckoned nothing. They were eschatologists waiting for the kingdom, and working hard for it; they saw it close at hand, in the chaste form of a garden city.

The Fabians—and both the Webbs and Wells agreed on this, even after their disagreements—took the sensible view that it was useless to attempt to build a just co-operative state out of impoverished or ill-nurtured human material. "We must first drain the morass of destitution," said Beatrice. Religious reformers from the saints to the Salvation Army agree with them: first feed and heal, then make holy. The starving *cannot* be made good. But the Fabians thought—as the Utilitarians before them had thought—that you only have to make human beings well and happy, and they *will* be good. "Evil is merely the non-adaptation of an organism to its condition," wrote Herbert Spencer. All the Fabians, whether of the "old gang" or of the Wells faction, had a great dislike of stupidity, but no idea of sin. Though, privately, G.B.S. and Beatrice Webb at least faced the fact of sin. But Beatrice thought sin could be counteracted by living, as she did, on six ounces of food a day, working unceasingly, and constantly attempting prayer. G.B.S. thought sin could be conjured away by vegetarianism, by the avoidance of stimulants, by chastity, and by intellectual fervor—that *amor intellectualis* or intellectual love of God which St. Thomas Aquinas predicates as the highest energy of the saints. Neither faced—except in rare moments of despair—the total bankruptcy of man, nor admitted his need of redemption.

And so, in spite of Beatrice's prayer and fasting, in spite of Sidney's selfless dedication and abnegation, in spite of Shaw's giving the best years of his life to committee work, in spite, indeed, of all that was just and true in Fabian doctrine, yet, as their contemporary A. E. Housman put it:

> The tears of all that be
> Help not the primal fault
> It rains into the sea
> And still the sea is salt.

Today's sea is half a century saltier and Hiroshima-heavier than when Wells and the Webbs and all the Fabians together worked and willed for it to become sweet. Both the Webbs and Wells held much the same view of the state as did an Oxford Platonist of the seventies, T. H. Green. Green, dissenting from Bentham's opposition between the state and the individual as artificial, suggested that the citizen could have no meaning apart from the state. But the state must guarantee to each man the powers without which he cannot realize himself, for the state is the instrument through and by which the citizens realize themselves, and its main function is to achieve the full moral development of its citizens. This view completely substituted the state for God as that in which (instead of Whom) we live and move and have our being.

H. G. Wells was "extraordinarily quick in his apprehensions," Beatrice noted, "and took in all the points we gave him in our 48 hours talk with him—he is a good instrument for popularising ideas, and he gives as many ideas as he receives." Wells has described himself as caustically as he had described Sidney Webb, "Bent, shabby, slovenly, and latterly a somewhat obese figure . . . a dumpy, irascible little man, who carried a shrivelled stomach on two short legs and tiny feet, with the big forehead jutting above." He came into the Fabian Society one dull February day, introduced by Shaw and Wallas. In a reedy, squeaky voice he presented his credentials, and in the following month gave his first lecture, "The Question of Scientific Administration of Areas in Relation to Municipal Undertakings" which was subsequently published as an appendix to *Mankind in the Making*. As a lecture it was by no means a success, E. R. Pease noted, but excused Wells with the suggestion that it was perhaps the first he ever gave, since he read his paper in a low monotonous voice, and addressed it to a corner of the hall.

Had H. G. Wells been by nature or practice as effective in speaking as he was in writing, the fate of the Fabian Society might have been quite other, Pease opined. As it was, Wells was at a great physical disadvantage when sharing the floor with the skilled debaters of the "Old Gang." These enduring members of the Fabian Executive were vaingloriously apt to crow over the Social Democratic Federation, whose members were always either seceding or getting thrown out. But, as happened, several of the "Old Gang" were variously dispersed about this time: Olivier left the Executive to become Governor of Jamaica, and Annie Besant, finding herself, as Shaw puts it, a fifth wheel in the Fabian coach, left to succeed Helena Petrovna Blavatsky. Shaw and Webb remained, but they had achieved positions and publicity that took them far beyond the limits of the Society, though Shaw still served as its pamphleteer, economist, star-turn, and general feelings-soother.

And now this small, vulgar dynamo of a Wells threatened to disrupt the placid Fabian waters, like a noisy motorboat on a peaceful lake. On January 12, 1906, Wells read to the Fabian Society an article, "This Misery of Boots," which had appeared in the *Independent Review* in December 1905. It is a most effective, and rather touching, discussion of human ills from the feet up, and is partly autobiographical.

> A very considerable part of my childhood was spent in an underground kitchen, the window opened upon a bricked-in space surmounted by a grating before my father's shop window. So that when I looked out of the window, instead of seeing, as children of higher upbringing would do, the heads and bodies of people, I saw their underside. I got acquainted with all sorts of social types as boots, simply, indeed as the soles of boots, and only subsequently and with care have I fitted heads and bodies and legs to these pediments.

Certainly, as G.B.S. said, whatever H. G. Wells writes is not only alive, but kicking. This article was later published as a Fabian special tract, but there were such delays (over a year) before publication, although Wells was paying the printer, that one Fabian suggested the title be changed to "This Misery of Wells," by H. G. Boots.

On February 9, the great controversy began. Wells read before the Society a paper entitled "Faults of the Fabian." E. R. Pease in his *History of the Fabian Society*, in his chapter "The Episode of Mr. Wells," notes that Wells complained that the society was still half a drawing-room society, lodged in a cellar, with one secretary and one assistant. Wells criticized it for lack of imaginative megalomania. Also for being so needlessly poor. "You have it from Mr. Bernard Shaw that poverty is a crime; if so, then by the evidence of your balance sheet ours is a criminal organization," Wells remarked, adding that in the United States such institutions as Columbia and the University of Chicago demonstrated the practicability of the remunerative sale of well-written books upon Socialism, while the Fabian society rested content with the publication of its sometimes admirable, often congested, insufficient, ill-written, and uninspiring penny tracts. He attacked the arid and undiscriminating catalogue of "what to read" and said that propaganda was quite the most vitalizing function of such a society as the Fabian. It gave every member something to do; if they could not speak, they could convene; if they could not persuade, they could lend books and tracts. Propaganda prevented the accumulation of a deadtail to the society of inactive members. "Your Committee," he complained, "discussed and dismissed as unfruitful the idea of accosting strangers and distributing tracts in a casual manner. But that would be only the first phase in making a convert. You neglect to go on with the half converted, and to attach and incorporate the converted. Partly this seems due to some odd, muddleheaded idea of keeping the Fabian Society 'select' but more to certain clumsinesses which surround the admission of members."

Wells took exception to the Fabian Basis, which he said, "ignores the express aim of Socialism to secure an ampler and nobler type of individual life, and a more beautiful way of living for all men and women. Its tone," he complained, "was materialistic, litigious, and not of such texture that our members may quote it with pleasure, learn it by heart for help and support or reread it with refreshment." For a revised basis he suggested emphasizing the idea that Socialism subordinates all private rights and property to the public welfare and that it further denies any private right of property whatever in human beings. Wells had already made exceedingly personal remarks about the Fabian Executive. "The personality that does reach the members is that of Mr. Pease," he had sneered. "It is impossible to ignore the role played by Mr. Pease in Fabian affairs. It is not too much to say that the powers and limitations of the Fabian Society so long as it is ruled upon its present lines, must necessarily follow the powers and limitations of Mr. Pease's character. What he can do, the Society can do, what he cannot, the Society cannot."

Wells felt the Fabian Society to be a waning organization: membership had dropped from 881 in 1899 to 730 in 1904. Some people objected then, too (as also later), to going into battle under the banner of an angry old-age pensioner. Wells decried the "constant flow of rather foolish laughter, or rather forced jesting. It flows over and obscures all sorts of grave issues, it chills and kills enthusiasm. . . . Our accursed giggle . . . an assumed pretence that this grave high business of Socialism, to which it would be a small offering for us to give our lives, is an idiotic middle-class joke." G.B.S. was the worst offender: the others copycatted Shaw. Wells also complained there was some deep feud between Pease and the Blands, and that G.B.S. often hesitated to act because of the dark riddle of "what the Blands would do about it." In his autobiography Wells said that by the time he came into the Society, Bland, an able politician, had established himself in the mind of Shaw as a necessary evil, and Pease as an unavoidable ally.

As a remedy for Fabian faults, Wells proposed larger and more commodious quarters, more and better-paid officials, and an active campaign for membership, which he declared would reach 10,000 in a year or so if properly handled —by him. He offered a "complete little gospeller's outfit," and added: "If I may make an unblushing proposal at this point, I would say that you had better give a good piece"— of the job of writing propaganda—"to me." Wells was impressed by the contrast between the small size of the Fabian Society and the large size of the Strand, in which its office was located. "Note the glare of the advertisements, note the abundance of traffic and the multitude of people . . . that is the world whose very foundations you are attempting to change. How does this little dribble of activities look then?" (No bigger, no doubt, than David did to Goliath.)

At the close of the meeting it was unanimously agreed that the Executive Committee be instructed to appoint a committee . . . to consider what measures should be taken to increase the scope, influence, income, and activity of the Society. The committee consisted, among others, of Mrs. Bernard Shaw, of H. G. Wells and his wife, and of Mrs. Pember Reeves. The committee met first on February 28, 1906, but did not present its report until October, as Wells had been away most of that time, lecturing in the U.S.A. Meanwhile the Parliamentary election of 1906, and the choice of Keir Hardie as leader of the Labor Party, gave point to many of H. G. Wells's criticisms: obviously, since Labor had arrived, and was now a political force supported, actively or passively, by the trade unions and other working-class organizations throughout the country, the Fabian Society should reappraise its relationship to Labor and its whole position in the Socialist movement. Mr. Pease notes that the Executive forwarded to the members the report of the committee, to which Mrs. Wells had acted as secretary, and which was also signed by Mrs. Bernard Shaw, among others—but accompanied it with a report of their own, "drafted by Bernard Shaw, and incomparably superior to the other as a piece of literature." But the real issue, as Mr. Pease notes, was a personal one: Was the Society to be controlled by those who had made it, or was it to be handed over to Mr. Wells? "We knew by this time that he was a masterful person, very fond of his own way, very uncertain what that way was, and quite unaware whither it necessarily led."

G.B.S. was in an equivocal position. He had sponsored Wells's entry into the Fabian Society; he admired him enormously as a novelist; he was "under well-founded suspicion of being too friendly to Wells," and certainly genuinely wanted to keep him a Fabian. But G.B.S. was also devotedly loyal to his old friends—of whom Pease was one—and he believed in such essentially Fabian tactics as permeation, and was prepared to fight for them. Wells had demanded, as G.B.S. said, "that the order of public meeting should be abolished, and he himself be both chairman and speaker when he addressed the public and, second, that the Fabian Society should pass a vote, not merely of censure, but of contempt, on its executive committee, in order that its old leaders should be compelled to resign and leave him sole Fabian Emperor." The trouble with Wells, as G.B.S. pointed out, was that he "is a spoiled child. His life has been one long promotion." The real issue between them was upstart Wells *versus* downstart Shaw. Wells called G.B.S. an ass, and lost his temper; G.B.S. treated him exactly as a gentleman treats an obstreperous valet. "There is," he wrote Wells, "an art of public life which you have not mastered, expert as you are in the art of private life. The fine part of private life consists almost wholly of taking liberties; the art of public life consists fundamentally in respecting political rights. Intimate as I am with Webb, I should no more dream of treating him as you have treated him than of walking into the House of Lords and pulling the Lord Chancellor's nose." [5]

Nor was that all: G.B.S. went on to try to cure H.G.'s platform manner by what he himself admits was a blow beneath the belt: he told Wells his terrible posture and delivery in public speaking came from his obsequiousness in the shop, from a lifetime of replying, "Anything more today, Madam?" Little wonder Wells exploded. And so, in his own quiet way, did G.B.S., who told the Fabians:

> The amendment by Mr. Wells is drawn in such a manner that if carried it will act as instructions to me and my colleagues on the executive committee . . . to resign

and not offer ourselves for re-election. Nothing but an overwhelming expression of opinion in a full meeting can avert the most serious consequences to the Society as matters cannot be settled by a mere majority in a small meeting.

Mr. Pease[6] gallantly admitted that at the full, general meeting on December 14, 1906, "Wells's speech, which occupied an hour and a quarter and covered the whole field, would have been great, had Mr. Wells been a good speaker. It was vigorous, picturesque, entertaining and imaginative, as his work always was." Wells has described his own delivery on this occasion: "myself speaking haltingly on the verge of the inaudible, addressing my tie through a cascading moustache that was no sort of help at all." At 9:00 P.M., G.B.S. replied to the whole debate. "Bernard Shaw's speech, probably the most impressive he has ever made in the Society, was delivered to a large and keenly appreciative audience in a state of extreme excitement," wrote Pease. G.B.S. related how Mr. Wells had complained of the long delay of the Old Gang in replying to his report. "But we took no longer than he," wrote Shaw. In a long letter to Wells, G.B.S. had already pointed out that Wells had taken a year to reply to the draft sent him for discussion by Webb and Shaw. During the committee's deliberations Wells produced a book on America. "And a very good book too," said G.B.S. He went on, "But whilst I was drafting our reply I produced a play." Here G.B.S. paused, glanced vacantly around the ceiling, and seemed to have lost his train of thought. When everyone was thoroughly uncomfortable he went on, "Ladies and gentlemen, I paused there to enable Mr. Wells to say, 'And a very good play too.' " The narrator of this incident describes how the assembled Fabians laughed and laughed and laughed. "Keats was snuffed out by an article; Wells was squelched by a joke." [7]

Later, G.B.S. "adroitly formulated Wells's real appeal to the society, which was to make a clean sweep of the Old Gang." [8] He declared that since Wells's amendment had been converted by his printed and circulated speech into a motion of want of confidence, if the amendment received one simple vote beyond those of its mover and seconder—Wells—G.B.S. and his colleagues would walk out, since Mr. Wells had asked the Society for an endorsement of his "wild description of the highly respectable and very efficient Old Gang as liars,

6 p. 174.
7 Hobson, pp. 106-07.
8 Henderson, p. 255.

tricksters, intriguers, die-hard reactionaries and enemies of the Socialist species generally." [9]

At the end of G.B.S.'s speech, H. G. Wells withdrew his amendment. Then the Executive Committee welcomed the co-operation of Mr. Wells and said that whilst they could not accept his report as a whole, they were willing to adopt any particular item after full discussion.

Twenty-six years later Wells[10] confessed that he had

> envisaged the reconditioned Fabian Society as becoming by means of vigorous propaganda mainly carried on by young people the direct element of a reorganised Socialist Party. The idea was as good as the attempt to realise it was futile. No part of my career rankles so acutely in my memory, with the conviction of bad judgment, gusty impulse and real, inexcusable vanity, as that storm in the Fabian teacup.

Some of the reforms for which Wells had pleaded—for example, making access into the Fabian Society as simple as into any political society, merely by joining, in fact, the encouragement of increasing membership merely for its own sake—came about. But the anticipated amelioration in the Society did not; on the contrary, the flooding or stuffing of the Fabian Society with the mere and the ordinary diluted its saltiness, removed its *raison d'être,* and led after a few years to a serious decline.

Sir Robert Ensor frankly declared to me that Wells's row with the Fabian Society was entirely due to Wells's inveterate habit of mixing pleasure with business. It was caused solely by

> his misconduct. Any attempt to cast an ideological veil over it is quite ridiculous and after the event. When Wells was brought into the Society by the Webbs, it was full of young people mostly engaged to each other. Among these was Amber Pember Reeves, the daughter of the New Zealand Government Agent. Wells had an illegitimate child by her, and then wrote a book about their affair, called *Ann Veronica.* Then he proceeded to have another affair with a daughter of Hubert Bland by a stray, one of those children brought up as her own by Mrs. Bland. Bland was a scamp clothed in a frock coat, striped trousers and a monocle, who preyed on his wife while having relations with other women. This Bland girl was engaged to Clifford Sharp, but Wells persuaded her to elope with

9 *Ibid.,* p. 254.
10 1934, p. 574.

him. Sharp found them together on a train at Paddington Station, and took the girl away. Thereupon Mrs. Pember Reeves and Hubert Bland—both of whose daughters had been seduced by Wells—were very angry, and said they would not attend executive meetings any more unless *Mrs.* Wells left the executive—which she did.

The illogicality of driving *Mrs.* Wells away because of her husband's conduct, which was like "a rabbit's—he even looked like a rabbit," as Sir Robert put it, does not seem to have occurred to the Fabians.

Wells's "paranoid" hatred of G.B.S. was not, according to Sir Robert, because G.B.S. called him a counter-jumper, but because of his own indiscretion. Bland had confessed to Wells that "I am a student, an expert, in illicit love." Wells notes that Bland was "sincerely disgusted at my disposition to take the moral fun out of his darling sins. My impulses were all to get rid of the repressions of sexual love, to minimise its import and to subordinate this stress between men and women as agreeably as possible to the business of mankind." In this case Wells proceeded to do this by telling Bland's illegitimate daughter about her father's pretty pastimes, and she, not unnaturally, repeated what Wells had told her to her father.[11] Wells then told Webb and Olivier of the girl's betrayal of his confidence to her, and they told G.B.S. Wells[12] admitted "the essential trouble of my life is its petty weaknesses." But he never forgave G.B.S. and later campaigned in Manchester for the Liberal candidate just because G.B.S. was backing the Labor man.

Actually, after his defeat in the Fabian Society, Wells tired of his excursion into Socialism and abandoned it altogether, although, luckily for the Fabians, he wrote several good books and pamphlets on the subject. The best of these, written while Wells was still a Fabian, was *New Worlds for Old*. He resigned from the Society in September 1908, explaining in his letter of resignation that: "I have had it in my mind that I might presently take part in a vigorous campaign for a revised Basis and a revived propaganda. But when I calculate the forces against such a campaign . . . I am forced to conclude that the effort is, for me at least, not worth making."

The essential difference between Shaw and Wells, as human beings, not as Socialists, is illustrated by Kingsley Martin's anecdote anent a certain correspondence between them which he wished to publish in the *New Statesman*. He asked both

11 *See* Note at the end of this chapter.
12 *First and Last Things*, p. 116.

their permissions, and from Wells got the reply "Of course you must make it public. GBS has behaved like a cad and ought to be exposed." Shaw wrote: "Certainly do not publish. I have the greatest respect for my old friend H. G. Wells. He has made a perfect ass of himself and I wouldn't like it put on permanent record."

Indeed, G.B.S. continued always to speak of Wells with the greatest kindness and courtesy, and to defend him when attacked. He refused an invitation from the *Daily Express* to write an obituary of Wells while living, to be published on his death, but Wells accepted the offer to do one of Shaw, and immediately after G.B.S.'s death, Wells's obituary appeared (Wells had predeceased Shaw by more than a decade), an uncivil blast, like a fart from a corpse, which added nothing to Wells's reputation. Yet, in spite of his breach with the Fabian Society, Wells made its views widely known in the United States, where his books had a tremendous sale and a considerable influence on the young. Indeed, it is through four Fabian writers—Shaw, Wallas, Wells, and Laski —that Fabianism "permeated" the United States, these four being avidly read in colleges and universities from the twenties on.

Until the New Deal era, when Franklin D. Roosevelt invented the fireside chat by radio, books influenced opinion even more in the States than in Europe, where personal influence was oftener a man than a book. For example, it was Henry George in person who influenced the Fabians; it was the Fabian writings—Shaw's *Major Barbara*, for example, and his other plays and Wells's Socialist novels— which brought Socialism in its English dress to the American campus. Wallas and Laski, too, though they both taught at Harvard, were tremendously read in universities several thousand miles from Cambridge, Massachusetts. Wallas's *Human Nature in Politics* and Laski's *A Grammar of Politics* educated and inspired many of the men who came to Washington in the New Deal years.

In England, too, Wells's campaign to widen and broaden Fabian membership, his journalistic flair, and his dramatic struggle with G.B.S. all publicized Fabian ideas, and brought many people into the Society. Pease, heaping coals of fire on Wells's head, admitted that in 1907 and 1908 the Society consisted largely of new members. Moreover "the propagandist enthusiasm of Mr. Wells and the glamour of his name had helped to attract a large number of distinguished people to our ranks." [13]

[13] Pease, p. 186.

The best epitaph on the Episode of Mr. Wells was written by George Standring, the Fabian Society's printer, and was entitled *Fables for Fabians No. X—The Frog*. The fable described how the frog emerged from his dark underground cellar into the bustle of the Strand, "and his heart became heavy within him, and he said, 'Lo, I must megalo.' So the frog increased by the patient and persevering inhalation of air, and busted. *Moral: All's well that ends Wells."*

NOTE

Nearly fifty years later, reviewing in the *New Yorker* (February 2, 1957), Henderson's life of Shaw and that of St. John Ervine together, one of Mr. H. G. Wells's children, Mr. Anthony West, accused the Webbs of circularizing the Fabian Society with the details of Wells's private affairs, apparently with the intention of destroying his reputation. Shaw, Mr. Anthony West said, liked both parties to the dispute, but felt that the Webbs' concept of the Society's role in affairs was the right one, and so, up to a point, became a consenting party to the campaign of slander. There seems to be no printed evidence of such statement or of such a campaign. The nearest Mrs. Webb gets in her diaries to mentioning Wells's private life (which his filial defender admits "was in some confusion at the time") is to comment that after hearing H. G. Wells end a lecture to the Fabian Society with an attack on the family, she read his *The Days of a Comet*, which, she says, "ends with a glowing anticipation of promiscuity in sexual relations. The argument is one that is familiar to most intellectuals—it has often popped up in my mind and has seemed to have some validity. Friendship between particular men and women has an enormous educational value to both, especially to the woman. Such a friendship is practically impossible . . . without physical intimacy; you do not, as a matter of fact, get to know any man thoroughly except as his beloved . . . if you could have been the beloved of the dozen ablest men you have known it would have greatly extended your knowledge of human nature and of human affairs. But there remains the question whether, with all the perturbation caused by such intimacies, you would have any brain left to think with. I know that I should not." (*Our Partnership,* pp. 359-60.)

In his *George Bernard Shaw, A Postscript*, Hesketh Pearson says that Shaw told him the Webbs had warned both Bland and Olivier to advise their daughters to keep clear of Wells, who would try to seduce them. In the case of Bland their warning came too late, and when Bland spoke to his daughter she calmly informed him that Wells had described *him* as a fearful roué. Bland was thereupon furious with Wells, who was furious with the Webbs. . . .

CHAPTER THIRTEEN

THE ONLY REALLY EFfective weapon of the press against Socialism is silence, G.B.S. noted in the 1908 reprint of *Fabian Essays,*[1] and the Fabians were painfully aware that although their lectures were crowded, were given by celebrities, and were financially successful, nary a one was ever covered by a single daily paper. Not a word about them "was allowed to leak through to the public through the ordinary channels of newspaper reporting." G.B.S. has described how the Society had permeated the Liberal press in the nineties, feeding it Fabian ideas:

> We collared the *Star* by a stage army stratagem and . . . had the assistant editor, Mr. H. W. Massingham, writing as extreme articles as Hyndman had ever written in *Justice.* Before the capitalist proprietors woke to our game and cleared us out, the competition of the *Star,* which was immensely popular under what I may call the Fabian regime, encouraged a morning daily, the *Chronicle,* to take up the running.

In 1899 the young Lloyd George, financed by George Cadbury and other Quakers, originated the anti-war syndicate which bought the *Daily News* and converted it to an antiimperialist, Liberal daily: the staff, Élie Halévy[2] noted, was Puritan as well as Radical.

In 1903, during the London education battle, inspired by Haldane "the *Times* came down on our side," as Beatrice put it, and for one glorious week, Sidney Webb himself dictated to the *Daily Mail.* He had written to Alfred Harmsworth, whom he had never met, when he was almost in despair of inducing the Cabinet to give London education to the LCC, telling him that the London M.P.'s would force the govern-

[1] p. 305.
[2] p. 108.

ment to give way, and why should not the *Daily Mail* take
the credit for making the government yield? Harmsworth
asked him round and then told him, "Very well, Mr. Webb,
we'll do it. But we don't know anything about the subject.
You must come in every night at 11 p.m., for a week, and
see that we say everything right." [3] Which, of course, Webb
did with the greatest pleasure.

But though these were triumphs and though Fabians wrote
a great deal, individually, and for almost all the current
"highbrow" weeklies, monthlies, and quarterlies, the Fabian
Society still had no organ of its own. In 1907, G.B.S. wrote,
"I and another person unknown to me put down £500
apiece to found a weekly magazine, to be called *The New
Age*, edited by my friend Holbrook Jackson and a mysteri-
ous man called Orage. The paper was in deep financial
straits from the moment this initial capital was spent, and
Jackson transferred his activities." Holbrook Jackson and
A. R. Orage in the same year also founded a Fabian arts
group that included philosophy (and, grumped E. R. Pease,
to tell the truth almost excluded Socialism).

This group met in Cliffords' Inn and included G.B.S., H. G.
Wells, Lowes Dickinson, Arnold Bennett, Gerald Gould, and
S. G. Hobson. "Bennett soon fell to puffery and log-rolling,
was squibbed and left in a huff," explained Beatrice Hastings, A. R. Orage's long-time mistress, who was assistant
editor at the *New Age*. She further declared that Orage's
"real and perfect passion" was to get into Parliament. Orage
has described Socialism as it was in England in 1907:

> Socialism was a cult, with affiliations in direction now
> quite disowned. With theosophy, arts and crafts, vege-
> tarianism, "the simple life." Morris had shed a medieval
> glamour over it with his stained glass *News from Nowhere*.
> Edward Carpenter had put it into sandals. . . . Cun-
> ninghame Graham had mounted it upon an Arab steed to
> which he was always saying a romantic farewell. Keir
> Hardie had clothed it in a cloth cap and red tie. And GBS,
> on behalf of the Fabian Society, had hung it with innumer-
> able jingling epigrammatic bells and cap. My brand of
> socialism was, therefore, a blend, or let us say an anthol-
> ogy, of all of these. [4]

Orage was essentially a pioneer in the world of ideas, but
it was generally assumed that the *New Age* would be a
Fabian organ, though only a few were aware that Shaw had

[3] Beatrice Webb, 1948, p. 258, n.
[4] Quoted in Mairet, p. 40.

helped to finance it. Sidney Webb, E. R. Pease, and H. G. Wells all contributed inaugural letters to the first issue. But the only trace of sectarianism was due to the editorial Fabian connection. Fabianism, in the first years, was never editorially attacked. Holbrook Jackson wanted the *New Age* to be geared to the middle class, to teach them Fabian Socialism and Fabian arts-group policy; Orage wanted it to be a Socialist *Spectator,* and even after Holbrook Jackson's departure, Orage remained Fabian on the whole. Orage, who came from very humble stock (one sister was a village postmistress, the other a housekeeper), presided over a sort of club at the Café Royal. He was a brilliant editor, and from the first day of the *New Age,* G. K. Chesterton and Hilaire Belloc rolled and wrestled all over the paper in warfare with G.B.S. and H. G. Wells. The "Chester-Belloc," as the doughty Catholic literary pair was called by G.B.S., openly abhorred the Fabians as arrogant, and despised them for trying to control the lives of the poor, which, they declared, could only lead to the Servile State. Some of the most successful Fabian debates ever held were between G.B.S. and Belloc, or G.B.S. and G. K. Chesterton. Mr. Harry Craven, a lifelong Fabian, says the best speeches he ever heard made in his life were during a debate between G.B.S. and G.K.C. on "A man who is not a socialist is no gentleman."

The Fabians and their challengers were gay in those days, when Chesterton and Belloc rode into the Savoy Hotel on donkeys demanding food, drink, and shelter for man and beast; when Belloc walked to Rome and G.B.S. bicycled to Land's End.

H. G. Wells wrote how G. K. Chesterton mocked valiantly and passionately against the oppressive and recurrent anticipation of himself in Socialist hands, hair clipped, meals of a strictly hygienic description at regular hours, a time for laughing, and austere exercises in several of the more metallic virtues daily. (Simone de Beauvoir's account of the daily routine of Red Chinese youth bears out this prophecy most accurately in 1958.) Max Beerbohm, who was as anti-Fabian as G.K.C., foresaw a Socialist state of an even more nightmarish nature: a hopeless, horrid flight from the present. Max said that Sidney Webb, whom Wells described as "like myself, both of us short inelegant men but for all that terribly resolute," indefatigably and incessantly tried to drag Max off to a mechanical Utopia, and there take his thumbmark, and his name; then number him distinctly in indelible ink and set him free to roam, under inspection of course, in a white, sanitary-tiled world.

J. Ramsay MacDonald accused G. K. Chesterton of having a "more than Fabian frigidity" but Chesterton has himself explained his views in his autobiography:

> I called myself a Socialist, because the only alternative to being a Socialist was not being a Socialist. And not being a Socialist was a perfectly ghastly thing. It meant being a small-headed and sneering snob, who grumbled at the rates and the working classes, or some hoary old Darwinian who said the weakest must go to the wall.

Certainly, however much G.K.C. might tilt at Fabians he has made them honorable amendment. "I have," he confessed, "in my time had my fling at the Fabian Society, at the pedantry, the schemes and the arrogance of experts, nor do I regret it now. But when I remember that other world against which it reared its bourgeois banners of cleanliness and common sense I will not end without doing it decent honor."

As well he might, for in 1907 Chesterton was himself a Fabian, as was his brother Cecil. As also was Eric Gill, who recalled those days when he wrote an obituary letter about A. R. Orage: "Nearly 30 years ago we met, Fabians both. We worked together on the Fabian Arts Group—we made vague efforts to deprive Fabianism of its webbed feet—vain efforts." [5] C. E. M. Joad led a procession of tram strikers to the Martyrs' Memorial while he was at Oxford, and was fined by the university authorities. He went daily out to Chipping Norton to address striking woodworkers, yet he hesitated to follow "our leader, G. D. H. Cole, who had already found the Fabians too slow, out of the Fabian fold." "My reluctance," he explained, "was due to G.B.S."

Among many currently well-known writers who were Fabians while young, are Robert Graves, who was one for two whole years at Oxford (a friend had put his name down, but he succeeded in never attending a meeting) and Ronald (later Monsignor) Knox, who joined the Fabians in 1907. Knox also joined a Socialist club run by his friend Charles Lister at Balliol (Lister had already joined the Labor Party at Eton), on condition that Lister join the Canning (the Balliol Conservative debating club). Together they had fun organizing a strike at a paper-bag factory at Banbury: Ronald Knox described himself as he was then:

> Conceive me if you can
> A fervid Etonian
> Anti-Gladstonian
> Down-with-the rich young man. [6]

[5] *New English Weekly*, Nov. 15, 1934.
[6] These facts I owe to the courtesy of Monsignor Knox's biographer, Mr. Evelyn Waugh.

D. H. Lawrence about this time was complaining that "in Croyden the Socialists are so stupid and the Fabians so flat." [7] Other Fabians of that era were G. M. Trevelyan, Patrick Braybrooke, St. John Ervine, and Hugh Dalton. This last avers he was a Socialist in the nursery, asking his nanny. "Who is the old lady picking up sticks?" Nanny replied, "That is an old woman, dear." Then asked Hugh, "Who is that old woman pouring tea?" "Hush, dear," replied Nanny, "that's a lady— that's your grandmama." Beatrice Webb's nephew, Stafford Cripps, and also the Woolfs, Leonard and Virginia, were other distinguished Fabians then at the beginning of their careers.

It is difficult for anyone today to realize how sheerly obstructive the Tories were, both in the brief Liberal Government of 1892-5 and in the triumphant Liberal Parliament of 1906-12. As Sir Robert Ensor points out, the Lords had used their veto power during the earlier, weak Liberal Administration to prevent the Liberals from carrying their bills. Then during the ten years of unionist rule, 1895-1905, the

> second chamber had as such, lain dormant, and allowed its power of revising bills to rust in almost complete disuse. Now it was to become wide-awake again, and to re-employ that power. Recalling the success of such tactics in 1883-5, Balfour even suggested that the House of Lords might be strengthened rather than weakened by a course of bill-wrecking.[8]

And he explains how practical men like Balfour and Lansdowne, the former of high and the latter of flexible intelligence, could be so shortsighted. Because both were aristocrats, born to the purple,

> they belonged to, they led in, and they felt themselves charged with the fortunes of, a small privileged class, which for centuries had exercised a sort of collective kingship, and at the bottom of its thinking instinctively believed that it had a divine right to do so. Passionately devoted to the greatness of England, these men were convinced she owed it to patrician rule. In their view, her nineteenth-century parliamentarism had worked successfully, because the personnel of parliament was still (with a few much-resented exceptions like John Bright) upper-class, and the function of the lower orders was limited to giving the system a popular *imprimatur* by helping to choose which of the two aristocratic parties should hold office.[9]

[7] Nehls, I, p. 134.
[8] Ensor, p. 387.
[9] *Ibid.*

Tory democrats believed that the more widely extended the franchise, the less chance the electorate would have of behaving as anything but an electorate, and the more the poor voted, the stronger would be the position of the popularly revered old families as against "middle-class upstarts run by dissenting shopkeepers." Men like Balfour and Lansdowne were therefore horrified by the 1906 election, which brought into the house fifty-three Labor M.P.'s, nearly all of whom had been manual workers and all of whom without exception had been reared in working-class homes. Worse still, as a result of this election, Lloyd George had been brought into the very Cabinet itself, and he the orphan son of an elementary schoolteacher, brought up by his uncle who was a village shoemaker. The great Tories quite sincerely could not believe that a House of Commons so composed and led, could effectively rule the nation; it was as contrary to nature as expecting a dray horse to win the Derby, or a common mongrel to course hares. "Scarcely distinguishing between the Constitution and the dominance of their own order, they felt justified in using any resource of the former . . . in order to crush the challenge to the latter." [10] But the newly victorious Liberals had had enough of privilege and of Balfour's golden oratory and their collective view was that "politics was a task for men, and not a sport for gentlemen." [11]

In this triumphant new government of 1906 the Liberals had 377 seats, a majority of 84 over all the other parties combined: the Conservatives had 132 and also counted as theirs 25 Liberal Unionists. Sir Robert Ensor says that more realistically the Members of Parliament should be classified as: 109 Chamberlainists, 32 Balfourians—although both Balfour and his brother lost their seats—and 83 Irish Nationalists under John Redmond. The 53 Labor members were divided into the 29 returned by the Labor Representation Committee to sit as an independent party and the other 24 who were ordinary Lib-Labs. Many of these were the officials of the miners' unions, elected like the Labor R.C. men on a class basis, though more cautious.

Socialism was now definitely in the general air; in May 1906, the French Chamber held 75 Socialists; in 1905, 300,000 Socialists had marched in perfect order in the Russian streets, and in 1906 in Denmark 76,566 Socialist voters—one quarter of the whole national poll—had sent 24 Socialist deputies to Parliament.

[10] *Ibid.*, p. 388.
[11] *Ibid.*, p. 391.

And how scared were the bourgeoisie! In his preface to the 1908 reprint of *Fabian Essays,* Shaw[12] describes how

> In 1906 a Fabian essayist stood one May morning in the Rue de Rivoli, and found himself almost the only soul in the west end of Paris who dared appear there. . . . There was much less danger of a revolution that day than there is of Primrose Hill becoming an active volcano at 6 P.M. this evening, and the purpose of the Government and its party newspapers in manufacturing the scare to frighten the bourgeoisie into supporting them at the general election just then beginning was obvious, one would have thought, to the dimmest political perspicacity. . . .

Lloyd George was very well aware that because of Gladstone's preoccupation with the Irish troubles, and Chamberlain's desertion of social welfare for tariff reform, Liberal social policy had been shelved for twenty years. He was therefore determined to enact all that Chamberlain had authorized, and more; in fact, to steal as much as he could of Fabian thunder. As R. K. Ensor[13] put it, "Had there been no home rule split, and had Chamberlain succeeded Gladstone as Liberal premier, social reform might have come to England twenty years sooner than it did. In that case the Labour Party—at least in the form which it actually took—might never have been born." But by the time Lloyd George had the majority he needed, Labor had been born and the Fabian Society had given it a program. All Lloyd George had to do was to follow up with legislation the outpouring of Fabian plans and blueprints, and to keep slightly ahead of the Labor Party barking at his heels.

The great Liberal budget of 1909, brought in by Lloyd George, around which, John Burns said, the Cabinet deliberated like "19 ragpickers around a 'eap of muck" brought in a national system of labor exchanges, children's allowances for payers of income tax; super-tax for the first time, and, above all, the land-value duties (20 per cent on the unearned increment of land value, to be paid when lands changed hands). Of these measures, R. K. Ensor wrote that their political value proved immense, both as slogans and as irritants.[14] This proposed 1909 budget scared the dukes so much that Cecil Chesterton described them as cutting down on their football subscriptions, and many capitalists threatened to emigrate to South America, carrying their railways and coal mines in their overcoat pockets.

12 p. xxxii.
13 p. 389.
14 *Ibid.,* p. 474.

But this great Liberal budget did not originate with the Liberals. Philip Snowden, the Labor Party's budget expert and a Fabian, had previously outlined a budget drawn up very much on Lloyd George's lines. For Lloyd George was a veering weathercock. The collectivist wind then was blowing, its air filling the nation's lungs with the heady breeze of social legislation, and he gyrated with it. But several of the Cabinet were already reefing their sails against the Socialist breezes. When Lloyd George brought in his insurance scheme, Charles Masterman and John Burns openly went about boasting that the best thing about the insurance scheme was that it had "spiked the Webb guns" and "dished the Webbs," by taking all the wind out of their sails. Certainly, Lloyd George, Winston Churchill, and Asquith too had picked the Webb brains at a series of breakfasts and lunches, to some purpose. The Webbs were under no illusion as to why they were asked out so much. Beatrice knew that in political life the Arab adage is true, "When they asked the ass to the wedding it replied, 'Is it to grind the corn or draw water?'" and she estimated their influence on legislation shrewdly, by the number of invitations she and Sidney received. At this time, her diaries are full of daily entries recording being "dined and wined" by various members of the Liberal Cabinet, none of whom, however, except for Haldane, she regarded as friends.

During these triumphantly Liberal years, Winston Churchill, then president of the Board of Trade, was another frequent visitor at the Webbs' table, and a real leader in social reform. When, in 1906, Herbert Gladstone, one of the sons of the great Prime Minister, as Home Secretary jibbed at accepting the principle of a legal minimum wage, the bill, in the more radical hands of Winston Churchill, passed during the next session. Winston had started as a Tory, and had crossed the floor of the house on tariff reform. He was to return to the Tory fold after World War I, but his radical interlude was a glorious one. Beatrice Webb thought that "to put Asquith and Lloyd George and Winston Churchill dead in front of Joe on the tariff and the colonies . . . are apt placements." Beatrice Webb had begun by finding Winston "restless, egotistical, bumptious, shallow-minded and reactionary, but with a certain personal magnetism, great pluck and some originality, not of intellect but of character. More of the American speculator than the English aristocrat." But by 1908 she was approving a really eloquent speech on the unemployed he had made the night before, and noted that he had mastered the Webb scheme, though not going the whole length of compulsory labor exchanges. "He is brilliantly able . . . and is definitely casting in his lot with the constructive state action." [15] A few days later, after breakfasting with Lloyd George, she wrote of the latter, "He has less intellect than Winston, and not such an attractive personality, more of the preacher, less of the statesman."

But perhaps the most important result of the Webbs' relationship with Winston was their telling him, "If you are going to deal with unemployment, you must have the boy Beveridge." The Webbs than gave a luncheon to introduce the two to each other, and Lord Beveridge later acknowledged that the access to the seat of power was given him mainly by the Webbs. "They owed both things—time for thought and social contact with power—to Beatrice's possession of £1000 a year from her father. Where will the next generation of young reformers find their Webbs?" [16]

However, the scheme produced out of his Welsh wizard's hat by Lloyd George after many consultations with the Webbs and with other Fabians, too, such as Morant and Beveridge, was financially antithetic and antipathetic to the Webbs' collectivist ideas, which were to be financed entirely out of general taxation. There was here too, as in the case of the Shaw-Wells conflict, a clash of personalities: the pragmatic, reasonable, logical Webbs found the Welsh witch, as Maynard Keynes dubbed Lloyd George, incomprehensible and unendurable. Keynes[17] has described Lloyd George as a *femme fatale,*

> this syren, this goat-footed bard, this half-human visitor to our age from the hag-ridden magic and enchanted woods of Celtic antiquity—one catches in his composition that final purposelessness, inner irresponsibility, that existence outside or away from our Saxon good and evil, mixed with cunning, remorselessness, and love of power.

And Keynes went on,

> he is rooted in nothing; he is void and without content; he lives and feeds on his immediate surroundings; he is an instrument and a player at the same time . . . he is a prism which collects light and distorts it, and is most brilliant if the light comes from many quarters at once; a vampire and a medium in one.

Against this mercurial minister were the "two typewriters that clicked as one"—Sidney, who "thought instinctively in terms of state and municipal action and of public administra-

---

[15] Beatrice Webb, 1948, p. 417.
[16] Beveridge, p. 70.
[17] 1933, p. 36.

tion," and Beatrice, "much more of a philosopher, for whom democratic local government was a bridge between the public and the private spheres of social action." [18]

From 1907 to 1912 the Fabian Society was the standard-bearer of Socialism in Britain—it was said then that all new political movements began in the Fabian Society, as all Spanish revolutions began in Barcelona.

The Fabian Society at that time was largely made up of new members, many of whom already showed the promised brilliance that later carried them to great heights: among these were Arthur Henderson, Philip Snowden and his wife —they met at a Fabian meeting at Leeds—William Temple (later Archbishop of Canterbury), Leo Chiozza Money, L. S. Amery, Aylmer Maude, Harold Laski, R. H. Tawney, Jerome K. Jerome.

At the same time the Fabian Women's Group, the Fabian Nursery (started by the young Blands, who had every reason to wish to escape the overmastering presence of the elderly and experienced),[19] and the University Fabian Societies all burgeoned.

The leadership of the Labor Party, as it soon came to be called, in the House of Commons devolved on Keir Hardie, and, indeed, the Parliamentary Labor Party may be said to be his creation. G.B.S. described him as

> a simple fellow. He couldn't understand how Sir Edward Grey could tell the most appalling lies without a flicker of shame, and then leave the House of Commons with the impression that it was his opponent was the liar. Keir Hardie was not adroit, he could not handle people . . . the very opposite of J. Ramsay MacDonald.[20]

Keir Hardie, who was most violent in debate, was a most reasonable and conciliatory committee man. He muttered, "Well-fed beasts," when Conservatives interrupted him in debate, and declared he would not belong to any club of which Lord Salisbury was a member—thus proving himself equal to any Tory in class consciousness. Indeed, G.B.S. called him "the damnedest aristocrat of the lot." Only once in his life did he put on evening dress—when he was in France for a congress of the Second International, Jean Jaurès sent him tickets for the opera. Hardie borrowed a tuxedo and a scarf from the waiter in the *bistro* where he was dining, and arrived to find he was the only man in the whole opera who had changed.

[18] G. D. H. Cole, 1956, p. 210.
[19] Pease, p. 196.
[20] Pearson, p. 110.

Before the 1906 election it had been said that: "Socialism
was little more than a middle-class fad. It had no existence
outside of debating societies, Trade Unions, and obscure borough councils. It had no organic connection with the world
outside. Socialism, in brief, was Fabianism, and Fabianism
was mainly talk." [21] It was Keir Hardie who changed all that.

After 1906 the question of the propriety of Socialists standing as Liberals, or giving support to Liberals, became increasingly acute. From 1906 to 1910 the Labor members'
position in Parliament was that of a left wing to the enormous
Liberal majority. Labor candidates had by then been elected
as Liberals for over twenty-five years; very few indeed had
been elected only by Labor votes. Many sat for two-member
constituencies, sharing both votes and representation with a
Liberal; most of the others had won in a straight fight over
the Conservative candidate, in seats uncontested by a Liberal, so had received at least as many Liberal as Labor votes.
Yet even in the beginning some delegates wished membership
in the Labor Party forbidden to any member of the organization connected with any other political body. This *Clarion*
group put forward a resolution (known as the Fourth Clause)
declaring, "All members of the ILP shall pledge themselves
to abstain from voting as candidate for election for anybody
who is in any way a nominee of the Liberal, Liberal Unionist
or Conservative Party" and this "Fourth Clause" became a
hardy annual at Labor Party Conferences, always raised by a
steadfast group of *Clarionettes*.

Pease mentions as a reason for the "anomaly" of the Fabian Society as a whole being affiliated to the Labor Party,
while some of its members were Liberal Members of Parliament, the fact that the Labor Representation Committees
had been founded as a group, and not as a party. The trade
unions affiliated to the Labor Party were in the same position.
He adds that in several instances the same member who first
tried to get the Fabian Society to expel all members who
worked with any party other than the Labor Party, then
shortly after suggested the Fabian Society should leave the
Labor Party altogether—a comical example of human political inconsistency. Robert Blatchford, then president of the
Manchester Fabians, produced a resolution that no member
was acceptable who was a member of either the Liberal or
Conservative parties. This was heresy to the London Fabians.

G.B.S. delightfully mocked those "simon-pure" Fabians who
would not demean themselves by working with anyone but
Labor candidates. "When I think of my own unfortunate char-

[21] Raymond, p. 354.

acter," he wrote, "smirched by compromise, rotted with opportunism, mildewed by expediency, blackened by ink contributed to Tory and Liberal papers, dragged through the mud of Borough Councils, stretched out of shape with wire-pulling, putrefied by permeation, worn out by 25 years pushing to gain an inch here or straining to stem back a rush there, I think John Burgess might have put up with just a speck or two on those white robes of his. . . ." [22]

But the Fabian Sir Henry Slesser worried because the ILP excluded all who were not loyal to the Labor Party, and the Webbs also boggled when a Liberal M.P. was elected to the Executive of the Fabian Society at the same time that Harry Snell at Huddersfield, Will Crooks at Woolwich, and Stephen Sanders at Battersea (all straight radicals) were all also Fabian-supported candidates. At the 1912 Labor Party Conference, St. John Ervine asked awkward questions: "Is it decent for an officer of a party to speak for the opponent of a nominee of that party? May a Fabian work for the return of a Liberal in the interests of Socialist legislation?"

The Labor Party's spectacular success in forcing its own Trades Disputes Bill onto the Liberal Party, and getting it past the vast Conservative majority in the House of Lords made even such men as Haldane declare that "we had underestimated the extent to which the Labour spirit had operated on the candidates at the (1906) election." Labor might thereafter be only a pendant to the triumphant Liberals, but it was the tail that wagged the dog. Keith Hutchison[23] declared that the outpouring of social legislation during the period from 1906 to 1917 makes it comparable to the New Deal era in the United States. Old-age pensions, the enactment of an eight-hour day for miners, the institution of trade boards to regulate conditions in sweated industries, the provision of labor exchanges, progress in public housing, and town planning . . . each of these measures added a new brick to the rising structure that Beatrice Webb called "the housekeeping state." And while Labor cannot take all the credit for these measures, the Liberals, had the Labor members not been breathing hotly down their necks, would never have dared sponsor them, for the Liberal leader was the vacillating wait-and-see Asquith, with his bland and weary face, in which frankness and reserve had long fought themselves to a standstill.[24] Lloyd George without Labor prodding from the rear would have achieved far less.

[22] Quoted from a letter regarding Burgess, in Joad.
[23] p. 93.
[24] Dangerfield, p. 4.

Today it is hardly possible to realize what a hard time Labor had in reaching the English people. Keir Hardie, who intuitively felt that a beginning must be made with throwing the Liberal rider off the trade-union horse, was the first "working man" to think in terms of the Labor Party as His Majesty's loyal Opposition. "Nicknamed Queer Hardie . . . he serenely was wending his way, destroying Liberal-Labourism, and giving the British working class an independent political existtence." [25] The crucial difference ten years had made in feeling can be gauged by the fact that in 1897 at Barnsley, a mining town in Yorkshire, the ILP candidate, Peter Curran, was opposed by a Liberal employer *and* a Conservative. The local miners' leaders worked for the Liberal. The ILP candidate was stoned by the miners and mobbed by their women and children, whistling and yelling and shouting him down. Ten years later, Peter Curran got into Parliament as M.P. for Jarrow, and in 1908 the Miners' Federation, which had opposed him, joined the Labor Party. But the assumption that the working class will vote Labor is one that can never be made in England. I remember when I was official Labor Party candidate for St. George's, Westminster, in the 1935 election and thought I would get some votes from the working-class homes in the slums of Pimlico down by the river (flooded in winter and rat-ridden), Herbert Morrison, the Labor "boss" of London and a very wise man, told me the only votes I would get were above stairs in the big houses in Belgravia, and how right he was!

[25] Beer, II, p. 311.

CHAPTER FOURTEEN

IN 1900 THERE HAD BEEN only 62,698 Labor voters in England. The Reform Bill of 1832 had established a businessman's world, in which his unlimited economic possibilities were secured to him by legislation, and thereafter England in the nineteenth century became the leading mercantile and banking power in the world. As the fifteenth-century civil wars in England had ended the feudal, hierarchical type of society, by eliminating so many people that the value of labor rose to unprecedented heights, so the seventeenth-century wars disposed of Tudor absolutism, "by proving no king divine without his head." The Napoleonic wars freed the commercial classes from whatever vestiges of aristocratic control had survived the French Revolution. Thereafter, the wasteful horrors of unlimited cutthroat competition, bringing with them a terrible deterioration of the standard of living of the laboring classes, together with an immense increase in their numbers and in their purchasing power, resulting from the Industrial Revolution, brought into dangerous juxtaposition employers ever more dependent on a cheap supply of labor, and laborers richer and yet more miserable than ever before. The friction between the employed whose labor was necessary to the capitalist, and the capitalist whose plant or industry was necessary to the worker, led to the increasing participation of the trade unions in political action. But the natural conservatism of the British workingman is so strong, as is his dislike of the new, commercial middle classes (far harder taskmasters than the aristocracy, which paid less in wages and gave more in comfort—a house, a garden, produce, coal, water, often food) that the final conversion of the trade unions to the Labor Party had to be completed, as it had been begun, by the Tories themselves. For the British worker is naturally agin' Liberal bourgeoisie far more than he is against the Tory nobility or gentry. Had the Conservatives not deliberately antagonized the trade unions, first by the Taff Vale decision, which drove many unions to affiliate with the ILP, and then by the Osborne case, the trade unions might never have "gone Labor" at all, but might well have remained marginal to politics, as have the co-operatives. Until World War I, the trade unions of five countries—France, Great Britain, Italy and the United States, accounted for more than three-fourths of the trade union membership of the entire world.

At the time of the Taff Vale decision, both Houses of Parliament had been Tory; at the time of the Osborne case, it was the House of Lords' judges alone who single-handedly made it illegal for a trade union to provide for the salaries of its parliamentary representatives by compulsory contribution from all members. This completed the work Fabian propaganda had failed to do. One W. V. Osborne, heavily financed by his capitalist employers, took action against the Amalgamated Society of Railway Servants, of which he was a member. He wished to restrain it from spending any of its funds on political objects, declaring that this was beyond its powers as a trade union. The case was debated for more than a year, and on December 21, 1909, the law lords judged that the ASRS must not use funds for political objectives and must not levy contributions to help the Labor Party pay the election expenses of Labor Members of Parliament. The Webbs underlined the injustice of this judgment by their understatement: "That it should be illegal for the salaried president of the ASRS to sit in Parliament when it is perfectly legal for the much more generously salaried Chairman or Director of a Railway Company to do so is an anomaly hard for any candid man to defend." The Osborne decision almost wrecked the Labor Party financially, for the trade unions affiliated to it had been its main source of contributions toward meeting the election expenses of candidates, or for paying salaries to Labor-elected Members of Parliament. The clamor for remedial legislation was immediate and sustained, but "the Asquith Government, while promising eventual redress, was not sorry to see the Labour Party handicapped, and found reasons for delaying action." [1] The Finance Act of 1911, which began the payment of salaries to MPs from public funds, was some mitigation, but it was only by the Trade Union Act of 1913 that unions were allowed to set up special political funds, provided authorization had been given by a ballot of members.

The Second Annual Conference of Fabian Societies and Groups opened on July 6, 1907, under Hubert Bland's chairmanship. He began by recalling the First Annual Conference

[1] Hutchison, p. 99.

held way back in 1892. In 1908 the Third Annual Conference, attended by H. G. Wells, debated the ticklish problem of co-operation with the Labor Party. "A resolution favouring exclusive support of independent Socialist candidates was thrown out by a large majority, but another advocating preference for such candidates was only defeated by 26 to 21." [2]

The Fabian Society had made a careful study of the birth rate, the first and for a long time (until after World War I) the only statistical inquiry made on the subject. It was based on a survey of 316 marriages, and showed that from 1890-9 out of 120 marriages only 6 fertile marriages were recorded in which birth-control methods of one kind or another had not been used. This brought before the British public a fact of which they had hitherto been unaware; that probably the chief cause of the fall in the birth rate was the voluntary limitation of families. Sidney Webb published the available evidence in two special articles in *The Times* in October 1906. These were the great days of Fabian Tracts. G.B.S.'s *Rent and Value* and his *Fabianism and the Fiscal Question;* Henry W. Macrosty's *The Revival of Agriculture,* and his *State Control of Trusts;* (Sir) Leo Chiozza Money's *Riches and Poverty;* Percy Dearmer's *Socialism and Christianity;* and Sidney Webb's *The Necessary Basis of Society* all appeared and sold like hot cakes.

"But the *magnum opus* of Fabian reform is the Minority Report written by Mr. and Mrs. Sidney Webb, as the *Report of the Royal Commission on the Poor Law,* 1909," wrote Max Beer.[3] And E. R. Pease notes that the transformation of Mrs. Webb from a student and writer, "a typical Socialist of the chair," into an active leader and propagandist originated in December 1905, when she was appointed by the outgoing Conservative government (and actually personally by her friend Arthur Balfour, then Prime Minister), a member of the Royal Commission on the Poor Law. The Fabian Society "had nothing to do with the work of the Commission during the four years of the latter's labors, though as usual not a few Fabians took part in the work, both officially and unofficially." But from this point on, Mrs. Webb was on the whole the dominant personality in the Society.[4] She was elected to the Executive, however, only in 1912, in absentia, while on her world tour. Beatrice Webb's colleagues on the Royal Commission on the Poor Law included her former boss and cousin, Charles Booth, from whom she had become quite es-

[2] Pease, p. 198.
[3] II, p. 289.
[4] Pease, p. 214.

tranged since her marriage to a Socialist, and two Socialist members out of a total of twenty; George Lansbury, a fellow Fabian, and Francis Chandler, general secretary of the Amalgamated Society of Carpenters.

Arthur Balfour, who had appointed them all, explained to Beatrice that the Committee's chairman, Lord George Hamilton, was "not such a fool as he looks." Balfour made this remark when lunching with Beatrice and Sidney before going to see G.B.S.'s *Major Barbara,* which Beatrice castigated as "amazingly clever, grimly powerful, but ending . . . in an intellectual and moral morass."

The English Poor Law, as amended by the Poor Law Amendment Act of 1834, depended on three principles. That of *less eligibility*—i.e., that any able-bodied recipient of state aid should have a situation less eligible—that is, more uncomfortable—than the independent laborer of the lowest class. If the "condition of the pauper is ever elevated above the condition of independent labourers, the condition of the independent class is depressed, their industry is impaired, their employment becomes unsteady . . . such persons then received the strongest inducements to quit the less eligible class of laborers and enter the more eligible class of paupers." So read the law, and the first requisite of Poor Law administration had been constantly to scale down relief. The second principle was *national uniformity:* that paupers should be treated identically in town and country, and from parish to parish, to prevent discontent and to prevent them from shopping around trying to find the pleasantest or the least disagreeable officials and work hours. The third principle was the complete substitution of indoor for outdoor relief; every pauper was to be forced into the "workhouse" prior to receiving any relief at all. The new commission was predominantly a body of experts, either in Poor Law administration or social investigation, and during its first year of office, it drifted away "from being an enquiry into the disease of pauperism, into an investigation of the disease of destitution." [5]

Beatrice Webb infuriated her colleagues by more or less engineering the evidence in her own direction, as she described it,[6] and by making her own investigations at her own expense. The Commission's chairman actually asked her to give up such investigating on her own account, and for reply Beatrice gently but firmly said she was going to continue basing herself on the practice of the royal commissions and select committees she had known. Beatrice, as an observer of hu-

[5] Beatrice Webb, 1948, p. 369.
[6] *Ibid.,* p. 370.

man nature, was interested to find that she herself had become wholly indifferent to the Commission. She merely worked as hard as she knew how in her own direction without caring much what happened. She found herself perpetually watching her colleagues, dashing in when she saw an opening —she sometimes pushed or squeezed through, sometimes the door was jammed in her face—and she accepted either fate with equal equanimity. At first she confessed she had been so horribly sensitive to their dislike. Actually Beatrice with her Fabian crew of workers was preparing the ground for all the unemployment relief measures that have been passed since 1909 for the social disease of unemployment. That they all felt that somehow or another this disease ought to be treated outside the Poor Law was the dark background shadow against which the Commission worked. Lord George tried to forbid Beatrice to show her own productions to anyone else —but he was shutting the stable door after the horse had bolted, for "at present my two reports are being read by a committee of the cabinet," she wrote happily in October 1908. The Webbs started a newspaper campaign for "the break-up of the poor-law" and let L. S. Amery (then of the *Times*) have their Poor Law scheme. The *Times* printed the whole scheme—the last part verbatim. This, which Beatrice admitted was "a really indiscreet use of our composition" roused Lord George Hamilton to fury, but "the net result of our indiscreet, or as some would say, unscrupulous, activity has been to damage the Webbs but to promote their ideas." The government sent Haldane round in his car to the Webbs' house to ask whether they would object to the Cabinet's seeing their report. "Certainly not, I replied." [7]

The Royal Commission members really behaved very childishly, suggesting they would only provide Mrs. Webb with one set of her own proofs, to work on. "Tell the chairman," she sent word grandly, "that on the day I am refused the number of proofs that I think necessary for efficient working, the report goes off to my private printer, *and if that happens I will not be responsible for the consequences.*" Every one of the Royal Commission members seemed to be disgusted at the "amateurish, blotchy, majority report." "But what was the alternative? Mrs. Webb's dissent," said one disconcerted commissioner to the other. For the Webb document stared at them in a blue cover—300 pages of reasoned stuff with a scheme of reform at the end.

Work on the Royal Commission ended in 1909, and from that spring until the summer of 1911, the Fabian Society and the Webbs campaigned for the Minority Report. G.B.S., the Webbs, and the secretary, E. R. Pease, the de facto rulers of the Fabian Society, as A. R. Orage called them, threw themselves heart and soul into the formation of a National Committee for the Promotion of the Break-up of the Poor Law, inaugurated in May 1909. In 1910 the title was changed to the National Committee for the Prevention of Destitution. The Minority Report was drafted by Sir Henry Slesser at Sidney Webb's request. Two days before the bill was to be introduced in the House, Slesser got a telegram from Sidney: "We have forgotten the Scilly Isles"—showing Webb's minute attention to detail. The Minority Report was signed by Beatrice Webb, George Lansbury, the Rev. Russell Wakefield (late Bishop of Birmingham), and F. Chandler. E. R. Pease[8] describes what followed:

Mr. and Mrs. Webb reprinted the Minority Report with an introduction and notes in two octavo volumes, and they lent the Society the plates for a paper edition in two parts at a shilling and two shillings, one dealing with Unemployment and the other with the reconstruction of the Poor Law, some 6000 copies of which were sold at a substantial profit. The Treasury Solicitor was rash enough to threaten us with an injunction on the ground of infringement of the Crown copyright, and to demand an instant withdrawal of our edition. But Government Departments which try conclusions with the Fabian Society generally find the Society better informed than themselves, and we were able triumphantly to refer the Treasury Solicitor to a published declaration of his own employers, the Lords Commissioners of the Treasury, in which they expressly disclaimed their privilege of copyright monopoly so far as ordinary blue books were concerned, and actually encouraged the reprinting of them for the public advantage. And, with characteristic impudence, we intimated also that, if the Government wished to try the issue, it might find that the legal copyright was not in the Crown at all, as the actual writer of the Report, to whom alone the law gives copyright, had never ceded his copyright and was not a member of the Royal Commission at all. At the same time we prepared to get the utmost advertisement out of the attempt to suppress the popular circulation of the Report, and we made this fact known to the Prime Minister. In the end the Treasury Solicitor had to climb down and withdraw his objection. What the Government did was to undercut us by publishing a still cheaper edition, which did not stop our sales, and thus the public

8 *Op. cit.*

benefited by our enterprise, and an enormous circulation
was attained for the Report. The Minority Report . . .
though never, from first to last, mentioning Socialism, was
a notable and wholly original addition to Socialist theory,
entirely of Fabian origin. Hitherto, all Socialist writings on
the organisations of society, whether contemporary or
utopian, had visualised a world composed exclusively of
healthy, sane, and effective citizens, mostly adults. No
Socialist had stopped to think of how, in a closely popu-
lated and highly industrialised Socialist community, we
should provide systematically for the orphans, the sick, the
mentally or physically defective and the aged on the one
hand, and on the other, for the adults for whom at any
time, no immediate employment could be found. The Minority Report, whilst making immediately practicable proposals for the reform of all the evils of the Poor Law,
worked out the lines along which the necessary organisation must proceed, even in the fully socialised State.
We had, in the Fabian Society, made attempts to deal
with both sides of this problem, but our publications,
both on the Poor Law and the unemployed, had lacked the
foundation of solid fact and the discovery of new principles, which the four years work of the Fabians connected
with the Poor Law Commission now supplied.

The discreet editorial "we" of E. R. Pease here alludes to
the fact that the manuscript of the Minority Report was in
Sidney Webb's handwriting and thus "presumably, he himself
held the copyright." [9] Raymond Postgate[10] has pointed out
that no one has ever questioned the fact that Sidney Webb
wrote the actual text of the report. Only then perhaps did the
Treasury realize what a bargain the Royal Commission had
got by appointing Beatrice Webb and getting Sidney for free
. . . or perhaps it might be more accurate to say, for good
measure.

Beatrice has herself described the National Committee for
the Prevention of Destitution: "We started out with a small
staff of paid assistants and rapidly enrolled a large body of
voluntary organisers, journalists and lecturers, together with
some 20,000 members, contributing an income for office expenses of over £ 5,000 a year." [11]

Nor were the 20,000 members all Labor, or even all Socialists; Conservatives, Liberals, Nonconformist ministers,
bishops and other Church of England dignitaries, peers, and

[9] Margaret I. Cole, 1945.
[10] p. 89.
[11] Beatrice Webb, 1948, p. 422.

even Catholic priests were among them; in short, the National Committee claimed to be a non-party organization. When the National Committee named a National Conference for the Prevention of Destitution which opened in May 1911, with a mammoth meeting at the Albert Hall, the opening resolution was proposed by Mr. Arthur Balfour (Conservative!), seconded by Sir John Simon (Liberal—at that time Solicitor-General), and supported by Mr. J. Ramsay MacDonald. "To get these three leaders of the three political parties to formally adopt the policy of the national minimum of civilised life, was an apparent success for our cause. But looking back on it, I am inclined to think that it was a little too clever. It lost us the friendship of the Conservative leader, and did little to gain us any general support from the Liberal and Labour leaders, neither of whom were our personal friends," Beatrice Webb admitted.[12]

In fact, the apparent success was, temporarily at least, a total failure. For another eighteen years the defenders of the *status quo* maintained their position all along the line.[13] Moreover, the tremendous battery of Fabian agitation for the Minority Report meant that the Majority Report of which Beatrice had been so fearful ("the majority have got a magnificent reception," she had gloomed) was shelved—it was never "even considered to be a basis of discussion." Yet Beatrice was to realize that her real enemies were those who wished to maintain the status quo: "In our depreciation of the Majority Report . . . we overlooked the immense step which would have been made by sweeping-away of the deterrent poor law, in name, at any rate; and to some extent in substance, by municipalising its control."

Mary Agnes Hamilton first met Beatrice when campaigning for the Majority report. "She was magnificent in a great hat with ostrich feathers and of course swept her audience . . . she was not only a far better speaker but had a far better case" and she converted Mary Agnes there and then![14]

Le mieux est l'ennemi du bien—better is good's enemy, and Beatrice early admitted she felt a trifle foolish at having crabbed the Majority Report to her family and intimate friends and exalted at its expense the Minority Report. Yet during the first year of agitation the Webbs were wildly optimistic and were well served by the *Crusade*, the monthly magazine they founded as the publicity and propaganda organ of Beatrice's

12 *Ibid.*, p. 476.
13 *Ibid.*, p. 477.
14 Hamilton, 1944, p. 256.

committee. It appeared from February 10, 1910, and ran until February 1913, increasing from twelve to thirty-six pages during that time, under the very able editorship of Clifford Sharp. In April 1913 appeared the first issue of the *Crusade's* successor, the *New Statesman,* also edited by Clifford Sharp. This, still today gloriously Fabian, was to become the best-hated and best-loved weekly published in England—perhaps in English.

The trouble with the Minority Report agitation was that the Webbs, with their 20,000 signatories (which included all the members of the Fabian Society), overreached themselves. The *status quo* party were presided over by Beatrice's former chairman, Lord George Hamilton, who "foamed at the mouth" when she was mentioned, and they included representatives of the existing Boards of Guardians and also John Burns, then president of the Local Government Board, who was the Minority Report's bitterest enemy, for he regarded it as a censure on himself. These opponents gathered themselves into the National Poor Law Reform Association. Thereafter propaganda to retain and enlarge the power of the extant authority (the Boards of Guardians) altogether eclipsed the allied propaganda for the Majority Report. The Webbs, in their *English Poor Law Policy* wrote their own epitaph for their two years of "raging, tearing propaganda, lecturing or speaking five or six times a week."

> Our agitation, powerful as it became, was destined to be unfruitful in the political field. The Liberal Cabinet remained unfriendly to any legislative reform of the poor law. . . . Meanwhile Mr. Lloyd George, the most powerful force in the government, had become enamoured of an entirely distinct method of dealing with poverty, and was pressing forward the vast scheme of sickness insurance, to which the initial experiment in unemployment insurance promoted by Mr. Winston Churchill was eventually attached. Although these schemes of social insurance left untouched both the evils and the cost of the poor law . . . they presently absorbed the whole attention, not only of the Cabinet and the Legislature, but also of the public. All the steam went out of the movement for extinguishing the Boards of Guardians and transferring their powers to the county and municipal authorities and to the national government, whether according to the prescriptions of the majority or those of the minority.

But the Local Government Act of 1929, sponsored by Conservative Neville Chamberlain, then Minister of Health, in effect adopted the functional approach to the relief of destitution which the Webbs had advocated twenty years before in the Minority Report. It abolished the Boards of Guardians, transferring most of their duties to the county and borough councils, whose public health and education committees, in co-operation with new public-assistance committees, became responsible for destitute children and the destitute sick. "The Minority Report, read today, wears an air of major prophecy." For the Fabians it bridged the gap between the palliatives, dilatory and doled-out piecemeal, such as the eight-hour day, the child-labor acts, school meals, and pit-head baths, and Socialism, "the organisation of industry by the community for the community . . . which was obviously far off." [15] G. D. H. Cole[16] wrote: "The Minority Report of the Poor Law Commission is indeed a landmark: it is the first full working out of the conception and policy of the Welfare State, more comprehensive, because covering a wider ground, than the Beveridge Report of 1942, which in many respects reproduced its ideas."

Lloyd George's successful national-insurance scheme was gradually supported by the trade unions, which, like friendly society and insurance companies, could administer the benefits provided, thus increasing their influence by patronage. They were, also, in some selected industries, the administering authority for unemployment benefits, and were therefore categorically and professionally against collectivization. However, the Fabians were not the only Socialists who opposed Lloyd George and his elaborate web to trip the Webbs: a section of the ILP joined the Fabians in a vigorous campaign to defeat the bill. E. R. Pease was not pleased:

> This was a new role for the Society. Usually it has adopted the principle of accepting and making the best of what has already happened. . . . The Labour Party decided to . . . recognise the Insurance Bill as a great measure of social reform, and to advocate amendments. The Fabian Society attacked the bill . . . magnified its administrative difficulties, and generally encouraged the duchesses and farmers who passively resisted it; but their endeavour to defeat the Bill was a failure.

The duchesses actually came up from the country to address meetings at the Albert Hall, begging the people not to "lick stamps." But all in vain. Lloyd George won. And as Pease[17] wrote in 1916: "Anybody who today proposed to repeal the [Insurance] Act would be regarded as a lunatic."

[15] Pease, p. 218.
[16] 1956, p. 207.
[17] p. 224.

Among the Fabians' unexpected allies in this stand against insurance was Hilaire Belloc, who "saw in the compulsory deductions from wages, to be made by employers acting as the Government's agents, a dangerous step in the direction of the Servile State." [18] Belloc argued that for the state to make the employer its agent in obliging the workers to contribute out of their wages toward the cost of what should be, and essentially was, a public service, could, by giving the employer a disciplinary control over the worker, lead to a general system of state regimentation of all the workers. The Fabian Society's *The Insurance Bill and the Workers* argued the case for noncontributory health services and sickness and unemployment benefits, but it was not until the 1929 depression, when neither workers nor employers could keep up their insurance contributions any longer, that the real bankruptcy of Lloyd George's scheme became apparent.

The "plunge into propaganda" occasioned by going to town on behalf of the Minority Report had unforeseen consequences for the Fabian Society as an organization, as well as for the Webbs personally. The latter found they had to suspend their monumental history of English local government in the nineteenth century, which was never completed; they also lost touch with both the influential Liberal and Conservative leaders and superior civil servants. "We have been quite strangely dropped by the most distinguished of our acquaintances . . . I have never had so few invitations as this season," [19] wrote Beatrice in her diary. As she put it, "You cannot at one and the same time exercise behind-the-scenes influence over statesmen, civil servants and newspaper editors, while you yourself engage in public propaganda of projects which these eminent ones may view with hostility or suspicion." Personally, Beatrice "sometimes regretted this turning-point in Our Partnership . . . I should have preferred a life of continued research and non-party social intercourse."

The Webbs' adamant hostility to Lloyd George's great insurance scheme(though Sidney at the beginning had wished the bill to go through) was based on their recognition that the "issue is fairly joined—complete state responsibility with a view of prevention, or partial state responsibility by a new form of relieving destitution unconnected with the poor law, but leaving the poor law for those who fall out of benefit. It is a trial of strength between the two ideas." [20] But their Minority Report had come too late to stop insurance, and of

18 G. D. H. Cole, 1956, p. 209.
19 Beatrice Webb, 1948, p. 428.
20 *Ibid.*, p. 476.

insurance the Webbs remained disapproving because "the fact that sick and unemployed persons were entitled to money incomes without any corresponding obligation to get well and keep well, or to seek and keep employment, seemed to us likely to encourage malingering and a disinclination to work for their livelihood." [21]

No statement could more emphatically underline the definitely ethical appeal of Fabian Socialism than this of Beatrice Webb's: The eight-hour day, the minimum wage, the right to work were demands which, like those for better housing and health, stemmed from the uneasy guilt of the better-offs, quite as much as from the revolutionary demands of the proletariat. "In the realm of feeling and conscience, the realm of the spiritual, Socialism forms the religion of service to the people," wrote James Ramsay MacDonald, and Leon Trotsky,[22] quoting him with disgust, sneered,

> Together with theological literature, Fabianism is perhaps the most useless, and, in any case, is the most boring form of verbal creation. The cheaply optimistic Victorian epoch, when it seemed that tomorrow would be a little better than today, and the day after tomorrow still better, found its most finished expression in the Webbs, Snowden, MacDonald, and other Fabians. The ILPers, the conservative bureaucrats of the Trade Union represent . . . the most counter-revolutionary force in Great Britain. . . . Pacifism is the chief rallying point of British imperialism . . . at any cost, these self-satisfied pedants, these upstart liveried lackeys of the bourgeoisie must be shewn in their natural form to the workers.

But if Fabian Socialism aroused the conscience of the haves, it also insisted on a *quid pro quo* from the have-nots: the State that gave must also be able not only to take away, but to attach strings to its gift.

The Fabians exempted no one from the possibility of malingering: "How do I know I am not malingering?" Beatrice asked herself in her diary, when retiring to bed for a couple of days, and she was afraid the Insurance Act would lead to the "thoughtless manufacture of a parasitic class of chronically unemployed." As she saw it, the hopeless contradiction between the economic power of the few and the political power of the many stemmed from what Beatrice called the mutually destructive trilogy of the Christian ethic, profit-making capitalism, and political democracy. Only in the Wel-

[21] *Ibid.*, p. 430.
[22] pp. 88-89.

fare State, the Webbs felt, could these three safely become one.

For the Fabian Society as a whole, too, the Minority Report was a turning point. For until 1909 the Fabian Society had been the most successful ever of all nonpolitical British organizations of the we-whose-souls-are-lighted-with-wisdom-from-on-high type. (Strangely enough, these organizations, while starting on officially non-party lines, always seem to end up Conservative. Political and Economic Planning—PEP—is a good example of this tendency.) But from now on, the Fabian Society officially became the Labor Party's powerhouse. And that was a radical change and not, perhaps, one that ultimately benefited the Society.

As a postscript to the Minority Report, in his toy theater at Easton Glebe, H. G. Wells dramatized it for his friends. His play began by the Commission's taking Bumble the Beadle to pieces, and putting him in a cauldron and stewing him. Then out of the cauldron leaped a rejuvenated Bumble, several times larger than when he went in.

CHAPTER FIFTEEN

THE FIRST FABIAN SUM-
mer School opened at the end of July 1907 and was a great
success. Half a dozen Fabian Society members put up the
capital and agreed to accept financial responsibility, leaving
to the Society the arrangement of lectures. G.B.S. and
Charlotte were devoted in their attendance, and Beatrice
notes in her diary for 1907 that the Shaws had lent her and
Sidney their little week-end house at Ayot St. Lawrence for
two and a half months, as the Shaws had migrated to Wales,
to be near the Fabian Summer School, which looked over
the sea. The house had previously been a real school; it was
on the coast between Barmouth and Harlech. E. R. Pease[1]
considered the Summer School valuable in

> enabling leaders and officials to find out who there is who
> is good as a speaker or thinker . . . and many of our
> members have come to us through attendance at the
> school. One regular lecture a day for four days a week is
> the rule, but impromptu lectures or debates in the evening
> . . . are customary . . . frequent conferences on special
> subjects are held, either by allied bodies, such as the Com-
> mittee for the Prevention of Destitution, or by a Group,
> such as the Education Group or the Research Department.
> On these occasions the proportion of work to play is greater.

Two years later Beatrice Webb[2] described the goings on at
the Summer School with affectionate amusement:

> The Fabian Summer School has become an odd and in-
> teresting institution. Two or three houses on the mountain-
> ous coast of North Wales are filled to overflowing for
> seven weeks with some hundred Fabians and sympathisers
> —a dozen or so young university graduates and under-
> graduates, another strain of middle-class professionals, a

[1] p. 200.
[2] 1948, pp. 414-15.

stray member of Parliament or professor, a bevy of fair girls—and the remainder—a too large remainder—elderly and old nondescript females, who find the place lively and fairly cheap. The young folk live the most unconventional life—stealing out on moor or sand, in stable or under hay-ricks, without always the requisite chaperone to make it look as wholly innocent as it really is. Then the gym cos-tume which they all affect is startling to Methodist Wales, and the conversation is most surprisingly open. "Is dancing sexual?" I found three pretty Cambridge girl graduates discussing with half-a-dozen men. But mostly they talk economics and political science in the intervals of breaking off the engagements to marry each other they formed a year ago.

In 1910, the Webbs directed the Fabian Summer School for six weeks and found it very exhausting, although the ex-traordinarily mixed assembly were "all kindly and well-bred and interested, but not exciting in themselves, and some of them ugly and crude in mind and manners." The company included ILP organizers, medical officers of health, teachers, social workers, journalists, auctioneers, and unregistered den-tists, all living in extremely close quarters and yet not getting on each other's nerves. The general manager and the Webbs, however, differed radically as to the basic conception of the school: Miss Hankinson wanted a co-operative country holi-day, organized games, excursions, and evening entertain-ments, with a few lectures and discussions thrown in. "Our conception is that of an organised school-teaching, learning and discussing, with some off days and off hours, for recrea-tion and social intercourse," wrote Beatrice. The numbers present varied—from around 150 down to about 70, and sometimes one concept of the school, sometimes the other, prevailed. The Webbs wanted to attract members from the university Fabian Societies, but failed. A little group of half a dozen Cambridge men—Hugh Dalton, Rupert Brooke, Charles Sorley, James Strachey, Ben Keeling, Clifford Allen—came for a week, but the weather, being detestable, must have made the trip appear rather a bad investment for them and they were inclined to go away rather more critical and super-cilious than they came. "They won't come unless they know whom they are going to meet," sums up Rupert Brooke. "And I gathered that, even if they did come, they would only talk together and to us. They don't want to learn . . . they cer-tainly don't want to help others. The egotism of the young university men is colossal. Are they worth bothering about?" [3]

After four years the Welsh lease was up, and the original committee had repaid all the capital borrowed and was £100 to the good. In 1911 the Fabians moved their summer school abroad to Saas Grund, in the Rhone Valley, where they took over a small hotel for six weeks. One of the few French Fabians, Dr. Hertz, who was to be killed in World War I, addressed the large parties of Fabians who came out for a fortnight each. Barrow House, Derwentwater, in the Lake District, was taken for three years in 1912, with grounds sloping down to the lake, with its own boating pier and bathing place. A camp of tents for men was set up, and as many as sixty guests could be accommodated at one time. Harry Craven remembers walking in the lovely Lake District country with the Webbs and says the Fabian Summer School was one of his most delightful memories—the real intellectual stimulation, and the real camaraderie were most exhilarating to the then young among the Fabians.

For about this time the original Fabians began to feel distinctly old. "The Fabian Society," glooms Beatrice Webb in 1911, "is going through a crisis, not of dissent, but of indifference." Sidney had resigned, because he and Beatrice were going to the Far East for a year: "whereupon GBS not only announces his intention of resigning, but persuades some half-a-dozen of the old gang to resign also. All with the view to making room for young men who are not there."

A very important letter from G.B.S. to Sidney Webb suggests the main rearrangements on the Fabian Executive, resulting from the voluntary retirement of the most distinguished members of the old gang.

> AYOT ST. LAWRENCE
> 5 March, 1911

Since we agree on the main point, let me deal with those on which we disagree, that is, those on which you are totally wrong.

1. The withdrawal of Bland will be a shock. The withdrawal of Shaw will be a shock. The withdrawal of Webb will be a shock. What is more, these shocks will each be maximum shocks. If they occur simultaneously, the effect will be no worse than one of them would produce by itself —and one is already inevitable. But if they are separated from one another by a year's interval, the succession of shocks will reduce the Society to the condition of a village in an earthquake district . . . when we go, we must not go on tiptoe; and we must go together. . . . The present opportunity may never recur. Some other Wells, or some new political development, may next year produce a situation in which all the explanations in the world will not

avail against the suspicion that the resignation is a crossing of the House floor. It is probably now or never. Your voyage round the world is a perfect excuse for bringing a long pending difficulty to an issue. . . . Now for the real difficulty. Guest has been captured for the Theosophists, like Mrs. Besant, and will not stand again. That makes 10. Ten vacancies is much too steep a step for steady progress. We must mitigate it somehow. The following devices are possible:

(a) Induce Ensor and Barker to remain. And perhaps Guest.
(b) Reduce the Old Gang to Bland-Shaw-Webb, leaving Pease and Standring in office as officially indispensable, and not counting Headlam (who was off for many years) as a real oldganger.

Finally, G.B.S. concludes, if the above measures fail "and the worst comes to the worst, reduce the numbers of the Executive to (say) 15." [4]

"The Fabian Executive," E. R. Pease wrote, "was a wonderfully friendly and united body. In all my fifty years experience of it there was nothing that can be called a quarrel, and this harmony was largely . . . due to Webb's good temper and persistence in conciliation." After Pease resigned as secretary, William Sanders took Pease's place, both as secretary to the Fabian Society and as delegate to the Labor Party. Called up in the fall of 1915, he and Pease promptly went around to 41 Grosvenor Square and persuaded Sidney Webb to accept nomination. "I consider this my second best day," noted Pease. "My best was when I invited the future Fabians to meet at my rooms."

Twenty-two new candidates came forward at the election of April 1911, but on the whole the Society showed no particular eagerness for change, as Pease had put it. The retiring members were re-elected ahead of all the new ones, with Sidney Webb at the top of the poll.

By this time it was apparent that the self-denying ordinance of the veterans was not really necessary, and the Executive, loath to lose the stimulation of Shaw's constant presence, devised a scheme to authorize the elected members to co-opt as consultative members persons who had already held office for ten years. But this proposal was defeated on a show of hands. . . . Here then it may be said that the rule of the Essayists as a body came to an end. Sidney Webb alone remained in office. [5]

[4] Quoted in Henderson, p. 271.
[5] Pease, p. 223.

When the Webbs came back to England after their world tour, the Fabian Society had completed the change-over in its functions, from the permeation and education of all persons and parties, to the work of research and propaganda for the Labor Party. It had settled down "with admirable good temper," as Beatrice notes, and she adds, "the Standing Committee of the ILP and Fabian Society is a success and is controlling the policy of the Labour and Socialist movement in this country—in so far as this movement has any policy." And she adds, "What annoys me is the absence of any relationship, good or bad, between the Labour MP's and the Labour movement in the country. The Labour MP's seem to me to be drifting into futility, a futility that will presently be recognised by all whom it may concern." [6]

It was soon recognized, and Beatrice was indeed a true prophet.

So, on this occasion, was G.B.S., whose premonition of another Wells in the Fabian Society, or some new political situation outside of it, was exactly fulfilled within the year. Both occurred. The new Wells was G. D. H. Cole. The new political situation was the "direct action" of the syndicalists, expressed concretely in England by industrial unionism and theoretically, in an Anglicized version, by Guild Socialism.

In the fall of 1912 Beatrice Webb, recently returned from her world tour, took a long look at her now practically defunct National Committee for the Prevention of Destitution, and also at the Fabian Society, and decided that the Society's most useful and enduring function was research. In establishing the Fabian Research Bureau her idea was to "systematise research," to enlist the co-operation of social enquirers "not necessarily committed to the principles of the Society," and to obtain funds for this special purpose from those who would not contribute to the political side of the Society's operations. This Research Bureau proved a wonderful safety valve, becoming the natural outlet for the younger Fabians who were often impatient of, and rude to, the "Old Gang." But Beatrice Webb, at fifty-one, had no wish to be reckoned as a member of the old gang and insisted she would be the leader of the Fabian nursery. Yet, no sooner had she founded the Fabian Research Bureau than the Guild Socialists at once captured it, sidetracking it to it the keenest and most vigorous among the young Fabians, as Margaret Cole tells in her *Growing up into Revolution*.[7] Beatrice tried hard to keep the young rebels within the Society, but "the rebels

[6] Beatrice Webb, 1952, p. 6.

[7] pp. 63-64.

were unaccommodating; they would have nothing whatever
to do with collectivism; they manned the Fabian Research
Bureau, took it completely out of the control of the Executive, and away from the Society." [8] The split was accentuated
by the blank hostility of the Webbs to the Russian Revolution
in its early days, and was not healed for twenty years. But the
Fabian Society itself was never split: only a very few insur-
gents swarmed out, taking a new queen bee, Margaret Cole
(then Postgate) with them, who with her friends talked about,
and worked for, "the Movement" which was Guild Socialist.
Most of the Movement's adherents, though not quite all,

> worked in the Fabian Research Department, either for love
> or for very low pay, or as outside advisers. The Fabian Re-
> search Department was the work of the Webbs . . . who
> had decided that it was necessary to work out, preferably
> through the Fabian Society, a series of projects for turning
> Britain into a Socialist country. Beatrice Webb thought it
> would be a good way of utilising the ability of young men
> such as Hugh Dalton and other Cambridge Fabians whom
> she had met at the Fabian summer school. Unfortunately
> for her purpose there had simultaneously entered the Fa-
> bian Society young men, principally from Oxford, led by
> W. Mellor and G. D. H. Cole, who were Guild Socialists.
> The Webbs thought "workers control" vicious nonsense
> and said so; the Guild Socialists thought them wicked old
> bureaucrats and said so. One deeply stirred old member
> moved that "Mr. Cole be a cad." [9]

It was something of an irony, Margaret Cole admitted, that all
this anti-Webbian activity was conducted on the premises of
the Fabian Society itself, in a nest as it were of vociferous
young cuckoos located between the first floor office of
E. R. Pease, the shaggy, growling, elderly secretary, and the
residence of Mrs. Herbert, the caretaker and provider of
lunches to the Fabian common room, at the top. E. R. Pease,
wrote Earl Attlee in an obituary in the *Times* (London) in
June 1955, regarded him and his brother "as if we were bee-
tles" when they tried to join the Fabian Society. "We *are* Socialists," protested young Clement Attlee to the suspicious
Pease, who finally agreed to admit the future Prime Minister
and his brother to the Fabian Society! Margaret Cole, writing
of Mr. Pease and Mrs. Herbert, notes that:

> We were the bane of both their lives. Pease objected to
> the noise over his head, to the burning of lights and the

[8] Margaret I. Cole, "The Fabian Society," *Political Quarterly*, Vol.
XV, July-September, 1944.
[9] Margaret I. Cole, 1949, pp. 63-65.

creation of litter until all hours, and was inclined to accuse us of opening his letters and abstracting his postal orders. Mrs. Herbert, with better justification, suspected us of raiding her stores and eating up "Mr. Pease's jam" when we worked weekends, and there was a running feud between us and those elderly Fabians who, having grown old and rheumatic in the service of the Society, came to sit quietly in its commonroom, and found something between a revolution and a romp going on.

For Margaret, Beatrice Webb was a tall lady wearing a large and very ugly hat, with a beaked nose, a very thin pale face, a harsh high voice and a bright commanding eye. "I saw only a Bogie-woman, who wished to deny self-expression to the workers and increases of pay to Fabian research workers . . . there was a curious streak of stinginess in the Webbs which led them to exploit the willingness of the enthusiast to work for low pay."

G.B.S., in a letter to G. K. Chesterton, also describes the "goings-on" of G. D. H. Cole, Margaret Postgate, and their friends:

You know that there is a body called the Fabian Research Department of which I have the hollow honour to be Perpetual Grand, the real moving spirit being Mrs. Sidney Webb. A large number of innocent young men and women are attracted to this body by promises of employment by the said Mrs. Sidney Webb in work of unlimited and inspiring uplift, such as are unceasingly denounced, along with Marconi and other matters, in your well-written organ. . . . Well, Mrs. Sidney Webb summoned all these young things to an uplifting at home at the Fabian Office lately. They came in crowds and sat at her feet while she prophesied unto them, with occasional comic relief from the unfortunate Perpetual Grand. At the decent hour of ten, she bade them goodnight and withdrew to her own residence and to bed. For some accidental reason or other I lingered until, as I thought, all the young things had gone home . . . at last I started to go home myself. As I descended the stairs I was stunned by the most infernal din I have ever heard . . . coming from the Fabian Hall, which would otherwise be the backyard. On rushing to this temple I found the young enthusiasts sprawling over tables, over radiators, over everything except chairs, in a state of scandalous abandonment, roaring at the tops of their voices and in a quite unintelligible manner a string of presumably obscene songs, accompanied on the piano with frantic gestures . . . by a man I had always regarded as a respectable Fabian Researcher. A horribly sacrilegious character was given to the proceedings by the fact that the tune they were singing as I entered was Luther's Hymn *Ein feste Burg*. As they went on (for I regret to say my presence exercised no restraint whatever) they sang their extraordinary and incontinent litany to every tune, however august its associations, that happened to fit it. These, if you please, are the solemn and sour neophytes whose puritanical influence has kept you in dread for these many years. But I have not told you the worst. Before I fled from the building I did at last discover the words it was they were singing: the poem in *The Flying Inn* . . . a young maenad didn't care where the water went if it didn't get into the wine. . . .[10]

G. D. H. Cole rapidly became vice-president of the Fabian Research Bureau, and was the instigator of the Labor Year Book. As Margaret Cole has pointed out, at this time the Webb influence was at its nadir and even the Webbs admitted to themselves, "we have never been as unpopular as now." The Fabian Research Department, instantly captured by Cole, Mellor, and Tawney

proved that it would have been quite unthinkable for the young ones among us who came into the movement during the years of the Fabian Research Department, to have ranged ourselves on the Webb side. All the enthusiasm, all the *fun* of playing games with press-cuttings, of knowing by heart the initials of Trade Unions and their ramifications, of meeting with rebellious local leaders of industry . . . and the organisation of Parliamentary questions, resolutions, and other methods of embarrassing and annoying the Government and promoting the cause of workers control, were to be found in the opposition camp; and in that camp we were happy to serve, in office hours and outside.[11]

Beatrice Webb understood and almost sympathized with the impatient young. In her *Diaries, 1912-1924,*[12] she notes on May 2, 1922:

To some of the younger intellectuals our persistence as publicists, using up one subject after another, must be a cause of annoyance, an annoyance which Mrs. Cole freely expressed in her description in *The Guild Socialist* of Sidney Webb and his irritating "permanence" as a leader of Socialist thought. To a whole bevy of younger Socialists our energetic survival must be . . . tiresome.

[10] Quoted in Ward, p. 209.
[11] Margaret I. Cole (ed.), 1949, p. 158.
[12] p. 223.

All the "fun and games in politics" belonged to the rebels; it was the old members, such as the one who declared, "I've been a member of the Fabian Society for forty years, and now these young men make me come all the way from Streatham to vote against them," who stood by the Webbs. To the young ones the Webbs were stingy old bullies, who had never been to the university (neither Beatrice nor Sidney nor Shaw) and they thus had no experience either of prolonged and eager discussion of doctrine—throughout their lives they were impatient of time spent in philosophic talk; they just wanted to find an acceptable doctrine and then get on with the job—or with the irrepressible ragging and abusive controversy of serious-minded university youth. The elder Fabians were staid creatures by contrast—what Shaw called "our invaluable habit of laughing freely at ourselves" did not extend to horseplay.[13] Yet when Cole resigned from the Executive and from the Society, Mellor and other Guild Socialists stayed on, just in order to continue the work of the Fabian Research Department. As Beatrice didn't want to lose all of her brightest young people, she made no objection when the department dropped the word "Fabian," called itself the Labor Research Department, and attached itself to Transport House, Labor Party headquarters.

In 1917 the *Monthly Circular* of the no longer Fabian Labor Research Bureau began to appear. It is still published. The Bureau also undertook the preparation of long and detailed briefs for trade-union secretaries engaged in wage negotiations, and produced *Labour White Papers* for a penny each, summarizing facts, figures, and forecasts on immediately current questions. In the mid-twenties the Labor Research Department was captured by the Communists, and was disowned by Labor Party headquarters at Transport House.

Margaret Cole's opposition to "Sidneywebbicalism" was largely personal: Beatrice was not interested in young female Fabians; she thought them either socially unpresentable, like the wives of the trade-union leaders she later unsuccessfully tried to turn into ladies, or sirens likely to deflect the young male Fabians from their work. Margaret explains,

When I first saw Beatrice, I thought she looked infinitely frail and infinitely old—she was thirty years older than I was . . . and my only concern was how I could get out of the room, without either being sacked on the spot by the formidable old lady in the hideous hat, or doing anything violent,—such as sneezing, for example—which might cause her to disintegrate on the spot.

13 Margaret I. Cole (ed.), 1949, p. 156.

The young cuckoos wrote ribald rhymes:

> O that Beatrice and Sidney
> Would get in their kidney
> A loathsome disease
> Also Pease

was their type of effusion. Beatrice, however, had an immense admiration for G. D. H. Cole, who, she thought, regarded himself as Sidney's successor. In 1918 she visited the now young-married Coles and commended this "promising union of two devoted fellow workers."

Margaret Postgate, familiarly known as "Mop" because of the mop of short thick black wavy hair in which is set swarthy complexion, mobile mouth, sharp nose and chin and most brilliantly defiant eyes, is the daughter of a professor of classics. She succeeded Arnot as paid secretary to the Research Department and shocked us old folk with her daringly unconventional ways and rebellious attitude. She kept what hours she chose, smoked the most masculine pipe, was on affectionate terms, first with Arnot, then with Cole. . . . But though her manners have been disorderly her ways have been straight; she has wit and reasoning power of an unusual quality and she is fundamentally sweet-tempered and kind. . . . She and Cole seem perfect intellectual comrades. On both sides the marriage is an unworldly one. The little house in a bystreet in Chelsea is the interior of choice spirits, comfortable, even luxurious in lounges, restful in colouring, furniture solid and old, with a plenitude of books. These two are friendly with us. . . . Cole is preparing himself for political leadership. But he has a hard way to go. He is marked for life as a C.O. [conscientious objector] . . . the new shop-steward movement is not only indifferent but hostile to his elaborate proposals of centralised Guilds. . . . Meanwhile Cole, who is, from the intricate convolutions of his subtle brains to the tips of his long fingers, an intellectual and an aristocrat, is becoming disillusioned about the Labour Leaders, far more than we. All the same, I believe he will win through. But it will not be the old folk and the old movement that he will have to overcome; it will be the surge of the new interests and the demagogie of the new leaders, more extreme than himself.

G. D. H. Cole has also been described as he was at that time by a visiting French journalist. His guest found Cole living in Eccleston Square, alone in a big empty room, with a large table in the center. Outside the trees were bathed in the damp, infused London light. "A thin, well-dressed man, with a long grave idealist's face. He never smiles, has few gestures, no exaggeration; has a distinction, a simplicity untouched by success, a fine intellect strengthened by contact with the crowd." Cole had come up to Balliol College, Oxford, in 1908, and has described how he became converted to Socialism while a schoolboy by reading Morris's *News from Nowhere*. For him, Socialism was not a political theory, but a creed: "I am in effect a Socialist," he wrote recently. "By Socialist I mean fundamentally the entire body of principles, which I have set out. . . . They are good altogether and for good, and I am not arguing with anyone who denies them: I am simply telling him."

Cole was an absolutist: he was absolutely against the wage system, and absolutely against Parliamentary representation of any sort: he did not believe any human person could be represented and could still remain free: no one human being could represent another, no body could be representative of the whole of the people. Cole was thus irrevocably a pluralist. In his *New Statesman* pamphlet (published "in association with the Fabian Society" in 1954) querying whether this managerial welfare state was socialist, he categorically assumed that "it is the business of all good men to oppose tyranny either of man over men or of the ruling State over subject people." He prefixed his *World in Transition* with his credo: "What I take for granted." Item number 4 is the "duty of service." "Every person is under the obligation not merely to avoid being a burden on society but the positive one of contributing to the social well-being of others." And Cole's final point is

> I want people to have good nutrition, good housing, food, education, good work conditions, freedom of speech, self-government . . . sound moral notions whether they would vote for having them or not. To this extent I am prepared to assert that I know better what is good for people than they may know themselves, being mostly much more ignorant and much more held in mental subjection than I am.

Like so many other writers, Cole's first book was a "slim volume" of verse published at Oxford by Blackwell's in 1914. He remained a poet, as was shown by his *The Bolo Book* (1921):

> If the boss cuts wages, in spite of all the sages,
> We'll stop his blasted factories as we stopped them
>   long ago.

A serious flaw in *The Bolo Book* is its anti-Semitism, almost

as virulent as that of Belloc. For example, to the tune of
"Jerusalem the Golden" its readers were asked to sing:

> Beyond the Baghdad railway
> Thy Chosen people wait
>
> * * * * *
>
> They stand, those hills of Judah,
> Completely clothed in Jews
> Selections of the Samuels,
> And Leagues of Montagues
> Lord Rothschild's ever with them . . .
> There shines the wig of Reading
> From viceroy-ships released
> And Guggenheim and Mannheim . . .
> And Lewis, Levys, Lowes . . .

Perhaps the best song in the book, to be sung to the tune of
the Russian national anthem, was:

> Northcliffe the terrible, Peer, who ordainest,
> Asquith Thy scapegoat, Lloyd George Thy sword
> Flare forth Thy headlines, spread hate among nations,
> Lest we have peace in our time, my Lord.

A fine indictment of a terrible war-profiteer.

G. D. H. Cole repeatedly declared that he never wanted
a Parliamentary career, and this "sentimental Jacobin" influenced his generation, and his juniors, by his voluminous
writings, by being a most successful "don"—he was a Fellow
of All Souls and was Chichele Professor of Social and Political Philosophy at Oxford from 1944 to his death in 1959.
As a journalist he was one of the lights of the *New Age* under
A. R. Orage, and later of the *New Statesman* of which he
was chairman. But *New Standards,* the weekly founded by
G. D. H. Cole and his wife Margaret, on October 23, 1923,
to advocate workers' control, only lasted about a year, and was
singularly undistinguished. G.B.S. wrote for the first issue, and
G. K. Chesterton for one of the last, but neither contribution
was outstanding, and, for the rest, it was sorry stuff, faintly
religious in flavor, perhaps as a concession to the large number of Church of England clergy rooting for Guild Socialism.
Guild Socialism was a mishmashed British version of syndicalism which had grown out of a worsening of class relations
in Great Britain. This worsening was largely due to the fact
that, because the Liberals took so long a-dying, and Labor
so long a-growing, for a while there was real, unrepresented
and truly anarchic ferment among the British people expressing itself in direct action (since nature abhors a vacuum) and
in strikes and other violence.

CHAPTER SIXTEEN

THE ONLY TIMES THIS century when class feelings ran really high in England were immediately before and after World War I. The feeling before the war was largely directed against the obstructionist behavior of the House of Lords which tried to veto Lloyd George's social legislation. As Sir Llewellyn Woodward[1] puts it, "The action of the House of Lords between 1909 and 1911 was in a sedate form a strike against the constitution." The Liberals broke that strike, but success has its perils no less dangerous than defeat, and the triumphant Liberal Party never really recovered from their victory over the House of Lords. After the Lords had rejected Lloyd George's budget by 350 to 75 (it had passed the Commons by 379 votes to 149), the Liberals went to the country for the second time in a year, and won a triumphant endorsement of their proposals. The death of King Edward VII in 1910 postponed the showdown, and George V was reluctant to engage in a battle which he thought had shortened his father's life. But on July 24, 1911, he agreed to create 250 Liberal peers if the Lords proved intractable. The Parliament Act which was then passed by the growling, out-licked Lords, has been called by a leading Fabian, "The most decisive step in British constitutional development since the franchise extension of 1867." [2]

But meanwhile the working classes in Britain were turning both against the trade unions, who were being dragged along at the triumphant Liberal coattails, and against the permeative and meliorist Fabians. In fact, the workers were taking matters into their own hands. In 1904 less than two million working days were lost in strike; in 1912, forty million days were lost. And these strikes were, for the most part, unauthorized: they were a threat not only to the Labor Party but

[1] p. 248.
[2] Ensor, p. 430.

to the Trades Union Council. Socialism had up until then
been moving along its fourfold way quietly enough, increasing by (a) regulation of industries, hours, wages; (b) the
increase of communal services such as school lunches, pit-
head baths, old-age pensions; (c) the increased taxation of
unearned income, including land duties and death duties; and
(d) a wide variety of increases in public ownership—of
utilities, of parks, of education. Long before the first Labor
Government came into power in 1922 there were 10,000
elected Labor representatives in the various local and municipal bodies. But around 1910 the rising prices, without
corresponding wage advances, were resulting in widespread
industrial unrest. However, the trade unions, following the
two mandatory but undecisive elections of 1910, "were in
no mood to be prodded into Socialist paths." [3] Nineteen-
eleven proved to be the critical year, with great strikes
spreading like wildfire among seamen and waterside workers,
with a national railway strike and with the fiercely fought
struggle in the South Wales coalfield.[4]

Trade disputes certainly had multiplied. In 1910-14 they
averaged 1,029 a year, more than ever before. All this industrial warfare was the work of leaders who had no use at
all for permeation, gradualness, or the Webbs' discreetly regulated freedom. There was at this time nothing in Great
Britain comparable with the mass Socialist parties of Germany, Austria, and France—the Labor Party itself was still
uncommitted to Socialism, although the ILP and the Fabian
Society both had been so committed from the start. Syndicalists, Industrial Unionists, Guild Socialists, militant suffragettes, and ardent Home Rulers were all in their several ways
anti-Fabian, for one reason or another, and from 1911 on,
the most significant of these malcontented left-wingers were
the Guild Socialists. Since the Parliamentary Labor Party
had agreed to support the Liberals in the contest with
the House of Lords and in the demand for Irish Home Rule,
the Labor Party refused to bring down the government on
female suffrage, though they were pledged to it. Direct action
by trade unionists as well as by suffragettes was the result.

The Guild Socialists and the direct-action trade unionists
got their ideas from France, where Sorel's syndicalism
(*syndicat* being merely the French for "trade union") was the
new and aggressive political philosophy. It quickly spread,
and in England in 1910 the Industrial Syndicalist Educational League held an assembly of 200 delegates represent-

[3] Beatrice Webb, 1952, p. 2.
[4] G. D. H. Cole, 1956, p. 224.

ing 60,000 workers. It may be noted, in parentheses, that in the United States, during the years between 1908 and 1913, the IWW was making a trade-union history which was very far removed from the bland British version during the same decade.

The Guild Socialists started in England with the advantage of good press coverage and publicity. The *Daily Herald,* a newspaper started by a group of compositors, and instantly dubbed "the miracle of Fleet Street," incessantly derided the Labor Party and advocated women's franchise and some sort of syndicalism as a social panacea.[5] Meanwhile, A. R. Orage's *New Age* was a sturdy advocate of Guild Socialism as a purely British compromise with syndicalism, and the University Fabian Societies were converted, first Oxford by G. D. H. Cole, and later Cambridge by Clifford Allen.

The Guild Socialist movement's first statement was A. J. Penty's book *The Restoration of The Guild System.* Penty was a Christian Socialist, a disciple of William Morris, who began as a Fabian, and found, in the Fabian Society, A. R. Orage and S. G. Hobson to be kindred spirits. But Hobson was no medievalist; he had lived in the United States and his vision of guilds was of "vast democratically controlled agencies for the running of industry."[6] Hobson saw the guilds arising out of the trade unions, which would include "all workers by hand or brain." The *New Age* pushed all these ideas, to which G. K. Chesterton, Hilaire Belloc, and Arnold Bennett also subscribed, and about which they wrote brilliant articles. These, though much read by left-wing intellectuals, did not reach the working classes.

The real issue between collectivism and syndicalism had come to a practical head in 1907 during the railroad strike, when the Fabian attitude in approving the treaty imposed by Lloyd George upon the railroad industry pinpointed the problem of whether strikes would be allowed in state-owned industry. In the *New Age* for December 7, 1907, the Fabian viewpoint was expressed in a letter:

In the case of the nation's principal means of land transport, the resort to the chief Trade Union weapon of the strike was such a national calamity that no responsible statesman could nowadays treat it as a private matter. The nation can no more afford to let the railway industry be intimidated by the claims—however just—of the railway workers, than by the obstinacy—however dignified—of railway directors.

5 Pease, p. 230.
6 G. D. H. Cole, 1956, p. 243.

G. D. H. Cole's *The World of Labour*, published at the end
of 1913, attracted a lot of notice, and he was elected to the
Fabian Society Executive in April 1914. He at once began a
new reform movement, hostile to the Labor Party, from
within the Society. He gives a cogent explanation of Guild
Socialism (of which he was the chief formulator) in his
History of Socialist Thought, pointing out that Guild Socialism was fundamentally an ethical and not a materialist doctrine. It set out, he opined, as against both State Socialism
and what was soon to be called Communism, to assert the
vital importance of individual and group liberty, and the
need to diffuse social responsibility among all the people by
making them as far as possible masters of their own lives and
of the conditions under which their daily work was done.
Freedom from the fear of unemployment, freedom at work,
and the right to work under supervisors and managers of
their own choosing and to rid the work-places of rulers
appointed from above, whether by the capitalist employer
or by the State, were, he declared, the necessary foundations
of industrial democracy, without which political democracy
could only be a pretense.

Later it became clear that the idea of "workers' control"
meant very different things to the Guild Socialists, to the
Industrial Unionists, and subsequently to the Communists. To
the Communists, workers' control meant control by the
workers as a class; the Guild Socialists meant control by
the actual working group over the management of its own
affairs, within the framework of a wider control of policy
formulated and executed as democratically as possible, and
with the largest diffusion of responsibility and power. Sorel's
idea of the general strike always remained a myth for England, even when implemented in 1926, for reasons which
Sorel [7] himself saw clearly.

> That the general strike is not popular in contemporary
> England is a poor argument to make against the historical
> validity of the idea. For the English are distinguished by an
> almost total incomprehension of the idea of the class strug-
> gle . . . the corporation, privileged or at any rate pro-
> tected by the laws, always seems to them the ideal of work-
> ing-class organisation.

There was a constant danger in England, as Vernon Lee[8]
well saw, that "the parliamentary (what we call Fabian)
element of Society increasing, the reforms and reconstruc-

[7] p. 90.
[8] II, p. 114.

tions would catch up with Syndicalist aspiration and leave them with nothing to rage against in a disastrous dullness of logical give-and-take."

The Guild Socialists were diametrically opposed to the Fabians, yet they began as Fabians—"Gradgrinds in Socialist clothing" as Robert Blatchford called them—and tried hard, from within the heart of the Society, to convert the organization from what the Guild Socialists thought of as its state idolatry. The Guild Socialists, still speaking as Fabians, "coldly announced that the Fabians should give up Fabianism," and went about trying to dispel what they considered to be G.B.S.'s obstinate obsession that the meaning of history is Fabian. The Webbs had always feared and disapproved of any producer-directed organizations, believing that consumer control is the only truly democratic economy: if the producers, collected into guilds, are in control, the consuming public is at their mercy, and society can be held to ransom again and again by a few. The Guild Socialists, on the other hand, declared that the Fabians sought to

raise the poor, rather than to rouse them. The worker was to reach Socialism—if ever—after he had been brought, blindfold and bound, through the drear vista of the Servile State . . . the ideal of National Guilds . . . gives the worker something to work for, whereas the Collectivist only offered him someone to vote for. . . . Emancipation by capture, indeed, was the contribution of Fabianism to the problem of Socialist policy, the capture of the machinery of the State by the enlightened bureaucrat, capture of the Trade Unions by the progressive politician. . . . To every problem the State Socialists applied their flyblown formula, the nationalisation of the means of production, distribution and exchange, as if putting industry into the hands of the politicians were synonymous with putting it into the hands of the people.[9]

The main emphasis of Guild Socialism was therefore against any form of collectivization, and its energies were concentrated on the abolition of the wage system: the worker would remain, it declared, a passive instrument of production so long as he was bought with a wage—it did not basically alter his condition whether that wage was paid by a single capitalist employer or by the state. Authority and responsibility must be transferred *to* the producers, and the proprietors must be merged into the producers. This, the Guild Socialists declared, was the only way to graduate

[9] Reckitt and Bechhofer, p. 21.

from economic feudalism to Socialism, without sidestepping into the fell clutches of the Servile State.

G. D. H. Cole had barely been elected to the Fabian Society Executive before he proposed that the Society should disaffiliate from the Labor Party. His resolution was defeated by 92 votes to 4. He and Clifford Allen now combined to produce a new program for the Society, which was described as representing "several schools of thought" and was published in *Fabian News* for April 1915. The aim of the Society was to be simplified merely to the doing of research, and the whole Basis was to be replaced by the following brief phrase:

"The Fabian Society consists of Socialists and forms part of the national and international movement for the emancipation of the community from the capitalist system."

At the annual meeting in May 1915, G. D. H. Cole, "brash and young, attacked Beatrice Webb and used abominable language," Sir Robert Ensor recalls. W. N. Ewer is more specific. "Cole told the executive they were fools. Then, white with rage, he declared, 'I withdraw that statement. You are bloody fools. I resign from the Executive and from the Society.' Beatrice Webb whispered to Ensor, 'That young man is certain to become Prime Minister.'" But within the Fabian Society the revolt was crushed by the "suburban cohorts" who had come up for the annual meeting, and for once her prophecy proved false. As Pease put it, "Mr. Cole adopted the wise course of founding a society of his own for the advocacy of Guild Socialism." The Oxford Fabian Society severed its connection with the parent society, and a few London members also followed G. D. H. Cole out of the Fabian Society. Of these W. Mellor and Clifford Allen were the most able. All were to be conscientious objectors (C.O.'s) in the war.

Beatrice Webb[10] contrasted the young Socialists of 1912 with those of 1882:

Syndicalism has taken the place of old-fashioned Marxism. The angry youth, with bad complexion, frowning brow and weedy figure, is now always a Syndicalist; the glib young workman whose tongue runs away with him, today mouths the phrases of French Syndicalism instead of those of German Social Democracy. The inexperienced middle class idealist has accepted with avidity the ideal of the Syndicalist as a new and exciting Utopia. But . . . so far as we can foresee, Syndicalism will disrupt the British Socialist Party (formed in 1909 by a merger of Hyndman's Socialist Dem-

[10] 1952, p. 8.

ocratic Federation with some dissident ILP-ers), it will detach some branches of the ILP and some impatient Fabians; it will increase discontent with the Labour Party—but it will have no appreciable effect on the larger currents of Trade Unionism.

G. D. H. Cole's revolt and the rise of syndicalism, however camouflaged as Guild Socialism, made the Fabians realize more acutely than ever how essential it was to have a magazine of their own. The *New Age,* bold, brilliant and witty, had gone over entirely to the new dissidents, and was spreading Guild Socialist ideas in Fabian circles at a great rate, while as yet no official Fabian voice answered. After a great deal of preliminary "figurin'" as to costs, the Fabians came up with the *New Statesman* as their reply. The Webbs first built up a card catalogue of 20,000 possible subscribers from the Fabian Society, the old Minority Commission's National Committee mailing list, and personal friends: G.B.S. was said to be "good for" 1,000 subscribers, the Webbs for 500 and J. C. (later Sir John) Squire for 100. But only 150 subscribers were caught at the Webbs' first casting. The Liberal *Nation,* a far more serious rival under its brilliant ex-Fabian editor, H. M. Massingham, even than the *New Age,* estimated the *New Statesman's* chances as rather dim. The lowest sales the *Nation's* statisticians gave as compatible with survival were 3,000; the maximum expected by the Webbs was 5,000—after three years. Experts told the Webbs 1,000 subscribers would be a miracle, but the final total registered before the first issue appeared was 2,500, and after a year over 2,000 resubscribed. The capital available was only £5,000 —about $20,000—of which G.B.S. contributed £1,000. "Our plans are cut—I will not say dried—they are still moist with uncertainty as to detail," Beatrice Webb wrote at Christmas, 1912.

Massingham sneered that the new magazine would be one-idea'd, always harping on socioeconomic themes, just as the *New Witness,* whose stars were Chesterton and Belloc, was always hammering at the theme of political corruption. From the first there was no question who was to be the *New Statesman's* editor: Clifford Sharp had done the Fabians yeoman's service for several years as editor of the *Crusade,* and he was the Webbs' obvious and only choice. He was appointed editor and given a completely free hand. The first two staff members to be appointed were J. C. Squire as literary editor and Desmond MacCarthy as dramatic critic. The former left to found the *London Mercury,* a literary monthly; the latter remained with the *New Statesman* until his death. The first number, while announcing the new venture as determinedly Fabian, made it clear that it was not, and never would be, an organ of the Labor Party. The first number tacitly admitted that the Fabians shared the British public's "abysmal ignorance" of foreign affairs. Also from the first, Shaw refused to sign his articles. This meant, Clifford Sharp said, that the editorial blue pencil could, and would be, and it was, used on Shaw. G.B.S. acquiesced in this, but it soon became obvious that, as he said, "it is not my Organ, but it may be none the worse for that."

Clifford Sharp disliked Shaw for, as he thought, befriending Wells (who had unsuccessfully tried to elope with Sharp's fiancée), and mangled Shaw's articles out of sheer spite. Beatrice Webb thought Shaw showed extreme patience and tact, though she was devoted to Sharp, who had served her Poor Law Abolition Committee valiantly. The *New Statesman's* early supplements suffered from Webb-footedness. "Have you seen our Blue Book supplement?" Clifford Sharp asked A. R. Orage. "Which *is* your Blue Book supplement?" Orage replied, and described the *New Statesman* as "worse than the *Nation*—the Damnation." However, there were many such quips flying around, as when A. R. Orage offered for example to speak for G. D. H. Cole. "Do you speak?" asked Cole, and when Orage offered to write for Cole, the latter retorted, "Do you write?" All the Fabians helped the infant magazine: of course G.B.S. gave his articles "for free" as was only to be expected, but even such a commercial character as Arnold Bennett[11] notes in his diary: "Wrote *Phenomena at Covent Garden* for the *New Statesman* as a gift to the Webbs, due to skillful fascination of Beatrice Webb," and he faithfully attended directors' meetings, to which J. C. Squire also came with "Long hair, jaegerishly dressed." Again: "17 November 1915 Directors meeting. Shaw said we ought to attack Asquith. Said we ought to make Haldane P.M."

Thanks to its brilliant and enduring editors and to its galaxy of Fabian friends, the *New Statesman* has never ceased flourishing. Before it absorbed the *Nation* (in 1930) sales reached about 12,000, then rose to some 15,000. In 1931, Kingsley Martin became editor and proved to be one of the most brilliant in the history of English journalism. In 1934, the *New Statesman* took over the *Weekend Review* and now (1959) circulation is over 85,000, and G. D. H. Cole, the chairman of the *New Statesman's* board of directors, was simultaneously president of the Fabian Society.

11 II, pp. 474, 491, 574.

The most famous of all *New Statesman* supplements was Bernard Shaw's *Common Sense About the War,* published in the early fall of 1914. It created a terrific sensation, and it was greatly to Clifford Sharp's credit that he published it, for he was, as S. K. Ratcliffe has pointed out, of necessity hostile to Shaw's ideas, but "he could not be indifferent to a pamphlet of supreme brilliance and audacity . . . he accepted it unhesitatingly . . . there was no loss of circulation. The sales, indeed, attested the steadiness of the subscribers and a quiet incoming of new readers." [12]

Yet reader reaction against G.B.S. soon grew strong. Hall Caine had asked G.B.S. to contribute to *King Albert's Birthday Book,* but after *Common Sense About the War* the *Daily Telegraph* refused to accept G.B.S.'s chapter. Caine immediately offered to resign his editorship, but G.B.S. withdrew his piece. Seventy-five thousand copies of *Common Sense About the War* were quickly sold, but when the Germans started using it as propaganda the great British public began ostracizing G.B.S. His plays were withdrawn; old friends now cut him dead and publicly disowned him; H. G. Wells said his writing suggested "an idiot child laughing in a hospital." But G.B.S., undaunted, wrote "An Open Letter to President Wilson" which H. W. Massingham published in the *Nation* on November 7, 1914. Mr. Archibald Henderson[13] thinks this article had a pronounced influence on the American President, as it adumbrated many of his pronouncements on the freedom of the seas, and the League of Nations. The realistic Belgians meanwhile did not in the least object to G.B.S.'s assertions that England had entered the war to protect her own security, or as G. D. H. Cole succinctly put it: "The violation of Belgium was certainly a crime, but no less certainly it was for the [British] Government a very fortunate accident." In fact, the Belgian government later in the war hired G.B.S. to write propaganda.

[12] Margaret I. Cole (ed.), 1949, p. 14.
[13] p. 295.

CHAPTER SEVENTEEN

ON AUGUST 4, 1914,
the future of the Fabian Society, of Guild Socialism, of the
Labor Party, of the British Empire, and of the whole Western
world was radically changed, as Humbert Wolfe put it, by:

> The ineptitude
> Which, like a slattern bringing food
> Just slipped and let the whole world smash.

For one great historian of England, Élie Halévy, World War
I (or the War of 1914-18) was the sinister lever of tyrannical
Socialism, that did more to bring about Communism than
Marx himself. For other writers, the war gave organized
capital its supreme chance against both collectivism and
syndicalism—against the socialism of consumer and producer
alike, and created the totalitarian state, ruthless, but rarely,
if ever, radical. Halévy points out how in the war, the British
Parliament voted electoral reform and educational reform,
and that when the state took over the coal mines, the railways, and the munition factories, it effected a degree of collectivization the Webbs had hardly seriously hoped would
be achieved in their lifetime.

For how many years had the Webbs not indefatigably
worked to socialise and to bureaucratise England? For
this they multiplied Fabian tracts, for this they wrote their
great and admittedly tendentious histories, for this they
founded the London School of Economics and the *New
Statesman*. At the war's end, when for a few weeks in the
summer of 1919, the nationalisation of railways and coal
was virtually a fact, surely Sidney Webb, now a member
of the Sankey commission, could say his lifetime's work
had been a success.[1]

And yet, although during the war the workers who were
not sent to the front got high wages, all their rights were

[1] Halévy, Epilogue.

suspended for the war's duration, including the right to strike. And bureaucratic collectivism and Guild Socialism, instead of reinforcing each other, canceled each other out: capitalism brilliantly maneuvered the one against the other, and Lloyd George absolutely rejected the Sankey Committee's recommendations, and instead suggested a plan for unification which would include mixed councils of miners and owners, with the government as arbitrator.

The British Labor Party is of all workers' parties in the world the least doctrinal, but in 1913 the TUC leadership was dissatisfied because the Parliamentary Labor Party was "so coyly and inextricably tied to the apron strings of the mother of Parliaments." And so the workers began that series of strikes which but for the declaration of war would have culminated in a general strike—and did so a few years after the war was over, when the workers realised that all they had got for four years' hard fighting was a suspension of their hard-won privileges and a situation as bad, or worse, than before. As G. D. H. Cole put it in *The Bolo Book:*

> Diddled diddled donkeys, my son John
> Went to France with his khaki on
> Front line the first night and didn't last long
> So they gave me fifteen shillings for my son John.

In 1914 the workers had rightly diagnosed the fall in real wages in spite of the increase in the gold reserves as an attack on Labor: after the war the workers began their attempts to improve their situation by a request from the miners for a national pool of earnings and a national minimum wage, and they obtained neither.

But to take the sequence of war events as they directly concerned the Fabians it is necessary to go back to July 29, 1914, when the International Socialist Bureau held an emergency session in Brussels. Keir Hardie and two lesser lights represented Great Britain. After the meeting, the Bureau issued a manifesto saying in part that "with unanimous vote the Bureau considers it an obligation for the workers of all nations concerned not only to continue but even to strengthen their demonstration against war in favour of peace and a settlement of the Austrian-Serbian conflict by arbitration." Two days later, Jean Jaurès was assassinated in a Paris café by a war fanatic. On August 2 a big demonstration was held in Trafalgar Square, representative of every branch of the Labor and Socialist movement in England. The 15,000 people present passed a resolution protesting the "secret agreements and understandings which the democracies of the civilised world know only by rumour." The Webbs refused to sign this resolution.

"We are not experts," they Pilated. And they sauntered through the crowd to Trafalgar Square, where Labor, Socialist, pacifist demonstrators—with a few trade-union flags— were gesticulating from the steps of the monuments to a "mixed crowd of admirers, hooligan war-mongers and merely curious holiday-makers. It was an undignified and futile exhibition, this singing of the Red Flag and passing of well-worn resolutions in favour of universal peace." [2] G.B.S. called the "Red Flag" "the funeral march of a fried eel." On August 4, Arthur Ponsonby[3] listened to the declaration of war being announced in the House of Commons: "Members sprang to their feet, jumped on the seats, waved their hats and order papers and cheered till the rafters rang." He felt utterly disgusted and horrified by such an exhibition, and realized that he simply failed to understand the motivation of these his fellow countrymen.

The Labor Party National Executive passed a resolution on August 5 declaring the Labor movement had "opposed the policy which produced the war, and its duty is now to secure peace at the earliest possible moment." But the Parliamentary Labor Party refused to allow J. Ramsay MacDonald, its chairman, to read this resolution to the House. MacDonald thereupon resigned his chairmanship. Thereafter the Labor Party, except for the ILP, threw themselves into the war, Fabian Arthur Henderson even assisting with the recruiting campaign in order to prevent conscription. "Members of the Labour Party," he said in a speech at Wallsall on September 11, 1914, "were under a triple obligation to make the voluntary system commensurate with the present national needs." The ILP, however, preferred to use as its text a speech by Lord Welby, a high official of the Treasury, anent the Armaments Ring: "We are in the hands of an organisation of crooks. They are politicians, generals, manufacturers of armaments and journalists. All of them are anxious for unlimited expenditure, and go on inventing scares to terrify the public and Ministers of the Crown." G. D. H. Cole, then still a Fabian, writing on labor in wartime noted that

> between the organised workers of the European powers there is no quarrel capable of provoking war, no national antagonism strong enough to stand against the very real sense of inter-working-class solidarity. Here then is the problem which the revolution is compelled to face. Is alle-

[2] Beatrice Webb, 1952, p. 25.
[3] p. 17.

giance due first of all to the nation, which includes some of all classes, or to the class which includes some of all nations? The answer to this would provide the deepest insight into war psychology, for from it at last true relation between national and class consciousness might emerge.

Alas! What emerged was the "bastard internationalism of the Labour and Socialist movement collapsed like a house of cards." And as the *Labour Leader* prophesied gloomily on August 27, 1914: "This war is the beginning of a new military despotism in Europe, of new alarms, new hatreds and oppositions, new menaces and alliances, the beginning of a dark epoch dangerous, not only to democracy, but to civilization itself."

Among the Fabians, each member of the Society decided individually where his duty lay: Clifford Allen, for example, a member of the Fabian Executive, was one of the principal opponents of conscription, whereas W. Stephen Sanders, the general secretary, was one of the government's most devoted recruiting officers. Meanwhile, many young and distinguished Fabians, including Rupert Brooke and Charles Sorley, were being killed in action. Beatrice Webb noted that "the inner circle of the Fabian Society is distinguished for the intensity of the difference of opinion with regard to the cause of the war and the right way of ending it . . ." But she also noted that the Guild Socialists would be pro-war if they were not in rebellion against the government on principle.

The ILP was still pacifist, but the British Socialist Party (the rump of Hyndman's group) were violent anti-German patriots. Beatrice went on: "The ruck of the Trade Union officials are just sane and commonplace supporters of the British Government against its enemies." [4]

It must be remembered that at this time, unlike the other parties affiliated to the International Socialist Bureau (including, of course, the Fabian Society, Socialist since 1887), the Labor Party was not a Socialist body; the Socialists within it were in 1914 still a minority. During the war the dilution of labor, the employment of masses of unskilled and women workers in skilled trades, the rapid increase of automatic machinery and, above all, the increased tempo of the process of economic amalgamation and concentration accentuated the economic factor, so that the rich grew richer and the position of the middle classes grew more precarious. By 1915 conscription had been accepted in Britain and the government was already trying industrial coercion: "Imperial munitions of war urgently required by the navy and army are

[4] Beatrice Webb, 1952, p. 33.

being held up by the present cessation of work," wrote Sir George (later Lord) Askwith. Still, in those far-off days when the government ordered a resumption of work on Monday morning, March 19, people could and did ask "by what authority did the government order men back to work?" By the time World War II broke out, habeas corpus was suspended retroactively a few weeks after the outbreak of hostilities, and hundreds of thousands of British subjects were imprisoned instantly, many for the duration, and no one any longer dreamed of questioning the government's right to capture or to coerce them.

A terrible step forward into totalitarianism was the passing of the Defense of the Realm Act of 1914 (DORA) which brought in its wake secret police, spies, eavesdroppers, telephone tappers, and letter openers—all innovations in twentieth-century Britain. The war mood was hysterical and bitter: DORA became the symbol of oppression: G. D. H. Cole caught the feeling of the Fabians with his:

> How we do dote on DORA
> She's the heaviest scorer
> There are some who deplore her
> But the Cabinet's for her.

When the 1917 Club was started as a meeting place for Liberal and Labor people who felt the same about the war, the members asked for *Allezdora* as telegraphic address. When this was refused, *Antedora* was suggested. "You sure do like the name Dora," said the official approached. "It's the name of our chairman's girl friend," was the answer given him.

The war mood then was hysterical and bitter. Many a blameless dachshund was sacrificed to it, and one noble lord cried out, "We have actually been dining off German plates," as he hurled his to the floor and was followed by all the other members of his club. Nursemaids daily took their charges to Hyde Park to watch the Tommies charging sawdust-stuffed sacks with fixed bayonets. "It'll be Germans next —their blood will spurt out like that," Nanny would say. Robert Graves[5] has given the words of his sergeant as he and the other men charged the dummies: "Hurt him now. In at his belly! Tear his guts out. . . . Now that upper swing at his privates with the butt. Ruin his chances of life. No more little Fritzes. Bite him, I say. Stick your teeth in him and worry him. Eat his heart out." Children were given mechanical gadgets that hung the Kaiser, musical boxes that played Hate-the-Hun tunes. And hundreds of tots were roused to watch the just-struck Zeppelin flaming in the 1916

5 p. 295.

sky like a great lighted cigar, while their nannies loudly rejoiced at the thought of the burning Boches therein.

With this mood generally prevalent, the pacifist Fabians, such as Bertrand Russell and Clifford Allen, had a grim time in jail. I remember their coming to us for their first meal after being released. Their accounts of the stomach pump used forcibly to feed them was awe-inspiring to a six-year-old. I turned to my neighbor and asked him if he too had just come out of jail. Montagu Norman, governor of the Bank of England, was not amused. J. Ramsay MacDonald, perhaps then the most hated man in England because of his views, came to lunch at my special request on my seventh birthday. Pink, our butler, turned white when approaching him to serve the potatoes, set the silver dish beside him, and said to my mother, "Please excuse me, Madam, but I cannot serve a traitor," and left the room. (Fourteen years later, J. Ramsay MacDonald, then Prime Minister, came to dine on my twenty-first birthday, and Pink did not refuse to serve him.) Pacifists were discriminated against in World War I and treated scurvily, but compared with the ghastly conditions endured at the front, where men lived in the trenches knee-deep in rat-ridden water for weeks at a time, the pacifists had it so easy no one could get too worked up about them.

Many Liberals belonged to the Lansdowne Movement. The Marquis of Lansdowne had sent a letter to the *Times* suggesting a negotiated peace—the *Times* had refused to publish it, but the *Daily Telegraph* did; of these not a few joined the ILP either during or after the war, as it was the only political body that was as a whole unanimously and consistently pacifist.

It may be said that the British workingman became Europe-conscious only during World War I. The Fabian Society then also turned its attention to foreign (international) affairs with its customary efficiency. The anti-British might still quip that "Fog in the Channel: Continent Isolated"—an actual newspaper headline—represented a national attitude, but already in 1915 Beatrice noted that the Fabian Research Bureau, with G. D. H. Cole as vice-president, was showing signs of healthy development, Leonard Woolf was starting on an inquiry into possible developments of supranational law, and H. N. Brailsford too was already working on his book on international peace problems.

In 1916 G.B.S. discussed Leonard Woolf's report on international government for the Fabian Society.

War can do many things, but it cannot end war. The rights of the Nation are at present wiped out . . . the English-

man is forced to fight as a pressed man for Russia, though
his father was slain by the Russians at Inkerman, and for
the French though his grandfather fell at Waterloo charging shoulder to shoulder with Blücher's Prussians. The
German is compelled by the Prussians, whom he loathes, to
die for Turkey and the Crescent, against Anglo-Saxon
Christendom. Every one of the belligerents is holding down
some conquered race or nation. . . . Let us not deceive
ourselves with good natured dreams; unless and until Europe is provided with a new organ for supranational action,
provided with an effective police, all talk of making an end
of war is waste of breath. . . . How it may all be done?
. . . it is the peculiar role of the Fabian Society to supply
progressive aspirations with practical methods.

He then recommended the report, financed by the Quaker
pacifist J. Rowntree, and written by Leonard Woolf. It was
published as a supplement to the *New Statesman,* after a
summer-school meeting at Lake Derwentwater. It had first
been submitted to a non-Fabian group under the presidency
of Lord Bryce—among them were J. A. Hobson, Graham
Wallas, and Lowes Dickinson. As a result of this meeting, and
of their approval of Leonard Woolf's work, the Bryce
group joined the Fabian Research Committee as consultative members. This report was, G.B.S. said, "as good as
the Fabian Society can at present make it." Sir Robert Ensor
considers it was very good, and avers that it was "seminal" to
the League of Nations, and was on President Wilson's
table at the end of the war. For, as G.B.S. put it, "it still is the
vocation of the Fabian Society to chart all the channels into
which the State is being irresistibly driven by social evolution," but it was galling to members of the Society to find that
British Cabinet ministers were prepared to think good intellectual work was only done abroad: they would eagerly
seize on foreign theory or practice, ignoring the selfsame
blueprints clearly marked for them at home. The diligent
Fabian Mary Agnes Hamilton noted that during the war the
Social Democratic Federation went jingoist, and finally van-
ished; the Fabians kept quiet and avoided splits; while the
real center of Socialist life was the ILP. The ILP leaders
were the uncertainly yoked J. Ramsay MacDonald and the
"sea-green incorruptible"—so-called for his paper-white face
and burning eyes—Philip Snowden, Fabians both, though
both of the anti-Webb variety.

In 1917, Herbert Samuel and Edwin Montagu sent Graham
Wallas (who no longer had any use for the Fabian Society
or the Labor Party or the trade-union movement, disliked all
vocational organizations, and regarded them as conspiracies

against the public[6]) to ask Clifford Sharp if the *New States-man* would become the official organ of His Majesty's Opposition. Sharp insisted the magazine remain independent, but indicated that it had no objection to consultations or to receiving communications.

On the British Government's 1917 Reconstruction Committee there were, out of a total of fifteen persons, three Fabians and two other Labor men besides—and the assistant secretary, Arthur Greenwood, was also a Fabian. Beatrice Webb, who had previously been on the Statutory Pension Committee (which she dismissed with: "petting the ex-soldier on the cheap is the note of all its activities"), found the swollen world of Whitehall seething, and was nauseated by Lloyd George's technique—should it better be called perhaps trick?—of handing over each department of the civil service to the interest with which it was concerned. "The insurance Commission is controlled by the great Industrial Companies, the Board of Trade by the Shipowners, the Food Controller is a wholesale Grocer, the Ministry of Munitions is largely managed by the representatives of the munitions manufacturers, a Duke's land agent has been placed at the head of the Board of Agriculture," she wrote.

But if Lloyd George was corrupt, the Socialists were confused. Ideologically, Guild Socialism, syndicalism, and distributism (Hilaire Belloc's version of syndicalism) with their anti-state propaganda, confused the simple Fabian collectivists, raised and trained to be consumer-centered. And the natural aims of working-class Labor, its practical defense of the laborer and his hire, were deflected by the Parliamentary Labor Party's concern with the suffrage movement, the Irish rebellion of 1916, and the two Russian revolutions of March and October, 1917. These were variously greeted in Socialist circles, from tepidly, almost timidly, to enthusiastically. The Leeds Conference of June 1917 was "the direct outcome of the first Russian Revolution; it was a large, somewhat heterogeneous and enthusiastic gathering which passed, among others, a resolution calling for the immediate creation in Britain of Councils of Workers and Soldiers on the Russian model. It produced little concrete results." [7] The Webbs themselves declared that so long as the Russian Revolution went in for any kind of nonsense like workers' control they had no interest in it: their interest dated only from Lenin's abandonment of this whole idea. The British Socialists were divided into those who came out in full cry against the

[6] Beatrice Webb, 1952, p. 66.
[7] *Ibid.*, p. 88, n. 1.

Bolshevists and those who became Communists; the Guild
Socialists supported the Revolution but decried the tendencies
already apparent toward centralization. After Arthur Henderson had been driven out of the War Cabinet, he warmly
supported the idea of the Stockholm Conference at which a
meeting was proposed with the Bolshevist leaders. At the
Labor Party's annual conference in Nottingham in January
1918, Henderson engineered Alexander Kerensky's appearance, and Kerensky made a "great oration" in Russian,
listened to in dead silence. Henderson's management of the
Kerensky episode, it was conceded, amounted to genius.

The Labor Party's acceptance in 1918 of Sidney Webb's
program "Labour and the New Social Order" meant that it
could go to the country at the next election with a program
more complete than that of either of its rivals, Conservatives
or Liberals. The Labor program was a cautious, truly Fabian,
commitment to Socialism. The "Four Pillars of the House"
Labor proposed to erect were:

a. The universal enforcement of the national minimum
wage.

b. The democratic control of industry (nationalization).

c. The revolution in national finance.

d. The use of surplus wealth for the common good.

Many of the Labor "left" thought that this "detailed and
practical" program had been imposed on the Labor Party by
Sidney. This new constitution declared the objectives of the
Labor Party to be: "To secure for the producers by hand and
by brain the fruits of their industry and the most equitable
distribution thereof that may be possible, upon the basis of
the common ownership of the means of production and the
best obtainable system of popular administration and control
of each industry or service." As E. R. Pease pointed out,
nothing could possibly be more Fabian and thus in 1918, at
war's end, he concludes the Labor Party at length became "a
definitely Socialist organisation."

The "Hang the Kaiser" election of 1918, fought on the
widely extended franchise which included women for the first
time, brought 57.6 per cent of the electorate to the polls.
The coalition between the Conservatives and the Lloyd George
Liberals polled over five million votes and elected 338 Conservatives, 136 Coalition Liberals and other Coalition supporters. The Asquith Liberals only elected 26 members, so
the Labor Party, with 59 members, became the official Opposition. "Almost twenty years of undistinguished Tory rule
began with this adventitious victory," notes Charles Mowat.[8]

8 p. 7.

For Ramsay MacDonald, who lost by 14,000, "the haunting memory is of the women, bloodthirsty, nursing their hate, issuing from the courts and alleys crowded with children, reeking with humanity, the sad flotsam and jetsam of wild emotion." [9] One working woman trying to explain why the working classes had not voted Labor, explained that the British people were afraid the Labor Party would be too lenient to the Germans, that they really endorsed the "squeeze them till the pips squeak" mentality. Beatrice Webb noted that she felt physically sick when reading the frenzied appeals of the Coalition leaders to destroy the Hun forever and felt that "the one outstanding virtue of the Labour Party, a virtue which is its very own, not imposed upon it by its intellectuals, is its high sense of international morality."

The Fabian Society suffered severely in this 1918 election. Only three of its Labor-nominated candidates were successful out of forty-two, and altogether only four Fabians won or kept their seats. But by the time the February 1919 coal strike threatened, the Fabians were back again playing at the top table. Lord Haldane, now once again in the Cabinet, was instructed by the Prime Minister, Lloyd George, to arrange another dinner with the Webbs. The four dined at Haldane's, whose discreet butler was told by Lloyd George to telephone home for the list of names the Prime Minister was proposing to appoint to the Royal Commission on the Mines. But the telephone at Number 10 Downing Street did not answer, "an odd incident in a Prime Minister's abode," wrote Beatrice. Lloyd George told her, "We will beat them [the miners] if they strike. We have the food." Who would the Webbs suggest be appointed to the Commission? he asked. Naively Beatrice admitted: "Here we were in a difficulty, as we could hardly give Sidney's name. We proposed Cole: the PM had never heard of him." Next day, Tom Jones was sent round with the PM's list: "He let the cat out of the bag and a very ugly cat it was: The persons on the list were all hostile to nationalisation." The strike was averted only by the appointment of a much more conciliatory commission under Lord Justice Sankey. Of its nine members, three represented the owners, three were miners' officials, three—R. H. Tawney, Sir Leo Chiozza Money, and Sidney Webb—were Fabians. The three Fabians were chiefly responsible for drafting the majority report advocating the nationalization of the mines, signed also by the three miners' representatives.

During the war the state had run the railways, the mines, the ships: between the wars, however, the Sankey report

[9] *Forward,* December 21, 1918.

was shelved, and there was no nationalization for twenty years. But collectivist measures had mushroomed during the war under the Coalition, and the state had swollen until it was under the Conservatives in World War II that this "new Leviathan" first became a welfare state led by that arch-Tory, Sir Winston Churchill. In 1944 his party machine declared that "the Government accepts, as one of their primary aims and resolves, the maintenance of a high and stable level of employment after the war." The young man Beatrice Webb had approved as making sound speeches on unemployment in 1910, whom she and Sidney had thought the best man available to put at the top in May 1917, whom she had castigated as a "sinister reactionary" in 1920, had learned their lesson well. Though perhaps he had already forgotten his own statement that "the Tory party is the party of the rich against the poor, of the classes and their dependents against the masses, of the lucky and wealthy, the happy and the strong against the left out and shut out, the millions of the weak and the poor" (January 30, 1909).

CHAPTER EIGHTEEN

From the Congress of Vienna in 1815 to the Versailles Conference in 1919 is a century plus World War I. During this time many ideas and existences came around full circle. France the victim at Vienna became France the victor at Versailles, and just twenty years later was victim again at Vincennes. Perhaps the real victim in 1918 was the "bamboozled old Presbyterian," as Lord Keynes called President Wilson, who had hoped to establish, by his Fourteen Points, the democracy to make the world, for which so many millions of men had died, safe. Instead, he was led down the garden path—a not so primrose path to the everlasting bonfire. During the latter part of the same one hundred years, the various Socialist parties in England had been doing some boxing of the compass too. The Fabians had started off as anti-Marxist as it was possible to be, yet they had come to a position in 1918 where some of their leaders were prepared to accept not a few Marxist conclusions; whilst the syndicalist Guild Socialists, with their concern for individuals, for the little man, in factory or co-operative, were to find these ideas translated in Europe into the most grisly of Fascist realities. As Charles Mowat[1] has pointed out,

> to explain how Labour missed the opportunity to rule in the immediately postwar world—and to explain the weakening of Labour's interest in socialism, despite all protestations, for the next twenty years—we must notice the intervention of Lloyd George and the Coalition Government. . . . The Sankey Coal Commission and the National Industrial Conference were the principal means. Nothing was settled by them, but that did not matter. They had served their purpose: to get the leaders of the trade unions to talk rather than to act . . . Things settled back into their old grooves; 1919, the critical year of transition was safely passed.

[1] p. 31.

But if Labor thus fumbled its catch, so too, and more so, did the Liberals.

Perhaps the trouble was partly the unexpected boom of 1920, partly the equally unexpected reaction of both Capital and Labor to the Russian Revolution. As Sir Llewellyn Woodward sees it, the Right hated Bolshevism, and could not see the need for revolution, while the Left was embarrassed by Russian cruelties, but said they were necessary. Between them the Liberals lost their golden chance: "Never was an occasion more favourable; never was the opportunity so completely missed." [2] The Liberal leaders, Asquith, Grey, and Haldane, had absolutely no influence: they had been jockeyed out of position by Lloyd George in 1916 and thereafter had been laid aside by the public; Lloyd George himself after 1918 disquieted and alienated almost all his quondam supporters by his obvious hostility to Labor and by his irresponsibility in scattering promises lightheartedly without attempting or even pretending to keep them.

The postwar era began inauspiciously. There was a coal shortage, and everyone in England shivered over fires that were tinier than usual. In London, the demobilized troops found "the streets dirty and shabby . . . there were holes even in the main thoroughfares. The decent, orderly, good-natured Londoners had become as snappy and selfish as the far more sorely tried French. There was a shortage of everything except returning soldiers and debts." [3] And on top of this there were the two influenza epidemics, which killed 150,000 people in England and Wales, besides laying low about half the whole population.

International issues dominated the elections of 1918, 1922, and 1924 and even 1929—though perhaps during 1929 it was more specifically international economics that loomed as the largest single issue. And during all these years at home, the rich grew richer, the poor grew poorer, and the unemployed just grew in numbers: the average annual percentages of unemployed among trade-union members making returns were: 1911, 3%; 1919, 2.4%; 1921, 14.8%; 1922, 15.8%.

The spring of 1919 was considered by the Fabians as a favorable time to change the Basis for the first time in the Society's history. The new Basis[4] was submitted to a members' meeting on May 23, was confirmed six months later, and remained in force until it was once again amended, by

[2] Woodward, p. 108.

[3] Aldington, p. 204.

[4] *See* Appendix A.

postal ballot, in 1949.[5] In 1920, W. Sanders, the Society's secretary, became an official of the League of Nations, and F. W. Galton, once the Webbs' secretary, was elected general secretary to the Fabian Society in Sanders' stead. Beatrice Webb[6] wrote:

> Galton is now a middle-aged man, but exactly like his old self: strong, cynical and full of cheerful energy; . . . he dismisses ideas and sentiments with the same good-natured tolerance to weaker brethren, and he is a faithful friend and admirer of the Webbs except that he regards them as very distinctly "Old Folk" who may be a little past their work. He has plans for the Fabian Society and declares that it still has life left in it: but his mind runs on somewhat commercial lines. He scans the new movements and wonders whether they have anything in them: "I have seen four and twenty leaders of revolt" is his attitude to Cole and Co. "You won't get the better of the Webbs, I think." He is disgusted with the old political parties, and does not much believe in the Labour Party. . . . But with all these shortcomings for the Secretaryship of a Socialist Society, he has remained a clean-minded, clear-headed man—good to look at and good to work with.

In the Parliament of 1920 a sympathetic outsider, David Low,[7] the cartoonist, newly arrived from his native Australia, noted that

> Labour was only the fag-end of a party. It looked a pretty inadequate lot to take on Lloyd George's clustered hosts . . . no leaders. Not that that mattered since outside the House they didn't seem to be speaking to one another anyway. Ramsay MacDonald is reputed to have said he hated the Labour Party. Snowden had become sour and tiffy, and even Keir Hardie was losing enthusiasm. The bright boys of the Labour Party brains trust appeared to gyrate around the Webbs.

When the government tried to sound the tocsin during the 1919 railway strike by declaring a national emergency and calling for Citizen Guards, requisitioning 25,000 lorries and arranging for food distribution, it was the Labor Research Department, manned and trained by Fabians, which supplied the National Union of Railwaymen with facts and enabled it to match the government in the arts of publicity.

[5] *See* Appendix B.
[6] 1952, p. 180.
[7] p. 119.

In 1917, when the British Labor Party proposed to send delegates to an international conference in Stockholm, Lord Hugh Cecil stated that the Labor Party was unfit mentally and by training to deal with such questions as would be discussed there, and he would as soon send up a child of three in control of an airplane as entrust those policies to their guidance. In 1920 Winston Churchill contemptuously asked, "Is Labour fit to govern?" Four years later it was governing, and even Lord Grey was agreeing it had a perfect right to do so. Only eighteen years after its genesis, the Labor Party had not, indeed, a majority, yet it was running the country. As Sidney Webb pointed out in his article discussing the Labor Party on the threshold of power (in *Fabian News,* 1923), the Labor Party was the largest political organization in England, and the poorest. It was locally organized in all but half a dozen of the 600 constituencies in the country, and it had 10,000 elected representatives in various municipal and other local offices. In 1922 it polled 4¼ million votes, only a million fewer than the Coalition. In 1906 there were 40 Labor Members of Parliament elected; in 1918, 70; in 1922, 140; and in 1924, 200.

The special job of the Fabian Society, Sidney Webb pointed out in the same article, which also contained his most famous phrase, "the inevitability of gradualness," was to provide the Labor Party with a collective body of doctrine. Twenty-odd years later Herbert Morrison, another devout Fabian, when Lord President of the Council in the first Labor Government that really ruled, pointed out that "the Fabians had succeeded in doing that valuable job of work." Even their most bitter enemy, the American McCarthyist John T. Flynn,[8] agrees. Writing of the "British Fabian Socialists" who "never had more than 4000 members," he declares that "their plan had one thing to be said for it: it succeeded."

Meanwhile, as Max Beer[9] points out, "The conversion of organised Labour to socialism was one of the phenomena of the years 1917-1928. Henceforth trade union history forms a part of socialist history." Beer also notes how the young Liberals at that time were coming into the Labor Party in droves: "We young Liberals find our ideals in the Labour Party," one wrote to the *Manchester Guardian* on November 13, 1924. It was a kind of permeation in reverse: the Liberals, split on free trade by Chamberlain, split by Lloyd George again in 1916, were leaving their own sinking ship

[8] p. 14.
[9] II, p. 403.

in order to climb aboard the Labor craft, and the permeated of the 1890's became the permeators of the 1920's.

While Leonard Woolf's *International Government* (1916) and the Labor Party's *War Aims* of 1917 had, it was said, greatly influenced President Wilson, the concrete results of the Versailles Treaty, so diametrically the antithesis of Wilson's pronouncements, shocked many people, even among those who disapproved of Lord Keynes's *Economic Consequences of the Peace* because it shifted responsibility for the war from the Germans to the conquerors whose mistakes had fouled up the peace. Two wrongs don't make a right, and many felt there was no need to whitewash the Hun because the victors were behaving like Hunnish vultures.

Yet the British had made so many public statements, individual and collective, such as "We have no desire to add to our Imperial burdens either in area or in responsibility" (Asquith, October 1914) and "We are not fighting for territory" (Bonar Law, December 1916), that when the total British Empire loot was announced as 1,415,929 additional square miles,[10] this amount caused qualms of conscience among members of the war generation, including not a few of the hitherto imperialist young Fabians. But the older generation gave no sign of suffering from any sense of sin, neither the Right, that smugly was preparing to administer the spoil, nor the Left, which had so signally failed to prevent the outbreak of war. Indeed, the Second International, that had collapsed into obedient national jingoistic units so completely and instantly in 1914, had the gall to linger on after its failure, its members passing the buck like children playing cobbler, cobbler, mend my shoe. "Exactly as we blame France for the wicked treaty [of Versailles]," Beatrice Webb[11] wrote, "the French blame us: we are each of us vividly con-

---

[10] Territories added to the British Empire after World War I:

	Square Miles
Egypt (became part of the British Empire)	50,000
Cyprus (became part of the British Empire)	3,584
German West Africa (mandated to South Africa)	322,450
German East Africa (mandated to Britain)	384,180
Togoland and Cameroons, divided between Britain and France	112,415
Samoa (mandated to New Zealand)	1,050
German New Guinea (mandated to Australia)	90,000
Palestine (mandated to Britain)	9,000
Mesopotamia (mandated to Britain)	143,250
Total:	1,415,929

[11] 1952, p. 172.

scious of the other one's 'imperialistic greed' at the expense of the fallen enemies. They don't love us, these foreign allies. . . . They are angry, too, with the United States. Will there gradually arise an anti-Anglo-Saxon bloc in Europe, Asia, Africa?" It has taken less than forty years to prove the inevitability of Beatrice Webb's prophetic pen. For the Left of the twenties, there were three centers of enthusiasm (as Kingsley Martin noted in his life of Laski): the Labor Party, on the edge of power, after only eighteen years of existence; the Soviet Union, not yet visibly drenched in the blood of its own that it had purged; and the League of Nations, incomplete and frail, yet a tribute from the victors to the ideals in whose name they had vanquished.

The great influence on the young Oxford and Cambridge Fabians of those days—and they were an astonishingly brilliant batch—was that of G. E. Moore. First published in 1912, reprinted twice in 1925, and several times since, his *Ethics* nourished such diverse thinkers as G. Lowes Dickinson, R. H. Tawney, E. M. Forster, G. D. H. Cole, Irene Cooper Willis, Henry Slesser, Lytton Strachey, Leonard Woolf, Harold Laski, and, above all, J. Maynard Keynes, who has paid his mentor magnificent tribute in his *Two Memoirs*. Moore's *Ethics* was, in fact, for the Fabians of the twenties as focal a book as those of Henry George or Stanley Jevons had been for the Founding Fabians of the 1890's.

Moore, according to Leonard Woolf, abolished the Absolute. The Universe was divided into things that were true or false (i.e., absolute) and those that were good or bad (i.e., relative). For the former were matters of fact, the latter of opinion: it is always true that the earth is round, but whether loyalty is a good thing or a bad depends on whether you wish to hire a soldier or a spy. But Keynes, Woolf, and also Sir Henry Slesser and Sir Llewellyn Woodward all noted that Moore, and the Fabians who followed him, thought—as poor Bentham had before them, and Pelagius before him—that if the total consequences of a thing were clearly seen to be good, human beings would always want that thing. That if you could educate people out of the fogs of ignorance, and elevate them above the pangs of hunger and other kindred miseries, they would seek truth and ensue it. Like Keir Hardie, they simply could not understand Lord Grey's deliberately telling lies; they could not—or would not—face the fact that it was in, and from, *Paradise* that man fell: that it was at the moment of man's greatest possible happiness that he willfully, deliberately, chose evil. For the Fabians, man's homesickness for the slime was as incomprehensible as the original sin which caused it. This inability to see human nature clearly and whole made many of the Fabians—noble, brilliant, and virtuous though many of them were—fumbling dupes. Some were duped by the single and simple vision of the "housekeeping" welfare state, that "ubiquitous officialdom" as Auberon Herbert called it. Some, like the Webbs and Shaw, became the senile dupes of Soviet Communism, because they loved good blueprints, and Soviet blueprints are admirable; they only suffer from being untranslatable into comparable action.

The Fabians could not believe in the deliberate misuse of power. Wickedness, unconnected with underprivilege, discrimination, or sickness, they honestly could not imagine: power for them was as beneficent as domestic electricity or the patient ox; of lightning and mad bulls they distantly but incredulously disapproved. Yet Beatrice wrote:

Somewhere in my diary—1890?—I wrote *I have staked all on the essential goodness of human nature.* Looking back I realise how permanent are the evil impulses and instincts in man—how little you can count on changing some of these—for instance the greed of wealth and power—by any change in machinery. We must be continually asking for better things from our own and other persons' human nature—but how shall we get sufficient response? And without this how can we shift social institutions from off the basis of brutal struggle for existence and power on to that of fellowship? No amount of knowledge or science will be of any avail unless we can curb the bad impulses and set free the good.

This, written before her conversion to the Soviet system, shows that Beatrice had at that time arrived at a deeper insight and wisdom than was granted to many of her fellow Fabians.

The Fabians, in the twenties, were in a fine frenzy of writing and publishing. The Webbs produced their *A Constitution for the Socialist Commonwealth of Great Britain* in 1920, their *Consumers' Co-operative Movement* in 1921, and their *The Decay of Capitalist Civilisation* in 1923. More readable, and much more widely read, was R. H. Tawney's *The Acquisitive Society*, as trenchant a Fabian indictment of the capitalist system as Lord Keynes's *Economic Consequences of the Peace* had been of the Versailles Treaty, or Norman Angell's *The Great Illusion* had been of World War I, or Harold Laski's *A Grammar of Politics* was to be of "mobocracy"— all Fabian masterpieces.

R. H. Tawney married a sister of Lord Beveridge, and Margaret Cole's brother, Raymond Postgate, married a daughter of George Lansbury; thus the Fabian tradition of inter-group marriages was carried into the third generation.

Harold Laski was perhaps the most important of the younger Fabians: many regarded him as a new Webb. His sentences were "epic in phrase, and epic in meaning" and he was to have more influence in the United States than any other single Fabian. Laski[12] has described his own debt to the Webbs: "I learned a good deal from books, especially from those of Sidney and Beatrice Webb. They made me realise that a whole class of human beings was overlooked in the traditionally liberal family to which I belonged." And he added, "I devoted a good deal of time at Oxford to the Fabian Society and to propaganda on behalf of woman suffrage." He left the Panks—the suffragist followers of Mrs. Pankhurst—for the milder Peths—the devotees of Mrs. Pethick-Lawrence. He married a woman eight years his senior when he was eighteen, and after coming down from Oxford in 1914, and doing some leader writing for the *Daily Herald*, then the organ of the Guild Socialists, where he hobnobbed with Mellor, G. D. H. Cole, and G. K. Chesterton, he volunteered when war broke out, but was rejected as unfit. He then went to McGill, and later to Harvard, only returning to England after the war was over. On December 3, 1919, Graham Wallas, lecturing at the New School in New York, wrote to Laski to tell him that Sir William Beveridge had written from the London School of Economics asking for a reference on Laski: Sidney Webb wrote too. As a result Laski was offered Graham Wallas' job in 1920. Wallas wrote: "I suppose if I had not known you, you would not have got the job, but I don't think that would have been enough without Haldane's help." [13] Laski was an innovator in England, since he thought American institutions as important as British ones, and talked more of the Supreme Court than of Aristotle. In 1920 Frida and Harold Laski "went down to the Fabian Summer School for a day. Cole was the chief gazebo and I never saw such a crowd. Cole himself had obviously a most distinguished mind, but his henchmen are rather like third-rate Greenwich villagers who echo him wonderingly. I felt that National Guilds are not for me." [14]

They really were no longer for anyone very much. Guild Socialism died in the twenties for three reasons. The postwar slump; the coal strikes of 1920-21, followed by the Gen-

[12] p. 178.

[13] Quoted in Martin, p. 44.

[14] *Ibid.*, p. 57.

eral Strike of 1926—which were failures, and discredited direct action; and the foundation of the British Communist Party in 1921. The Communists were bidden to go all out, disrupting and recruiting among the Socialists, and Guild Socialists succumbed in large numbers. The Fabians, smugly, did not.

In fact, the Fabians were becoming positively pontifical.

Fabianism was spreading also abroad. The Second International's Conference at Geneva in August 1920 was masterminded by the British delegation, which was presided over by Tom Shaw, with Sidney Webb as chairman. Webb was chairman also of the Commission for the Political Systems of Socialism and Socialisation, "whilst I was on the sub-commission on Socialisation. Fabianism was in fact dominating the Second International through the medium of British trade unionism," wrote Beatrice Webb[15] in her diary for August 20. There was, she added, a "defiant repudiation of the Russian Soviet system and the dictatorship of the Communist Party." And she herself was certain then that the Soviet was the "servile state" in being. But a servile state run by fanatics who refuse any compromise with the "bourgeois fetish" of personal freedom. The influence of the Fabian Society on political thought was already the theme of doctoral theses, especially in America, wrote E. R. Pease.

Of President Franklin D. Roosevelt, R. G. Tugwell wrote, "He had a good Harvard education when Fabianism was developing, and he probably knew quite well the work of Wells and Shaw. Miss Perkins was literate in the Fabian tradition, and so were some of the rest of us." But Dr. Tugwell describes it as a diffused influence and did not think it advisable to make much of it. Mrs. Roosevelt, who knew the Webbs, meeting them both in London and in the States, doubts whether her husband had ever read their books, as she herself had not. Graham Wallas' influence at Harvard was never Fabian, but Harold Laski's was definitely so.[16] In the 1920's Stuart Chase tried to establish a Fabian Society in Boston, and in the 1930's in Chicago, but failed on both occasions. The League for Industrial Democracy, founded in 1905 on Fabian lines in New York by H. Laidler, has always kept closely in touch with British Fabians: the Fabian Society's Annual Report from 1925 to 1930 listed it under *Provincial Societies*. Laidler attended an early Fabian Summer School in the Lakes, and, when he was en route for Russia in 1930, Mrs. Webb gave

---

[15] 1952, p. 186.
[16] When Laski died he was President of the Fabian Society (having succeeded Sir Stafford Cripps); he was succeeded by G. D. H. Cole.

a luncheon for him in the Fabian common room. At th League's fortieth anniversary in 1945, A. Creech-Jones, M.P. spoke at their dinner in New York on the British Labo Party.

The League had begun in 1905, at a time when socia workers—Jacob Riis, Jane Addams, Robert Hunter, and oth ers—were stirring thoughtful Americans with tragic tales o how most Americans lived. Meanwhile, the Socialists, unde Eugene Debs, were growing: Debs got 400,000 votes as Pres idential candidate of the Socialist Party in 1904. The League' objective was to promote "an intelligent interest in Socialism among college men and women, graduate and undergraduate through the formation of study clubs in the colleges and uni versities." Among the founders of the League were Jack Lon don, Upton Sinclair, and William English Walling. Upto Sinclair said his college had failed to give him any under standing of the fundamental social problems of the day, an had decided that "since the professors would not educate th students, it was up to the students to educate the professors. Unlike the Fabian Society, the League for Industrial Democ racy has never affiliated with any political party, nor does it basis insist on Socialism; it operates solely at the instructiona and collegiate level. Harold Laski called the LID "America Fabian" and compared the *New Republic* with the *New Statesman* as expressive of Fabian policy.

Among League members, past or present, are Walter Lipp mann, Norman Thomas, Babette Deutsch, Sidney Hook Freda Kirchwey, Max Lerner, William Shirer, and Vid Scudder. Many efforts to track down, or even to estimate, Fa bian influence on American political thought have proved un availing. Walter Lippmann, Norman Thomas, and R. G. Tug well all admit there *was* an influence, but all warn agains overemphasis. Fabian permeation, as far as these Unite States are concerned, consisted mostly in importing *peopl* from England—the Webbs, G.B.S., Graham Wallas, Laski G. D. H. Cole—for longer or shorter periods; but above al it consisted in getting their books read. There was also con stant visiting between such people as Jane Addams and th Webbs. Perhaps the most pervasive influence of all was tha of Shaw's plays, performed in New York earlier and oftene than even in London, on the young people who later becam the New Dealers. The New Deal, however, it must not b forgotten, came *before* the Beveridge Plan and the Labo majority, so that it is just as possible that the New Deal in fluenced the British welfare state as vice versa.

"A general election on a purely class basis" was how Bea trice Webb described that of 1922 in which her Sidney, a

sixty-three, found himself elected for Seaham Harbour, a
north-country mining constituency. She found the prospect
of Parliament unpleasing, although she was glad that the
miners were grateful to Sidney for his work on the Sankey
Commission. Webb got in by almost a 12,000 majority over
the Conservatives: the sitting Liberal member trailed with
only 5,000 votes.

The permeation of Seaham was done on the best Fabian
lines. Clubs, religious and semi-religious bodies, League of
Nations, Union branches, friendly societies, Welfare Leagues,
were card-indexed; pubs as well as clubs canvassed. The result was that, during the nine years Sidney represented the
constituency, he had record majorities; Beatrice notes that
the miners "from the first regarded Sidney as their property:
the serious ones regarded him as their local preacher, and the
younger ones as their 'professional' football player whom
they had acquired at a high price and had to look after."

The Fabian Society meanwhile kept the Webbs busy: Beatrice hoped their *The Decay of Capitalist Civilisation* would
"be a big piece of propaganda and give lift to the Fabian
Society and its doctrines." G.B.S. was gallantly generous in
devoting days of his time to the Webbs' proofs "pointing and
repairing our style and adding one or two paragraphs of his
where he thought we have not made our meaning clear."
G.B.S. also gave not only his own lecture that year at the
Kingsway Hall, but also Hugh Dalton's. Beatrice conceded
that he was a real dear of a friend and comrade. The Fabian
lectures were now a social success as well as a financial one:
two Rothschilds, peers, princes, and a minor royalty attended them in 1922. Another old friend and fellow Fabian,
Lord Haldane, had courageously come out for the Labor Party.
A younger Fabian, P. Hastings (later Sir Patrick Hastings,
Q.C.), then a novice, gives in his autobiography an amusing
account of "my initiation into the ranks of my new found
party. It was necessary that I should be passed as fit for service. I was, therefore, invited to dinner by Mr. and Mrs. Sidney Webb." At that time, he points out, Sidney Webb was the
leader of the intellectuals in the Labor Party. "He was a man
of great ability, but suffered somewhat from a disposition to
regard human nature as a fitting subject for a Blue Book. He
was an undoubted authority on Blue Books." In appearance,
Hastings notes, Webb was not impressive, as he insisted upon
wearing a peculiar beard of the kind generally associated
with a goat.

The first time I heard him speak in the House of Commons an opposing Member so far forgot himself as to make

goat-like noises, and finally to remark, "Speak up, Nanny." This might have passed unheard, had not David Kirkwood, always ready to die in a forlorn cause, leapt to his feet. "Mr. Speaker," he roared. "Is it in order for an Hon. Member to describe my revered leader as a nanny goat?" This perhaps unfortunate interruption was drowned in roars of laughter.

Sidney performed an act of quiet heroism; he continued his speech to the end.

Sir Patrick feared that he did not pass his dinner-party exam with high honors. The only thing he remembered was G.B.S. skillfully eating nuts with his soup. "Personally I enjoyed the evening with the Webbs enormously. It was the first time I had ever been cross-examined, and I had the advantage of not being upon oath. I fought the next election as a Labor candidate, and was elected for Wallsend."

In 1920 Beatrice Webb started her "Half-Circle Club, so called because it was for one sex only. Its object was to groom Labor women and the wives of Labor men to feel at ease in society. Over 100 persons turned up and we had a rollicking evening," Beatrice wrote in 1921. Arthur Henderson ("the ideal methodist") acted as chairman, and R. Ellis Roberts read from Vachel Lindsay's poems. At the next meeting there were 170 women and their husbands: Mrs. Clynes was a dignified hostess. Beatrice notes that "the Half-Circle Club, if it has done nothing else, has led to something like personal friendship between the little group of women who form the Executive, and to friendliness among some hundred others." The Club began because Mrs. Frank Hodges had confided to Beatrice how lonely she was in London. "At first the menkind were hostile; now Henderson and Clynes are the keenest supporters of the Club." J. Ramsay MacDonald remained actively against it and George Lansbury was suspicious. Desmond MacCarthy declares these parties for the wives of Labor members were not a success; but G. D. H. Cole approves the validity of an endeavor "to protect the members of the new governing class at once from social isolation and from the insidious risks of patronage." Some of the Labor wives thought Mrs. Webb "too bloomin' patronising by 'arf": there was even an "anti-Beatrice fellowship." Yet Beatrice was to be proven terribly right—in the persons of no less than the first Labor Prime Minister and the first Labor Chancellor of the Exchequer and his wife—in her fear of the "aristocratic embrace" by which the Tories disarmed the new Labor members (and their wives) by simply asking them to dinner. Some of the wives, however, were naturally well protected against

the "insidious risks of patronage." For example, Catholic
Mrs. Clynes, of whom Beatrice writes in her diary that she
was well dressed, "carrying herself like a duchess," staying
with the King and Queen both at Windsor and at Sandring-
ham, and never mentioning it; discreet, courteous, kind. At
the other end of the social scale was Lady Warwick, who put
Easton Lodge at the disposal of the executive of the Labor
Party for week-end conferences and consultations. The press
invaded the first house party "as our hostess obviously desired
these attentions" and the Webbs, Hendersons, MacDonald,
et al. "appeared in groups not only in the newspapers but also
on newsreels." Beatrice approves Lady Warwick who "cannot
help being a Countess" and who had "become an old woman
like myself—a benign and hard-working old woman who has
gained the respect of her neighbours by a sterling public
spirit—supporting a secondary school—turning a medieval
barn into a fine hall for plays and meetings, promoting the
local Labour Party."

In 1922 Lloyd George's government, with its endorsement
of the sadistic (and ineffective) Black-and-Tans in Ireland,
with its colossal sale of honors at home (15,000 pounds for a
knighthood, 50,000 pounds for a peerage) and its monstrous
handing over to Greece of the lands Lloyd George himself
dubbed as the Turkish homeland of Anatolia, went out when
the Conservatives decided to retire from the Coalition and go
to the country on their own. "Lloyd George remained in public life, admired, distrusted, unused, and stonily watched the
country sink in the hopeless morass of depression and unemployment, while lesser men frittered away Britain's power in
the world." [17]

The Conservatives went to the country on protection in
1923. Mowat[18] thinks Baldwin's advocacy of protection was
essentially sound: that if it lost him an election, it staved off a
Labor majority until after World War II and completely disrupted the Liberals, who might otherwise have come out for
protection themselves. The country rejected protection: 258
Conservatives, 158 Liberals, and 191 Labors were returned.
The Labor Party decided to accept Liberal support and form a
government: Neville Chamberlain agreed with Asquith that
to keep Labor out would strengthen it, whereas, in office "it
would be too weak to do much harm but not too weak to get
discredited." [19]

J. Ramsay MacDonald was now once more cordial to the

[17] Mowat, p. 142.
[18] p. 167.
[19] *Ibid.*, p. 169.

Fabians—though Mary Agnes Hamilton[20] writes that "the Webbs he disliked; Cole he snubbed; Laski he detested"—mainly because he found his fellow Scots, the Clydesiders, impossible. The *Times* reported MacDonald as sitting on the front bench "white with anger at the folly of his own followers" when Jimmie Maxton accused the Conservatives of murdering children by cutting grants to child-welfare centers. It was the forty-year-old distaste of the Fabians for sentimentalizing over the very real and legitimate miseries of the poor that now joined together MacDonald, the Webbs, Henderson, Snowden, Herbert Morrison, Lords Parmoor and Haldane, Arthur Creech-Jones, and Phillip Noel Baker in uneasy fellowship against such sob-brothers as Maxton, Jack Jones, and George Lansbury. Lansbury above all had no use for Fabians, especially for either G.B.S. or H. G. Wells. "If they had spoken their most uncharitable thoughts," wrote Raymond Postgate (Lansbury's biographer and his son-in-law, who was also Margaret Cole's brother), "the two writers would have described Lansbury as sentimental and he would have described them as self-centred. Socialism was for Lansbury above all a means for ensuring the security and independence for the ordinary man." Yet of all the attacks the Conservatives made upon Fabianism, only one ever disgusted Lansbury and that was "The charge that State Socialism as the Webbs and the elder Fabians advocated it, might make men the slaves of the state as soon as they had escaped from being the slave of the employer." [21] Beatrice Webb[22] was not too sanguine about Labor's taking office. "For Labour to accept the responsibilities of government is a big risk; it may lead to immediate disaster. But its leaders will become educated in the realities of political life and in the work of administration," she wrote. Sidney Webb was first offered the Ministry of Labor, but settled for the Board of Trade in order to preside over unemployment. Early in 1924, Arnold Bennett[23] met the Webbs walking. He asked them about the first Labor Government. "O, I think it's a jolly lark," Beatrice said, then added, in reply to a question from Bennett about Labor Ministers, "Well, they do work. You see, they have no silly pleasures." Sidney, smiling, added, "Talking of silly pleasures, here she is, taking me out for a constitutional." Meanwhile in the Foreign Office—which MacDonald had reserved for himself—everyone was delighted by his good manners, after Lord Curzon's

[20] 1944, p. 125.
[21] Postgate, p. 94.
[22] 1952, p. 258.
[23] III, entry for February 4, 1924.

deplorable ones, and King George V is alleged to have said, when MacDonald kissed hands, that it was nice to have a gentleman as Prime Minister, for a change.

Of the twenty-two Fabians elected to Parliament, four became Cabinet Ministers: Sydney Olivier (India), Brigadier General Thomson (Air), Sidney Webb (Board of Trade), and Philip Snowden (Chancellor of the Exchequer). Over two hundred Fabians attended the Fabian dinner to honor these under R. H. Tawney's chairmanship. Susan Lawrence, Parliamentary private secretary to the Minister of Education, toasted the government; Arthur Henderson, party whip, and Lord Olivier, Secretary of State for India, replied for it. There were also many Fabians in minor offices in 1924: Margaret Bondfield, Under-Secretary of Labor; A. V. Alexander (from the co-operative movement), Parliamentary private secretary to Webb; Arthur Greenwood, Minister of Health; Josiah Wedgwood, Chancellor of the Duchy of Lancaster; Ernest Thurtle, Minister of Pensions; Sir Patrick Hastings, Attorney General.

The Labor Party had polled four and a half million votes out of the fourteen million cast. Unfortunately, MacDonald's policy was far from Socialist: except for Wheatley's Housing Act, MacDonald, without a working majority, nibbled at health, education, and unemployment plans where he should have nailed Labor's colors firmly to the mast. As Max Beer[24] put it: "The weaning of Labour from Liberalism was a long and painful process."

At the Labor Party's Annual Conference in 1924 the Communist Party of Great Britain, formed in 1920 from the rump of the Social Democratic Federation, applied for affiliation to the Labor Party. Their application was refused by 3,185,000 votes to 193,000, and it was also decided that no member of the Communist Party would be eligible for membership of the Labor Party. A year later, in 1925, the trade unions were asked not to send members of the Communist Party as delegates to Labor Party conferences or meetings.

The record of the MacDonald Government in foreign affairs included *de jure* recognition of the Soviet Government, acceptance of the Dawes Plan for Germany and of the Geneva Protocol. At home, wages increased, and "Fabian policy, formulated by the Essays in 1888, holds the field and for the moment governs the country," as E. R. Pease put it. It was indeed, only for the moment. "The end of the Labour Government was sudden and messy," wrote Mowat.[25] When the gov-

24 II, p. 379.
25 p. 183.

ernment fell on the Campbell case (Campbell, a Communist
had been arrested and charged under the Incitement to Mu-
tiny Act, but under pressure from Maxton, Lansbury, and
Jack Jones, Sir Patrick Hastings withdrew the prosecution)
MacDonald was accused, particularly by the Liberals, of rat-
ting, of being tired of office without power. Heavy-footed
and square-toed, he has been likened to Samson; everyone
wanted him to accept Asquith's olive branch. "There are 614
men of this House who do not want an election and one who
does—and means to have it," a colleague said.

During the ensuing election campaign, the *Times* under the
headlines "Soviet plot" published the "Red Letter" purporting
to be from Zinoviev, President of the Presidium of the Communist International in Moscow, to the Central Committee of
the British Communist Party, and marked "Very secret." This
letter is supposed to have caused the Conservative victory. It
was given to the *Times* by Sir Eyre Crowe, permanent head
of the Foreign Office. Crowe had not consulted either Mac-
Donald, who was in Wales, or Lord Haldane, who had been
left in charge in London, before giving the letter to the press,
and no one ever saw, or has since ever seen, the original.
Later, Sir Austen Chamberlain was unable to prove the letter
authentic. Mowat suggests that the style of the letter proves
nothing, but

> its matter tells against it. It is all so pat, as if intended for
> publication. It contains everything that the professional
> anti-bolshevist could want . . . the references to the pro-
> letariat and the capitalists and the *bourgeoisie,* to British
> imperialism in the Middle East, to Ireland and the colonies,
> to the need for cells in the army (especially at munitions
> factories and "military store depots") and for finding "the
> future director of the British Red Army." It doesn't miss a
> bet. If it was not a forgery, it might just as well have
> been, for all the credence such a puerile concoction was
> worth. Not that it matters; it did its work anyway, and that
> work was much less than many people assumed it to be.[26]

Forty-two seats were lost by Labor, reducing the number of
Labor seats to 152, but Labor votes rose by more than a
million, to over five million. The Conservatives gained 2 1/4
million votes, the Liberals lost 1 1/4 million votes and 110
seats. Only eighteen Fabians were returned to the House of
Commons, while three peers represented Labor in the Lords.
MacDonald asked Lord Haldane to take charge of the Opposition in the upper house as its leader. Haldane, being of the

[26] *Ibid.*, p. 194.

same race as his "Claymore and Shorter-catechismed" leader, accepted.

The Conservative Government rejected the Geneva Protocol on March 12, 1925, and so took the first step "In bringing about a decadence in the power of the Council and Assembly of the League." [27] The resolution accepting the Protocol had been unanimously passed at Geneva. Even before the Conservative Government finally announced its decision not to support it, the Locarno Treaties had been mooted-treaties to which India and the British Dominions—which had accepted the Protocol—did not assent.

The group of Fabian "Conshies" (conscientious objectors) who during the war had, many of them, lived for longer or shorter periods at Garsington Manor, near Oxford, working on the farm of the brewer Philip Morrell and his wife Lady Ottiline (both pacifists) were, in the twenties, producing great literature, as well as many books. Aldous Huxley's *Point Counter Point* gives the classic description of this group, which included D. H. Lawrence and Augustus John, Clive Bell, Lytton Strachey, Bertrand Russell, Desmond MacCarthy, Maynard Keynes, and Leonard and Virginia Woolf. The Morrells gave to all these brilliant men and women a haven which, one of them confessed, was almost too cozy, too removed from the sanguinary realities an hour's boatride away.

In the twenties, too, the "Bloomsbury Group," led by Virginia Woolf, were almost all Fabians, and all "Left" in politics. The Woolfs, outwardly not unlike the Webbs, were actually very different. Both couples were well-to-do, literate, childless, devoted to each other and to their work. Their descriptions of each other give their climate richly. In her *A Writer's Diary*, Virginia Woolf,[28] who had no allegiance save to her own genius, describes how "Lytton [Strachey] lunched here on Sunday with the Webbs [in 1919]. And when I told him my various triumphs did I imagine a little shade, instantly dispelled . . . the luncheon was a success." Lytton Strachey had proposed to Virginia on February 17, 1909. "I proposed and was accepted. It was an awkward moment . . . especially as I realised the very minute it was happening that the whole thing was repulsive to me," [29] he wrote. Virginia and Leonard's announcement of their engagement, sent to Lytton Strachey and preserved by him, read: "Ha! Ha! June 6, 1912."

[27] Parmoor, p. 268.

[28] p. 12.

[29] Virginia Woolf and Lytton Strachey, p. 37.

In February 1927, the Leonard Woolfs spent the week
end, Beatrice wrote from Passfield Corner (she had just
turned seventy). "We had lost sight of them and were glad
to renew relations with this exceptionally gifted pair." Earlier
"they had been living under a cloud, Virginia had been on the
borderline of lunacy; now she had altered into a spare, self-
contained ascetic-looking creature with a refined, almost narrow and hard intellectuality of expression. Woolf also is
matured and has lost his nervous shyness." In one matter Beatrice notes they "are not up-to-date, for they are rigid secularists, regarding theology or even mysticism as *l'infâme*. Here
his Jewish blood comes in—he is quite clearly revolted by the
Christian myth," and Beatrice does not blame him. He is

> an anti-imperialist fanatic but otherwise a moderate in
> Labour politics, always an opponent of "workers control"
> and "proletarianism." . . . The last hours with them were
> spent in a raging argument about denominational educa-
> tion and the validity of religious mysticism—they were
> against toleration—what was "manifestly false" was *not* to
> be taught at the public expense . . . I pleaded for the "en-
> dowment of error" and threatened them with fundamental-
> ism—Roman Catholicism—if they insisted on universal
> and compulsory sectarianism.[30]

Leonard Woolf has added a note to this account to the effect
that Beatrice

> seemed to get angry, and marched up and down, faster and
> faster, and whisking herself around at each turn, until at
> one of the whisks her skirt gave way, and fell, entangling
> her feet; she stooped, picked it up, and holding it against
> her waist, continued her march up and down, never for a
> moment interrupting her passionate argument in favour
> of the teaching of religion in schools. Sidney and Virginia
> sat silent all through the discussion.

"We dined with the Webbs," Virginia wrote later, in 1929.

> [They] are friendly, but can't be influenced about Kenya.
> We sit in two lodging house rooms(the dining room had a
> brass bedstead behind the screen), eat hunks of red beef,
> and are offered whisky: it's the same enlightened, imper-
> sonal, perfectly aware of itself atmosphere. "My little boy
> shall have his toy, but don't let that go any further. That's
> what my wife says about my being in the Cabinet." No, they
> have no illusions.[31]

30 Beatrice Webb, 1956, p. 131.
31 Virginia Woolf, 1953, p. 149.

Leonard Woolf, born in 1880, and for twenty-four years "subjected to the process which is called education," entered the Ceylon Civil Service in 1904; in 1911 he resigned.

During those six and a half years I was almost a purely political animal for 10, 12 or 14 hours a day and every day I was occupied with politics, first as assistant to the administrator of the district, and later, for two and a half years, as the police magistrate, judge and administrator of a district. When I escaped from the civil service and returned to live in London and England I did not escape from politics; they have pursued me, or I them, ever since . . . by politics I mean the governmental framework or organisation of society.

Leonard Woolf was a typical Fabian of the twenties. The contrast between so potent and fulfilled, so efficacious and valuable a social life as his and that of his contemporary Jewish intellectual, Franz Kafka, living in the Austro-Hungarian Empire, explains a little not only the success of the Fabians, but their absolute Englishry. "You do not realise how much the Fabian name has meant to the Socialists of Europe" was a phrase much used by foreigners attending the Fabian Jubilee in 1944. For Fabianism was, is, and evermore shall be, British to the core.

CHAPTER NINETEEN

IN ENGLAND, EVERYTHING goes to the left, except the Labor Party," quipped a French observer, and this was especially true of the twenties. J. Ramsay MacDonald, "A magnificent substitute for a leader" if ever sincerely a Socialist (which some doubted), had become, by the time of the messy fall of the first Labor Government, a radical with social ambitions, literary aspirations, and a fine presence. The first result of the letdown by Labor—the government's deliberate riding for a fall in the Campbell case—was that the Trade Union Council became more definitely Socialist. And then in 1926 the General Strike, postponed since 1921, occurred. The Fabians were solidly against the General Strike, as was consistent with their constant opposition to direct action. In 1921 the Triple Alliance of miners, railwaymen and dockers had seemed a solid union. But when Thomas and Cramp for the railwaymen and Bevin and R. Williams for the dockers, decided—with the approval of their executives—on "Black Friday," April 16, 1921, "that an incautious speech of Frank Hodges [the miners' secretary] gave them sufficient reason to refuse to strike on the miners' behalf," the *Daily Herald* came out with a leader written by Gerald Gould:

> Yesterday was the heaviest defeat that has befallen the Labour movement within the memory of man. It is no use trying to minimize it. . . . We on this paper have said throughout that if the organised workers would stand together they could win. They have not stood together and they have reaped their reward.[1]

This had left ragged sores, and the Fabians foresaw worse to come. The real reason for the 1926 strike was the end of the postwar boom. This recession followed the end of the Allied occupation of the Ruhr. The Fabians had not faced the loss of foreign markets—nor had the British nation yet been converted to Keynes's extraordinarily subtle finessing of foreign

[1] Quoted in Postgate, p. 214.

exchanges. "On June 30, 1925, the owners served notice to end the 1924 agreement in one month . . . the national minimum percentage addition to standard wages was to go. The men were offered more if they would return to an eight-hour day." [2]

Baldwin, himself one of a coal-and-steel-owning family, backed down on "Red Friday," July 31. During the next winter, twelve Communists, including Harry Pollitt, the leader of the British Communist Party, were sent to jail for from six to twelve months—put, in fact, out of harm's way. Meanwhile, the miners' leaders, Herbert Smith and A. J. Cook, proceeded on the slogan, "Not a penny off the pay, not a minute on the day." The owners and the government were not less intransigent, and Baldwin told the Trades Union Congress that before His Majesty's Government could continue negotiations, they must require "an immediate and unconditional withdrawal of the instructions for a general strike." Yet the strike began on Tuesday, May 4, 1926, and lasted for nine days. The workers called out came out almost to a man. Undergraduates from Oxford and Cambridge assisted in maintaining essential social services and had a lovely week's holiday while several of the heads of colleges—notably of Balliol and of Lady Margaret Hall, Oxford—were on the strikers' side. The undergraduates and other volunteers unloaded ships at the docks, drove trains, buses, trucks, milk vans, etc. Soon in many cases the strikers took back their jobs because the volunteers were ruining the rolling stock; everywhere, at the week end, there were cricket and football matches of strikers versus amateurs (i.e. black-legs). "On the railways many a businessman realised a lifetime's ambition by driving an engine, acting as a guard, or manning a signal box." [3]

The general strike was conducted with "complete inefficiency by both sides," which, as Richard Aldington described it, "led to the happiest result, an early peace." He had received a telegram from the *Times* to come and help the paper to continue, and, though he now feels "I suppose I really ought to have been on the other side," he hitchhiked to London—there being no regular transport available. He had, he said, "no particular liking for Mr. Baldwin and his friends or what they represented. On the other hand, a diet of wooden-headed trade-union leaders seemed no great happiness, while contact with the labor-minded intellectuals had made them positively distasteful to me." [4]

[2] Mowat, p. 292.

[3] *Ibid.*, p. 313.

[4] Aldington, p. 204.

Beatrice found the hall of the Fabian bookshop occupied by a dozen or so men—the strike committee of the London Branch of the Railway Clerks' Association—on the eighth day of the strike, when she had dropped in to see Galton, the Fabian secretary. She overheard the words, "I recommend that we go in," on the phone, and asked Galton, "What's up?" "The usual thing," he said in his cheery cynical voice, "they've got cold feet." That same day, at a meeting at Fabian head-quarters of about fifty strikers, the majority determined to stay out. But fifteen, including the chairman and secretary, left the room for their respective offices.

The strike cost the government only three-quarters of a million pounds, "a sum which the death of a couple of million-aires will pay," snorted Beatrice, while "the three million strikers will have spent some three million pounds of trade union money and lost another four or five in wages. . . . A strike which opens with a football match between the police and the strikers and ends in unconditional surrender after nine days with densely packed reconciliation services at all the chapels and churches . . . will make continental Social-ists blaspheme," she added. The sorry conclusion has been well put: "Opinion on both sides agreed the General Strike was a terrible mistake and a failure which created a mechani-cal reaction. Every genuine labor leader deplored it except the head of the miners. Every real liberal worked to avert it and then to settle it fairly." [5]

"When all is said and done we personally are against the use of the General Strike in order to compel the employers of a particular industry to yield to the men's demands," Beatrice Webb[6] wrote on May 4, "however well justified these claims may be. Such methods cannot be tolerated by any Govern-ment—even a Labour Government would have to take up the challenge. A General Strike aims at coercing the whole com-munity and is only successful *if it does so* and in so far as it does so." And she added,

For the British Trade Union Movement I see a day of ter-rible disillusionment. The failure of the General Strike of 1926 will be one of the most significant landmarks in the history of the British working class. Future historians will, I think, regard it as the death gasp of the pernicious doctrine of "worker's control" of public affairs through the Trade Unions, and by the method of direct action. This absurd doctrine was introduced into British working class

[5] Sister McCarran, p. 416.
[6] 1956, p. 91.

life by Tom Mann and the Guild Socialists and preached
insistently, before the war, by the *Daily Herald* under
George Lansbury. In Russia it was quickly repudiated
by Lenin and the Soviets. . . . In Italy, the attempt to
put this doctrine into practice by seizing the factories led
to the Fascist revolution. . . . Popular disgust with the
loss and inconvenience of a General Strike will consider-
ably check the growth of the Labour Party in the country,
but will lead to a rehabilitation of political methods and
strengthen J.R.M.'s leadership within the party itself. On
the whole . . . it was a proletarian distemper which had
to run its course and like other distempers it is well to
have it over and done with at the cost of a lengthy conva-
lescence. . . . The Worker's Control Movement has led
throughout the world to the extension and strengthening of
state bureaucracy—a form of government which the Syndicalists and the Guild Socialists were intent on superseding
by the vocational organisation of the workers.

During the twenties Beatrice and Sidney Webb made their
little country house, Passfield Corner, a nucleus for Fabians.
The country was "somehow not their natural setting; they
went for walks from a sense of duty" commented Mary
Agnes Hamilton, but the walks became celebrated.

Louis Fischer, traveling back from the U.S.S.R. (where he
had met the quiet Webbs and contrasted them favourably with
G.B.S. and Lady Astor's noisy party), stopped by for lunch.
After lunch, Beatrice retired upstairs for a nap; Sidney took
his guest for a walk. Arriving (on a cold winter day) at a
clearing in the woods, Lord Passfield announced, "Here I
throw myself upon the ground" and did so. Opinions on the
quality of the lunch provided varied: Louis Fischer's was un-
enthusiastic, E. M. Forster's, ecstatic. "For lunch," wrote the
latter, "we had mutton, greens, potatoes, rice pudding—simplest of menus but supreme in quality and superbly cooked;
never have I eaten such mutton, greens, potatoes, rice. Then
Sidney Webb took me for a walk . . . Into the silence he ut-
tered a sentence about himself and his wife: "Our age this
year is a hundred and fifty-seven," he said, adding, "Our combined ages." [7]

G.B.S. and Charlotte were the most frequent, as the most
welcome, of the Webbs' visitors: they came constantly, as
they preferred it to Ayot St. Lawrence—they took a fancy to
her cottage, as Beatrice put it, but sometimes there is just a
little trace of fatigue in the kindliness of her entries: the
Shaws have stayed three days, and are coming back for the

[7] Forster, p. 218.

next week end; the Shaws came for a week . . . the Shaws have been staying, but G.B.S. is ill; G.B.S. has read her book; G.B.S. is full of fantastic ideas. But "Charlotte is as good a wife to G.B.S. as I am to Sidney! We have a great respect for each other as wives, and a long standing good comradeship which has stood the test of years." Beatrice notes too, "Graham Wallas and Audrey came too, but Sidney was frankly bored with *them";* it was the young visitors who delighted both the Webbs. Kingsley Martin with his "attractive young wife . . . he is one of the Tawney-Laski group"; Susan Lawrence; Ellen Wilkinson; "Our relation with the younger folk is all that can be desired." [8] Beatrice boasts. H. G. Wells and the Webbs made it up, too, though with reservations on either side, and in 1929 G. D. H. Cole came back to the Fabian fold. "It was too difficult to make a new party," he told me, and so he again tried to work with the Fabians. In 1927 R. H. Tawney drafted the new Labor Party program: "a revised, longer and more imprecise version of *Labour and the New Social Order,*" Mowat [9] calls *Labour and the Nation.* But it did the trick: In 1929 Labour won 287 seats, the Conservatives 261, the Liberals 59. Baldwin resigned, and MacDonald made up a Cabinet of whom eight were Fabians, and there were also ten other Fabians in the government but not in the Cabinet. The total membership of the Fabian Society in 1930 was 1,862. Little wonder the *Evening Standard* on November 17, 1930, carried the headline: "Government by Fabians," and said:

> Many Labour members are talking about the dominance in the Government of that very academic body, the Fabian Society . . . practically every recent appointment, either to high or low office, in the Labour administration, has been made from the membership of the Society, the latest examples of which are the new Air Minister, Lord Amulree, and the new Solicitor General, Sir Stafford Cripps[10] . . . at least 90% of the members of the Government are on the rolls of the Society, and . . . contrary to regulations, so are a good many highly placed Civil Servants. . . . This ascendancy is, of course, due to the all-powerful influence of Lord Passfield and his wife, Mrs. Sidney Webb, with whom the Fabian Society has been the passion of their lives.

In 1929 Sidney Webb, who had not contested his seat in the House of Commons, accepted a peerage in order to be-

[8] Beatrice Webb, 1956, p. 134.

[9] p. 350.

[10] Beatrice Webb's nephew.

come Colonial Secretary, but Beatrice refused to be called Lady Passfield. Sidney was a failure as Minister: as Mrs. Cole[11] puts it, he was "too much in the hands of his officials . . . his innate trust of the 'expert' served him ill." Yet Laski noted "Webb is the best administrator" though he was to disagree with him violently over the White Paper on Palestine. Indeed, most Jews understandably excoriated Webb thereafter. The morning after it appeared, when J. Ramsay MacDonald telephoned L. Namier, the Oxford historian, who was tutor to MacDonald's son Malcolm at the time, Namier refused to speak to the PM "now or ever." That sort of pressure—and there was a good deal of it at that time—may have influenced MacDonald to take Palestine out of Webb's hands and put it under a committee of the Cabinet.

But the Labor Government was really doomed by the depression, which it inherited, and by foreign affairs, about which it was inept. Arthur Henderson, at the League of Nations, did a magnificent job; but it was Gandhi and Mussolini, not Albert Thomas or Aristide Briand, who were the world's star performers in 1931. The Cabinet crisis of August 1931 was almost wholly a financial one: it occurred when the Bank of England announced it could get no more credits from J. P. Morgan and Co. The prospects (said the telegram from New York read by MacDonald to the Cabinet) of a loan subscribed by the American public "would not be good unless Parliament should already have enacted economy legislation." The larger economies proposed included a 10 per cent cut in the dole to the unemployed; and all this would save was 12¼ million pounds sterling. Eleven ministers were ready to accept the reduction in unemployment payments: these included Webb, Sankey, Amulree, Wedgwood Benn, Parmoor, Herbert Morrison—all the Fabians except Henderson, Addison, and Alexander. No one expected MacDonald to stay on as Prime Minister: The announcement of the National Government to be led by him caused "utter stupefaction." MacDonald, Snowden, and Sankey, who remained in the National Government, have been regarded, even by Conservatives and of course by Labor, as complete renegades. But a reaction in favor of MacDonald seems to be setting in, at least among historians. Dr. Medlicott, of the London School of Economics, exonerates MacDonald for consulting the Opposition and not his own party during the financial crisis: he had to, because of the minority position, Medlicott declares. Gladstone did the same thing on occasion, and in 1939 Chamberlain also consulted Attlee as to whether the Labor Party would back the

11 In Beatrice Webb, 1956, p. xiii.

guarantee to Poland, before discussing the matter with his
Cabinet. Harold Laski, discussing the *Crisis and the Constitution,* said that the crisis arose because of two unanswered
questions: What is the relation of the Prime Minister to his
Cabinet—is he *primus inter pares* or their master? And what
is the actual position of the monarch in the British political
system? Certainly, the Prime Minister was becoming increasingly dictatorial: already, in 1924, when he had decided on
dissolution after the Campbell case, not every member of his
Cabinet was consulted. This trend to the center had started
with the shifting of emphasis from the House of Commons to
the Cabinet, and was enormously assisted by the superb improvement in the quality of the civil service. Also, the old
system of party government had by now really become obsolete. G.B.S., in his introduction to the 1931 edition of *Fabian
Essays,* firmly says, "The Party system must be scrapped ruth-
lessly" because "the effect of this system is that measures
brought before the House by the Government are never voted
on their merits, but solely on the question whether the Government shall remain in office or not: experience soon
proved," G.B.S. concludes, "that the System strengthens the
hands of the Prime Minister and his Cabinet . . . at the cost
of spoiling the quality of the Government by reducing the
King's choice of capable ministers; reducing their supporters
to the rank of operatic choristers; and making all Government factious and lop-sided." [12]

King George V, who had much enjoyed the wartime truce
to party strife, and much approved Coalitions and the whole
idea of a "National Government" used his influence strongly
to persuade MacDonald to head one. The personal friendship
between MacDonald and Baldwin made the merger easier
than it could have been at any other time.

Beatrice Webb's reaction to the National Government was
that, alas, she regretted Sankey, but was glad MacDonald,
Thomas, and Snowden would disappear from the Labor
world, as they were rotten stuff. She makes on September
23, 1931, the most telling comment of all on the sticky ends
of the two Labor Governments:

It is certainly a striking coincidence . . . that the first
Labour Cabinet fell because of the forged Zinoviev letter,
implying Soviet propaganda in Great Britain, and the
second Labour Cabinet fell on the express and openly
acknowledged ground that the Federal Bank of the U.S.A.
practically demanded this dismissal of the Labour Cabinet
as *a condition of their financial loans.* It looks as if Great

[12] Shaw, 1948, p. xii.

Britain is to be a pawn in the struggle between the two great forces in the world of today—Russian Communism and American Capitalism.[13]

MacDonald took only eight Labor members out into the wilderness of the National Government with him, including his own son, Malcolm MacDonald. In 1932 the ILP was steam-rollered out of the Labor Party by 2,000,000 votes to 200,000. But "the Labour Party had lost one gadfly only to find another: the Socialist League." The most important members of the new League were Sir Stafford Cripps, Sir Charles Trevelyan, H. N. Brailsford, and Harold Laski, who were Fabians, and William Mellor, who was not.

G.B.S. had returned from his trip to Russia quite determined to convert the Fabian Society to Communism. Louis Fischer, who met him in Russia, says he was simply an *oppositionsgeist:* his talk to the Thieves' Reform School in Moscow in 1931 was as purely mischievous as his talk to the British propertied classes apostrophizing them as burglars in 1891. His lecture to the Fabians on November 26, 1931, (after the election) began by sweeping away Fabians, Social Democrats, Collectivists, Socialists, and so on.

All that has gone. There is now nothing but Communism, and in future it is quite futile to go about calling yourselves Fabians. Henceforward, because of what has happened in Russia, you are either Communists or what MacDonald and Snowden are, whatever that exactly may be. . . . Anarchism is simply liberty in its last ditch. Syndicalism is a thing of which I am very much afraid. If a revolution were to break out in this or any other country, the first thing that would embarrass and hamper it would be an outbreak of practical syndicalism.

G.B.S. went on to say that Communism was simply successful Fabianism and that over Lenin's great tomb should be written "the inevitability of gradualness." Mr. Stalin, he pointed out, "had a vivid remembrance of the time when we spent a hundred million of our money to destroy the Soviet Government. He explained to me that perhaps it was one of the reasons for the need for a strong Soviet army." The Fabians were singularly unconvinced by G.B.S.'s conversion, or by his eloquence. Very little applause, noted Beatrice in her journal, but in a letter to Tom Jones in 1931 she remarked that "the Fabians who have been over to the U.S.S.R. this summer, among them C. M. Lloyd, S. K. Ratcliffe, D. C. Somervell, Patrick Hastings and others, have all come back enthusiastic, which

[13] Beatrice Webb, 1956, p. 290.

impresses me rather more than G.B.S.'s brilliant testimony, as he has always a bias in favor of anything that is new."

Sidney Webb went twice to Russia, once with Beatrice, and once with her niece, Barbara Drake. They went quietly, with none of the fanfare of publicity that surrounded G.B.S. and the Astors. The Russians could not believe their eyes when they saw the Webbs alive, for Lenin had translated their books in the eighteen nineties. Could they be real? Really *alive?* The Webbs thought that the U.S.S.R. was just like England, where what is written down on paper is so: they thought that when a regulation was printed, or a statement made in the Soviet constitution, then that regulation took daily effect, that statement was carried out in practice. They were, of course, sadly wrong. Also, like many visitors to Russia from England before them, they had a complete and abysmal ignorance of what had gone on before the Revolution. They knew little of Russian history, and what they knew of Russian administration they had learned from exiles, from Kropotkin and Stepniak. Which was about as much use as learning about the U.S.S.R. from Countess Tolstoy or the Grand Duchess Xenia. Little wonder that writers who met the Webbs in Russia, like Louis Fischer and Maurice Hindus, found them naïve.

A new, very Fabian venture was the Left Book Club, founded in London by Victor Gollancz, with John Strachey and Harold Laski as its editors, which started in 1936. Members received a book each month, and all the books were specially commissioned: the Webbs' *Soviet Communism* was the most distinguished but the most *communisant*. The Left Book Club had 50,000 members within a year; 400 local groups met monthly to discuss each choice. *Left News* spread the Club's influence further. The young people at the universities read George Orwell's *The Road to Wigan Pier* and Huberman's *Man's Worldly Goods* avidly. War in Spain, when it broke out, became "their" war in a way no foreign war ever has become before or since in England. The poets and playwrights of the day, too, were all political: W. H. Auden, Stephen Spender, Cecil Day Lewis, and Christopher Isherwood, whose plays were performed by the Group Theater, all emphasized how widely radical ideas had spread.

In the thirties, against the pro-Nazism of the *Times* and the Cliveden set, against the terrified waiting for war of the average decent person, from the time of the failure of sanctions against Italy on, there was only the unorganized, but increasingly literate, Left. Their leaders were Ernest Bevin and Hugh Dalton, who both tried to make the Labor Party more realistic about rearmament, and Sir Stafford Cripps, as ascetic as G.B.S., but without a trace of humor: brilliant, saintly, stiff—"there," said Churchill of him, "but for the grace of God goes God."

During appeasement Labor's stock went up and up: the whole Labor movement came out for war rather than surrender in 1938: there were no Municheers on the Left. But when at last the rot was halted by Chamberlain's swing-around to guarantee Poland (March 31, 1939), Attlee, consulted by Chamberlain as to whether Labor would back the guarantee, asked Maisky, the Russian Ambassador, whether the U.S.S.R. would march. Yes, said Maisky, and Chamberlain went ahead alone with the guarantee instead of stipulating that Britain would come in directly the U.S.S.R. did. As Lloyd George sourly remarked, "We have undertaken a frightful gamble." Great Britain had promised to defend a farther-away country than that Czechoslovakia of which Chamberlain had said they knew nothing. When the declaration of war was imminent, it was L. S. Amery, once a Fabian, now an arch-Tory, who called across the Commons for the Opposition leader Fabian Arthur Greenwood to "speak for England" and Greenwood did: the Labor vote of censure followed by Lloyd George's great speech brought down the government. On May 10, 1940, Churchill formed a Cabinet including Attlee and Greenwood. That day was for the Labor Party "a day of fulfillment and promise: for the first time in its history of forty years it was accepted as the full equal of the other parties in the counsels of the nation." [14]

[14] Mowat, p. 656.

CHAPTER TWENTY

I N 1930 THE NEW FABIAN Research Bureau had come into existence. It was completely independent of the Fabian Society, "now torpid and middle-aged, but beaming like a kindly jaded uncle on the youngsters. It was to do again what the Fabian Society had done in its brisk heyday: to temperate youth; to inquire; to amass facts; to produce research papers, and so to plan the formulation of socialist policy." [1] Clement Attlee was chairman, G. D. H. Cole honorable secretary, and Cripps was a very active member of the Executive. A younger generation of Socialist economists rallied to it: men such as E. Durbin, Hugh Gaitskell, T. Balogh, and Douglas Jay.

The NFRB was staffed by an eager group of young Socialist thinkers many of whom, John Parker says, "had received their Socialist baptism in the very practical test of the 1926 General Strike." [2] In the thirties it was the NFRB which carried on the Fabian tradition rather than the Fabian Society. The collapse of the second Labor Government had shown tragically clearly how much work was to be done. The NFRB was very small in 1933—it had only 130 members—but, as Margaret Cole[3] has pointed out, by the late thirties:

> The new Fabian Research Bureau was coming to be recognised as the best place for young intellectuals to serve their apprenticeship for work in the Labour movement. In 1938 there were only 800 or so members, but it was a membership which pulled its full weight. As the NFRB grew, however, confusion between its name and that of the old established yet somnolent Fabian Society began to cause inconvenience.

[1] Estorick, p. 140.
[2] Margaret I. Cole (ed.), 1949, p. 238.
[3] 1949, p. 203.

When the Fabian Society's general secretary, F. W. Galton, was about to retire on a pension, and all Fabian debts had been wiped off, and the Fabians—thanks to G.B.S.'s generosity—owned their own premises, an amalgamation was arranged. At the time—1938—the Fabian Society was itself in the doldrums. As Margaret Cole notes,

> the Society was really magnificently elderly. It seemed singularly appropriate that of its occasional Tracts, the last published before its amalgamation with the New Fabian Research Bureau, was entitled *Our Aging Population.* There were the Fabian lectures, which drew a large crowd to listen to Bernard Shaw; there were the Annual Reports, parts of which appeared year by year in identical phrasing, as though they had been kept in standing type; there was the *Fabian News,* a small parish magazine with its title-piece drawn by Walter Crane. There was also the Fabian Summer School, which dated back to 1907, but when in 1938 I went to visit it I rubbed my eyes, because it seemed to be peopled with exactly the same faces as I had seen on my last previous visit in 1921. After that experience we were not surprised to find a good deal of the nominal membership of the Society had to be written off for nonpayment of subscription. . . . We did not, however, strike off any member who was 80 in 1939; this preserved quite a few; the others who were not struck off appeared, after some blinking, quite to like the idea of being bustled into a great deal of new activity.[4]

The amalgamation resulted in John Parker, G. D. H. and Margaret Cole becoming the officers of what Margaret Cole calls the *Fabian Society Redivivus,* with an executive drawn from both the NFRB and the Society. Beatrice Webb, whose influence had weighed greatly in persuading the Fabian Society's Executive to vote in favor of amalgamation, became president, and her last public utterance was her presidential address to the Fabian Conference of 1941.

The newly revived society got a

> good deal of help from the electoral truce. For there being no elections to fight, and much civil defense work, there was no place left for Socialists to work and discuss among themselves without getting into political rivalry with the Labour Party, as did the Commies, the ILP or Commonwealth at a later date, until the Fabian Society came along. Stimulated by these conditions and by an eloquent appeal made by Victor Gollancz to the 1941 Summer School, we went ahead with the founding and re-founding of local

4 *Ibid.*

Fabian Societies in close connection with the local Labour movements, enrolling as members, as well as the local workers, people such as solicitors, civil servants and local government officers, who for professional reasons might not be able to advertise themselves as members of the Labour Party but might suffer no harm from joining a body with so fortunately non-committal a name as the Fabian Society. The local Fabian Societies seem still to be fulfilling a real need; there are over 130 of them, and the number could easily be increased if the standard were lowered.[5]

In order to make sure that the Fabian Society should not repeat the experience of the ILP and the Socialist League and get pushed by a few persistent politicians into endeavoring to force a policy upon, or in opposition to, the Labor Party leaders

we introduced into the new rules a proviso, known as the "self-denying ordinance" which forbade the Society as such to pass or move any resolution on political subjects, and proclaimed that any pamphlet or article must be put out under the signature of its author and authors and must not commit the Society as a whole. This had the great advantage of making the Fabian Society now a poor hunting ground for Communism: for if you cannot make a Society pass a political resolution, what advantage is there to be gained by going to the trouble of capturing it?[6]

Therefore the Society now never speaks as, or for, the Society: it promulgates no policy and mandates no delegates to any conferences or gatherings.

In 1945 the 230 Fabians (out of 394 Socialists elected to the House of Commons) were this time in power. The triumphant Labor Government (41 Fabians in the government helping materially) succeeded in nationalizing:

1. The Bank of England
2. Cables and wireless
3. Civil aviation
4. Transport (both rail and road)
5. Coal mines
6. Electricity
7. Gas
8. Medical services.

This time, neither from the U.S.S.R. did there come a Red scare, nor from the U.S.A. a threat that loans could not be

[5] *Ibid.*, p. 206.
[6] *Ibid.*

arranged. On the contrary, between 1946 and 1948, production increased in England in every section of industry.

In 1947 the Fabian Society had a total membership of 8,400. The Society celebrated its Diamond Jubilee (postponed owing to the war) with a great Sunday evening meeting and concert at the Albert Hall, attended by 6,000 people. Harold Laski presided: Clement Attlee, the Prime Minister; Herbert Morrison, Lord President of the Council; Ellen Wilkinson, Minister of Education; and John Strachey, Minister of Food, spoke. That same year G. D. H. Cole resigned the chairmanship he had held since the reorganization in 1939, to reassume it on Harold Laski's death.

A new phase of the work of the Fabian Colonial Bureau began with the coming to power of the Labor Government. "We were aware," said the Annual Report, "that we would henceforth find ourselves in a key position, and also, perhaps, a delicate one. It might have been attractive to follow a line of uncritical support and sympathetic exposition of Government policy. We felt, however, that we would be truer to Fabian tradition if we maintained an attitude of independence and acted as a friendly critic and spur, rather than as an uncritical supporter. This has not been an easy role . . . we believe, however, that we have had some success, and that our reputation for independence and sincerity has been maintained."

With the coming into power of the Labor Government, the Fabian Society did indeed take on a new role: no longer was it the "thinking power-house" of the Loyal Opposition; it had become instead an "independent Socialist society working in close conjunction with, and trusted by, the wider Labour movement" (Fabian Society, 66th Annual Report). The need for such a society became increasingly apparent as the Labor Party faced its urgent problems—such as the economic crisis of 1948, the severity of which, in terms either of money or of manpower, had not been anticipated. The trade unions, too, proved that old enemies are often better than new friends. They rallied financially to the Fabian Society's side. For example, the Amalgamated Engineering Union contributed £200 for Fabian research in 1950, and trade union societies and co-operatives also contributed. Indeed, the financial future—almost, it might be said, the continued existence—of the Fabian Society now depends on these Labor organizations. This is a new thing, that these groups should be prepared to endow Fabian research for its own sake, but "it is a thing which must go on if Fabian research is to survive. For the day of the private patron is waning . . . the Fabian Society, a political body, cannot hope to obtain assistance from 'impartial' donors. It is up to the Labour Movement," noted the Fabian Society's 68th Annual Report, "if it wants research to continue, to provide the very modest wherewithal; it is up to individual Fabians to see that the branches of organised Labour with which they are connected are made aware of this necessity."

The Fabian Society is as hard working as ever. For example, today the local societies are responsible for about 180 meetings every month, and sales of Fabian literature average £ 200 a month. They conduct week-end conferences, day schools and local research. Meanwhile headquarters deals with such new problems as automation, the UN, the underdeveloped countries, and world-wide illiteracy.

But it was in the field of foreign affairs that the Fabians had been most negligent in the past; and it is in this field that they have become most active. As Beatrice Webb wrote to her nephew, Sir Arthur Hobhouse, on September 26, 1938, "I always knew that I know nothing about foreign affairs." And she knew more than most Fabians. It was, indeed, the Munich crisis that woke the Fabians from their island-mindedness, though it was not until the years 1945-8 that the Labor Party came of age in international affairs. During those three crisis-packed years, Foreign Secretary Ernest Bevin's achievement in filling the power vacuum between the U.S.S.R. and the U.S.A. by economic aid and political integration, by assisting America's entry into the said power vacuum, and by preventing the U.S.S.R.'s entry there until America was established, equaled, the Fabians aver, Churchill's wartime miracles.

The most important policy that Fabians can work for today, many of them agree, is the concept of a World Plan for Mutual Aid. For this is enlightened self-interest. Britain has strong reasons of national interest to urge international investment in the underdeveloped areas. The World Plan, launched by the Labor Party in 1950, "is impeccable in aim and general conception," though there are a tremendous number of practical problems in the way. But, as Denis Healey points out,

> all the particular problems exercising the democracies dwindle into insignificance beneath the decisive general challenge: can they, without sacrificing the essentials of their way of life, construct out of the present anarchy of independent nation states an international society which, however rudimentary, at least gives hope of avoiding a major catastrophe, and of providing foundations on which future generations may build? [7]

[7] McKitterick and Younger, p. 148.

The Fabians have an almost proprietary interest in working for such a society, for it was a Fabian tract in 1915 that first outlined its scaffolding.

In 1943 Beatrice Webb died, and in 1947, Sidney. In December 1947 their ashes were buried together in Westminster Abbey, the highest honor a grateful nation can bestow. G.B.S. wrote on a postcard to Bardie Drake, "How B. must be sizzling to hear the name of Jesus spoken over her."

In 1950 a number of American students, mostly sponsored by Americans for Democratic Action, joined the Fabian Summer School. In the same year Sir Stafford Cripps accepted the honorary office of president: on his death he was succeeded by G. D. H. Cole. When G.B.S. died in 1950 the lights on Broadway were lowered: he was, as Beatrice Webb had written on his seventieth birthday, among the men and women responsible for the birth and education of the Labor movement in Great Britain, "the greatest of all, wit and mystic, preacher and dramatist." At the outbreak of World War II, H. G. Wells refused to work for the government—even to take part in civil defense—because, he said, they had picked his brains in World War I and he wasn't such a fool as to be caught twice. He died in 1946.

In 1951 the Conservatives came in again. The main effect, so far as the Fabian Society was concerned, was that there was a renewed demand for the reformulation of Fabian policy in the light of changing economic and social circumstances and in preparation for the fourth Labor Government. *New Fabian Essays,* published in 1952, met this demand and was a best-seller, being favorably commented upon even by the *Times.* In 1957 *Fabian International Essays* showed that the younger Fabians were coming of age in foreign affairs. But perhaps the most active work of the Fabian Society today is done by the Fabian Colonial Bureau, which is deeply involved with the problem of the Central African Federation, and with Kenya and Nigeria. Among its experts are Rita Hinden, Margery Perham, the Earl of Listowel, and Lord Faringdon, and it regularly publishes tracts on such topics as Labor in the Colonies. Many Africans, such as Tom Mboya, secretary of the Kenya Federation of Labor, write for, or are associated with, the Fabian Colonial Bureau, which publishes its own separate Annual Report. The Fabian Society, the oldest Socialist society in the world, is still today the creative brain of the Labor Party that was largely its creation. What do Fabians consider are the tasks ahead to which they must devote themselves?

Denis Healey, in *New Fabian Essays,* notes that

> the founders of British Socialism never conceived that external factors would one day dominate British politics. Their very parochialism was their strength: they found socialism wandering aimlessly in Cloud Cuckoo land and set it working on the gas and water problems of the nearest town or village. The modern Welfare State is their monument.[8]

But its very success in domestic reform prevents Fabianism from being a successful guide to world politics. Its utopianism makes it tend to discount power politics, dismissing them as a disease to which only capitalists or capitalist states are liable, and regarding all social ills as springing from a bad system of property relations. The Labor Party met the first great post-World War I crisis of collective security in Manchuria with an ostrichlike policy of total war resistance. On the other hand, the transfer of power in India under a Labor Government made Great Britain the only white power with genuine friends in Asia; the government acted with understanding too in dealing with the Chinese Revolution, and British policy helped change Dutch policy toward Indonesia. Suez was so ridiculous a fiasco that it served to prove Labor's point to all except the dead. But just what is that point? Denis Healey makes it very clear:

> The essence of British socialism lies not in its contingent analysis or techniques, but in its determination to apply moral principles to social life. It belongs to that stream of Christian thought which, while insisting that the individual human personality is an end in itself—indeed the only temporal end in itself—believes that all men are brothers, and must realise their brotherhood in this world by creating a society in which they enjoy an equal right and duty to freedom and responsibility. It is in this sense that our socialism is inseparable from democracy.[9]

Thus, today, the Fabians' first job is a rethinking back to ethics, because Socialism is primarily an ethical concept.

Fabianism as a doctrine began with the conviction of the value of the human person and a belief that all men and women have an equal right to live their lives in a manner which seems to them morally good. The state exists for the individual, and the maintenance of his rights is its first duty: each citizen has an equal claim on the common good in respect of equal needs.

[8] Crossman, p. 161.
[9] *Ibid.*, p. 165.

The citizen's rights are the conditions he feels are necessary to the fulfillment of his best self. But these rights cannot be equal unless freedom is equal, and to get equal freedom equal economic opportunity is necessary. This economic equality of opportunity must be imposed by collective control and implies the common control for the common good of the means of production and distribution. The Fabian Society provided Great Britain with a body of Socialist doctrine that owed nothing to Karl Marx—as the Frenchman Ernest Pfeiffer said, the Fabians were the first critics of Marx, and they have constantly maintained that one could be a Socialist without even having read *Das Kapital.* Sidney Webb regarded any and all social reforms as a beginning of Socialism within the framework of capitalist society. But there was no room in his ideas either for increasing misery, or revolution, or war. The Fabians followed Jevons in seeing the source and measure of value not in labor but in utility, for the Fabians were above all utilitarians. But while Bentham had used the idea of "the greatest happiness of the greatest number" to justify the abolition of the bad forms of state interference, the Fabians used it to justify the good forms.

The Fabians, most of whom were very long-lived, and all of whom were very hard-working (the seven essayists alone produced over 100 books among them), lived to see their political plans carried out with a success beyond all their reasonable hope: "Our general social policy is to construct a base to society in the form of a legally enforced minimum standard of life, and to develop all forms of shooting upwards," wrote Beatrice Webb[10] in 1903. As far as England is concerned, this has been achieved. "What the founders of the Fabian Society did was to destroy the immense prestige and authority of Cobdenist Liberalism. . . . We really did knock *Laissez Faire* into a cocked hat, and Sidney Webb made John Bright obsolete. State enterprise, state control, state finance, factory legislation and municipal trading . . . rose . . . to be the only hope of survival for civilisation," wrote G.B.S.

E. R. Pease had said that the work of the Fabian Society had not been to make Socialists, but to make Socialism, and this has been done by municipalization and nationalization. The capitalist's gasworks and waterworks, docks, trams, mines, railways, banks, and buses have been taken over, and the state has secured the profits of management and unearned increment. The capitalist has been compensated with interest-bearing securities, until in fact he has become a recipient of unearned income, and now is taxed and supertaxed precisely

[10] 1948, p. 272.

because his income is unearned. G.B.S. chuckled because this has all been done in so thoroughly English a way; "it was a big success, but did it produce the result we were aiming at?" he asked.

The answer is perhaps both yes and no. England today is certainly much nearer the "chaste form of a garden city" than it was in the sooty, grimy nineteenth century. But whether the people who inhabit it are better for being cleaner, healthier, richer, better-housed, with far less work to do and far more to eat than their grandparents, is another question. Certainly the Fabians, who permeated all classes "with a common opinion in favour of social control of socially created values" insisted that the society which was to exert control must be democratic, and taught that democratic control must be reconciled with expert guidance.

Socialism of the Fabian type has made representative democracy its creed. It has adopted the sound position that democracy flourishes in that form of state in which people freely produce, thanks to an equality of educational opportunity, and freely choose, thanks to a wide and active suffrage, their own members for their guidance, and since they have freely produced and chosen them, give them fully and freely the honor of their trust.

The Fabians who so influenced their country have been both cordially admired and bitterly detested. But a more vigorous, hard-working, and alive succession of individuals it would be hard to find elsewhere in British history, and today there is every indication that George Bernard Shaw, at ninety-two, was quite right in concluding his *Fabian Essays* with the proud boast that "the name of Fabian may perish, but not the species."

APPENDIX A

BASIS OF THE FABIAN SOCIETY
(To be signed by all Members)
(*Adopted May 23rd, 1919*)

The Fabian Society consists of Socialists.

It therefore aims at the reorganisation of Society by the emancipation of Land and Industrial Capital from individual ownership, and the vesting of them in the community for the general benefit. In this way only can the natural and acquired advantages of the country be equitably shared by the whole people.

The Society accordingly works for the extinction of private property in land, with equitable consideration of established expectations, and due provision as to the tenure of the home and the homestead; for the transfer to the community, by constitutional methods, of all such industries as can be conducted socially; and for the establishment, as the governing consideration in the regulation of production, distribution and service, of the common good instead of private profit.

The Society is a constituent of the Labour Party and of the International Socialist Congress; but it takes part freely in all constitutional movements, social, economic and political, which can be guided towards its own objects. Its direct business is (*a*) the propaganda of Socialism in its application to current problems; (*b*) investigation and discovery in social, industrial, political and economic relations; (*c*) the working out of Socialist principles in legislation and administrative reconstruction; (*d*) the publication of the results of its investigations and their practical lessons.

The Society, believing in equal citizenship of men and women in the fullest sense, is open to persons irrespective of sex, race or creed, who commit themselves to its aims and purposes as stated above, and undertake to promote its work.

The Society includes:—

I. Members, who must sign the Basis and be elected by the Committee. Their Subscriptions are not fixed; each is expected to subscribe annually according to his means. They control the Society through the Executive Committee (elected annually by ballot through a postal vote), and at its annual and other business meetings.

II. Associates, who sign a form expressing only general sympathy with the objects of the Society and pay not less than 10s. a year. They can attend all except the exclusively members' meetings, but have no control over the Society and its policy.

III. Subscribers, who must pay at least 5s. a year, and who can attend the Society's Ordinary Lectures.

The monthly paper, *Fabian News,* and the Tracts from time to time published in the well-known Fabian Series, are posted to all these classes. There are convenient Common Rooms, where light refreshments can be obtained, with an extensive library for the free use of members only.

Among the Society's activities (in which it places its services unreservedly at the disposal of the Labour Party and the Local Labour Parties all over the country, the Trade Unions and Trades Councils, and all other Labour and Socialist organisations), may be mentioned:

(i.) Free lectures by its members and officers;

(ii.) The well-known Fabian Book-boxes, each containing about three dozen of the best books on Economics, Politics and Social Problems, which can be obtained by any organisation of men or women for 15s. per annum, covering an exchange of books every three months;

(iii.) Answers to Questions from Members of Local Authorities and others on legal, technical or political matters of Local Government, etc.;

(iv.) Special subscription courses of lectures on new developments in thought;

(v.) Economic and social investigation and research, and publication of the results.

Lists of Publications, Annual Report, Form of Application as Member or Associate, and any other information can be obtained on application personally or by letter to the Secretary.

APPENDIX B

RULES OF THE FABIAN SOCIETY

As Amended by the Postal Ballot held in April, 1949.

1. The name of the Society shall be the Fabian Society.

2. The Society consists of Socialists. It therefore aims at the establishment of a society in which equality of opportunity will be assured and the economic power and privileges of individuals and classes abolished through the collective ownership and democratic control of the economic resources of the community. It seeks to secure these ends by the methods of political democracy.

The Society, believing in equal citizenship in the fullest sense, is open to persons irrespective of sex, race or creed, who commit themselves to its aims and purposes and undertake to promote its work.

The Society shall be affiliated to the Labour Party. Its activities shall be the furtherance of socialism and the education of the public on socialist lines, by the holding of meetings, lectures, discussion groups, conferences and summer schools, the promotion of research into political, economic and social problems, national and international, the publication of books, pamphlets and periodicals, and by any other appropriate methods.

3. The Society as a whole shall have no collective policy beyond what is implied in Rule 2; its research shall be free and objective in its methods.

No resolution of a political character expressing an opinion or calling for action, other than in relation to the running of the Society itself, shall be put forward in the name of the Society. Delegates to conferences of the Labour Party, or to any other conference, shall be appointed by the Executive Committee without any mandatory instructions.

4. Full Membership of the Society shall be open to those who are willing to accept the Rules and By-Laws of the Society. The acceptance of candidates is subject to confirmation by the Executive Committee.

The Executive Committee may, in special cases, elect Honorary Members of the Society.

Those who do not desire, or are ineligible for, full membership of the Society may become Associates, if in general sympathy with the objects of the Society. The acceptance of candidates is subject to confirmation by the Executive Committee. Associates shall have the same rights as full members in regard to the publications, schools, conferences and lecture meetings of the Society, but shall have no voting rights, shall not be eligible for membership of the Executive Committee and shall not be entitled to attend Annual and Special General Meetings of the Society. Federations of Labour Parties, Borough, Divisional and Local Labour Parties, Trade Unions and their branches, Co-operative organisations and other bodies may become subscribing bodies to the Society. The acceptance of candidates is subject to confirmation by the Executive Committee.

5. The Society shall be governed by an Annual Meeting of members to be held at a time and place to be determined by the Executive Committee. Members shall be invited to submit Resolutions. The Resolutions shall be circulated and the members invited to submit Amendments. The full Agenda, including the Resolutions and the Amendments thereto, together with copies of the Annual Report, shall be circulated not less than a fortnight before the meeting. The Chairman of the meeting shall have the right to accept emergency Resolutions and Amendments with the consent of the meeting. The Executive Committee shall announce the dates by which Resolutions and Amendments must be received. All National members, fully paid up members of recognised Local Societies and the representative from each subscribing body shall have the right to attend and vote at the meetings.

6. The Executive Committee may at any time call a Special General Meeting to discuss any business of the Society.

If 5 per cent. of all members entitled to vote in the election of the Executive Committee send to the General Secretary in writing a request for a Special General Meeting, the Executive Committee shall appoint for the meeting the earliest convenient date thereafter and shall circulate any Resolutions submitted.

7. The Executive Committee may, and on a requisition signed by not less than 5 per cent. of all members entitled to vote in the election of the Executive Committee shall, refer any question to the decision by Postal Ballot of all the members entitled to vote in the election of the Executive Committee.

8. The Rules may be revised by an Annual Meeting or by a Special General Meeting, provided the proposals have been circulated 14 days before the meeting, or by a Postal Ballot.

Any alterations of or addition to Rules 1-6 shall be adopted only if supported by not less than three-quarters of the members present and voting at the Annual or Special General Meeting or by a simple majority of those voting in a Postal Ballot.

9. The Executive Committee, including Officers, shall consist of not more than 24 members, of whom the Hon. Treasurer and 17 other members shall be elected as provided in Rule 10 following.

The Executive Committee shall have the right to co-opt additional members and to fill casual vacancies provided that the membership of the Committee does not at any time exceed 24 in number. The Executive Committee shall elect such officers for the year as it thinks necessary. Five members shall be a quorum for the Executive Committee. Any member absent from four consecutive meetings of the Committee or its standing sub-committees without obtaining leave of absence shall be deemed, upon a resolution to that effect being passed by the Executive Committee, to have vacated his seat on the Committee or sub-committee.

10. Before the Annual Meeting, the Society shall elect by ballot an Hon. Treasurer and 17 other members of the Executive Committee to hold office for one year. Nominations for these shall be invited from national members and fully paid up members of Local Societies whose names have been received at the Central Office one month before voting papers are sent out. All ballot papers must be returned within 28 days of issue. Scrutineers shall be appointed by the Executive Committee, whose duty it shall be to open the ballot box, to count the votes, and to certify to the General Secretary the results. In the event of a tie the Chairman of the Society shall have the casting vote. All members of Local Societies whose names have been received at the Central Office shall be entitled to vote in the Annual Postal Ballot for the election of the Executive Committee. The new Executive Committee shall come into office immediately after the Annual Meeting.

11. The Executive Committee shall conduct the general business of the Society, appoint such paid officers and staff as it deems necessary, create such sub-committees and groups as are considered desirable from time to time, sanction publications and appoint all delegates to represent the Society.

The Executive Committee shall, subject to the Rules of the Society, have the power to make and revise By-Laws for the composition and procedure of Committees, Bureaux, Groups, Local Societies (and their Regional or other Committees) and other organs of the Society. Such By-Laws shall be published in *Fabian News* and shall come into force as determined by the Executive Committee, but may be amended or annulled by a resolution at an Annual or Special General Meeting of the Society.

Subject to the decision of the Annual or any Special Meeting, the Executive Committee shall have full control over the affairs of the Society.

12. No book, pamphlet or tract submitted to the Society shall be published unless approved as of a suitable standard according to rules made by the Executive Committee. All publications sponsored by the Society shall bear a clear indication that they do not commit the Society, but only those responsible for preparing them.

13. Members are expected to subscribe annually to the funds of the Society in accordance with their means. The minimum annual subscription for members of the Society and for all subscribing

bodies and associates shall be 20/- which shall entitle the subscriber to receive a copy of *Fabian News* and all pamphlets priced 6d. or less issued by the Society. A subscription of 30/- or more shall entitle the subscriber to receive a copy of the *Fabian News* and all pamphlets priced 1/- or less. A subscription of 50/- or more shall entitle the subscriber to receive a copy of the *Fabian News* and all pamphlets priced 2/- or less. A subscription of 60/- shall in addition make the subscriber a member of the Colonial and International Bureaux receiving all publications to which Bureau members are entitled. Persons undergoing a full-time course of instruction and members of the ranks of H.M. Forces shall be allowed to be members for the period in which they are so engaged for an annual subscription of half the rate applicable in each category. The Executive Committee shall have the right in exceptional cases to decide that a pamphlet should be issued either to a greater or a lesser number of members than is specified in this rule. The Executive Committee shall have power to strike off the books any member who, after notice, fails to pay his subscription.

14. The Executive Committee shall have the power to recognise a Local Society and to approve its Rules and to make By-Laws for the regulation of such societies.

A fee of 1/- per year per member shall be paid by a Local Society to the National Society. The minimum payment shall be 20/-.

15. Any question as to the interpretation of these Rules shall be settled by the Executive Committee subject to appeal to a meeting of members qualified to effect an alteration of rules.

FABIAN PUBLICATIONS 1884-1958

TRACTS

1884	1	*Why Are the Many Poor?* W. L. Phillips (Amended G. B. Shaw).
	2	*A Manifesto.* G. B. Shaw.
1885	3	*To Provident Landlords and Capitalists.* G. B. Shaw.
1886	4	*What Socialism Is.* Mrs. Wilson.
1887	5	*Facts for Socialists.* S. Webb (Ed. J. F. Oakeshott).
	6	*The True Radical Programme.* G. B. Shaw.
1888	7	*Capital and Land.* Sir Sydney Oliver.
1889	8	*Facts for Londoners.* S. Webb.
	9	*An Eight Hours Bill.* S. Webb.
	10	*Figures for Londoners.* S. Webb.
1890	11	*The Workers' Political Programme.* S. Webb.
	12	*Practical Land Nationalisation.* S. Webb.
	13	*What Socialism Is.* G. B. Shaw.
	14	*The New Reform Bill.* J. F. Oakeshott.
	15	*English Progress towards Social Democracy.* S. Webb.
	16	*A Plea for an Eight Hours' Bill.* S. Webb.
	17	*The Reform of the Poor Law.* S. Webb.
1891	18	*Facts for Bristol.* Sir Hartman W. Just.
	19	*What the Farm Labourer Wants.* S. Webb.
	20	*Questions for Poor Law Guardians.* S. W. Group (London).
	21	*Questions for London Vestrymen.* J. C. Foulger.
	22	*The Truth about Leasehold Enfranchisement.* S. Webb.
	23	*The Case for an Eight Hours' Bill.* S. Webb.
	24	*Questions for Parliamentary Candidates.* S. Webb.
	25	*Questions for School Board Candidates.* S. Webb.
	26	*Questions for London County Councillors.* S. Webb.
	27	*Questions for Town Councillors.* Rev. C. Peach.
	28	*Questions for County Councillors (Rural).* P. Hudson.
	29	*What to Read.* G. Wallas.
	30	*The Unearned Increment.* S. Webb.
	31	*London's Heritage in the City Guilds.* S. Webb.
	32	*The Municipalisation of the Gas Supply.* S. Webb.
	33	*Municipal Tramways.* S. Webb.
	34	*London's Water Tribute.* S. Webb.
	35	*The Municipalisation of the London Docks.* S. Webb.
	36	*The Scandal of London's Markets.* S. Webb.

37 *A Labour Policy for Public Authorities.* S. Webb.
38 *Paham Mae Y Lluaws Yn Dlawd?* (a translation into Welsh of No. 1.)

1892   39 *A Democratic Budget.* J. F. Oakeshott.
40 *Fabian Election Manifesto, 1892.* G. B. Shaw.
41 *The Fabian Society: What It Has Done and How It Has Done It.* G. B. Shaw.
42 *Christian Socialism.* Rev. Stewart D. Headlam.
43 *Vote! Vote!! Vote!!!* G. B. Shaw.

1893   44 *A Plea for Poor Law Reform.* Fred Wheeler.
45 *The Impossibilities of Anarchism.* G. B. Shaw.
46 *Socialism and Sailors.* B. T. Hall.
47 *The Unemployed.* John Burns.

1894   48 *Eight Hours by Law.* Henry W. Macrosty.
49 *A Plan of Campaign for Labour.* G. B. Shaw.
50 *Sweating: Its Cause and Remedy.* H. W. Macrosty.
51 *Socialism: True and False.* S. Webb.
52 *State Education at Home and Abroad.* J. W. Martin.
53 *The Parish Councils Act.* H. Samuel.
54 *The Humanizing of the Poor Law.* J. F. Oakeshott.
55 *The Workers' School Board Programme.* J. W. Martin.
56 *Questions for Parish Council Candidates.* H. Samuel.
57 *Questions for Rural District Council Candidates.* H. Samuel.
58 *Allotments and How to Get Them.* H. Samuel.
59 *Questions for Candidates for Urban District Councils.* H. Samuel.
60 *The London Vestries.* S. Webb.

1895   61 *The London County Council: What It Is and What It Does.* J. F. Oakeshott.
62 *Parish and District Councils.*
63 *Parish Council Cottages and How to Get Them.*
64 *How to Lose and How to Win an Election.* J. Ramsay MacDonald.
65 *Trade Unionists and Politics.* F. W. Dalton.
66 *A Programme for Workers.* Edward Pease.

1896   67 *Women and the Factory Acts.* Beatrice Webb.
68 *The Tenant's Sanitary Catechism.* A. Hickmott.
69 *The Difficulties of Individualism.* S. Webb.
70 *Report on Fabian Policy.* G. B. Shaw.
71 *The (London) Tenant's Sanitary Catechism.* Miss Grove.
72 *The Moral Aspects of Socialism.* Sidney Ball.

1897   73 *The Case of State Pensions in Old Age.* G. Turner.
74 *The State and Its Functions in New Zealand.* W. P. Reeves.
75 *Labour in the Longest Reign (1837-1897).* S. Webb.
76 *Houses for the People.* A. Hickmott.
77 *The Municipalization of Tramways.* F. T. H. Herle.
78 *Socialism and the Teaching of Christ.* Rev. J. Clifford.

79 *A Word of Remembrance and Caution to the Rich.* John Woolman.

80 *Shop Life and Its Reform.* W. Johnson Woolman.

1898 81 *Municipal Water.* C. M. Knowles.

82 *The Workmen's Compensation Act.* G. R. Allen.

83 *State Arbitration and the Living Wage.* H. W. Macrosty.

84 *The Economics of Direct Employment.* S. Webb.

85 *Liquor Licensing at Home and Abroad.* Edward Pease.

86 *Municipal Drink Traffic.* Edward Pease.

1899 87 *Sosialaeth a Dysgiediaeth Christ.* (a translation into Welsh of No. 78.)

88 *The Growth of Monopoly in English Industry.* H. W. Macrosty.

89 *Old Age Pensions at Work.* J. Bullock.

90 *The Municipalization of the Milk Supply.* Dr. McCleary.

91 *Municipal Pawnshops.* C. Charrington.

92 *Municipal Slaughterhouses.* G. Standring.

93 *Women as Councillors.* G. B. Shaw.

94 *Municipal Bakeries.* Dr. McCleary.

95 *Municipal Hospitals.* Dr. McCleary.

1901 96 *Municipal Fire Insurance.* Mrs. F. MacPherson.

97 *Municipal Steamboats.* G. D. Shallard.

1899 98 *State Railways for Ireland.* Clement Edwards.

1900 99 *Local Government in Ireland.* G. R. Allen, Jr.

100 *Metropolitan Borough Councils.* H. W. Macrosty.

101 *The House Famine and How to Relieve It.*

102 *Questions for Candidates: Metropolitan Borough Councils.* H. W. Macrosty.

103 *Overcrowding in London and Its Remedy.* W. C. Steadman.

104 *How Trade Unions Benefit Workmen.* Edward Pease.

1901 105 *Five Years' Fruits of the Parish Councils Act.* S. Webb.

106 *The Education Muddle and the Way Out.* S. Webb.

107 *Socialism for Millionaires.* G. B. Shaw.

108 *Twentieth Century Politics.* S. Webb.

1902 109 *Cottage Plans and Common Sense.* R. Unwin.

110 *Problems of Indian Poverty.* S. S. Thorburn.

111 *Reform of Reformatories and Industrial Schools.* H. T. Holmes.

112 *Life in the Laundry.* Dr. McCleary.

1903 113 *Communism.* Wm. Morris.

114 *The Education Act, 1902.* S. Webb.

115 *State-Aid to Agriculture.* T. S. Dymond.

1904 116 *Fabianism and the Fiscal Question.* G. B. Shaw.

117 *The Education Act, 1903: How to Make the Best of It.* S. Webb.

118 *The Secret of Rural Depopulation.* Lt. Col. D. C. Pedder.

1912 161 *Afforestation and Unemployment.* Arthur P. Grenfell.
162 *Family Life on a Pound a Week.* Mrs. Pember Reeves.
163 *Women and Prisons.* Helen Blagg and Mrs. Wilson.
164 *Gold and State Banking.* E. Pease.
165 *Francis Place.* St. John G. Ervine.
166 *Robert Owen.* Miss B. L. Hutchins.
167 *William Morris.* Mrs. Townsend.

1913 168 *John Stuart Mill.* J. West.
169 *The Socialist Movement in Germany.* W. S. Sanders.
170 *Profit-Sharing and Co-Partnership.* E. Pease.
171 *The Nationalisation of Mines and Minerals Bill.* H. H. Slesser.
172 *What About the Rates?* S. Webb.
173 *Public Versus Private Electricity Supply.* C. Ashmore Baker.

1914 174 *Charles Kingsley.* C. E. Vulliamy.
175 *The Economic Foundations of the Women's Movement.* M. Atkinson.
176 *The War and the Workers.* S. Webb.

1915 177 *Socialism and the Arts of Use.* A. Clutton Brock.
178 *The War: Women: and Unemployment.* Womens E. C. Group.

1916 179 *John Ruskin.* Edith Morley.
180 *The Philosophy of Socialism.* A. Clutton Brock.
181 *When Peace Comes; the Way of Industrial Reconstruction.* S. Webb.

1917 182 *Robert Owen, Idealist.* C. E. M. Joad.
183 *The Reform of the House of Lords.* S. Webb.
184 *The Russian Revolution and British Democracy.* J. West.

1918 185 *The Abolition of the Poor Law.* Beatrice Webb.
186 *Central Africa and the League of Nations.* R. C. Hankin.
187 *The Teacher in Politics.* S. Webb.

1919 188 *National Finance and a Levy on Capital.* S. Webb.

1920 189 *Urban District Councils.* C. M. Lloyd.
190 *Metropolitan Borough Councils.* C. R. Attlee.
191 *Borough Councils.* C. R. Attlee.
192 *Guild Socialism.* G. D. H. Cole.
193 *Housing.* C. M. Lloyd.
194 *Taxes, Rates and Local Income Tax.* Robert Jones.
195 *The Scandal of the Poor Law.* C. M. Lloyd.
196 *The Root of Labour Unrest.* S. Webb.

1921 197 *The International Labour Organisation of the League of Nations.* W. S. Sanders.

1922 198 *Some Problems of Education.* Barbara Drake.
199 *William Lovett.* Mrs. L. B. Hammond.
200 *The State in the New Social Order.* H. J. Laski.
201 *International Co-operative Trade.* L. S. Woolf.

RESEARCH PAMPHLETS

172 *The New Towns.* Norman MacKenzie.
173 *A Socialist Education Policy.* H. D. Hughes.
174 *Rents and Social Policy.* D. Eversley.
175 *Food Policy: From Farmer to People.* Norman Wood.
176 *Plan for the Aircraft Industry.* Frank Beswick.
177 *The Future of Retailing.* R. W. Evely.

1956 178 *Financing Local Government.* A. H. Hanson.
179 *The West Indian in Britain.* Clarence Senior and Douglas Manley.
180 *Leasehold Enfranchisement.* Arthur Skeffington.
181 *Plan for Cotton.* John Murray.
182 *Plan for Coal Distribution.* A Fabian Group.
183 *Bulk Purchase & the Colonies.* T. F. Betts.
184 *Facts for Socialists.* G. D. H. Cole.

1957 185 *Justice and the Administration.* Gordon Barrie.
186 *Colonial Development Corporation.* G. W. Dumpleta.
187 *The Control of Inflation.* Geoffrey Maynard.
188 *Home Ownership.* D. L. Munby.
189 *Wage Policy Abroad.* H. A. Turner.
190 *Reform of the Tax System.*
191 *The Future of Legal Aid.* Peter Benenson.
192 *Plan for Rented Houses.* James MacColl, M.P.
193 *Trade Unions and the Individual.* Cyril Grunfeld.

1958 194 *Speed-up Land Reform.* R. S. W. Pollard.
195 *Aid for Development.* David Blelloch.
196 *The Child and the Social Services.* D. V. Donnison.
197 *No Cheers for Central Africa.* R. Hinde and Mary Stewart.
198 *Plan for Steel Re-Nationalisation.* John Hughes.
199 *Efficiency and the Consumer.* C. D. Harbury.

BOOKS AND OTHER PUBLICATIONS

1886 *The Government Organisation of Unemployed Labour.* Report by a Committee of the Fabian Society.

1889 *Fabian Essays in Socialism.* Edited by Bernard Shaw.

1898 *Report on Municipal Tramways.* Presented to the Richmond (Surrey) Town Council by Ald. Thompson.

1900 *Fabianism and the Empire. A Manifesto of the Fabian Society.* Edited by Bernard Shaw.

1907 *This Misery of Boots.* H. G. Wells.

1908 *Those Wretched Rates, a Dialogue.* F. W. Hayes.
Ballads and Lyrics of Socialism 1883-1908. E. Nesbit.
The Commonsense of Municipal Trading. Bernard Shaw.

1909 *Break Up the Poor Law and Abolish the Workhouse.* S. and B. Webb. Being Part I of the Minority Report of the Poor Law Commission 1909.
The Remedy for Unemployment. Being Part II (See above) Sidney and Beatrice Webb.

1923   *The Decay of Capitalist Civilisation.* Sidney and Beatrice Webb.

      Representative Government and a Parliament of Industry. H. Finer.

1924   *Social Insurance: What It Is and What It Might Be.* A. Gordon.

1925   *History of the Fabian Society* (revised). E. R. Pease.

      The Co-operative Movement in Italy. Edward A. Lloyd, B.A.

1927   *The British Civil Service: An Introductory Essay.* H. Finer.

1929   *Mind Your Own Business: The Case for Municipal Housekeeping.*

1930   *The Socialist Tradition in the French Revolution.* H. Laski.

1932   *The Constitution and the Crisis 1931 and After.* H. Laski.

      Abridgement of the Minority Report of the Royal Commission on Unemployment Insurance.

      Where Stands Socialism Today? Autumn Lectures 1932.

1934   *The Nationalisation of Banking* by Mrs. Blanco-White.

1937   *What Is Ahead of Us?* Autumn Lectures 1936.

1938   *Dare We Look Ahead?* Autumn Lectures 1937.

1939   *Hitler's Route to Bagdad.* Edited by Leonard Woolf.

1940   *The Unemployment Services.* By Polly Hill.

      Where Stands Democracy? Autumn Lectures 1939.

      Britain's Food Supplies in Peace and War. Charles Smith.

1942   *Evacuation Survey.* Edited by Richard Padley and Margaret Cole.

      Programme for Victory. Autumn Lectures 1940.

      Victory or Vested Interest? Autumn Lectures 1941.

      Plan for Africa. Rita Hinden.

      Social Security. Evidence submitted to the Beveridge Committee.

      Education for Democracy. Margaret Cole.

      Downing Street and the Colonies. Colonial Bureau.

1943   *American Labour.* Ernest Davies.

      War over West Ham. E. Doreen Idle.

      Retail Trade Association. Professor Hermann Levy.

      Social Security. W. A. Robson.

      Plan for Britain. Autumn Lectures 1942.

      Our Soviet Ally. Edited by Margaret Cole.

      When Hostilities Cease. Papers on Relief and Reconstruction.

      Commodity Control. P. Lamartine Yates.

1944   *Can Planning be Democratic?* Autumn Lectures 1943.

1945   *Fabian Colonial Essays.* Prepared for the Fabian Colonial Bureau.

      What Labour Could Do. Autumn Lectures 1944.

      Co-operation in the Colonies. Report to the Fabian Colonial Bureau.

      The Changing Conditions of the British People 1911-1945. Mark Abrams.

Population and the People. A National Policy. Evidence submitted to the Royal Commission on Population by a Committee under the Chairmanship of Dr. W. A. Robson.

Towards a Socialist Agriculture. Edited by F. W. Bateson.

1946   *Forward from Victory.* Autumn Lectures 1945.
Co-operation in the Soviet Union. N. Barou.

1947   *Transport for the Nation.* A Broadsheet prepared by the Fabian Society for the Labour Party.
Czechoslovakia. Six Studies in Reconstruction.
The Reform of the Higher Civil Service.

1948   *Co-operative Movement in a Labour Britain.* Edited by N. Barou.
The Road to Recovery. Autumn Lectures 1947.
The Fate of Italy's Colonies. J. C. Gray and L. Silberman.

1949   *Regionalism.* Peter Self.
Principles of Economic Planning. Professor A. Lewis.

1950   *Behind the Ration Book.* Jack Blitz.

1951   *Industrial Democracy and Nationalisation.* Hugh Clegg.

1952   *New Fabian Essays.* Edited by R. H. S. Crossman.

1953   *Shaw and Society.* C. E. M. Joad.

1957   *Fabian International Essays.* Edited by T. E. M. McKitterick and Kenneth Younger.

Fabian Special

1942   1 *Take Over the War Industries.* Populus.
        2 *Let's Talk it Over—An Argument about Socialism for the Unconverted.* Raymond Postgate.
        3 *How the Russians Live.* Wright Miller.
        4 *The Colonies and Us.* Rita Hinden.
        5 *Beveridge Quiz.* Joan Clarke and Laurence Coward.
        6 *A Guide to the Health Plan.* Fabian Medical Service Group.
        7 *The British Working Class Movement.* G. D. H. Cole.

1951   8 *British Labour Movement.* G. D. H. Cole. (Retrospect and Prospect). (Ralph Fox Memorial Lecture).

1946   *Socialists and the Empire.* Rita Hinden.

Letter Series

1942   1 *To an Industrial Manager.* G. D. H. Cole.
        2 *To a Soldier.* A Comrade in Arms.
        3 *To a Student.* Margaret Cole.
        4 *To a Shop Steward.* Guild Socialist.
        5 *To a Woman Munition Worker.* Susan Lawrence.
        6 *To a Doctor.* Brian Thompson, M.D.
        7 *To a Country Clergyman.* Sidney Dark.
        8 *To a Teacher.* Michael Stewart.

Science and Social Affairs Series

1946 1 *The Atom and the Charter.* P. M. S. Blackett.

Colonial Controversy Series

1946 1 *Domination or Co-operation.*
1947 2 *Crisis in Africa.* L. Silberman.
     3 *Labour's Colonial Policy.* Arthur Creech Jones.
     4 *Kenya Controversy.*
     5 *Friendship and Empire.*
     6 *Troubled Uganda.* E. M. K. Mulira.
1950 7 *The Way Forward.* J. Griffiths.

Webb Memorial Lectures

1945 1 *The Webbs and Their Work.* R. H. Tawney.
1946 2 *The Social Services and the Webb Tradition.* M. Cole.
1947 3 *The Webbs and Soviet Communism.* Harold Laski.

Study Guides

1954 *About Equality.* W. T. Rodgers.
1956 *Essentials of Socialism.* W. T. Rodgers.

Biographical Series

Year	Tract No.	Title and Author
1912	165	*Francis Place.* St. John G. Ervine.
	166	*Robert Owen.* Miss B. L. Hutchins.
	167	*William Morris.* Mrs. Townsend.
1913	168	*John Stuart Mill.* J. West.
1914	169	*Charles Kingsley.* C. E. Vulliamy.
1916	179	*John Ruskin.* Edith Morley.
1917	182	*Robert Owen, Idealist.* C. E. M. Joad.
1922	199	*William Lovett.* Mrs. L. B. Hammond.
1925	215	*William Cobbett.* G. D. H. Cole.
	217	*Thomas Paine.* Kingsley Martin.
1926	221	*Jeremy Bentham.* Victor Cohen.
1941	—	*James Keir Hardie.* G. D. H. Cole.
1942	—	*Richard Carlisle.* G. D. H. Cole.
1943	—	*John Burns.* G. D. H. Cole.
1956	297	*Beatrice & Sidney Webb.* Margaret Cole.

BIOGRAPHICAL INDEX

Bakunin, Mikhail A. (1814-1876). Russian aristocrat and property owner, advocate of collectivism, atheism, and radical anarchism. He studied and agitated abroad, was handed over to the Tsar and exiled to Siberia, from whence he escaped to Switzerland in 1855. A member of the First International, he came into conflict with Marx and was expelled in 1872.

Balfour, Arthur James, 1st Earl of (1848-1930). British statesman, author, Tory politician. Prime Minister from 1902-5, and Foreign Secretary in Lloyd George's coalition government. Author of the "Balfour Declaration" supporting the establishment of a Jewish national home in Palestine.

Balfour, Gerald William (1853-1945). Politician, Chief Secretary for Ireland, and holder of other offices. Member of the Royal Commission on Trade Unions. Brother of Arthur Balfour.

Balfour, Lady Elizabeth Edith (1867-1945). Daughter of the Earl of Lytton, wife of Gerald Balfour, and, as "Lady Betty," a noted society hostess.

Barnes, George Nicoll (1859-1940). By profession an engineer, he rose to Secretary General of A.S.E. Labor M.P. from 1906-22. In the coalition government during the war, he opposed the Labor Party's break with the coalition.

Beerbohm, Sir Max (1872-1956). English author and caricaturist. Among his works are *A Book of Caricatures; Zuleika Dobson*, a satirical novel; *A Christmas Garland*.

Bellamy, Edward (1850-1898). American author, best known for his utopian novel *Looking Backward*.

Belloc, (Joseph) Hilaire (Pierre) (1870-1953). English writer, born in France, lively exponent of Catholic point of view. Author of light verse, essays, travel books, biography, and fiction. *On Nothing; On Everything; On Anything; On Something;* etc.

Bennett, Enoch Arnold (1867-1931). English journalist, playwright, and novelist. His best-known work is *The Old Wives' Tale*. Also: *Clayhanger; The Clayhanger Family; Lord Raingo; Accident;* etc.

Benson, Msgr. Hugh (1871-1914). Catholic writer and apologist. Wrote historical fiction: *By What Authority*, etc.

Bentham, Jeremy (1748-1832). Founder of the school of Philosophic Radicalism ("the greatest good for the greatest number"). *Fragment on Government* (1776); *Introduction to Principles of Morals and Legislation* (1789).

Bentinck, Lord Henry (1863-1931). M.P. for South Nottingham for many years between 1885 and 1929.

Bernstein, Eduard (1850-1932). Leader of the Revisionist wing of the German Social Democratic Party.

Besant, Annie (1847-1933). One of the seven Fabian Essayists. Early propagandist of birth control. Led a successful strike of underpaid match-girls at Bryant & May's in 1888. In 1889 abandoned Socialism for theosophy.

Beveridge, Sir William Henry (1879-   ). British economist and so-
   cial scientist, from 1919-37 director of the London School of
   Economics and, from 1937-45, master at Oxford University.
   The guiding force behind social legislation coverage "from the
   cradle to the grave," he is the author of *Social Insurance and
   Allied Services,* and *Full Employment in a Free Society.*

Bismarck, Prince Otto (1815-1898). Prussian statesman who, in
   1871, brought about the unification of Germany. He became
   the first Chancellor ("Iron Chancellor") of the German Reich.

Bland, Hubert (1856-1914). Author, journalist, Socialist and a
   founder-member of the Fabian Society.

Bland, Mrs. Hubert. *See* Nesbit, Edith.

Blavatsky, Helena Petrovna (1831-1891). Famous spiritualist and
   founder of the theosophic movement. Generally known as
   Mme. Blavatsky.

Blücher, Gebhard Leberecht von (1742-1819). Prussian general
   who supported Prussia's entry into the war against Napoleon
   (1805). In 1806 he had to surrender at Ratkau, but took part
   in the defeat of Napoleon at Waterloo, 1815.

Blunt, Wilfred Scawen (1840-1922). English poet, author, explorer,
   and translator of Oriental poetry. He was opposed to the imperialistic British policies. His works include: *The Future of
   Islam; Secret History of the English Occupation of Egypt;
   Diaries;* etc.

Boole, George (1815-1864). Mathematician; professor Queens University, Cork, 1849-64; LL.D., Dublin; D.C.L., Oxford. Published *The Laws of Thought* (1854), in which he employed
   symbolic language in a generalization of logical processes. He
   is considered founder of philosophical school of logical posi-
   tivism.

Booth, Charles (1840-1914). Shipowner and manufacturer. He organized—at his own expense—the eighteen-volume study: *The
   Life and Labour of the People of London.*

Bradlaugh, Charles (1833-1898). Secularist leader and propagandist of birth control, woman suffrage, and trade unionism. Insisted on and won the right to take his seat in Parliament on
   affirmation rather than Bible oath.

Brailsford, H. N. (1873-   ). Socialist journalist and war corre-
   spondent. Editor of the ILP weekly, the *New Leader,* 1922-6.

Bright, John (1811-1889). Orator and statesman; son of Rochdale
   miller; Member of Cabinet and privy council, 1868-70. Bright
   and Cobden were two leading representatives of the emerging
   manufacturing class after Reform Bill of 1832.

Broadhurst, Henry (1840-1911). General secretary of the Stone-
   mason's Union. Sat as a Liberal from 1880 to 1886 and from
   1894 to 1896. An extremely left trade unionist in his youth, he
   later became a strong opponent of efforts to introduce Socialism into the unions.

Brooke, Rupert (1887-1915). English poet. Socialist at Cambridge. Fell in active duty during World War I. *Grantchester; The Great Lover; 1914* (war sonnets).

Bryce, James, Viscount Bryce (1838-1922). English historian. Liberal politician and holder of various offices in Liberal Governments. Ambassador to U.S.A., 1907-13. *The American Commonwealth, Holy Roman Empire,* and *Studies in History and Jurisprudence,* are among his works.

Burns, John (1858-1943). Trade unionist, pacifist, chief leader of the Dock Strike of 1889. Elected to Parliament as a Socialist in 1892. He fought against the Webbs in the Poor Law agitation. "The Man with the Red Flag."

Buxton, Charles Roden (1875-1942). Brother of Noel Buxton, Liberal pacifist who later turned Labor.

Buxton, Noel (1869-1948). Minister of Agriculture in first two Labor Governments.

Buxton, Sydney Charles, Viscount (1853-1934). Radical politician, friend of Lord Haldane. President of the Board of Trade, 1910-14.

Cadbury, George (1839-1922). Cocoa and chocolate manufacturer and social reformer. Founded Bournville Village Trust, 1900. Quaker and keen Liberal.

Caine, Sir Hall (1853-1931). Novelist. Son of a ship's smith, born on Isle of Man. In 1878 delivered lecture on Rosetti's poetry which brought him the poet's friendship. Books: *The Deemster* (1887); *The Manxman* (1894); *Eternal City* (1901).

Campbell, Mrs. Patrick, *née* Stella Tanner (1865-1940). English actress, famous beauty, player of many leading parts, notably Eliza Doolittle in Bernard Shaw's *Pygmalion* (1912). The correspondence between her and Bernard Shaw was published and widely read.

Campbell-Bannerman, Sir Henry (1836-1908). Liberal Prime Minister, 1906. Responsible for granting self-government to the Transvaal and Orange Free State, 1907.

Carpenter, Edward (1844-1929). Socialist and anarchist, author. His most famous book is *Love's Coming of Age.* He also wrote *Civilisation, Its Cause and Cure.*

Carr-Saunders, Sir Alexander (1886-   ). Population expert.

Cassel, Sir Ernest (1852-1921). Financier and philanthropist. Born in Germany, naturalized 1872. Created State Bank of Morocco and National Bank of Turkey. Gave away 2 million pounds sterling during lifetime. Great friend of Prince of Wales (later Edward VII).

Chamberlain, Joseph (1836-1914). Radical politician. Mayor of Birmingham, 1870-3. Formed the Liberal Unionist Group. The early Fabians were influenced by his ideas.

Chamberlain, Neville (1869-1940). British statesman. After holding different positions in Conservative Governments he succeeded Baldwin as Prime Minister in 1937. His policy of "appeasement" led to the Munich Pact. On May 10, 1940, after the defeat of Norway, he lost the premiership to Winston Churchill.

Champion, Henry Hyde (1859-1928). Socialist organizer and artillery officer. One of the leaders of the SDF, he agitated for Socialist M.P.'s and was violently opposed to Liberalism. Left England for Australia in 1893.

Chandler, Francis W. (1849-1938). Woodworker. General Secretary of the Amalgamated Society of Carpenters and Joiners. He represented the industrial workers at the Royal Commission on the Poor Law.

Chesterton, Gilbert Keith (1874-1936). English journalist, writer of poetry, essays, fiction. His works include *The Man Who Was Thursday; Come to Think of It; Autobiography;* etc. In 1922, Chesterton was converted to Catholicism and frequently expressed his religious opinions as an author.

Chubb, Percival (1860-1920). Ethical Culturist, author.

Churchill, Lord Randolph Henry Spencer (1849-1895). British statesman. Secretary for India (1885). Chancellor of the Exchequer (1886). Resigned his posts in protest against the government budget. Father of Sir Winston Churchill.

Churchill, Sir Winston Leonard Spencer (1874-). English statesman and author. After military service in Cuba, India, South Africa, he entered Parliament as a Tory in 1901. He broke away and became Home Secretary and First Lord of the Admiralty under Asquith. Returned to Tories after World War I. An opponent of Neville Chamberlain's policy of appeasement, he became First Lord of the Admiralty in 1939 and Prime Minister in 1940. Received Nobel Prize for Literature in 1953. Books: *Marlborough,* a biography of his ancestor; *The Second World War* (5 vols.); *A History of the English-Speaking Nations;* etc.

Clarke, William (1852-1901). Political journalist and Fabian. Writer for *The Spectator.* Wrote life of Walt Whitman, 1892.

Clynes, J. R. (1869-1949). Worked as a boy in a cotton mill. Won a seat in the House of Commons, 1906. Food Controller, 1918; Lord Privy Seal, 1924; Home Secretary, 1929-31.

Cole, George Douglas Howard (1889-1959). Professor of Social and Political Theory in the University of Oxford. Supporter of Syndicalism and Guild Socialism. Author of *The World of Labour* (1913); *An Intelligent Man's Guide to the Post-War World* (1947); etc.

Costello, Benjamin Francis (1855-1899). A barrister, member of the LCC (Progressive) and lecturer for the Fabian Society.

Courtney, Leonard Henry, Baron Courtney of Penwith (1832-1918). Political economist and writer. Liberal parliamentarian, leader of the anti-war party during the Boer War and, subsequently, an independent pacifist.

Crane, Walter (1845-1915). English painter and illustrator of the romantic school. His best-known illustrations are for Spenser's *Faërie Queene* and for children's books.

Craven, Harry (1886-   ). Journalist. Educ. London University. Joined Fabians, 1907.

Cripps, Charles Alfred (1852-1941). Lawyer, husband of Theresa Potter. Sat in Parliament as Tory and was made Baron Parmoor. Resigned at the outbreak of World War I from his party and became one of the leaders of the pacifist and internationalist movement. In 1924 and 1929, Lord President of the Council in the Labor Government.

Cunctator, Quintus Fabius Maximus (d. 203 B.C.). Name is Latin for "the delayer." Roman general who fought Hannibal by wearing him out by marches, skirmishes from a distance, and by avoiding direct contact.

Cunninghame Graham, Robert Bontine (1852-1936). Son of a Scottish landowner. Artist, author, and one of the most colorful personalities of the Socialist movement. Starting out as an extreme Liberal, he soon joined the SDF.

Dalton, Hugh (1887-   ). Leader of the Cambridge Fabian Society in his youth, he became Chancellor of the Exchequer in 1945.

Darwin, Charles Robert (1809-1882). English naturalist. His most important work is *On the Origin of Species by Means of Natural Selection* (1859), in which he explained the evolution of higher species through the survival of the fittest. Darwinism was one of the leading theories of the nineteenth century.

Davidson, Thomas (1840-1900). Founder of the Vita Nuova, or Fellowship of the New Life, from which the Fabian Society developed as a splinter group.

Dearmer, Rev. Percy (1867-1936). Broad Churchman, social reformer, Fabian. Secretary of London Christian Social Union, later Canon of Westminster. Chairman of the League of Arts (1920). Contributor to many publications. Fabian Tract: *Socialism and Christianity*.

Dicey, Albert Venn (1835-1922). Jurist. Vinerian Professor of English Law, 1882-1909. Principal books: *Introduction to the Study of the Law of the Constitution* (1885); *Law and Public Opinion in England,* 1905.

Dickinson, G. Lowes (1862-1932). Author, pacifist. Wrote *The Magic Flute,* etc.

Dilke, Sir Charles, Baronet (1843-1911). Politician, proprietor of *Athenaeum.* Friend of Gambetti. M.P. for Forest of Dean, 1892-1911. Co-respondent in divorce suit, 1885.

Desborough, Lady, *née* Ethel Fane. Wife of William Henry Grenfell, 1st and last Baron Desborough. was a noted society hostess. She was the mother of poet Julian Grenfell V, killed in action 1915, as was his brother Gerald; the third son, Ivo, also fought in World War I and was killed in a motor accident in 1926.

Disraeli, Benjamin, 1st Earl of Beaconsfield (1804-1881). English statesman and author. Prime Minister of England in 1868 and from 1874 to 1880. Wrote novels, biography, political essays. *Vivian Grey; The Infernal Marriage; Endymion;* etc.

Donisthorpe, Wordsworth (1847-?). Expert on local government. Author of *Individualism, A System of Politics* (1889), etc.

Eaton, Walter Prichard (1878-   ). American author, essayist, dramatic critic. Successor of G. P. Baker as Professor of Drama at Yale University.

Edward VII (1841-1910). Eldest son of Queen Victoria, he spent most of his life as Prince of Wales. Reigned from 1901-10. A promoter of agreements with the Great Powers, he was responsible for the *entente cordiale*. His second child became George V of England.

Elcho, Lady, *née* Mary Constance Wyndham (d. 1937). Society hostess and one of the leaders of the "Souls."

Eliot, Thomas Stearns (1888-   ). American poet, naturalized British citizen. Most influential poet of his generation. Nobel Prize for literature in 1948.

Ellis, Havelock (1859-1939). English author and literary critic. One of the first to write on sexual psychology. *Studies in the Psychology of Sex* (6 vols., 1900-1910); *The Dance of Life;* etc.

Engels, Friedrich (1820-1895). German political philosopher, collaborator of Marx, with whom he wrote the *Communist Manifesto* (1848). Editor and publisher of Marx's work. *Entwicklung des Sozialismus von der Utopie zur Wissenschaft* (English edition is entitled *Socialism, Utopian and Scientific*) is his most important independent work.

Ensor, Robert Charles Kirkwood (1877-1959). Journalist, Fabian, political theorist, member of LCC. He is "Scrutator" of the *Sunday Times.* Author of *England, 1870-1914.*

Ervine, St. John Greer (1883-   ). Irish dramatist and critic, associated with the Dublin Abbey Theater. Among his plays are *The Ship; The First Mrs. Fraser; People of Our Class;* etc. He also wrote novels: *Changing Winds; Foolish Lovers;* etc.

Fletcher, Sir Walter Morley (1873-1933). Physiologist and administrator. FRS, 1915. Secretary of Medical Research Committee under Lloyd George, 1913. Chairman of Indian Government Committee on medicine, 1928.

Fourier, François Marie Charles (1772-1837). Founder of Fourierism, a communistic system according to which the world was to be divided into "phalansteries," with one central government and one language for all.

Frankfurter, Felix (1882-   ). U.S. jurist, born in Vienna. Professor of law at Harvard from 1914 to 1939, in which year he was appointed Associate Justice of the Supreme Court. Prominent in liberal causes, notably the Sacco and Vanzetti case.

Galsworthy, John (1867-1933). English novelist and dramatist, best known for *The Forsyte Saga,* a series of novels describing the fortunes of the Forsyte family. Among his plays are: *Justice; Strife; Escape; The Roof.* Also collections of short stories.

Gardiner, Alfred G. (1865-   ). Liberal writer and journalist, editor of the *Daily News,* author of *Pillars of Society* and many other pen portraits of famous contemporaries.

Garland, Hamlin (1860-1940). American novelist and short-story writer with strong emphasis on social problems. In one of his novels, *An Average* Man (1892), he set forth Henry George's single-tax idea.

Garnett, Edward (1868-1937). English critic, essayist, and biographer. Reader for all great publishing houses. His wife, Constance, was the famous translator of Russian novels.

George V (1865-1936). His reign, from 1910 to 1936, was the perfect example of constitutional monarchy. Assumed the family name of Windsor during the First World War. Father of George VI.

George, Henry (1839-1897). American political economist, known for his "single tax" and his study of the problems of poverty. *Progress and Poverty* (1879). Also: *Social Problems* (1884); *Science of Political Economy* (1897); etc.

Gibbons, James Cardinal (1834-1921). Catholic Archbishop of Baltimore. Wrote *The Faith of Our Fathers* (1877).

Gill, Eric (1882-1940). English sculptor and engraver, author of essays on art and social and religious problems. Pacifist, Christian anarchist. Wrote *Christianity and Art; Money and Morals;* etc.

Gladstone, Herbert, Viscount Gladstone (1854-1930). Son of the Liberal Prime Minister. Home Secretary, Chief Liberal Whip, Governor-General of South Africa.

Gladstone, William Ewart (1809-1898). British statesman. A Tory and, as such, Member of Parliament in 1833, he changed to Liberalism and became the dominant figure in that party. Served four times as Prime Minister, between 1868 and 1894. Sponsor of many reforms: disestablishment of the Church of Ireland, secret ballot, Irish land-reform act, etc.

Gordon, Charles George (1833-1885). "Chinese Gordon." English general. Captured Soochow. Thwarted by Ismail Pasha in his efforts to suppress the slave trade in Africa, 1876. Governor-General of the Sudan, 1877. Killed at Khartoum after having sustained a siege for 317 days.

Grant-Duff, Sir Mountstuart (1829-1906). Statesman and author. Liberal M.P. for the Elgin Boroughs, 1857-81. Under-secretary of State for India, 1868-74; Governor of Madras, 1881-6. *Notes from a Diary* (1897-1905).

Granville-Barker, Harley (1877-1946). Actor and dramatist, Fabian and crony of G.B.S. during early years. His wife was actress Lilah McCarthy.

General Theory of Employment, Interest and Money; The Economic Consequences of the Peace; etc. Created Baron 1942.

Kingsley, Charles (1819-1875). English clergyman and novelist, greatly interested in social reforms. He is the author of the children's classic, *Water Babies.* Involved in a famous controversy with Cardinal Newman.

Knox, Mgr. Ronald (1888-1958). Protonotary Apostolic, 1951. Son of Rt. Rev. C. A. Knox; ed. Eton and Balliol. *Caliban in Grub Street; Reunion All Round,* 1914. Translator of the Bible, etc.

Kropotkin, Prince Peter A. (1842-1921). Russian social philosopher, anarchist, and geographer; explorer in Finland, Manchuria, Siberia. He joined the revolutionary movement in 1872 and, from then on, was in and out of prison, in Russia and France, until he settled in London in 1886. He returned to Russia in 1917. He wrote works on anarchism, the terror in Russia, and the *Memoirs of a Revolutionist.*

Lammenais, Félicité Robert, Abbé de (1782-1854). French philosopher and theologian. He wrote an *Essay on Indifference in the Matter of Religion* after his ordination and was condemned in 1832. His most famous book was *Paroles d'un croyant.*

Lansbury, George (1859-1940). Socialist and lifelong champion of the workingman. Socialist M.P. from 1922 to his death.

Lansdowne, 5th Marquess (1845-1927). Henry William Edmund Petty-Fitzmaurice, 5th Marquess. Leader of Tory opposition in the House of Lords from 1906. Minister without portfolio in Asquith Coalition.

Laski, Harold Joseph (1893-1950). English political scientist, member of the Fabian Society, professor of political science in the University of London, connected with the London School of Economics, editor of the works of Edmund Burke and John Stuart Mill. Among his works are *The American Presidency: An Interpretation; Reflections on the Revolution of Our Time;* etc.

Lassalle, Ferdinand (1825-1864). German Socialist. Founder, in 1863, of the General Association of German Workers, the forerunner of the German Social-Democratic Party.

Le Bon, Gustav (1841-1931). Sociologist and scholar; author of *La Psychologie des Foules,* etc.

Lee, Vernon (Violet Paget) (1856-1935). Author; born in France. Published *Studies of the Eighteenth Century in Italy* (1880); *Satan the Waster* (1920), anti-war book; etc.

Lessner, Friedrich (1825-1910). Author of *Sixty Years in the Social-Democratic Movement; Recollections of an Old Communist;* etc.

Lippmann, Walter (1889-   ). American editor and journalist. Column in the New York *Herald Tribune* since 1931. Author of *The Method of Freedom,* etc.

Marryat, Captain Frederick (1792-1848). Writer of sea stories: *Mr. Midshipman Easy; Peter Simple;* etc.

Martin, Kingsley (1897-   ). Editor of *New Statesman* since 1931. Son of Unitarian minister. M.A., Princeton University. Wrote a life of Harold Laski.

Marx, Karl (1818-1883). German political philosopher, founder of the German Social Democratic Labor Party (1869). Author of *Das Kapital,* which furnished the theoretical underpinning for the Socialistic (Marxist, Communist) movements.

Massingham, Henry William (1849-1924). Journalist of liberal views, editor of the *Daily Chronicle* and the *Nation.* A Fabian in the nineties, he broke with the Society at the time of the Boer War.

Masterman, Charles Frederick Gurney (1873-1927). Lecturer, journalist, and radical politician. Liberal M.P. from 1906-14; Parliamentary Secretary to Local Government Board; etc.

Maude, Aylmer (1858-1938). Translator and expounder of the works of Leo Tolstoy. Employed in large carpet factory in Moscow 1884-97. Wrote *Life of Tolstoy* (1908), and also a biography of Marie Stopes (1924).

Maurice, Frederick Denison (1805-1872). Protestant divine; writer; published *Subscription no Bondage* (1836); professor of English literature and history at Kings College, London, 1840; edited Christian Socialist magazine; 1854 inaugurated Working Men's College; professor of moral theology at Cambridge, 1866.

Maurois, André (1885-   ). French novelist and biographer of the Lytton Strachey school of "the new biography." His life of Shelley, *Ariel,* is his best-known biographical study.

Meinertzhagen, Daniel (1842-1910). Senior partner in a banking firm. Brother-in-law of Mrs. Sidney Webb.

Mellor, William (1888-1942). Fabian and Guild Socialist. Secretary of Fabian Research Department, 1913-15; later, editor of the *Daily Herald.*

Meredith, George (1828-1909). English novelist and poet with deep interest in social problems. His work includes many volumes of poetry (*Ballads and Poems of Magic Life; A Reading of Earth;* etc.), novels (*Rhoda Fleming; The Amazing Marriage; Richard Feverel;* etc.), and essays.

Mill, John Stuart (1806-1873). English philosopher and economist, exponent of Utilitarianism. Among his best-known treatises are *System of Logic* (1843); *On Liberty* (1859); *Representative Government* (1861); *Utilitarianism* (1863).

Money, Sir Leo Chiozza (1870-1944). Journalist, Fabian, and Liberal M.P. Parliamentary private secretary to David Lloyd George, and Parliamentary secretary to the Ministry of Shipping, 1916-18. Wrote *Riches and Poverty.*

Montagu, Edwin (1879-1924). Statesman; son of first Lord Swaythling. Liberal M.P. 1906-22. Under-Secretary for India 1910-14;

O'Brien, William (1852-1928). Irish nationalist, journalist, and M.P. for Cork.

Olivier, Sydney, Baron Olivier (1859-1943). One of the seven Fabian Essayists. Governor of Jamaica. Wrote *White Capital and Coloured Labour,* and other books on problems of native emancipation. Secretary of State for India in the Labor Government of 1924.

Orage, A. R. (1873-1934). With Holbrook Jackson, edited the *New Age* until 1909. Met Major Douglas in 1918 and was converted to his Social Credit scheme. In 1922 fell under influence of P. D. Ouspensky and through him of Russian mystic George Gurdjieff. Founded *New English Weekly,* 1932.

Orwell, George (1903-1950). English novelist of extreme liberal views. His *Homage to Catalonia* grew out of his experience as a fighter on the Republican side during the Spanish Civil War. Two satirical novels, *Animal Farm* and *Nineteen Eighty-four,* depict the threat of totalitarianism.

Owen, Robert (1771-1858). Educationalist, factory reformer, Socialist. Founder of unsuccessful "owenite" communities in Britain and the U.S.

Pease, Edward R. (1858-1955). One of the founders of the Fabian Society and its general secretary from 1889-1914. Wrote a *History of the Fabian Society.*

Parnell, Charles Stewart (1846-1891). Irish nationalist leader, agitator for Home Rule, highly controversial figure. He won Gladstone and the Liberal Party over to his side.

Pearsall Smith, Alys (1867-1951). Daughter of Mary Pearsall Smith, American evangelist and author of many pious tracts. Married Bertrand Russell.

Pearsall Smith, Mary (1864-1945). Daughter of Mary Pearsall Smith and sister of Alys. Married, first, Frank Costelloe (Fabian) and, second, Bernard Berenson. Author of *A Vicarious Trip to the Barbary Coast,* etc.

Penty, A. J. (1875-1937). Christian Socialist who, after having started out as a Fabian, became one of the exponents of Guild Socialism. His major work is *The Restoration of the Guild System.*

Plato (427?-347 B.C.). Greek philosopher. Disciple of Socrates, founder of the Academy (Athens), where he taught philosophy, mathematics, government, etc. Aristotle was one of his pupils. His works, all in dialogue form, include: *Apology; Crito; Republic; Symposium.*

Podmore, Frank (1856-1910). Civil servant. Author of *Apparitions and Thought Transference* and *The Life of Robert Owen.*

Postgate, Margaret (Mrs. G. D. H. Cole) (1893-   ). Author; chairman of Education Committee, LCC.

Potter, Beatrice (Mrs. Sidney Webb) (1858-1943). With her husband, the main founder of the Fabian Society.

Proudhon, Pierre Joseph (1809-1865). Philosopher, anarchist, wrote *What Is Property?* ("Property is theft!") Imprisoned in 1849-52 for attacking Louis Napoleon.

Rauschenbusch, Walter (1861-1918). American Baptist clergyman, leader in social interpretation of Christianity. Author of *Christianity and the Social Crisis* and *The Social Principles of Jesus*.

Reeves, Amber Pember. Daughter of New Zealand representative; had a child by H. G. Wells, who wrote *Ann Veronica* about her. Author of *The New Propaganda* (London, Victor Gollancz, Left Book Club, 1939). Married Blanco White.

Reeves, William Pember (1857-1932). A native of New Zealand, where he was Minister of Labor, Education, and Justice. Agent-General in London. Socialist and Fabian, he wrote on state experiments in the colonies.

Ricardo, David (1772-1823). Economist. Successor, in thought, to Jeremy Bentham and James Mill.

Rosebery, Archibald Philip Primrose, Earl of Rosebery (1847-1929). Liberal peer. Prime Minister in 1895, first chairman of the London County Council, 1889.

Rosmini-Serbati, Antonio (1797-1855). Priest, founder of Instituto della Carita, generally called Rosminian Order. Born of a noble family in Trentino. His *Treatise on the Moral Conscience* was approved, and his order also, by Gregory XVI. But after the accession of Pius IX, owing to the enmity of Cardinal Antonelli, he was condemned for having sided with the *Risorgimento*. He greatly influenced Cavour and Manzoni, and died at Stresa in the odor of sanctity.

Ruskin, John (1819-1900). English painter, essayist, and art critic, connected with the Pre-Raphaelite Brotherhood. Very interested in social movements and reform, he also wrote on these subjects. His works include *Modern Painters; The Seven Lamps of Architecture; The Stones of Venice;* etc.

Russell, Bertrand, 3rd Earl Russell (1872-   ). Philosopher, author, mathematician, Socialist. Famous *enfant terrible* with unorthodox opinions about sex, education, religion, etc. His many works include *Introduction to Mathematical Philosophy; Marriage and Morals; Analysis of Mind;* etc. Nobel Prize for literature, 1950.

Saint-Simon, Comte de (Claude Henry de Rouvroy) (1760-1825). French philosopher and social reformer. His disciples developed his social doctrine into a system, Saint-Simonianism, which demands that all property be owned by the state.

St. Thomas Aquinas (ca. 1225-1274). Known as the Angelic Doctor. Italian scholastic philosopher, he taught at Bologna, Paris, Rome. His most important work is the *Summa Theologica*. His philosophy, Thomism, is the most influential school of thought in the Catholic Church.

Salisbury, Lord (1861-1947). Fourth Marquis; President of the Board of Trade, 1905; Lord President of the Council, 1923.

Squire, J. C. (Sir John) (1884-   ). English poet and journalist. Founder of the London *Mercury*.

Stacy, Enid (d. 1903). Socialist, member of the Fabian Society, Hutchinson lecturer, and member of the ILP. Died soon after her marriage to the Socialist curate, Rev. P. E. T. Widdrington.

Stead, W. T. (1849-1912). Journalist and author. Editor of *Pall Mall Gazette*, 1883-90. With Viscount Milner inaugurated "new journalism." Directly responsible for dispatch of General Gordon to Khartoum (1884).

Stepniak, Sergei M. (1852-1895). Pseudonym of Sergei Kravchinski, a Russian writer, member of the Nihilist party, who lived in exile in Italy, Switzerland, and England. Wrote *Underground Russia; The Career of a Nihilist;* etc.

Stevenson, R. L. (1850-1894). Scotch novelist, poet and essayist. His *Treasure Island* has become a children's classic. Other works are *Kidnapped; David Balfour; A Child's Garden of Verses;* etc.

Strachey, John (1901-   ). Son of St. Loe Strachey, editor of the *Spectator*. M.P. for Dundee West; Secretary of State for War, 1950-1.

Tagore, Rabindranath (1861-1941). Hindu artist, poet, author, and social reformer. Awarded Nobel Prize for literature in 1913. Founder of an international university at Bolpur, Bengal. Translator of Hindu works—among them, his own—into English. Author of *Gitanjali; Lectures on Personality; The Child; The Golden Boat;* etc.

Tawney, R. H. (1880-   ). Born in Calcutta. Educated at Balliol. Member of executive of Workers Educational Association, 1908-47. Professor of Economic History, University of London, 1931-49. Author of *The Acquisitive Society; Religion and the Rise of Capitalism;* etc.

Temple, William (1881-1944). Archishop of Canterbury. Married Frances Anson.

Tennant, Margot. See Asquith, Emma.

Tennyson, Alfred, Lord (1809-1892). English poet, immensely popular and considered most outstanding of the Victorian poets. His works include: *Poems* (1832); *Poems* (1842); *Maud; Idylls of the King;* etc.

Terry, Dame Ellen (1847-1928). English actress, known for her long, close association with Bernard Shaw, who wrote many plays for her. Their extensive, romantic correspondence is famous.

Thomas, J. H. (1874-1949). Born in Newport, Wales. Engine-driver on Great Western Railroad. General secretary, National Union of Railwaymen, 1918-31. Colonial Secretary, 1924, 1931, 1936.

Thompson, Henry Yates (1838-1928). Secretary to W. E. Gladstone and distinguished bibliophile. Author of several books on illuminated manuscripts.

Thorne, Will (1857-1946). Gasworker. Founder and general secretary, National Union of General & Municipal Workers. M.P. for Plaistow from 1906.

Tillett, Benjamin (1860-1943). Organizer of the Transport Workers. Active in the 1889 Dock Strike and subsequent strikes. Labor M.P., 1917-24 and 1929-31.

Tocqueville, Count Alexis de (1805-1859). French political theorist, historian, and civil servant. After a tour of the United States he published *Democracy in America,* a classic study of American institutions.

Townshend, Charlotte Payne (d. 1944). Irish millionairess, member of the Fabian Society, who later became Mrs. Bernard Shaw.

Toynbee, Arnold (1889-   ). English historian and lecturer. His monumental work *A Study of History* appeared in 1947 in a condensed version and became a best-seller. Editor of *Greek Historical Thought* and *Greek Civilization and Character.*

Trevelyan, George Macaulay (1876-   ). Member of the famous family of statesmen and historians. Historian and professor of history at Cambridge. *British History in the Nineteenth Century; England Under Queen Anne;* etc.

Trevelyan, Sir George Otto (1838-1928). English historian and statesman. *The American Revolution* (6 vols.) is one of his works.

Trotsky, Leon (Lev D. Bronstein) (1877-1940). Russian revolutionary leader. Commissar of Foreign Affairs and Minister of War during the Russian Civil War (1918-20). Opposed Stalin's theory of "Socialism in one country" and was driven into exile in 1929. Settled in Mexico, 1937, where he continued his political activity and founded the Fourth International. Was assassinated. *History of the Russian Revolution* (3 vols.) is one of his many works.

Turner, Sir Ben (1863-1942). General president of the National Union of Textile Workers (wool). M.P. for Batley. Secretary for Mines, 1929-30.

Voynich, Ethel Lillian Boole (1864-   ). English novelist and translator from the Russian. Her best-known novel, *The Gadfly,* has been translated into many languages.

Wakefield, Rev. Henry Russell (1854-1933). Broad Churchman, Bishop of Birmingham, 1911-24. Chairman of the Central Committee on the Unemployed. He signed the minority report as member of the Poor Law Commission.

Wallas, Graham (1858-1932). Sociologist; author of *Human Nature in Politics;* lecturer at the London School of Economics. One of the "Big Four" of the Fabian Executive, 1888-95.

Ward, Barbara (Lady Jackson) (1914-   ). Married Robert Jackson, 1950. Assistant editor, *The Economist,* 1936-9. Governor, BBC, 1946-50. Publications: *The West at Bay* (1948); *Faith and Freedom* (1954); etc.

BIBLIOGRAPHY

Aiken, Henry D. (ed.). *The Age of Ideology: The 19th Century Philosophers*. Vol. V of *Great Ages of Western Philosophy*. Boston: Houghton Mifflin Co., 1957; New York: The New American Library (Mentor Book No. MD 185), 1956.

Aldington, Richard. *Life for Life's Sake: A Book of Reminiscences*. New York: The Viking Press, Inc., 1941.

Amery, L. S. *My Political Life*. 3 vols. London and New York: Hutchinson & Co. (Publishers), Ltd., 1953-55.

Barker, Sir Ernest. *Political Thought in England from Spencer to the Present Day*. New York: Henry Holt & Co., Inc.; London: Williams and Norgate, Ltd., 1915.

Beer, Max. *A History of British Socialism*. 2 vols. Introduction by R. H. Tawney. London: George Allen & Unwin, Ltd.; New York: Harcourt, Brace & Co., Inc., 1919-20.

Bellamy, Edward. *Looking Backward: 2000-1887*. London: F. Warne & Co., 1890; New York: Random House, Inc. (The Modern Library No. 22).

Bennett, Arnold. *The Journals of Arnold Bennett*. 3 vols. London: Cassell & Co., Ltd.; New York: The Viking Press, Inc., 1932-33.

Bentham, Jeremy. *An Introduction to the Principles of Morals and Legislation*. London: 1789.

Bernstein, Eduard. *Die Volkswirtschaftslehre der Gegenwart in Selbstdarstellung*. Leipzig: Heiner, 1924.

————. *My Years of Exile: Reminiscences of a Socialist*. New York: Harcourt, Brace & Howe; London: Leonard Parsons, 1921.

Beveridge, William Henry. *Power and Influence: An Autobiography*. New York: Beechhurst Press, Inc., 1955; London: Hodder & Stoughton, Ltd., 1953.

Blunt, Wilfred Scawen. *My Diaries: Being a Personal Narrative of Events*. 2 vols. London: Martin Secker, 1920; New York: Alfred A. Knopf, Inc., 1921.

Boole, George. *The Laws of Thought*. London: Smith, Elder & Co., 1854; Chicago and London: The Open Court Publishing Co., 1940.

Burnham, James. *The Managerial Revolution: What Is Happening in the World*. New York: The John Day Co., Inc., 1941; London: Putnam & Co., Ltd., 1942.

Chesterton, Mrs. Cecil. *The Chestertons*. London: Chapman & Hall, Ltd., 1941.

Chesterton, G. K. *Autobiography*. London: Hutchinson & Co. (Publishers), Ltd., New York: Sheed & Ward, Inc., 1936.

———. *George Bernard Shaw*. New York: John Lane Co., 1909.

Colbourne, Maurice Dale. *The Real Bernard Shaw*. New York: Dodd, Mead & Co., Inc., 1940; London: J. M. Dent & Sons, Ltd., 1939.

Cole, G. D. H. *The Second International, 1889-1914*. Vol. III of *A History of Socialist Thought*. London: Macmillan & Co., Ltd.; New York: St Martin's Press, Inc., 1956.

———. *World in Transition: A Guide to the Shifting Political and Economic Forces of Our Time*. New York: Oxford University Press, 1949.

Cole, G. D. H. and Margaret I. *The Bolo Book*. London: The Labour Publishing Co., 1921.

Cole, Margaret I. *Beatrice Webb*. London: Longmans, Green & Co., 1945; New York: Harcourt, Brace & Co., Inc., 1946.

———. *Beatrice and Sidney Webb*. London: The Fabian Society, 1955.

———. *Growing Up into Revolution*. London and New York: Longmans, Green & Co., 1949.

Cole, Margaret I. (ed.). *The Webbs and Their Work*. London: Frederick Muller, Ltd., 1949.

Crossman, R. H. S. (ed.). *New Fabian Essays*. Preface by C. R. Attlee. London: Turnstile Press, Ltd.; New York: Frederick A. Praeger, Inc., 1952.

Dalton, Hugh. *Call Back Yesterday: Memoirs 1887-1931*. London: Frederick Muller, Ltd., 1953.

Dangerfield, George. *The Strange Death of Liberal England*. New York: Random House, Inc., 1935; London: Constable & Co., Ltd., 1936.

Ensor, Sir Robert. *England, 1870-1914*. Oxford: The Clarendon Press, 1936.

Ervine, St. John. *Bernard Shaw, His Life, Work, and Friends*. New York: William Morrow & Co., Inc.; London: Constable & Co., Ltd., 1956.

Estorick, Eric. *Stafford Cripps, Master Statesman*. New York: The John Day Co.; London: William Heinemann, Ltd., 1949.

Feiling, Keith. *The Life of Neville Chamberlain*. New York: The Macmillan Co., 1946.

Flynn, John T. *The Road Ahead: America's Creeping Revolution*. New York: The Devin-Adair Co., 1949.

Forster, E. M. *Two Cheers for Democracy*. New York: Harcourt, Brace & Co., Inc.; London: Edward Arnold, Ltd., 1951.

Gardiner, A. G. *Pillars of Society*. New York: Dodd, Mead & Co., Inc., 1914.

Garnett, David. *The Flowers of the Forest*. Vol. II of *The Golden Echo*. London: Chatto & Windus, Ltd., 1955; New York: Harcourt, Brace & Co., Inc., 1956.

George, Henry. *Progress and Poverty*. New York: D. Appleton & Co., 1880; Random House, Inc. (Modern Library No. 36), 1938.

Graubard, Stephen Richards. *British Labour and the Russian Revolution, 1917-1924*. Cambridge: Harvard University Press, 1956.

Graves, Robert. *Good-bye to All That: An Autobiography*. London: Jonathan Cape, Ltd., 1929.

Graves, Robert and Hodge, Alan. *The Long Week-end: A Social History of Great Britain, 1918-1939*. London: Faber & Faber, Ltd., 1940; New York: The Macmillan Co., 1941.

Haldane, R. B. *An Autobiography*. London: Hodder & Stoughton, Ltd.; New York: Doubleday, Doran, 1929.

Halévy, Élie. *Imperialism and Rise of Labour* Vol. V of *A History of the English People in the Nineteenth Century*. Translated by E. I. Watkin. 2nd ed. rev. London: Ernest Benn, Ltd.; Gloucester, Mass.: Peter Smith, 1949-52.

Hamilton, M. A. *Arthur Henderson: A Biography*. London: William Heinemann, Ltd., 1938.

————. *J. Ramsay MacDonald: A Biographical Sketch*. London: Jonathan Cape, Ltd.; New York: Peter Smith, 1929.

————. *Remembering My Good Friends*. London: Jonathan Cape, Ltd., 1944.

————. *Sidney and Beatrice Webb: A Study in Contemporary Biography*. Boston: Houghton Mifflin Co.; London: Sampson Low, Marston & Co., 1933.

Harrod, R. F. *Life of John Maynard Keynes*. London: Macmillan & Co., Ltd.; New York: Harcourt, Brace & Co., Inc., 1951.

Hastings, Sir Patrick. *Autobiography*. London: William Heinemann, Ltd., 1948.

Henderson, Archibald. *George Bernard Shaw: Man of the Century*. New York: Appleton-Century-Crofts, Inc., 1956.

Hewins, W. A. S. *The Apologia of an Imperialist: Forty Years of Empire Policy*. 2 vols. London: Constable & Co., Ltd., 1929.

Hobson, S. G. *Pilgrim to the Left: Memoirs of a Modern Revolutionist*. New York: Longmans, Green & Co.; London: Edward Arnold, Ltd., 1938.

Hutchison, Keith. *The Decline and Fall of British Capitalism*. New York: Charles Scribner's Sons, 1950; London: Jonathan Cape, Ltd., 1951.

Hyndman, H. M. *England for All*. London: Gilbert & Rivington, 1881.

————. *The Record of an Adventurous Life*. New York: The Macmillan Co., 1911.

Industrial Remuneration Conference. London: Cassell & Co., Ltd., 1885.

Jackson, Holbrook. *Bernard Shaw*. London: G. Richards, 1909.

Joad, C. E. M. (ed.). *Shaw and Society: An Anthology and a Symposium.* London: Odhams Press, Ltd.; Hollywood-by-the-Sea, Fla.: Transatlantic Arts, Inc., 1953.

Jones, Thomas. *A Diary with Letters 1931-1950.* London and New York: Oxford University Press, 1954.

Keynes, John Maynard. *Essays in Biography.* New York: Harcourt, Brace & Co., Inc.; London: Macmillan & Co., Ltd., 1933.

———. *Two Memoirs: Dr. Melchior, a Defeated Enemy,* and *My Early Beliefs.* Introduction by David Garnett. London: Rupert Hart-Davis, Ltd.; New York: A. M. Kelley, Inc., 1949.

Kropotkin, Prince Peter. *An Appeal to the Young.* Girard, Kansas: People's Pocket Series, 1931.

———. *Memoirs of a Revolutionist.* Boston: Houghton Mifflin Co., 1899.

Laski, Harold Joseph. *I Believe.* London: George Allen & Unwin, Ltd., 1942.

Lee, Vernon, *pseud. Vital Lies: Studies of Some Varieties of Recent Obscurantism.* London: John Lane the Bodley Head, Ltd., 1912.

Leslie, Sir Shane. *Cardinal Manning, His Life and Labours.* Preface by Sir Henry Slesser. New York: P. J. Kenedy & Sons, 1954.

Lovett, William, and Collins, J. *Chartism.* London: J. Watson, 1840.

Low, David. *Autobiography.* London: Michael Joseph, Ltd., 1956; New York: Simon & Schuster, Inc., 1957.

McCarran, Sister Margaret Patricia. *Fabianism in the Political Life of Britain, 1919-1931.* Chicago: Heritage Foundation, Inc., 1957.

Mackenzie, Norman. *Socialism: A Short History.* London: Hutchinson & Co. (Publishers), Ltd.; New York: Longmans, Green & Co., 1949.

McKitterick, T. E. M. and Younger, Kenneth (eds.). *Fabian International Essays.* London: Hogarth Press; New York: Frederick A. Praeger, Inc., 1957.

Maritain, Jacques. *Reflections on America.* New York: Charles Scribner's Sons, 1958.

Markham, S. F. *A History of Socialism.* New York: The Macmillan Co.; London: A. & E. Black, Ltd., 1931.

Martin, Kingsley. *Harold Laski, 1893-1950; A Biographical Memoir.* London: Victor Gollancz, Ltd.; New York: The Viking Press, Inc., 1953.

Marx, Karl. *Das Kapital.* New York: L. W. Schmidt, 1867.

Mill, John Stuart. *Utilitarianism.* London: Parker, Son, and Bourn, 1863.

Moore, Doris Langley. *E. Nesbit, A Biography.* London: Ernest Benn, Ltd., 1933.

Morris, William. *News from Nowhere*. London: Reeves & Turner, 1891; New York: Longmans, Green & Co., 1902.

Mowat, Charles L. *Britain Between the Wars, 1918-1940*. Chicago: The University of Chicago Press; London: Methuen & Co., Ltd., 1955.

Nehls, Edward. *D. H. Lawrence: A Composite Biography*. 3 vols. Madison: University of Wisconsin Press, 1957-59.

Nevill, Lady Dorothy. *Under Five Reigns*. London: Methuen & Co., Ltd., 1910.

Parmoor, Lord. *A Retrospect: Looking Back Over a Life of More Than Eighty Years*. London: William Heinemann, Ltd., 1936.

Pearson, Hesketh. *G.B.S.: A Postscript*. New York: Harper & Brothers, 1950; London: William Collins Sons & Co., Ltd., 1951.

Pease, Edward R. *The History of the Fabian Society*. London: George Allen & Unwin, Ltd., 1924; New York: International Publishers Co. (new and rev. ed.), 1926.

Pelling, Henry. *America and the British Left: From Bright to Bevan*. London: A. & C. Black, Ltd., 1956.

————. *The Origins of the Labour Party, 1880-1900*. London: Macmillan & Co., Ltd.; New York: St Martin's Press, Inc., 1954.

Ponsonby, Arthur. *Now Is the Time: An Appeal for Peace*. London: L. Parsons; New York: Albert & Charles Boni, 1925.

Postgate, Raymond. *The Life of George Lansbury*. London: Longmans, Green & Co., 1951.

Rauschenbusch, Walter. *Christianity and the Social Crisis*. London and New York: The Macmillan Co., 1907.

Raymond, E. T. *Portraits of the New Century*. New York: Doubleday, Doran, 1928; London: George Allen & Unwin, Ltd., 1924.

Reckitt, M. B., and Bechhofer, C. E. *The Meaning of National Guilds*. London: C. Palmer & Hayward, 1918; New York: The Macmillan Co. (2nd rev. ed.), 1922.

Robertson, Walford Graham. *Life Was Worth Living: Reminiscences*. Foreword by Sir Johnston Forbes-Robertson. New York: Harper & Brothers, 1931; with title *Time Was: Reminiscences*, London: Hamish Hamilton, Ltd., 1931.

Russell, Bertrand. *Portraits from Memory and Other Essays*. New York: Simon & Schuster, Inc.; London: George Allen & Unwin, Ltd., 1956.

Salt, Henry S. *Seventy Years among Savages*. New York: Thomas Seltzer, Inc.; London: Allen & Unwin, Ltd., 1921.

Shaw, George Bernard. *The Fabian Society: What It Has Done and How It Has Done It*. London: The Fabian Society (Tract No. 41), 1892.

————. *Fabianism and the Empire. A Manifesto of the Fabian Society*. London: The Fabian Society, 1900.

————. *Sixteen Self Sketches*. New York: Dodd, Mead & Co., Inc.; London: Constable & Co., Ltd., 1949.

Shaw, George Bernard (ed.). *Fabian Essays.* Jubilee Edition. London: George Allen & Unwin, Ltd.; New York: The Macmillan Co., 1948.

Simon, Yves. *Nature and Functions of Authority.* Milwaukee: Marquette University Press, 1940.

Slesser, Sir Henry. *Judgment Reserved: Reminiscences.* London: Hutchinson & Co., Ltd., 1941.

Slesser, Sir Henry, and Baker, Charles. *Trade Union Law.* London: Nisbit & Co., Ltd., 1927.

Snowden, Philip. *An Autobiography.* London: I. Nicholson and Watson, Ltd., 1934.

Sorel, Georges. *Réflexions sur la Violence.* Paris: M. Riviere, 1912; Translated by T. E. Hulme, New York: The Viking Press, Inc., 1914.

Sorley, Charles. *The Letters of Charles Sorley.* Cambridge: University Press; New York: The Macmillan Co., 1919.

Spender, J. A. *Between Two Wars.* London: Cassell & Co., Ltd., 1943.

———. *The Life of the Right Hon. Sir Henry Campbell-Bannerman, G.C.B.* 2 vols. London: Hodder and Stoughton, Ltd., 1923; Boston: Houghton Mifflin Co., 1924.

Trevelyan, G. M. *British History in the Nineteenth Century.* London and New York: Longmans, Green & Co., 1922.

Trotzky, Leon. *Whither England?* New York: International Publishers Co., 1925.

Voynich, Ethel. *The Gadfly.* New York: Henry Holt & Co., Inc., 1897.

Ward, Maisie. *Gilbert Keith Chesterton.* New York: Sheed & Ward, Inc., 1943; London: Sheed & Ward, Ltd., 1944.

Webb, Beatrice. *Diaries, 1912-1924.* Edited by Margaret I. Cole, Introduction by Lord Beveridge. London and New York: Longmans, Green & Co., 1952.

———. *Diaries, 1924-1932.* Edited with an Introduction by Margaret I. Cole. London and New York: Longmans, Green & Co., 1956.

———. *My Apprenticeship.* New York and London: Longmans, Green & Co., 1926.

———. *Our Partnership.* Edited by Barbara Drake and Margaret I. Cole. London and New York: Longmans, Green & Co., 1948.

Webb, Sidney. *The Difficulties of Individualism.* London: The Fabian Society (Tract No. 69), 1896.

———. *The Necessary Basis of Society.* London: The Fabian Society (Tract No. 159), 1911.

———. *Socialism: True and False.* London: The Fabian Society (Tract No. 51), 1894.

Webb, Sidney and Beatrice. *A Constitution for the Socialist Commonwealth of Great Britain*. London and New York: Longmans, Green & Co., 1920.

————. *The Consumer's Co-operative Movement*. London and New York: Longmans, Green & Co., 1921.

————. *The Decay of Capitalist Civilization*. New York: Harcourt, Brace & Co., Inc., 1923.

————. *English Local Government*. 15 vols. London and New York: Longmans, Green & Co., 1906-22.

————. *English Poor Law History*. 3 vols. London and New York: Longmans, Green & Co., 1927-30.

————. *English Poor Law Policy*. London and New York: Longmans, Green & Co., 1910.

————. *The History of Trade Unionism*. London: Longmans, Green & Co., 1894.

————. *Industrial Democracy*. London: Longmans, Green & Co., 1920.

————. *The Prevention of Destitution*. London: Longmans, Green & Co., 1911.

————. *Problems of Modern Industry*. London: Longmans, Green & Co., 1898.

Wells, H. G. *Ann Veronica*. New York and London: Harper & Brothers, 1909.

————. *Experiment in Autobiography*. 2 vols. London: Victor Gollancz, Ltd. and The Cresset Press, Ltd.; 1 vol., New York: The Macmillan Co., 1934.

————. *First and Last Things*. New York and London: G. P. Putnam's Sons, 1908.

————. "G.B.S.: A Memoir." *The New York Times*, Nov. 5, 1950.

————. *The New Machiavelli*. London: John Lane the Bodley Head, Ltd., 1911; New York: Duffield & Company, 1919.

————. *New Worlds for Old*. New York: The Macmillan Co., 1919.

————. *This Misery of Boots*. Boston: Ball Publishing Co., 1908.

Wingfield-Stratford, Esmé. *If "Labour" Wins*. London: Selwyn & Blount, Ltd., 1928.

————. *Those Earnest Victorians*. New York: William Morrow & Co., Inc.; with title, *Victorian Tragedy*, London: George Routledge and Sons, Ltd., 1930.

Woodward, Sir Ernest Llewellyn. *Short Journey*. London: Faber & Faber, Ltd., 1942.

Woolf, Virginia. *A Writer's Diary*. Edited by Leonard Woolf. London: Hogarth Press, Ltd., 1953; New York: Harcourt, Brace & Co., Inc., 1954.

Woolf, Virginia and Strachey, G. L. *Letters*. Edited by Leonard Woolf and James Strachey. New York: Harcourt, Brace & Co., Inc.; London: Chatto & Windus, Ltd., 1956.

INDEX